Fundamental Philosophy
Vol. 1

by

Jaime Luciano Balmes

Double9
BOOKS

Fundamental Philosophy
Vol. 1
by Jaime Luciano Balmes

ISBN: 978-93-60469-45-0

Published by

DOUBLE 9 BOOKS
2/13-B, Ansari Road
Daryaganj, New Delhi – 110002
info@double9books.com
www.double9books.com
Tel. 011-40042856

ABOUT THE AUTHOR

Spain's Jaime Luciano Balmes y Urpiá was a philosopher, theologian, Catholic defender, sociologist, and political writer who lived from August 28, 1810, to July 9, 1848. Balmes was an original philosopher who did not follow any particular school or line. He knew about the ideas of Saint Thomas Aquinas and was known as the Prince of Modern Apologetics by Pope Pius XII. He was born in Vic, Spain, in the Catalonia region. On the same day he was born, Balmes was baptized in the church of that city with the name Jaime Luciano Antonio. He passed away in the same place. Starting in 1817, Balmes went to the college in Vic to study. He took three years of Latin grammar, three years of rhetoric, and starting in 1822, three years of philosophy. In Solsona in 1825, the Bishop of that city, Manuel Benito Tabernero, gave him the tonsure. Balmes also took courses in theology at Vic Seminary from 1825 to 1826. It was free for him to take four courses in theology at the University of Cervera's College of San Carlos. Because the University of Cervera had to close in 1830, Balmes continued to study on his own in Vic for two years. He got his degree in religion on June 8, 1833.

CONTENTS

BOOK SECOND
ON SENSATION

BOOK THIRD

INTRODUCTION

The following translation of the great work of the lamented James Balmes on Philosophy, was undertaken at my suggestion and recommendation, and thus far I hold myself responsible for it. I have compared a considerable portion of it with the original, and as far as I have compared it, I have found it faithfully executed. The translator appears to me to have rendered the author's thought with exactness and precision, in a style not inferior to his own.

I have not added, as was originally contemplated, any Notes to those of the author. To have done so, would have swelled the volumes to an unreasonable size, and upon further consideration, they did not seem to me to be necessary. They would, in fact, have been an impertinence on my part, and the reader will rather thank me for not having done it. The work goes forth, therefore, as it came from the hands of its illustrious author, with no addition or abbreviation, or change, except what was demanded by the difference between the Spanish and English idioms.

James Balmes, in whose premature death in 1849, the friends of religion and science have still to deplore a serious loss, was one of the greatest writers and profoundest thinkers of Spain, and indeed of our times. He is well and favorably known to the American public by his excellent work on European civilization,—a work which has been translated into the principal languages of Europe. In that work he proved himself a man of free and liberal thought, of brilliant genius, and varied and profound learning. But his work on the bases of philosophy is his master-piece, and, taken as a whole, the greatest work that has been published on that important subject in the nineteenth century.

Yet it is rather as a criticism on the various erroneous systems of philosophy in modern times, than as containing a system of philosophy itself, that I have wished it translated and circulated in English. As a refutation of Bacon, Locke, Hume, and Condillac, Kant, Fichte, Schelling, and Spinoza, it is a master-piece, and leaves little to desire. In determining the fundamental principles of philosophy, and constructing a system in accordance with the real world, the author is not always, in my judgment, successful, and must yield to his Italian contemporary, the unhappy Abbate Gioberti.

When criticizing the errors of others, the distinguished author reasons as an ontologist, but when developing his own system, he is almost a psychologist. His ontology is usually sound, indeed, and his conclusions are for the most part just, but not always logically obtained. He recognizes no philosophical formula which embraces the whole subject-matter of philosophy, and does not appear to be aware that the *primum philosophicum* is and must be a synthesis; and hence he falls into what we may call, not eclecticism, but syncretism. This is owing to the fact that his genius is critical rather than constructive, and more apt to demolish than to build up.

What I regard as the chief error of the illustrious Spaniard, is his not recognizing that conceptions without intuitions are, as Kant justly maintains, empty, purely subjective, the mind itself; and hence, while denying that we have intuition of the infinite, contending that we have a real and objectively valid conception of it. Throughout his book the reader will find him maintaining that the human mind may, by discursion, attain to valid conceptions of a reality which transcends intuition. This I regard as an error. Discursion is an act of reflection, and though there is always less there can never be more in reflection than in intuition. If we have no intuition of the infinite, we have and can have no proper conception of it, and what is taken to be a conception of it is simply the human mind itself, and of no objective application or validity.

The excellent author is misled on this point, by supposing that in intuition of the intelligible the mind is the actor and not simply the spectator, and that an intuition of the infinite implies an infinite intuition. In both cases he is mistaken. In intuition we are simply spectators, and the object affirms itself to us. In intuition of the infinite, it is not we who perceive and affirm the infinite, by our own intellectual act, but the infinite that reveals and affirms itself to our intellect. In apprehending the infinite as thus revealed and affirmed, we of course apprehend it in a finite, not in an infinite manner. That which is intuitively apprehended is infinite, but the subjective apprehension is finite. The limitation is on the part of the subject, not on the part of the object.

The error arises from failing to distinguish sharply between intuition and reflection. In intuition the principal and primary actor is the intelligible object. In reflection it is the intellective subject; in the intuitive order the object presents itself as it is, with its own characteristics; in the reflective order it is represented with the limitations and characteristics of the thinking subject. As the subject is limited, its conceptions are limited, and represent the infinite not as infinite, but as the not-finite; and it is in the reflective order, if we operate on our conceptions, instead of our intuitions, only by a discursive process that we can come to the conclusion that the not-finite is the infinite. The author not distinguishing the two orders, and taking conceptions which belong to the reflective order as if they belonged to the intuitive order, supposes that we may have valid conceptions beyond the sphere of intuition. But a little reflection should have taught him that, if he had no intuition, he could have no conception of the infinite.

Following St. Thomas and all philosophers of the first order, the author very properly maintains that it is by the divine intelligibility, or the divine light, that the human mind sees whatever it does see; but he shrinks from saying that we have intuition of God himself. So far as we are to understand intuition of God as intuition, or open vision of him as he is in himself, he is undoubtedly right. But objects are intelligible only in the light of God, and it is only by this light that we apprehend them. Do we ever apprehend objects by the light of God without apprehending the light which renders them apprehensible? In apprehending the object, we apprehend first of all the light which is the medium of its apprehension. The light of God is God, and if we have intuition of the light, we must have intuition of him who is the true light that "enlighteneth every man coming into this world." We cannot see God as he is in himself, not because he is not intelligible in himself, but because of the excess of his light, which dazzles and blinds our eyes through their weakness. So, very few of us can look steadily in the face of the sun without being dazzled, yet not therefore is it to be said we cannot and do not see the sun.

The author does not seem to be aware that *substance* as distinguished from being or existence is an abstraction, and therefore purely subjective, and no object of intuition. Abstract from a thing all its properties or attributes, and you have remaining simply zero. The substance is properly the concrete thing itself, and in the real order is distinguishable simply from its phenomena, or *accidents*,—an abstract term,—not from its so-called attributes or properties. Hence, the question, so much disputed, whether we perceive substances themselves, is only the question, whether we see things themselves or only their phenomena. This question the Scottish school of Reid and Sir William Hamilton, have settled forever, and if it had not, Balmes has done it, making the correction I have suggested, in a manner that leaves nothing further to be said.

The author's proofs of the fact of creation are strong and well put, but fail to be absolutely conclusive in consequence of his not recognizing intuition of the creative act. They all presuppose this intuition, and are conclusive, because we in reality have it; but by denying that we have it, the author renders them formally inconclusive. We have intuition of God, real and necessary being, we have also intuition of things or existences, and therefore must have intuition of the creative act, for things or existences are only the external terminus of the creative act itself. Hence it is that Gioberti very properly makes the ideal formula, or *primum philosophicum*, the synthetic judgment, *Ens creat existentias*. Real and necessary Being creates existences. This formula or judgment in all its terms is given intuitively, and simultaneously, and it is because it is so given we are able at one blow to confound the skeptic, the atheist, and the pantheist. The illustrious Spaniard, uses in all his argument this formula, but he does so unconsciously, in contradiction, in fact, to his express statements, because he could not reason a moment, form a single conclusion without it. His argument in itself is good, but his explication of it is sometimes in fault.

If the learned and excellent author had recognized the fact that we have intuition of the creative act of the first cause, and the further fact that all second causes, in their several spheres and degree, imitate or copy the first, he would have succeeded better in explaining their operation. He does not seem to perceive clearly that the *nexus* which binds together cause and effect is the act of the cause, which is in its own nature causative of the effect, and by denying all intuition of this *nexus*, he seems to leave us in the position where Hume left us, because it is impossible to attain by discursion to any objective reality of which we have no intuition.

These are all or nearly all the criticisms I am disposed to make upon the admirable work of Balmes. They are important, no doubt, but really detract much less from its value than it would seem. It has, in spite of these defects, rare and positive merits. The author has not indeed a synthetic genius, but his powers of analysis are unsurpassed, and as far as my philosophical reading goes, unequalled. He has not given us the last word of philosophy, but he has given us precisely the work most needed in the present anarchical state of philosophical science. Not one of the errors to be detected in his work is peculiar to himself, and the most that the most ill-natured critic can say against him is, that, while he retains and defends all the truth in the prevailing philosophy of the schools, he has not escaped all its errors. Wherever he departs from scholastic tradition he follows truth, and is defective only where that tradition is itself defective. He has advanced far, corrected innumerable errors, poured a flood of light on a great variety of profound, intricate, and important problems, without introducing a new or adding any thing to confirm an old error. This is high praise, but the philosophic reader will concede that it is well merited.

The work is well adapted to create a taste for solid studies. It is written in a calm, clear, and dignified style, sometimes rising to true eloquence. The author threw his whole mind and soul into his work, and shows himself everywhere animated by a pure and noble spirit, free from all pride of opinion, all love of theorizing, and all dogmatism. He evidently writes solely for the purpose of advancing the cause of truth and virtue, religion and civilization, and the effect of his writings on the heart is no less salutary than their effect on the mind.

I have wished the work to be translated and given to the English and American public, not as a work free from all objections, but as admirably adapted to the present state of the English and American mind, as admirably fitted to correct the more dangerous errors now prevalent among us, and to prepare the way for the elaboration of a positive philosophy worthy of the name. We had nothing in English to compare with it, and it is far better adapted to the English and American genius than the misty speculations we are importing, and attempting to naturalize, from Germany. It will lead no man into any error which he does not already entertain, and few, perhaps none, can read it without positive benefit, at least without getting rid of many errors.

With these remarks I commit these volumes to the public, bespeaking for them a candid consideration. The near relation in which I stand to the translator makes me anxious that his labors should be received with a kindly regard. He who translates well a good book from a foreign language into his own, does a service to his country next to that of writing a good book himself.

O. A. BROWNSON.

August 7, 1856.

BOOK FIRST
ON CERTAINTY

CHAPTER I
IMPORTANCE AND UTILITY OF THE
QUESTION OF CERTAINTY

1. We should begin the study of philosophy by examining the question of certainty; before raising the edifice, we must lay the foundation.

Ever since there has been philosophy, that is, ever since men first reflected on themselves and the beings around them, they have been engaged with those questions which have for their object the basis of human knowledge, and this shows that on this subject serious difficulties are encountered. Inquirers, however, have not been discouraged by the sterility of philosophical labors; and this shows that in the last term of the investigation an object of high importance is discovered.

Philosophers have cavilled in the most extravagant manner upon the questions of certainty; on few subjects has the history of the human mind presented such lamentable aberrations. This consideration may excite suspicion that such investigations offer nothing solid to the mind, and serve only to feed the vanity of the sophist. But here, as elsewhere, we attribute no exaggerated importance to the opinions of philosophers, and we are very far from believing that they ought to be regarded as the legitimate representatives of human reason. It cannot, however, be denied that they are in the intellectual order the most active portion of the human race. When the whole body of philosophers dispute, humanity itself may be said to dispute. Every fact affecting the human race merits a thorough examination; to undervalue it, on account of the sophisms which envelop it, is to fall into the worst of all sophisms. There should be no contradiction between reason and common sense; yet such a contradiction there would be, if we should, in the name of common sense, contemn what occupies the reason of the most enlightened minds. Oftentimes it happens that what is grave and significant, that which makes a thinking man meditate, is the result neither of a disputation, nor of the arguments therein adduced, but the simple existence of the dispute itself. In itself it is sometimes of little importance, but by reason of what it indicates, of great consequence.

2. All philosophical questions are in some manner involved in that of certainty. When we have completely unfolded this, we have examined under one aspect or another all that human reason can conceive of God, man, and the universe. At first sight it may perhaps seem to be the simple foundation of the scientific structure; but in this foundation, if we carefully examine it, we shall see the whole edifice represented: it is a plane whereon is projected, visibly and in fair perspective, the whole body it is to support.

3. However limited may be the direct and immediate result of these investigations, they are of incalculable advantage. It is highly important to acquire science, but not less important to know its limits. Near these limits there are shoals which the navigator ought to know. It is by examining the question of certainty that we ascertain the limits of human science.

In descending to the depths to which these questions lead us, the understanding grows dim, and the heart is awed with a religious fear. A moment ago we were contemplating the edifice of human knowledge, and grew proud to see it with its colossal dimensions, its beautiful forms, its fine and bold construction; we enter it, and are led through deep caverns, and, as if by enchantment, the foundation seems to be subtilized, to evaporate, and the superb edifice remains floating in the air.

4. It must be remarked that in entering on the examination of the question of certainty, we do not conceal from ourselves its difficulties. To conceal would not be to solve them; on the contrary, the first condition necessary to their complete solution, is to see them with perfect clearness, and to feel their full force. It is no humiliation to the human understanding to seek those limits beyond which it cannot pass, but it is to elevate and confirm it. Thus the intrepid naturalist, when in search of some object he has penetrated to the bowels of the earth, feels a mixture of terror and pride to be thus buried in subterranean caverns, with just light enough to see immense masses barely suspended above his head and unfathomable abysses beneath his feet. There is something sublime, something attractive and captivating in the obscurity of the mysteries of science, in uncertainty itself, in the very assaults of doubt, threatening to destroy in one instant the work accomplished by the human mind only in the space of long ages. The greatest men have at all times enjoyed the contemplation of these mysteries. The genius which spread its wings over the east, over Greece and Rome, over the schools of the Middle Ages, is the same we now behold in modern

Europe. Plato, Aristotle, St. Augustine, Abelard, St. Anselm, St. Thomas of Aquin, Luis Vives, Bacon, Descartes, Malebranche, and Leibnitz, all, each in his own way, felt the sublime inspiration of philosophy.

Whatever tends to raise man to lofty contemplation in the sanctuary of his soul, contributes to his aggrandizement; for it separates him from natural objects, reminds him of his noble origin, and proclaims to him his high destiny. In a mechanical and sensual age, when every thing seems opposed to the activity of the powers of the soul, except when they administer to the wants of the body, it is well to renew those great questions in which the mind roams free and untrammelled over unbounden realms of space.

Only intellect can examine itself. The stone falls, but knows not that it falls; the ray calcines and pulverizes, ignorant of its power; the flower knows not that its beauty is enchanting; and the brute beast follows his instincts, but asks not the reason of them. Man alone, a fragile organization, appearing for a moment on earth again to return to the dust, harbors a spirit, which first inspects the external world, and then, anxious to ascertain its own nature, enters into itself as into a sanctuary, and becomes its own oracle. What am I? What do I do? What do I think? What phenomena do I experience within myself? Why am I subject to them? What is their cause, their order of production, their relations? The mind asks itself these questions,—serious and difficult indeed, but noble and sublime questions; an unfailing proof that there is within us something superior to inert matter susceptible only of motion and a variety of forms, that there is something, which, by an internal activity, spontaneous and rooted in our very nature, presents us an image of that infinite Activity, a single act of whose will created the world from nothing.(1)

CHAPTER II
TRUE STATE OF THE QUESTION

5. That we have certainty, common sense assures us, but what is its basis, and how it is acquired, are two difficult questions, which it is for philosophy to answer.

Three very different questions are involved in that of certainty; and if confounded, they contribute not a little to the creation of difficulties, and the confusion of matters which, even when they have their various aspects most accurately marked, are sufficiently hard and complicated.

It will greatly conduce to the due determination of our ideas, carefully to distinguish between the existence of certainty, its basis, and the mode in which it is acquired. Its existence is an indisputable fact; its basis the object of philosophical researches, and the mode of acquiring it frequently a concealed phenomenon not open to observation.

6. That bodies exist is a fact that no man of sane mind can doubt. No questions raised upon this point can ever shake our firm conviction in the existence, without us, of what we call the corporeal world. This conviction is a phenomenon of our existence. Explain it, perhaps we cannot; but we certainly cannot deny it; we submit to it as to an inevitable necessity.

What is the basis of certainty? Here we have not a simple fact, but a question solved by every philosopher in his own way. Descartes and Malebranche recur to the veracity of God; Locke and Condillac to the peculiar character and evolution of certain sensations.

How does man acquire this certainty? He knows not: he had it before reflecting on it; he is astounded to hear it made a matter of dispute, and he might never have suspected it could be asked, why we are certain that what affects our senses exists. It is of no use to ask him how he made so precious an acquisition; he regards it as a fact scarcely distinct from his own existence. He has no recollection of the order of sensations in his infancy; he finds his mind now developed, but is as ignorant of the laws of its development as he is of those which presided over the generation and growth of his body.

7. Philosophy should begin by explaining, not by disputing the fact of certainty. If we are certain of nothing, it is absolutely impossible for us to advance a single step in any science, or to take any part whatever in the affairs of life. A thorough-going skeptic would be insane, and that too with insanity of the highest grade. To such a one, all communication with other men, all succession of external actions, all thoughts, and even acts of the will would be impossible. Let us, then, admit the fact, and not be so extravagant as to say that madness sits on the threshold of philosophy.

It is the part of philosophy to analyze, not to destroy its object; for by destroying its object it destroys itself. Every argument must have a resting-point, which must be a fact. Whether it be internal or external, idea or object, the fact must exist: we must begin by supposing something, and this something we call a fact. Whoever begins by denying or doubting all facts, is like the anatomist, who, before dissecting a corpse, burns it, and casts its ashes to the wind.

8. Philosophy then, it may be said, commences not with an examination, but with an affirmation. Granted, and this is a truth whose admission closes the door on much sophistry, and sheds a brilliant light over the whole theory of certainty.

Philosophers are deceived when they imagine that they begin by doubting. Nothing is more false; when they think, they affirm, if nothing else, at least their own doubt: whenever they reason, they assert the connection of ideas, that is, the whole logical world.

Fichte, who certainly was not easily satisfied with anything, begins to treat of the basis of human knowledge by making an affirmation, and this he confesses with an ingenuousness that does him honor. Speaking of reflection, the foundation of his philosophy, he says: "The rules to which this reflection is subject, are not proved to be valid, but are tacitly presupposed to be known and admitted. They are, in their remotest origin, derived from a principle, the legitimacy of which can only be established on condition that *they are valid*. This is a circle, but an *inevitable circle*. But supposing it to be inevitable, and that we frankly confess it so to be, it is, in order to establish the highest principle, allowable *to trust all the laws of general logic*. We must start on the road of reflection with a proposition conceded by all the world without any contradiction."[1]

9. Certainty is to us a happy necessity; nature imposes it, and philosophers do not cast off nature. Pyrrho once came very near being hit by a stone, but he very naturally took good care to get out of its way, without stopping to examine whether it was a real stone, or only the appearance of one. The bystanders laughed at him for this, and, at the same time, showed how inconsistent this act was with his doctrine; but he gave this answer, which, under the circumstances, was exceedingly profound: "It is hard entirely to throw off human nature."

10. In sound philosophy, then, the question turns not upon the existence of certainty, but upon its motives, and the means of acquiring it. It is an inheritance of which we cannot divest ourselves, although we repudiate those very titles which guaranty its possession to us. Who is not certain that he thinks, feels, wills; that he has a body, and that there are around him others similar to his, of which the corporeal universe consists? Prior to all systems, humanity was in possession of this certainty, so, also, is every individual, although he may never during his whole life have once asked himself what the world is, what bodies are, or in what sensation, thought, and will consist. Not even if we examine the foundations of certainty and acknowledge the serious difficulties concerning them, which arise from ratiocination, is it possible to doubt everything. There never was, in all the rigor of the word, a true skeptic.

11. It is the same with certainty as with other objects of human knowledge. The fact is presented to us in all its magnitude, and with all clearness; but we do not penetrate to its innermost nature. Our understanding is as well provided with means to acquire knowledge of phenomena in the spiritual as in the material order, and it is sufficiently perspicacious to detect, delineate, and classify the laws to which they are subject; but when it would ascend to the cognition of the very essence of things, or would investigate the principles of the science which makes its boast, it feels its strength fail, and the ground whereon it stands, tremble and sink beneath its feet.

Happily, man possesses certainty independently of philosophical systems, not limited to phenomena of the soul, but extending as far as is needed in order to direct his conduct, both with regard to himself and to external objects. Before inquiring if there is certainty, all men were certain that they thought, willed, felt, that they had a body whose motions were governed by the will, and that there existed an assemblage of various bodies, called the universe. Since inquiries with regard to certainty were first instituted, it has remained the same with all men, even with those who disputed it; not one of whom could ever go farther than Pyrrho, and succeed in casting off human nature.

12. We cannot determine to what extent the force of mind of some philosophers, engaged in combatting nature, may have succeeded in creating doubt on many points, but certain it is: first, that no one ever went so far as to doubt the internal phenomena whose presence he felt inwardly; second, that if indeed any one ever did persuade himself that no external object corresponded to these phenomena, this must have been so strange an exception as to merit, in the history of science, and in the eyes of sound philosophy, no more weight than the illusions of a maniac. If Berkely went so far as to deny the existence of bodies, thus making the sophisms of reason

triumph over the instincts of nature, he is alone, and in opposition to all mankind, and richly merits to have this saying applied to him: "Insanity is insanity still, no matter how sublime it may be."

Those very philosophers, who carried their skepticism the farthest, agreed upon the necessity of accommodating themselves in practice to the appearances of the senses, and of reserving doubt for the world of speculation. Philosophers may dispute on every thing as much as they please, but, the dispute over, they cease to be philosophers, and are again men, similar to other men, and, like them all, enjoy the fruits of certainty. This, Hume, who denied with Berkely the existence of bodies, confesses: "I dine," he says; "I play a game at backgammon; I converse, and am happy with my friends; and when, after three or four hours of amusement, I would return to these speculations, they appear so cold, so strained, and so ridiculous, that I cannot find it in my heart to enter into them any farther. Here, then, I find myself absolutely and necessarily determined to live, and talk, and act, like other people, in the common affairs of life."[2]

13. We must, in discussing certainty, guard against the feverish desire of shaking the foundations of human reason. We should, in this class of questions, seek a thorough knowledge of the principles of science, and the laws which govern the development of our mind. To labor to destroy them is to mistake the object of true philosophy: we have only to make them a matter of observation, just as we do those of the material world, without any intention of disturbing the admirable order prevailing in the universe. Skeptics, who, in order to render their philosophy more solid, begin by doubting every thing, resemble the man, who, desirous of ascertaining, and exactly determining the phenomena of life, should bare his bosom, and thrust the knife into his heart.

Sobriety is as necessary to the health of the mind, as to that of the body: there is no wisdom without prudence, no philosophy without judgment. In the soul of man there is a divine light which directs him with admirable certainty. If we do not persist in extinguishing it, its splendor guides us, and when we reach the term of science it shows it to us, and makes us read in distinct characters the words, —*enough, you can go no farther.* These words are written by the Author of all beings; he it is that has given laws to the body as well as to the mind, and he contains in his infinite essence the ultimate reason of all things.

14. The certainty which is prior to all examination is not blind; on the contrary, it springs either from the clearness of the intellectual vision, or from an instinct conformable to reason: it is not opposed to reason, but is its basis. Our mind, in discursive reasoning, knows truth by the connection of propositions, or by the light which is reflected from one truth upon another. In primitive certainty the vision is by direct light, and does not need reflection.

When, then, we note the existence of certainty, we do not speak of a blind fact, nor do we seek to extinguish the light in its very source; we would rather say, that it is more brilliant there than in its radiations. We see a body whose splendor illumines the world in which we live; ought we, if requested to explain its nature and its relations with other objects, to begin by destroying these? When naturalists would examine the nature of light, and determine its laws, they do not begin by removing the light itself, and placing themselves in darkness.

15. True, this method of philosophizing is somewhat dogmatic, but dogmatic as it is, it has on its side, as we have seen, Pyrrho, Hume, and Fichte. It is not simply a method of philosophy, it is the voluntary submission of our very nature to an inevitable necessity, the combination of reason with instinct, a simultaneous attention to different voices calling from the depths of our soul. According to Pascal, "nature confounds the Pyrrhonians, and reason the dogmatists." This passes for a profound saying, and is so under a certain aspect; but it is notwithstanding somewhat inexact. The confusion is not the same in both cases: reason does not confound the dogmatist, unless he separates it from nature; but nature confounds the Pyrrhonian, either alone or joined with reason. The true dogmatist founds his reason upon nature; it knows itself, confesses the impossibility of proving every thing, and does not arbitrarily assume any principle that it needs unless nature itself furnishes it. And thus it does not confound the dogmatist, when guided by it he seeks a sure foundation for it. Nature, when it confounds the Pyrrhonian, attests the triumph of the reason of dogmatists, whose principal argument against Pyrrhonians, is the voice of nature itself. Pascal's thought would have been more exact if thus worded: nature confounds the Pyrrhonian and is necessary to the reason of dogmatists. This is less antithetical, but more true. Dogmatists do not deny nature; reason without it is impotent; to exercise its strength it needs a resting point. With such, Archimedes offered to move the earth, without this his immense lever could not stir a single atom.(2)

CHAPTER III
CERTAINTY OF THE HUMAN RACE, AND PHILOSOPHICAL CERTAINTY

16. Certainty does not originate in reflection; it is the spontaneous product of man's nature, and is annexed to the direct act of the intellectual and sensitive faculties. It is a condition necessary to the exercise of both, and without it life were a chaos; we therefore possess it instinctively, and without any reflection, and we enjoy the fruit of this as of all those other benefits of the Creator, which are inseparably joined to our existence.

17. It is, then, necessary to distinguish between the certainty of the human race and philosophical certainty, although, to speak frankly, it is not easy to conceive what can be the value of any human certainty distinct from that of the human race. If we set aside the efforts which the philosopher sometimes makes to discover the basis of human knowledge, we shall readily find him confounded with the rest of mankind. This cavil leaves no trace in his mind with respect to the certainty of all that the human race is certain of. He then discovers that the doubt which he felt was not a real doubt, although he may have deluded himself into a contrary belief. His doubts were simple suppositions, nothing more. When his meditation is over, and perhaps even while it lasts, he finds that he is as certain as the most ignorant individual of his internal acts, the existence of his own body, of other bodies around him, and of a thousand other things, which constitute the amount of knowledge requisite to the wants of life.

Question all, from the infant of a few summers, to the sage of many years and mature judgment, on the certainty of their own existence, their acts internal or external, their friends and relatives, the people among whom they dwell, objects seen or heard of, and you will not detect any hesitation in their answers, or any kind of difference in the grades of their certainty. If they have no knowledge of the philosophical questions touching these matters, you may read in their countenances wonder and astonishment that any one should seriously investigate things so *evident*.

18. Impossible as it is for us to know in what manner the sensitive, intellectual, and moral powers of children are developed, it is equally

impossible to prove a *a prior,* by analyzing the operations of his mind, that reflex acts do not concur to the formation of certainty; but it will not be difficult to find proofs of this in the exercise of these faculties when well developed. If we observe attentively, we shall see that the child's faculties habitually operate in a direct, not a reflex manner; which shows that the development is made directly, not by reflection. Were the primitive development the work of reflexion, the reflective power would be great in the child. But this is not the case. Very few men are ever endowed with it, and in the greater part of them it is very nearly null. They who attain to it, acquire it only by assiduous labor, and not without great violence to himself, can any one pass from direct to reflex cognition.

19. No matter what you teach a child, he perceives it indeed, but call his attention to the perception itself, and his understanding is at once obscured and confused. Let us make the experiment. Suppose we would teach a child the elements of geometry.

"Do you see this figure bounded by three lines? It is called a triangle; the lines are called sides, and the points where they unite the vertices of the angles." — "I understand that." — "Do you see this other figure bounded by four lines? It is called quadrilateral, and, like the triangle, has its sides and vertices of angles." — "Very well." — "Can a quadrilateral figure be a triangle, or *vice versa?*" — "It cannot." — "Never?" — "Never." — "Why not?" — "One has three, and the other four sides: how then can they be the same thing?" — "Who knows? It may seem so to you, but—" — "See here! This has three, and this four sides; and three and four are not the same thing."

Torture his understanding as much as you please, but you cannot drive him from his position: and thus we see that his perception and his reason operate directly, that is, by direct application to the object. Of himself he does not direct his attention to his own internal acts, does not think upon his own thoughts, does not combine reflex ideas, nor seek in them the certainty of his judgment.

20. And here we detect a vital error in the art of thinking as it has hitherto been taught. The young intellect is exercised in reflection, the most difficult part of science, which is as inconsiderate as it would be to commence his physical development by the most painful gymnastic exercises. Man's scientific development should be governed by his natural development, which is direct not reflex.

21. Let us apply this remark to the exercise of the senses. "Do you hear that music?" asks the child. — "What music?" — "Did you not hear it? Are you deaf?" — "It *seems* to you that you hear it." — "But, sir, I hear it so distinctly! How can it be possible?" — "But how do you know?" — "I hear it."

From his *I hear it* you cannot drive him: he will not hesitate a moment, nor will he appeal to any reflex act in order to avoid your importunities. "*I hear it*: do not you hear it?" He asks nothing more, and all your philosophy cannot equal the *irresistible force* of sensation which assures him that there is music, and that whoever doubts it is either deaf or in jest.

22. Had the faculties of the child been developed by alternate direct and reflex acts; had he, when acquiring knowledge of things, thought of something besides the things themselves; evidently a continuation of such acts would have left some impression on his mind, and urged to assign the motives of his certainty, he would indicate those very means that he made use of in the gradual development of his faculties; he would abstract the object, retire into himself, think upon his own thought in one way or another, and thus encounter the difficulty. Nothing of this character takes place, which proves that no such reflex acts have been performed, that there have been only perceptions accompanied by internal consciousness and certainty of their existence; but all in a confused, instinctive manner, without any thing like philosophical reflection.

23. What has been said of the child, may be proved true also of adults, however clear and perfect their intellect. If not initiated into questions of philosophy, they will give very nearly the same answers to difficulties proposed on the same matters, and even upon many others more exposed to doubt. Experience proves better than all ratiocination that no one acquires certainty by reflex acts.

24. Philosophers teach that the sources of certainty are the internal sense or consciousness of acts, the external senses, common sense, reason, and authority. A few examples will show us that there is reflection in all these, and how most men, and even philosophers, when they act like men and not like philosophers, think.

25. Suppose a clear-headed person, one however who is ignorant of the questions of certainty, has just seen some monument, the *Escurial* for instance, which leaves a lively and lasting impression on his mind, and while he recollects his gratification on seeing it, try to make him doubt the existence of this recollection in his mind, and its correspondence as well with the act of seeing as with the edifice itself, and he will very certainly think you are in jest, or will be astounded, and will suspect you of being out of your senses. He discovers no difference between things different as are the actual existence of his recollection, its correspondence with the past act of seeing, and the agreement of both with the edifice seen. He knows in this case no more than a child of six years: "I recollect it, I saw it, it is as I recollect it." This is all his science: he neither reflects, nor separates; all is direct and simultaneous.

No matter what suppositions you make, you can never get from the majority of men any better account of the phenomena of the internal sense, than you got from the supposed individual's recollection of the *Escurial*: "all that I know is that it is so." There are here no reflex acts; certainty attends the direct act, and no philosophical considerations can add one iota to the security given by the very force of things, and the instinct of nature.

26. Example of the testimony of the senses.

If we see any object, no matter what, at a proper distance and in sufficient light, we judge of its size, figure, and color, and we are very confident of the truth of our judgment, although we may never, in all our life, have thought of a theory of sensation, or of the relations of our organs, either to each other or to external objects. No reflex act accompanies the formation of our judgment; all is done instinctively, and without the intervention of philosophical considerations. We see it, and nothing else: this is enough for certainty. It is only after having handled books in which the question of certainty is agitated, that we turn our attention to our own acts; but this attention, it is to be remarked, lasts only so long as we are engaged in the scientific analysis; when this is forgotten, which it very soon is, we return to our general routine, and seldom recur to philosophy.

Note well that we speak here of the certainty of the judgment formed in consequence of sensation only in so far as it is connected with the uses of life, and not at all of its greater or less exactness with respect to the nature of things. Thus it matters little that we consider colors as inherent qualities of bodies, although in reality they are not; it is sufficient that the judgment formed does not in any sense change our relations to objects, whatever may be the philosophical theory.

27. Example of common sense.

In the presence of a numerous assembly, throw a quantity of printer's types at random upon the ground, and tell the bystanders that their names will all be found printed. They will all with one accord laugh at your folly. But what is the reason of this? Have they all reflected upon the basis of their certainty? Assuredly they have not.

28. Example of reason.

We all reason, and in many cases rightly. Without art or reflection of any kind, we often distinguish the solid from the futile, the sophistical from the conclusive. This does not require us to regard the course of our understanding; without scarcely noticing it we follow the right road; and a man may, in his life, have formed a thousand rigorous and exact ratiocinations without ever having once attended to his method of reasoning. Even those most versed in the dialectic art, repeatedly forget it; they perhaps follow it very correctly in practice, but they pay no express attention to any one of its rules.

29. Ideologists have written whole volumes on the operations of our understanding, and the simple rustic performs these operations without thinking that he performs them. How much has been written on abstraction, generalization, and universals! Yet this is all well regulated in the mind of every man, ignorant as he may be of a science which examines it. In his language you will find the universal and the particular expressed, and every thing occupying its proper place in his discourse: he encounters no difficulty in his direct acts. But call his attention to these acts themselves, to abstraction for example; and what was in the direct act so clear and lucid, becomes a chaos the moment it passes to the reflex order.

Thus we see that reflection, whose object is the act performed, is of very little importance even in reasoning, its most reflective medium.

30. Example of authority.

All civilized people know the existence of *England*, but most of them know this only from having heard or read of it, that is, by authority. Their certainty of the existence of England evidently is not surpassed by that of objects of their own vision; and yet how many of them have ever thought of analyzing the foundations of such a certainty? Yet is the certainty of those who have examined it greater than that of those who have not examined it? In the present case, as in an infinity of others analogous to it, there is no intervention of reflex acts: certainty is here formed instinctively, and needs no medium invented by philosophers.

31. These examples show that philosophers take a very different road to certainty from that taught by nature. He who created all things out of nothing, has provided them with all that is necessary to the exercise of their functions according to their respective positions in the universe; and one of the first necessities of an intelligent being is the certainty of some truths. What would become of us, if before beginning to receive impressions, and before the germination of primary ideas in our understanding, we were obliged to perform the painful task of elaborating some system capable of saving us from uncertainty? Were it thus, our intellect would perish at its very birth, for no sooner would it open its eyes to the light than it would be involved in the chaos of its own cavils, and it could never, with its scattered forces, succeed in dissipating the clouds which would arise on all sides, and which would finally sink it in total darkness.

If the greatest philosophers, the most clear and acute intellects, the strongest and most vigorous geniuses have labored to so little purpose to establish solid principles, such as might serve for the foundations of science, what would have happened had not the Creator succored us in this necessity, and given certainty to the tender intellect, just as he prepared for the preservation of the body the milk that nourishes and the air that vivifies it?

32. If any part of science ought to be regarded as purely speculative, it is undoubtedly the part which concerns certainty; and this proposition, paradoxical as it may seem at first sight, is true, and can be easily demonstrated.

33. What does philosophy here propose to do? To produce certainty? But it exists independently of all philosophical systems, and mankind were certain of many things before ever any one thought of such questions. Moreover, since the question was first raised, few, compared with the whole human race, have examined it; so it is now, and so it will be; and all the theories invented on this point can have no effect upon the fact of certainty. What has been said of its production may be said of the attempt to consolidate it. When have the generality of men had, or when will they have, time and opportunity to examine these questions?

34. Philosophy could here have produced nothing but skepticism, for the variety and opposition of systems were more calculated to create than to dissipate doubts. Happily nature is the most invincible opponent of skepticism; the sage's dreams pass not from his library to the every day uses of the life of ordinary men, or even of those who labor under or imagine them.

35. Philosophy here can propose to itself no more reasonable object than simply to examine the foundations of certainty, with the sole view of more thoroughly knowing the human mind, not of making any change in practice; just as astronomers observe the course of the stars, investigate and determine the laws to which they are subject, without therefore presuming to be able to modify them.

36. But even this supposition places philosophy in a very unsatisfactory position; for if we recollect what we have already established, we shall see that science observes a real and true phenomenon, but gives it a gratuitous explanation, by making an imaginary analysis of it.

Experience has in fact shown our understanding to be guided by no one of the considerations made by philosophers; its assent, when it is accompanied by the greatest certainty, is a spontaneous product of a natural instinct, not of combinations; it is a firm adhesion exacted by the evidence of the truth, the power of the internal sense, or the impulse of instinct; not a conviction produced by a series of ratiocinations. These combinations and ratiocinations therefore exist only in the mind of philosophers, not in reality; when, therefore, they attempt to designate the foundations of certainty, we are told what could or should have been, but not what is.

If philosophers would only be guided by their own systems, and would not forget them nor set them aside as soon as, or even before, they have finished explaining them, it might be said, that even if no reason can be given for human certainty, one can be given for philosophical certainty; but since these same philosophers make no use of these scientific means save when developing them *ex professo*, it follows that their pretended foundations are a mere theory, having little or no connection with the reality.

37. This demonstration of the vanity of philosophical systems relating to the foundation of certainty, far from leading to skepticism, has a directly contrary tendency; for it makes us appreciate at their true value, the emptiness of our cavils, compares their impotence with the irresistible force of nature, and thus destroys that foolish pride which would make us superior to the laws imposed upon our understanding by the Creator himself; it places us in the channel through which the torrent of humanity has for ages run; and it disposes us to receive with sound philosophy what the laws of our nature force us to accept.(3)

CHAPTER IV
EXISTENCE OF TRANSCENDENTAL SCIENCE IN THE ABSOLUTE INTELLECTUAL ORDER

38. Philosophers have sought a first principle of human knowledge; each has assigned his own, and now after so much discussion it is doubtful who is right, or even if any one is right.

Before inquiring what the first principle is, they ought to have ascertained whether there be any such principle. We cannot suppose this last question to be answered affirmatively; for it is, as we shall hereafter see, susceptible of different solutions, according to the aspect under which it is seen.

The first principle of knowledge may be understood in either of two senses; as denoting one first truth from which all others flow, or as expressing a truth which we must suppose if we would not have all other truths disappear. In the former sense it is a spring from which the waters flow, which fertilize the intellect; in the second sense it is a point whereon to rest a great weight.

39. Is there any one truth from which all others flow? There is in reality, in the order of beings, in the universal intellectual order; but in the human intellectual order there is none.

40. There is in the order of beings one truth, the origin of all truths; for truth is reality, and there is one Being, author of all beings. This being is a truth, — truth itself, — the plenitude of truth, — for he is being by essence, the plenitude of being.

Every school of philosophy has in some sense recognized this unity of origin. The atheist talks of the force of nature; the pantheist of an only substance, of the absolute, of the unconditioned; both have abandoned the idea of God, and now labour to replace it by something which may be made the origin of the existence of the universe, and of the development of its phenomena.

41. There is in the universal intellectual order one truth from which all others flow; it is, that the unity of origin of all truths is not only found

in realized truths, that is, in beings considered in themselves, but likewise in the concatenation of ideas representing these beings. And thus if our understanding could ascend to the knowledge of all truths, and embrace them in their unity and in all the relations uniting them, it would see them after arriving at a certain height, notwithstanding their dispersion and divergence as now perceived by us, converge to a centre, in which they unite, like rays of light in the luminous object from which they issued.

42. The most profound philosophical doctrines often appear in the treatises of theologians explaining the doctrines of the church. Thus St. Thomas, in his questions on the understanding of angels, and in other parts of his works, has left us a very luminous and interesting theory. According to him, spirits understand by a number of ideas smaller in proportion to the superiority of their order; and so the diminution goes on even to God, who understands by means of a single idea which is his own essence. And thus according to the holy doctor, not only is there one being, author of all beings, but also one infinite idea which includes all ideas. Whoever fully possesses this idea will see every thing in it; but since this full possession, called comprehension in theology, is solely a property of the infinite intelligence of God, creatures, when in the other life they shall have obtained the beatific vision, will see more or fewer objects in God according to the greater or less perfection in which they possess it. How wonderful! The dogma of beatific vision well understood, is also a truth which sheds much light upon philosophical theories. Malebranche's sublime dream about ideas was, perhaps, a reminiscence of his theological studies.

43. The transcendental science which embraces and explains them all, is a chimera to our mind so long as we inhabit this earth, but it is a reality to other spirits of a higher order, and it will also be so to us when, freed from this mortal body, we attain the regions of light.

44. So far as we may conjecture from analogy, we have proofs of the existence of this transcendental science, which includes all sciences, and is in its turn contained in one sole principle, or rather, in one only idea, in one only intuition. If we observe the scale of beings, the grades of distinction between individual intelligences, and the successive progress of science, the image of this truth will be presented to us in a very striking manner.

One of the distinctive characteristics of our mind is its power of generalization, of perceiving the common in the various, of reducing the multiplex to unity; and this power is proportional to its degree of intelligence.

45. The brute is limited to its sensations and the objects causing them. It has no power of generalization or of classification; nothing beyond the impression received or the instinct of satisfying its wants. Man, however,

as soon as he opens the eyes of his understanding, perceives unnumbered relations; he applies what he has seen in one case to different cases; he generalizes and infolds very many ideas in a single idea. The child desires an object above his reach; he immediately takes a chair or a stool, and improvises a ladder. A brute will watch the object of its appetite whole hours when placed beyond its reach, without ever thinking of doing like the child, and forming a ladder. If every thing be so disposed as to enable it to climb, it will climb, but it is incapable of thinking that in similar circumstances it ought to act in like manner. In the former case, we see a being having the general idea of a *means*, and its relation to the *end*, of which it makes use when necessary: in the latter we see another being having indeed before its eyes the end and the means, but not perceiving their relation, unable to go beyond the material individuality of objects.

In the former there is perception of unity; in the latter there is no bond to join the variety of particular facts.

It is seen by this simple example that the child will reduce all the infinity of cases, in which an object may be placed beyond his reach, to this one case; he possesses, so to speak, the formula of this little problem. True, he does not render himself an account of this formula, that is, does not reflect upon it; but he has it in reality; and if you give him an opportunity he will at once apply it, which proves that he has it. Or speak to him of things placed too high for his reach, and point rapidly from one to another of the objects before him; he will at all times instantly apply the general idea of an auxiliary medium; he will avail himself perhaps of his father's arm, or that of a servant, a chair, if in the house, a heap of stones, if in the fields; he discovers in all things *the relation of the means to the end*. When he sees the end, he immediately turns his attention to the means of attaining it: the general idea seeks individualization in a particular case.

46. Art is the collection of rules for doing any thing well; and is the more perfect in proportion as each rule embraces a greater number of cases, and consequently as the number of these rules is smaller. Doubtless, buildings that were solid, well proportioned, and adapted to the purpose for which they were destined, had been constructed before the rules of architecture were reduced to formulas; but the great progress of intelligence in the construction of buildings consisted in ascertaining what there was common to all well-built houses, in determining the cause of beauty and of solidity, in themselves considered, by passing from the individual to the universal, that is, by forming general ideas of beauty and solidity applicable to an indefinite number of particular cases, by simplifying.

47. The same may be said of all other liberal and mechanical arts: the progress of intelligence in all of them consists in reducing multiplicity to unity, and including the greatest possible number of applications in the least possible number of ideas. This is why lovers of literature and the fine arts labor to discover an idea of beauty in general, in order to attain a type applicable to all literary and artistic objects. It is also obvious that those engaged in mechanical arts always endeavor to govern their proceedings by a few rules, and he is held to be the most skilful who succeeds in combining the greatest variety of results with the greatest simplicity of means, by making that, which others connect with many ideas, depend upon one idea alone. When we see a machine produce wonderful effects by a very simple process, we praise the artificer not less for the means than for the end: this we say, is grand, and the simplicity with which it works is the most astonishing.

48. Let us apply this doctrine to the natural and exact sciences.

The merit of our actual system of numeration consists in including the expression of all numbers in a single idea, making the value of each figure ten times that to the right, and filling all intervals with zeros. The expression of infinite numbers is reduced to the simplicity of a single rule based upon a single idea; the relation of position with a tenfold value. Logarithms have enabled arithmetic to make a great advance by diminishing the number of its fundamental operations, since, with them it reduces multiplication and division to addition and subtraction. Algebra is only the generalization of arithmetical expressions and operations, their simplification. The application of algebra to geometry is the generalization of geometrical expressions; formulas of lines, figures, bodies, only the expression of their universal idea. In this idea as in a type, geometry preserves its first and generative idea, and it requires only the simplest applications in order to form an exact calculation of all lines belonging to the same class, which can possibly be met with in practice. In the simple expression $dz/dx = A$, called the differential coefficient, is contained the whole idea of infinitesimal calculus. It originated in geometrical considerations, but so soon as its universality was conceived, it poured a flood of light upon every branch of mathematical and natural science, and led to the discovery of a new world, whose confines are still unknown. The prodigious fecundity of this calculus emanates from its simplicity, its prompt generalization of both algebra and geometry, and its uniting them in a single point which is the relation of the limits of the differentials of any function.

49. It is to this unity of idea that the human intellect in its ambition aspires, and once obtained, it proves the cause of great progress. The glory of the greatest geniuses is that they discovered it: the advance of science

has consisted in profiting by it. Vieta explained and applied the principle of the general expression of arithmetical quantities; Descartes extended this to geometrical quantities. Newton established the principle of universal gravitation; and he, at the same time with Leibnitz, invented the infinitesimal calculus; and the exact and natural sciences march, by the light of a vast flambeau, with gigantic strides along paths never before trodden. And all this because intelligence has approached unity, and become possessed of a generative idea, involving infinite other ideas.

50. It is worthy of remark, that as we advance in science, we meet numerous points of contact, close relations, which no one at first sight would have suspected. Ancient mathematicians discussed the conic sections, but were far from imagining that the idea of the ellipse could be the basis of a system of astronomy: the foci to them were simple points, the curve a line, and the relations of both the object of combinations at once profitless and without application. Ages pass away, and these foci are the sun, the curve the orbit of planets. The lines on the geometrician's table represented a world!

The intimate connection of mathematical and natural science cannot be questioned; and who shall say to what extent both are connected with ontological, psychological, theological, and moral science? The extended scale over which beings are distributed may at first sight seem to be an assemblage of unconnected objects, but seen with the eyes of science, it is perceived to be a delicately worked chain, whose links present, as we advance, greater beauty and perfection. We see the different realms of nature united by close relations: the sciences, of which they are the objects, mutually borrow each other's light, and enter on each other's territory. The complication of objects among themselves involves this complication of science; and the unity of the laws imposed upon different orders of beings makes all sciences approach, and tend to form, one only science. If it were given us to see the identity of their origin, the unity of the end and the simplicity of the means, we should come into the possession of the true transcendental science, the only science which involves all others, or more correctly speaking, the only idea in which every thing is represented as it is, and every thing seen without any necessity of combination, or effort of any kind, just as a magnificent landscape, its outlines, form, and colors are pictured on a perfectly clear mirror. In the meantime, we must rest satisfied with shadows of reality, and must see in the instinctive tendency of our understanding to simplify, to reduce every thing or make it approach as much as possible to unity, the announcement, the sign of this single science, this intuition of the one infinite idea; just as in the desire for happiness which agitates our heart, the thirst after enjoyment which torments us we discover a proof that all is not ended here below, and that our soul has been created for the possession of a good not to be attained in this mortal life.

51. If we compare men with men, and pay attention to the character of genius, the most elevated point of human intelligence, we shall see the truth of what has been said of the scale of human beings, and the progress of science. Men of true genius are distinguished by the unity and extent of their conceptions. If they treat a difficult and complicated question, they simplify it, consider it from a high point of view, and determine one general idea which sheds light upon all the others. If they have a difficulty to solve, they show the root of the error, and with a word dispel all the illusion of sophistry. If they use synthesis, they first establish the principle which is to serve as its basis, and with one dash trace the road to be followed in order to reach the wished-for result. If they make use of analysis, they strike in its secret resort the point where decomposition is to commence, they at once open the object, and reveal to us its most obscure mysteries. If there is question of a discovery, while others are seeking here and there, they strike the ground with their foot, and exclaim, "the treasure is here." They make no long arguments, nor evasions; their thoughts are few but pregnant; their words are not many, but in each of them is set a pearl of inestimable value.

52. No doubt there is in the intellectual order a single truth from which all other truths emanate, one idea which includes all other ideas. This philosophy teaches, and the efforts, the natural and instinctive tendencies of every intelligence, toiling after simplicity and unity, show it: such also is the dictate of common sense, which considers that thought the highest and most noble which is the most comprehensive and the most simple.(4)

CHAPTER V
TRANSCENDENTAL SCIENCE IN THE HUMAN INTELLECTUAL ORDER CANNOT EMANATE FROM THE SENSES

53. In the human intellectual order, such as it is in this life, there is no one truth from which all others flow: philosophers have sought one in vain; they have found none, for there was none to be found. In fact, where could it be found?

54. Would it emanate from the senses?

Sensations are as various as the objects which produce them: by them we acquire knowledge of individual and material things; but no one truth, source of all other truths, can be found in any one of these, or the sensations proceeding from them.

55. If we observe our impressions received through sensation, we shall perceive that they are all equal so far as the production of certainty is concerned. We are just as certain of the sensation caused by any noise whatever, as we are of that produced by an object which we see, an odorous body which we smell, a savory morsel which we taste, or any thing which strongly affects our sense of touch. There is no gradation in the certainty produced by these sensations: they are all equal; for if we speak of sensation itself, we experience it in such a manner as to leave no uncertainty; and if we speak of the relation of sensation with the existence of the object causing it, we are just as certain that the sensation called *sight* corresponds to an external object *seen*, as we are that an external object *touched* corresponds to the sensation called *touch*.

Hence we infer that no one sensation is the origin of the certainty of other sensations; in this they are all alike: and most men have no other reason than their experience why they should be sure of this certainty. We are aware that what happens to individuals from whose eyes cataracts have been removed, shows that simple sensation does not suffice for the due appreciation of the object perceived, and that one sense aids another: but this does not prove any one of them to be preferable; for as the blind man, whose sight was suddenly restored, did not form an exact judgment as to the size and distance of objects seen by sight only, but required the assistance of touch; so is it very probable that if a person of good eyesight had been deprived from his birth of the sense of touch, he would not be able, were this sense given him suddenly, to form an exact judgment concerning objects touched, until, by the aid of sight, he had become accustomed to combine the new and the old order of sensations, and learnt by practice to determine the relations of sensation with its object, or to know by sensation the properties of its object.

56. This fact of the blind man is however contradicted by others which lead to a directly opposite result. The youth, upon whom the oculist, Jean Janin, performed the same operation, and other persons blind from their birth, whose eyesight Luigi de' Gregori partly restored, did not, like the blind man of Cheselden, deem these objects stuck to their eyes, but that they saw them as things really external and separate. Rosmini thus relates it,[3] although he gives the preference to the Cheselden case, which he says was repeated in Italy by the professor Giacomo di Pavia with precisely the same results.

57. It is not easy to ascertain how this combination of one sensation with another enables us to judge rightly of external objects; chiefly because the development of our sensitive and intellectual faculties is completed before we can reflect upon it: and thus we find ourselves certain of the existence and properties of things before we have thought of certainty, and much less of the means of acquiring it.

58. But even supposing us, after occupying ourselves with sensations and their relations with objects, to set aside the certainty which we already have, and to act as if we sought it, we can find no one sensation the basis of the certainty of the other sensations. We should meet in that all the difficulties to be encountered in the others.

59. One of the chief difficulties upon this point is to determine the relations of the sense of sight with that of touch, and how far the one depends upon the other. We propose hereafter to examine these questions at some length, and we shall therefore now refrain from entering upon them, as well because they are not of a character to be incidentally investigated, as because whatever their solution, it is not at all opposed to what we shall here establish.

60. It would be of no advantage to us to know that the certainty of all sensations was, philosophically speaking, founded upon that of some one sensation. Every sensation is a contingent, individual fact: how then are we to draw from it light to guide us to necessary truths? No matter under what

aspect we consider sensation, it is only an impression received through our organs. We are sure of the impression because it is intimately present to our mind; and its repetition aided by other sensations, whether of the same or another sense, makes us certain of its relations with the object producing it: but every thing is done instinctively, with little or no reflection; and we are always condemned, however much we reflect, to reach a point beyond which we cannot pass, for nature herself there stops us.

61. Far then from finding in any sensation a fundamental fact on which to found a philosophical certainty, we discover a collection of particular and mutually distinct facts, equal, however, so far as the production in us of that security which we call certainty is concerned. It is of no use to decompose man, and reduce him first to an inanimate machine, then allow him one sense, making him perceive different sensations, afterwards grant him another sense, making him combine the new and the old sensations, and so on synthetically to the possession and exercise of them all. These things may do to entertain one's curiosity, to nourish philosophical pretensions, or to give a show of probability to imaginary systems; but they are in reality of little or no use; the evolutions which the observer imagines do not resemble those of nature; and the true philosopher ought to examine what really is, not what is only in his conception.

Condillac, animating his statue by degrees, and making the whole sum of human knowledge flow from one sensation, is like those priests who got inside the statue of the idol, and thence emitted their oracles. It is not the statue which receives animation, that speaks and thinks, it is Condillac from within it. Let us, however, grant to the sensist all he demands; let us allow him to regulate as he pleases the mutual dependence of sensations; for the instant we require him to make use only of pure sensations in his discussions, he will be utterly disconcerted, how much soever he may suppose them to be transformed. But we reserve these questions to the place in which we shall examine the nature and origin of ideas.

62. Why are we sure that the agreeable sensation which we experience in our sense of smell proceeds from an object called a *rose*? Because we recollect having experienced the same sensation on a thousand other occasions; because both sight and touch confirm the testimony of smell. But how do we know that these sensations are something beside the impressions received in our soul? Why may we not believe them to come from some cause or other, without relation to external causes? Is it because other men say the contrary? Are we certain that they exist? How do they know what they tell us? How do we know that we hear rightly? There is the same difficulty with the other senses as with that of hearing, and if we doubt the testimony of three senses, why shall we not doubt that of four? Reasoning is here of no

avail; it would lead us to cavils which would require an impassible doubt, and would tear from us a security, of which, notwithstanding all our efforts, we cannot despoil ourselves.

Moreover, if we appeal to the principles of reason, in order to prove the truth of sensation, we leave the territory of sensations, and do not place in them the primitive truth, origin of all other truths, nor accomplish what we undertook.

63. Hence it follows: First, that there is no one sensation which is the origin of the certainty of all others; this we have only indicated here, reserving the demonstration of it to our treatise on sensations. Secondly, although such a sensation were to exist, it could not serve as the basis of any thing in the intellectual order, for with sensation alone it is impossible even to think. Thirdly, that sensations, so far from being able to serve as the basis of transcendental science, cannot serve of themselves alone to establish any science; because necessary truths cannot flow from them, since they are contingent facts.(5)

CHAPTER VI
TRANSCENDENTAL SCIENCE.—
INSUFFICIENCY OF REAL TRUTHS

64. We have thought proper briefly to refute Condillac's system, not on account of its intrinsic importance, or because it was not before in sufficiently bad repute, but in order to clear the field for higher and more strictly philosophical discussions. We should not omit to guard philosophy against the prejudice cast upon it by a system as vain as it is profitless. All that is most sublime in the science of the mind disappears with the *statue-man* and transformed sensations: we vindicate the rights of human reason by showing that before entering upon more transcendental questions it is indispensable to discard Condillac's system; just as it is necessary before making a good road to clear away the brushwood which obstructs the passage.

65. We come now to the proof that in the human intellectual order, such as it is in this life, there is no one truth the source of all truths; because no one truth includes them all.

Truths are of two kinds, real and ideal. We call facts, or whatever exists, real truths; we call the necessary connection of ideas ideal truths. A real truth may be expressed by the verb *to be*, taken substantively, or at least it supposes a proposition in which this verb has been taken in this sense: an ideal truth is expressed by the same verb taken copulatively, as signifying the necessary relation of a predicate with a subject, abstracting it, however, from both. *We are*, that is, *we exist*, expresses a real truth, a fact. *Whoever thinks exists*, expresses an ideal truth, for it does not affirm that there is any one who thinks or exists, but that if there is any one who thinks, he exists; or, in other words, it affirms a necessary relation between thought and being. To real truths corresponds the real world, the world of existences; to ideal truths the logical world, that of possibility.

The verb *to be*, is sometimes taken copulatively, although the relation expressed by it be not necessary: such is the case with all contingent propositions, and when the predicate does not belong to the essence of the subject. Sometimes the necessity is conditional, that is, it supposes a fact;

and then there is no absolute necessity, since the supposed fact is always contingent. When we speak of ideal truths, we refer to those that express an absolute necessary relation, abstracting it from all order of existence; and on the other hand, we understand by real truths all those that suppose a proposition in which a fact has been established. To this class belong the truths of natural science, for they all suppose some fact which is the object of observation.

66. No real finite truth can be the origin of all others. Truth of this kind is the expression of a particular contingent fact, and consequently can neither include other real truths or the world of existences, nor ideal truths which refer only to necessary relations in the world of possibility.

67. Were we to see intuitively infinite existence, cause of all existences, we should know a real truth, origin of all others; but as we know this infinite existence only by discursion and not by intuition, it follows that we do not know the fact of that existence in which the reason of all other existences is contained. Neither is it possible for us, after having by means of discursion reached this cognition, to explain from this point of view the existence of the finite by the sole existence of the infinite; for if we abstract the existence of the finite, the discursion, by which we attained to the cognition of the infinite, disappears, and then our whole scientific fabric tumbles to the ground. Demonstrate to a man by means of discursion the existence of God, and require him, setting aside the point of departure, and depending upon the sole idea of the infinite, to explain not only the possibility, but also the reality of creation; and he cannot do it. If he only sets aside the finite all his reasoning fails, and no effort can prevent its failing; he is like an architect who, after having built a superb cupola, is required to support it although the foundations of the edifice are removed.

68. Take any real truth whatever, the plainest and most certain fact, and yet we can derive nothing from it if ideal truth comes not to fecundate it. We exist, we think, we feel; these are indubitable facts, but science can deduce nothing from them; they are particular contingent facts, whose existence or non-existence neither affects other facts nor reaches the world of ideas.

These truths are of the purely sensible order, have not of themselves any relation with the order of science, nor can they be elevated to it if not combined with ideal truths. Descartes, when he brought forward the fact of thought and existence, driven as he was by his attempt to raise a scientific edifice, passed unawares from the real to the ideal order. *I think*, he said; and had he stopped here he would have reduced his philosophy to a simple intuition of consciousness; but he wished to go farther, he wished to reason, and then of necessity availed himself of an ideal truth: *whoever thinks exists.*

Thus with a universal and necessary truth he fecundated his individual and contingent fact; and as he needed some rule to guide him in his onward march, he sought one in the admissibility of the evidence of ideas. And thus also we see how this philosopher, who so toiled in search of unity, came all at once in contact with triplicity: *a fact, an objective truth, a criterion*: a fact in the consciousness of the subject; an objective truth in the necessary relation of thought with existence; a criterion in the admissibility of the evidence of ideas.

We may defy all the philosophers in the world to reason upon any fact whatever without the aid of ideal truth. We shall find in all facts the same sterility as in the fact of consciousness. This is no conjecture, but a rigid demonstration. Only one existence contains the reason of all other existences; if, then, we do not immediately and intuitively know it, we cannot discover any one real truth, origin of all others.

69. Even supposing there to be in the order of creation a fact of such a nature, that the whole universe is only a simple development of it, we should not therefore have found the real truth source of all science, for it would not enable us to make any advance towards the world of possibility, the ideal order, infinitely superior to that of finite existences.

If we suppose the progress of natural science to lead to the discovery of a single, simple law, which presides over the development of all others, and the application of which, varied according to circumstances, is a sufficient reason of all the phenomena now referred to many and very complicated laws; this would, without doubt, be an immense progress in sciences the object of which is the visible world; but what would it give us to know of the world of intelligences? What of the world of possibility?(6)

CHAPTER VII
THE PHILOSOPHY OF THE ME CANNOT PRODUCE TRANSCENDENTAL SCIENCE

70. The testimony of consciousness is sure and irresistible, but it has no connection with that of evidence. The object of the one is a particular and contingent fact; that of the other, a necessary truth. That I now think, is to me absolutely certain; but this thought of mine is not a necessary but a decidedly contingent truth; for I might never have thought, or even existed: it is a purely individual fact, is confined to me, and its existence or non-existence in nowise affects universal truths.

Consciousness is an anchor, not a beacon: it saves the understanding from shipwreck, but does not light it on its way; in the assaults of universal doubt, consciousness is at hand to shield it from destruction; but if asked to direct us, it gives us only particular facts.

These facts have no scientific value, except when made objective, or rather, when the mind, reflecting upon them, bathes them in the light of necessary truths.

We think, we feel, we are free; these are facts; but of themselves they are barren. If we would fecundate them, we must take them as a kind of material of universal truths. Thought becomes immovable, it congeals, if deprived of the impulse of these ideas; sensation is common to us and the brutes; and liberty, without combination of motives presented by reason, has no object, no life.

71. Here we discover the cause of the obscurity and sterility of German philosophy since Fichte. Kant fixed himself upon the subject, without, however, destroying objectivity in the internal world; and therefore his philosophy, although containing many errors, offers to the mind some luminous points: but Fichte went farther, planted himself upon the *me*, and made no use of objectivity, save when it was necessary to the more solid establishment of a fact of consciousness; and so he found only realms of darkness and contradiction.

Men of gifted minds have labored in vain to make some ray of light emanate from a point condemned to obscurity. The soul sees itself in its own acts; and that it presents immediately to itself facts conducing to its own cognition is the only title it has, more than other beings distinct from it, to be conceived by itself. What would it know were it not to perceive its own thought, its will, and the exercise of all its faculties? How is it to discuss its own nature, if not from data furnished by the testimony of its own acts? The *me* then does not see itself intuitively; is offered to itself only mediately, by its acts; that is, so far as it is known, it is in the same category as all other external beings, which are all known by their effects upon us.

The *me* in itself considered, is not a luminous point; it supports the fabric of reason, but is not the rule according to which it is to be constructed. The true light is found in objectivity, for it is properly the object of knowledge. The *me* can neither be known nor thought, save inasmuch as it makes itself its own object, and consequently places itself on a level with other beings subject to intellectual activity, which operates only by virtue of objective truths.

72. Intelligence cannot be conceived without at least internal objects; but if the understanding do not conceive relations and consequently truths in them, they will be sterile. These truths will have no connection, will be isolated facts, if they involve no necessity; and even those relations which refer to particular facts furnished by experience will not be susceptible of any combination if they do not, at least conditionally, involve some necessity. The brilliancy of the light in the room where I now write is in itself a particular, contingent fact, and science, as such, cannot make it its object except by subjecting the movement of the light to geometrical laws, that is, to necessary truths.

Science then may find a resting-point in the *me* itself as subject, but no point of departure. The individual is of no service to the universal, nor the contingent to the necessary. Assuredly there would be no such thing as the individual A's science, if the individual A himself did not exist; but the science which stands in need of the individual subject is not science properly so called, but the collection of individual acts by which the individual perceives science. This collection of acts is not the science perceived, which is something common to all intellects, and does not need this or that individual: the fund of truths constituting science does not spring from this collection of individual acts, particular facts, which are lost like minutest drops in the ocean of intelligence.

How then can science be based solely upon the subjective *me*? How can the object be made to spring from this subject? Consciousness has no connection with science, except in so far as it furnishes facts to which we may apply objective, universal, and necessary principles, independent of all finite individuality, constituting the patrimony of human reason, but not requiring the existence of any man.

73. No analysis of the facts of consciousness will produce the origin of the lights of science. Such an act would be either direct or reflex. If direct, its value is objective not subjective, the act does not found science, but the truth perceived, not the subject but the object, not the *me*, but that which is seen by the *me*. If reflex, it supposes another previous act, to wit, the object of reflection, which is primitive, and not the act.

Neither is the combination of the direct with the reflex act of any service to science, except as connected with necessary and objective truths, which are independent of the subject. An act individually considered, is an internal phenomenon, which, apart from objective truths, teaches us nothing. It has, indeed, a scientific value, if considered under the general ideas of being, cause, effect, principle or product of activity, modification, or its relations with its subject, which is the *substratum* of other similar acts; that is, if it be considered as a particular case, comprised in the general ideas as a contingent phenomenon, to be appreciated by the help of necessary truths, as an experimental fact to which a theory may be applied.

The reflex act is only a cognition of a cognition, feeling, or some other internal phenomenon; and therefore all reflection upon consciousness presupposes a prior direct act. The object of this direct act is not the *me*; the fundamental principle of the cognition therefore is not the *me*, as the object known, but only as the necessary condition, since there cannot be thought without a thinking subject.

74. These considerations destroy the very foundations of the system of Fichte, and that of all who take the human me as their point of departure on the voyage of science. The me, in itself, is not presented to us; we know it only by its acts; and herein it participates of a quality of other objects, the essence of which is not immediately offered to us, but only what emanates from it by the exercise of their activity upon us.

Thus guided by objective and necessary truths, which are the laws of our understanding, the type of the relations of beings, and consequently a sure standard of them, we ascend by reasoning to the cognition of things themselves. We know that our mind is simple, because it thinks, whereas the composite, the multiplex cannot think. It is thus we know the *me*. We are conscious of its thinking activity, and this is the material furnished by the fact, but then comes the principle, the objective truth to illumine the fact, and show the repugnance between thought and composition, and the necessary connection between simplicity and consciousness.

Upon examination, this reasoning will be found to apply not only to the *me*, but to every thinking being; and this is why we can extend our demonstration to all such beings: the *me*, therefore, which applies this truth, does not create, it only knows it, and knows itself to be a particular case comprised in the general rule.

75. To pretend that truth has its source in the subjective *me*, is to begin by supposing the *me* to be an absolute, infinite being, the origin of all truths, and the reason of all beings; which is equivalent to making philosophy commence by deifying the human understanding. But as one individual has no more right to this deification than another, to admit it is to establish a rational pantheism, which, as we shall hereafter see, is nearly, if not quite, identical with absolute pantheism.

If we suppose individual reason to be only a phenomenon of the one absolute reason, and consequently what we call spirits not to be true substances, but modifications of a single spirit, and each particular consciousness to be only a manifestation of the universal consciousness, we can then conceive why the source of all truth is sought in the *me*, and why we interrogate our own consciousness as a kind of oracle through which the universal consciousness speaks. But the difficulty is that such a supposition is gratuitous, and that they who thus seek the reason of all truths, begin by establishing the most incomprehensible and absurd of propositions. Who will persuade us that our consciousness is only the modification of another? Who will make us believe that what we call the *me* is common to all men, to all intelligent beings, and that the only difference between them is the difference of the modifications of one absolute being? Why, then, is not this absolute being conscious of every consciousness which it comprises? Why does it not know that which it contains, and by which it is modified? Why does it believe itself multiplex, if indeed it be one? Where is the bond of this multiplicity? If each particular consciousness were only a modification, would it preserve its unity, and a connected series of all that happens to it, when this series, this unity is wanting to the substance which it modifies?

76. However this may be, not even by supposing pantheism, can the friends of subjective philosophy at all advance their pretensions. With pantheism they legitimate, so to speak, their pretension, but do not realize it. They call themselves gods, and as such, have a reason for the source of truth being in them; but as there is in their consciousness only one apparition of their divinity only one phase of the orb of light, they can only see in it what it presents to them; and their divinity finds itself subjected to certain laws which make it impossible for it to give the light demanded by philosophy.

77. If we interrogate our consciousness upon necessary truths, we shall perceive that, far from pretending to found or to create them, it both knows and confesses them to be independent of itself. If, thinking of this proposition: "It is impossible for a thing to be, and not be at the same time;" we ask ourselves if the truth of this originates in our thought, consciousness at once answers that it does not. The proposition was true before our consciousness existed; and should it now cease to exist, the proposition would still be true; true, also, when we do not think of it: the soul is as an eye which contemplates the sun, but is not, therefore, necessary to the existence of the sun.

78. Another consideration demonstrates the sterility of all philosophy which seeks in the *me* alone the sole and universal origin of human knowledge. Every cognition requires an object; purely subjective cognition is inconceivable; although we suppose the subject and object to be identified, duality of relation, real or conceived, is still necessary; that is, the subject as known must stand in a certain opposition, — opposition at least conceived, — with itself as subject knowing. Now, what is the object sought in the primitive act? Is it something not the subject? Then the philosophy of the subject falls into the current of other philosophies, since in this something which is not the subject are objective truths. Is it the subject itself? Then we ask, is it the subject in itself or in its acts; if the subject in its acts, then the philosophy is reduced to ideological analysis, and has no special characteristic; if the subject in itself, we say it is not known intuitively, and least of all can they who call it the *absolute* pretend to this cognition; it is for them even more than for others a dark abyss. In vain will you stoop over this abyss, and shout for truth; the dull rumbling which reaches your ears is only the echo of your own voice; the profound cavern rolls back to you only your own words still more hollow and mysterious.

79. Eminent among the philosophers most given to empty cavils is the author of the *Doctrine of Science*, Fichte, of whose system Madame de Staël ingenuously remarked, that it very much resembled the awakening of Pygmalion's statue from sleep, which, turning alternately to itself and to its pedestal said, *I am, I am not.*

Fichte says, in the beginning of his work entitled *Doctrine of Science*, that he proposes to seek the most absolute principle, the absolutely unconditioned principle of all human knowledge. This his method is erroneous: he begins by supposing what is unknown, and does not even suspect that there may be a true multiplicity in the basis of human cognitions. We believe that there may be, and that there really is such a multiplicity, that the sources of our knowledge are various, and of different orders, and that we cannot reduce them to unity without leaving man and ascending to God. We repeat it, this equivocation has become exceedingly general, and its only result has been uselessly to fatigue inquiring minds or to drive them to extravagant systems.

Few philosophers have toiled harder than Fichte after this absolute principle; and yet, to speak plainly, he accomplishes nothing; he either repeats Descartes' principle, or amuses himself with a play upon words. We feel pity at seeing him labor so earnestly to so little purpose. We beg the reader to follow us with patience in our examination of the German philosopher's doctrine, not with the hope of finding a thread to serve as a clue to the Dædalus of philosophy, but in order to judge, with a knowledge of the cause, doctrines which have made so much noise in the world.

"If this principle," says Fichte, "is absolutely the first, it can neither be defined nor demonstrated. It must express the act, which neither is nor can be presented among the empirical determinations of our consciousness, but rather lies at the bottom of all consciousness, and alone makes consciousness possible."[4]

Without any antecedent, or any reason, without even taking the trouble to show on what he bases it, Fichte assures us that the first principle must express an act. Why may it not be an objective truth? This, at least, would have deserved some attention, for all preceding schools, the Cartesian included, located the first principle among objective truths, not among acts. Descartes himself needed an objective truth in order to establish the fact of thought and existence. "Whoever thinks exists," or, in other words, "whoever does not exist cannot think."

80. This last remark shows one of the radical vices affecting the doctrine of Fichte and other Germans, who attribute an altogether unmerited importance to subjective philosophy. They accuse others of too easily making the transition from the subject to the object, but forget that they, at the same time pass, unauthorised by any reason or title, from objective thought to the pure subject. Confining ourselves to the passage of Fichte just cited, what, we ask, will an act be which neither is nor can be presented among the empirical determinations of our consciousness? The principle in question is not exempted from being known because it is absolute; for if we do not know it, we cannot assert that it is absolute; and if it is not, and cannot be presented among the empirical determinations of our consciousness, it neither is nor can be known. Man knows not that which is not present in his consciousness.

The absolute principle upon which all consciousness rests, and which makes it possible, either does or does not belong to consciousness. If the former, it is liable to all the difficulties affecting the other acts of consciousness; if the latter, it cannot be the object of observation, and therefore we can know nothing of it.

Fichte confesses that in order to arrive at the primitive act, and separate from it all that does not really belong to it, we must suppose the rules of all reflection to be valid, and start with some one of the many universally admitted propositions. "Conceding us," he says, "this proposition, you must, at the same time, concede as act that which we desire to place as the principle of the whole *Doctrine of Science*; and the result of the reflection must be that this act is conceded to us as the principle together with the proposition. We take any fact of empirical consciousness, and strip it one after another of all its empirical determinations, until reduced to all its purity it contains that only which thought cannot absolutely exclude, and from which nothing further can be taken."[5]

These words show that the German philosopher proposed ascending to a perfectly pure and wholly indeterminate act of consciousness, which, however, is impossible. Either he takes the act in a very broad sense, and understands by it the *substratum* of all consciousness, in which case he only expresses in other words the idea of substance; or else he speaks of an act properly so called, that is, of some exercise of that activity, that spontaneity which we feel within ourselves; and in this sense the act of consciousness cannot be separated from all determination without destroying its individuality and existence. Man cannot think without thinking something, desire without desiring something, feel without feeling something, or reflect upon internal acts without fixing his reflection upon something. There is some determination in every act of consciousness: an act perfectly pure, abstracted from every thing, and wholly indeterminate, is impossible, absolutely impossible; subjectively, because the act of consciousness, although considered in the subject, requires some determination; objectively, because such an act is inconceivable as individual, and consequently as existing, since it offers nothing determinate to the mind.

81. Fichte's indeterminate act is only the idea of act in general. He imagined he had made a great discovery when he conceived nothing in the groundwork but the principle of act, that is, the idea of substance applied to that active being whose existence consciousness itself makes known to us.

If we may be allowed to say candidly what we think, our opinion is, that Fichte, with all his analytical investigations, has not advanced philosophy one step towards the discovery of the first principle. We see from what has already been said how easy it is to stop him by simply demanding an account of the suppositions made on the first page of his book. Still, wishing, as we do, to oppose him with all fairness, we will not take up his ideas without allowing him to explain them himself.

"Every one admits the proposition: A is A; just as that A = A, because such is the meaning of the logical copula; and indeed without the least deliberation we perceive and affirm its complete certainty. Should any one ask a demonstration of it, we should by no means give any, but should maintain that the proposition is absolutely certain, that is, without any further foundation. Thus incontestibly proceeding with general consent, we claim the right to *suppose something absolutely.*

"We do not, in affirming the preceding proposition to be certain in itself, suppose that A *is*. The proposition A is A, is not equivalent to this: A *is*, or, *there is an* A. (*To be* placed without a predicate has an entirely different meaning from *to be* with a predicate, whereof more hereafter.) If we make A denote a space contained between two straight lines, the proposition remains exact, although the proposition, A *is*, be evidently false. But, we assert: *if* A *is*, A *is thus*. The question is in no wise whether A is in general or not. The question is not of the *contents* of the proposition, but only of its *form*; not whereof we know something, but what we know of any object whatever.

"Consequently, by the above assertion, that the proposition is absolutely certain, this is established, that between the *if* and the *thus* there is a necessary connection; and it is this necessary connection between both which is supposed *absolutely* and *without other foundation*. I call this necessary connection provisionally = X."

All this show of analysis amounts only to what every logical student knows, that in every proposition the copula, or the verb *to be*, denotes not the existence of the subject, but its relation to the predicate. There was no need of so many words to tell us so simple a thing, nor of such affected efforts of the understanding in treating of an identical proposition. But let us arm ourselves with patience, and continue to listen to the German philosopher:

"But to return to A itself, *whether* A is or not; nothing is as yet affirmed thereon. The question then occurs: under what condition is A?

"X at least is supposed *in* and *by* the *me*, for it is the *me* which judges in the above proposition, and indeed judges by X as by a law, which consequently being given to the *me*, and by it established absolutely and without other foundation, must therefore be given to the *me* by the *me* itself."

82. What does all this Sanscrit mean? We will translate it into English: in identical or equivalent propositions there is a relation which the mind knows, judges, and according to which it decides upon the rest: this relation is given to our mind; identical propositions need no proof in order to obtain assent. All this is very true, very clear, and very simple; but, when Fichte adds that this relation must be given to the *me* by the *me* itself, he asserts

what he neither does nor can know. Who told him that objective truths come to us from ourselves? Is one of the principal philosophical questions, such as is that of the origin of truth, to be thus easily solved with a dash of the pen? Has he, perchance, defined his *me*, or given us any idea of it? Either his words mean nothing, or they mean this: I judge of a relation; this judgment is in me; this relation, as known and abstracted from real existence, is in me; all which may be reduced to Descartes' more natural and simple expression: "I think, therefore I exist."

83. Upon carefully examining Fichte's words, we clearly see that he made no more progress than the French philosopher. He goes on: "*Whether* and *how* A in general is supposed, we know not; but as X must mark a relation between an unknown supposition of A and an absolute supposition of A under the condition of this supposition, in so far at least as that relation is supposed, A exists *in* the *me*, and is supposed *by* the *me*, just as X. X is possible only in relation to an A: but X is really supposed in the *me*, therefore A also must be supposed in the *me* in so far as X is referred to it."

What confusion and mystery in the expression of the commonest things! How great Descartes appears beside Fichte! Each makes the fact of consciousness revealing existence the beginning of his philosophy. The one expresses his thoughts clearly, with simplicity and in a language which all the world does or may understand; the other, in order to seem an inventor, and to show that he has no master, envelops himself in a cloud of mystery, with darkness all around, whence in a hollow voice he pronounces his oracles. Descartes says: "I think, I cannot doubt it, it is a fact attested to me by my internal sense; no one can think without existing; therefore I exist." This is clear, simple, and ingenuous; it manifests a true philosopher, one without affectation or pretension. Fichte says: "Take any proposition whatever; for example, A is A:" and then goes on to explain how the verb *to be* in propositions does not express the absolute existence of the subject, but its relation with the predicate; the whole with a show of doctrine, wearisome in its form, and ridiculous in its sterility; and this too when he only wants to inform us that A is in the *me*, because the relation of the predicate with the subject, that is, X, is possible only in a being, since A denotes some being or other. Let us compare the two syllogisms. Descartes says: "No one can think without existing; but I think; therefore I exist." Fichte says literally what follows: "X is only possible in relation to an A; but X is really supposed in the *me*; therefore A must also be supposed in the *me*." There is at bottom no difference at all, and the only difference in form is that which exists between the language of a vain man and that of a sensible man.

At bottom the syllogisms are not different, we repeat it. Descartes' major proposition is: "Whatever thinks exists." He does not prove it, and admits that it cannot be proved. Fichte's major is: "X is possible only in relation to an A," or, in other words, no relation of a predicate with a subject, in so far as it is known, is possible without a being which knows. "X must mark a relation between an unknown supposition of A and an absolute supposition of the same A, *at least in so far as that relation is supposed*," that is, inasmuch as it is known. And how does Fichte prove a relative supposition to suppose an absolute supposition, that is, a subject in which it is supposed? Like Descartes, he does not prove it at all. There is no relative A without an absolute A; what does not exist cannot think. This is clear and evident; farther than this neither Fichte nor Descartes goes.

Descartes' minor is: "*I think;*" this he does not prove, but refers to consciousness beyond which he confesses that he cannot pass. Fichte's minor is this: "X is really asserted in the *me;*" which is equivalent to saying: the relation of the predicate with the subject is really known by the *me;* and as, according to Fichte himself, the proposition may be selected at pleasure, to say that the relation of the predicate with the subject is known by the *me,* is the same as to say that any relation whatever is known by the *me;* which in clearer terms may be expressed thus, *I think.*

84. Here we would remark, that the difference, if any there be, is altogether in favor of the French philosopher, who understands by thought every internal phenomenon of which we are conscious. In order to establish this fact, he has no need of analyzing propositions, and confusing the understanding upon those very points where it most requires clearness and precision. Fichte, to arrive at the same point, takes a roundabout way. Descartes points his finger to it, and says: *this is it.* The one acts like a sophist, the other like a true man of genius.

Had the German philosopher confined his forms, little calculated as they are to illustrate science, to what we have thus far examined, their greatest inconvenience would have been to weary both the author and his readers; but unfortunately his mysterious *me,* which makes its appearance at the very vestibule of science, and which, in the eyes of sound reason, can only be what it was to Descartes,—the human mind, knowing its existence by its own thought,—goes on dilating in Fichte's hands, like a gigantic spectre, which, beginning in a single point, ends by hiding its head in the heavens and its feet in the abyss. This *me,* absolute subject, is then a being which exists because it supposed itself: it is a being which creates its own self, absorbs every thing, is every thing, and is revealed in the human mind as in one of the infinite phases of its infinite existence.

What we have thus far said, suffices to show the tendencies of Fichte's system. We are here treating of certainty and its foundations; this, then, is not the place to anticipate what we propose to say more at length upon this system when we come to explain the idea of substance and refute pantheism: for this is one of the gravest errors of modern philosophy; everywhere, and under all aspects, it must be combatted, but to do this we must attack it in its roots. This is why we have examined at such length Fichte's fundamental reflection in his *Doctrine of Science*, and stripped it of the importance which he claimed for it, so as to make it the basis of a transcendental science; for he flattered himself with being able to determine the absolutely unconditioned principle of all human knowledge.(7)

CHAPTER VIII
UNIVERSAL IDENTITY

85. In order to give unity to science, some appeal to universal identity; this, however, is not to discover unity, but to take refuge in chaos. Universal identity is not only an absurdity, but a groundless hypothesis. Excepting the unity of consciousness, we find in ourselves nothing that is one; but multiplicity of ideas, perceptions, judgments, acts of the will, impressions of various kinds; and in relation to external objects, we perceive multitude in the beings which surround us, or as some pretend, in their appearances. Where then are unity and identity, for we can neither find them within nor without ourselves?

86. If it be said that nothing is offered to us but phenomena, and that we do not attain to the reality, the absolute and identical unity hidden beneath them, we can reply with this dilemma: either our experience is confined to phenomena, or it reaches the very nature of things: if the former, we cannot know what is concealed under the phenomena, nor absolute and identical unity; if the latter, then nature is not one but multiplex, for we everywhere encounter multiplicity.

87. It is curious to observe how easily men, the most skeptical in the simplest things, suddenly become dogmatic at the very point where the greatest motives of doubt are presented. With them the external world is either a pure appearance, or a being having no resemblance to the conception formed of it by the human race: the criterion of evidence, that of consciousness, and that of common sense have little power to command assent: the crowd alone should be satisfied with such weak foundations; the philosopher demands others far more solid. But strange as it may seem, the very philosopher who styled reality a deceitful appearance, and saw obscurity in what the human race considered luminous, so soon as he quitted the world of phenomena and arrived in the dominions of the absolute, finds himself illumined by a mysterious splendor, he requires no discussion, but by a most pure intuition, he sees the unconditioned, the infinite, the one in which every thing multiplex is involved, the great reality, the basis of all phenomena, the great All which re-unites in its breast all existences, re-assumes every thing, and absorbs every thing into most perfect identity.

He fixes his philosophic eye upon this focus of light and life, sees it roll out like the ocean of existence in vast billows, and thus explains what is various by what is one, the composite by the simple, the finite by the infinite. All these prodigies do not require him to leave himself; he has only to go on destroying all that is empirical, to ascend even to pure act by mysterious by-paths unknown to all except himself. This *me*, which may have believed itself an existence perishable and dependent on another superior existence, is astounded at finding itself so great; it discovers in itself the origin of all beings, or, more correctly speaking, the only being, of which all others are but phenomenal existences; it is the universe itself become by a gradual development conscious of itself: whatever is without itself, and at first appears distinct, is only itself, a reflection of itself, presented to its eyes, and unfolded under a thousand different forms like a magnificent panorama.

Let not the reader think we have imagined a system for the sake of combatting it; the doctrine which we have here exposed, is the doctrine of Schelling.

88. One cause of this error is the obscurity of the problem of knowing. To know, is an immanent action, having, at the same time, relation to an external object, excepting those cases in which the intelligent being becomes, by a reflex act, its own object. In order to know a truth, whatever it may be, the mind does not quit itself; it does not operate beyond itself; its own consciousness tells it that it remains, and that its activity is developed, within itself.

This immanent action extends to objects the most distant in time and place, and the most unlike in their nature. How is the mind to come in contact with them? How is it to ascertain whether their representation conforms to reality? There can be no cognition without this representation; without conformity, there is no truth, cognition is a pure illusion to which nothing corresponds, and the human understanding is unceasingly the sport of vain appearances.

Undeniably this problem is liable to very serious difficulties, which perhaps the science of man, while in this life, cannot solve. Here arise all the ideological and psychological questions ever treated by the most eminent metaphysicians. However, as it is not our intention to anticipate what is to be hereafter considered, we shall confine ourselves to the point of view indicated by our present question of certainty and its fundamental principle.

89. Consciousness attests the fact of representation; without this there is no thought; and the affirmation *I think* is, if not the origin of all philosophy, at least its indispensable condition.

90. Whence comes the representation? How is a being placed in such communication with other beings, and this not by a transient but by an immanent act? How explain the conformity between the representation and the object? Does not this mystery indicate that there is unity, identity, at the bottom of all things, that the being which knows, is the very being known, which appears to itself under a distinct form, and that what we call realities are only phenomena of one and the same being, always identical, infinitely active, which develops its strength in various ways, and forms by its development what we call the universe? No! This neither is nor can be! It is an absurdity which the most extravagant reason cannot accept: it is a resource as desperate as it is impotent to explain a mystery, if you will, but one a thousand times less obscure than the system which pretends to clear it up.

91. Universal identity explains nothing, but greatly confuses everything; it does not dissipate the difficulty, but strengthens it, and renders it insolvable. It certainly is no easy matter to explain how the mind obtains the representation of things distinct from itself; but it is no easier to show how the mind can have the representation of itself. If there is unity, complete identity between the subject and the object, how are the two presented to us as distinct things? How can duality proceed from unity, or diversity spring from identity?

It is a fact testified by experience, not the experience of external objects, but that of consciousness, by that which is most hidden in our soul, that there is in every cognition a subject and an object, perception and the thing perceived, and without this difference the act is not possible. Even when by an effort of reflection, we take ourselves for our own object, the duality appears; if it does not exist, we imagine it, for without this fiction we cannot think.

92. Even in the most intimate and concentrated reflection, duality, upon careful examination, is to be found, not by fiction, as it might seem at first sight, but in reality. When the understanding turns upon itself, it does not see its own essence, for it has no direct intuition of itself: it sees its acts, and these it takes for its object. The reflex act is not the act reflected. When I think that I think, the first thought is distinct from the second, and so distinct that one succeeds the other, for the reflective thought can exist only subsequently to the thought reflected.

93. This is confirmed by a profound analysis of reflection. Is reflection possible without an object reflected upon? Evidently not. What is this object in the present case? The thought itself: then this thought must have preceded the reflection. If it be supposed that they must not of necessity

follow in different instants of time, and that the dependence is saved, notwithstanding the simultaneousness, still the force of the argument is not lost; we grant, but do not concede, that the simultaneousness is possible; but the dependence at least is not possible without distinction. Dependence is a relation; relation supposes opposition of extremes; and this opposition draws with it distinction.

94. That these acts are distinct, although simultaneous, may be demonstrated in another manner. One of them, that reflected upon, may exist without the reflex act. We continually think, without thinking that we think; and the same may be proved true of every reflection whatever, whether it is occupied with the act thought, or it disappears and leaves only the direct act: these acts are, therefore, not only distinct but separable; therefore, the duality of the subject and the object exists not only in the external world, but also in that which is the most intimate and pure in our soul.

95. It avails not to say that the object of reflection is not any determinate act, but thought in general. This is in many cases false; for we not only think that we think, but that we think a determinate thing. Moreover, although the object of reflection is sometimes thought in general, not even then does the duality disappear: in that case the subjective act is an individual act, existing in a determinate instant of time, and its object is thought in general, that is, an idea representative of all thought, an idea which involves a sort of confused recollection of all past acts, or of what is called activity, intellectual force. The duality then exists more evidently, if possible, than when the object is a determinate thought. In one instance at least two individual acts are compared; but in this case an individual act is compared with an abstract idea, a thing existing in one instant of time with an idea that either abstracts it, or confusedly embraces all that has passed since the epoch when the consciousness of the reflecting being commenced.

96. These arguments have much greater weight when directed against those philosophers who place the essence of the mind not in the power of thinking but in thought itself; who give to the *me* no other existence than what springs from its own knowledge, affirming that it exists only because it *supposes* itself, by knowing itself, and only in so far as it *supposes* itself, that is, in so far as it knows itself. With this system there is duality, or rather plurality, not only in the acts, but even in the *me* itself; because this *me* is an act, and acts follow like a series of fluxions developed to infinity. Thus, far from saving the unity and identity of subject and object, plurality and multiplicity are established in the subject itself; and the unity of consciousness itself, in danger of being broken by the cavils of philosophers, is forced to take refuge in the obscurity of invincible nature.

97. We have thus incontestably proved that there is in us a duality of subject and object, that without it knowledge is inconceivable, and that representation itself is a contradiction unless in one sense or another we admit things really distinct in the recesses of intelligence. We beg to observe that we have a sublime type of this distinction in the august mystery of the Trinity, the fundamental dogma of our holy religion, covered, indeed, with an impenetrable veil, but which sends forth light to illustrate the profoundest questions of philosophy. This mystery is not explained by feeble man, but is for him a sublime explanation. Thus Plato availed himself of glimmerings from this focus as a treasure of immense value to philosophical theories; thus the Holy Fathers and theologians, in endeavoring to throw some light upon it by arguments of congruity, have illustrated the most occult mysteries of human thought.

98. The upholders of universal identity, besides contradicting a primitive and fundamental fact of consciousness, signally fail in their efforts to explain by it either the origin of intellectual representation or its conformity to its object. Evidently no man has an intuition of the nature of the individual *me*, and still less of the absolute being which these philosophers suppose as the *substratum* of whatever exists or appears. It is impossible for them to explain *a priori*, without this intuition, the representation of objects or their conformity to the representation. The fact, therefore, on which they would base their whole philosophy, either does not exist, or is unknown to us: in neither case can it serve as the foundation of a system.

Were this fact to exist, it could not be presented to our mind by any enunciation to which we could arrive by reasoning. It must be seen rather than known; either occupy the first place or none. If we begin to reason without taking this fact for our basis, we start from the apparent in order to attain to what truly is; we make use of an illusion to arrive at reality. Thus it evidently follows from the system of our adversaries that philosophy must either start with the most powerful intuition, or else it cannot advance a single step.

99. The schools distinguish between the principle of being and the principle of knowledge, *principium essendi et principium cognoscendi*; but this distinction has no place in the system which we oppose; being is there confounded with knowledge; what exists, exists because it is known, and it exists only in so far as it is known. To draw out the series of cognitions, is to develop the series of existences. They are not even two parallel movements; they are but one movement; the *me* is the universe, and the universe is the *me*; whatever exists is a development of the primitive fact, is the fact itself which is displayed under different forms, extending like an infinite ocean; its position is unlimited space; its duration eternity.(8)

CHAPTER IX
UNIVERSAL IDENTITY,—CONTINUED

100. These systems, as absurd as they are fatal, although under distinct forms, and by various means, they tend to prepare the way for pantheism, contain a profound truth which, disfigured by vain cavils, seems to be an abyss of darkness, whereas it is in itself a ray of most brilliant light.

The human mind seeks that by reason to which it is impelled by an intellectual instinct; how to reduce plurality to unity, to re-unite, as it were, all the variety of existences in a point from which they all proceed, and in which they are all absorbed. The understanding knows that the conditioned must be included in the unconditioned, the relative in the absolute, the finite in the infinite, the various in the one. In this, all religions, all schools of philosophy agree. The proclamation of this truth belongs to no one of them exclusively; it is to be met with in all countries of the world, in primitive times, back even to the cradle of the human race. Beautiful, sublime tradition! Preserved through all generations, amid the ebb and flow of events, it offers us the idea of the Divinity presiding over the origin and destiny of the universe.

101. Yes! The unity sought by philosophers is the Divinity itself,—the Divinity whose glory the firmament declares, and whose august face of ineffable splendor appears to us in our inmost consciousness. Yes! it is the Divinity which enlightens and guides the true philosopher, but blinds and confounds the proud sophist; it is what the true philosopher calls God, and venerates and adores in the sanctuary of his soul, but what the insensate philosopher, with sacrilegious profanation, calls the *me*. Considering its personality, its consciousness, its infinite intelligence, and its most perfect liberty, it is the foundation and the copestone of religion: distinct from the world, it produced the world from nothing, and preserves and governs it, and leads it by mysterious paths to the destiny assigned in its immutable decrees.

102. There is then unity in the world; there is unity in philosophy. In this all agree; the difference is that some separate, with the greatest care, the finite from the infinite, the thing created from the creative power, unity

from multiplicity, and maintain the necessary communication between the free will of the omnipotent agent and finite existences, between the wisdom of the sovereign intelligence and the fixed course of the universe: while others, affected with melancholy blindness, confound the effect with the cause, the finite with the infinite, the various with the one, and reproduce in the domain of philosophy the chaos of primeval times; but all scattering and in frightful confusion, without any hope of order or union: the earth of these philosophers is void, and darkness is upon the face of their deep; the spirit of God has not moved over the waters to fecundate the chaos, and produce oceans of life and light out of darkness and death.

The absurd systems invented by philosophical vanity explain nothing; the system of religion, which is that also of sound philosophy, and of all mankind, explains everything: the intellectual, as well as the corporeal world, is a chaos to the human mind the instant it abandons the idea of God: restore this and order reappears.

103. The two capital problems: whence the intellectual representation, and whence its conformity to objects, have with us a most simple explanation. Our understanding, although limited, participates in the infinite light; this light is not that which exists in God himself, but a semblance communicated to a being created according to his image.

Illumined by this light, objects shine upon the eyes of our mind, whether because they are in communication with it by means unknown to us, or because the representation is given to us directly by God, in the presence of objects.

The conformity of the representation to the thing represented, results from the divine veracity. An infinitely perfect God cannot take pleasure in deceiving his creatures. Such is the theory of Descartes and Malebranche, eminent thinkers, who took no step in the intellectual order, without looking to the Author of all light, and who never wrote a page on which the name of God was not traced.

104. As will hereafter be seen, Malebranche admitted that man sees every thing in God, even in this life; but his system, far from identifying the human *me* with the infinite being, carefully distinguishes them, not finding other means to sustain and enlighten the former than by approximating and uniting it to the second. To read the great metaphysician's immortal work is enough to convince one that his system was not that of this pure, primitive intuition, which is an act required of all empiricism, and which seems to rise within the limits of philosophy, from that intuition of the simple fact, the origin of all ideas and all facts, in which one of the dogmas of our religion, the beatific vision, seems realized upon earth in the domain of philosophy. These are senseless pretensions, and as far from the mind as from the system of Malebranche.(9)

CHAPTER X
PROBLEM OF REPRESENTATION:
MONADS OF LEIBNITZ

105. The pretension to find a real truth, the fountain of all others, is dangerous in the extreme, however indifferent it may at first sight appear. Pantheism, and the deification of the *me*, two systems which coincide at bottom, are a consequence not easy to be avoided if it be attempted to establish all human science upon one fact.

106. The real truth or fact, which would serve as the basis of all science, should be immediately perceived, otherwise it would lack the character of origin and basis of other truths; because the medium by which it should be perceived would itself have the better right to the title of first truth. If this intermediate fact were the cause of the other, evidently this latter would not be primitive; and if the priority were given to the order of knowledge instead of the order of being, we should still have the same difficulty as now to explain the transition from subject to object, or the legitimacy of the medium by which we perceive the primitive fact.

Since then, the immediate presence, the intimate union of the understanding with the thing known is necessary, it is clear that as the *me* has this immediate presence only for itself and its own acts, the fact sought for must be the *me* itself. That which is immediately present to us is the facts of consciousness; by them we place ourselves in communication with what is distinct from us. In case then that we must find a primitive fact, the origin of all others, this fact must be the *me*. If we deny this consequence, we must deny the possibility of finding any fact which may be the source of transcendental science. Here we see how the apparently most innocent philosophical pretensions lead to fatal results.

107. There is here certainly very little chance for evasion, but there is one so specious as to merit an examination.

The fact, which is the scientific origin of all others, is not necessarily their true origin. By distinguishing between the principle of being and the principle of knowledge, all difficulty seems to be avoided. It is absurd and contrary to common sense, that the *me* is the origin of all that exists; but not that it is the representative principle of all that is or can be known. Representation is not synonymous with causality. Ideas represent but do not cause the objects represented. Why, then, is it not possible to admit a fact representative of all that the human understanding can know? It is certain that the perception of this fact must be immediate, that is, it must be supposed intimately present to the understanding perceiving it; for which reason, it can be nothing else than the *me*: this, however, is not to deify the *me*, but only to concede to it a representative force, which may have been given to it by a superior being. It makes the *me* not an universal cause, but a mirror which reflects the internal and external worlds.

This explanation reminds us of the famous system of *monads* advanced by Leibnitz; an ingenious system indeed, the lofty flight of one of the mightiest geniuses that ever honored the human race. The whole world formed of invisible beings, all representative of the same universe, whereof they are a part, but by a representation adequate to their respective categories, and in conformity to their corresponding point of view, according to the place which they occupy, unrolling themselves in an immense series, which, commencing with the lowest order, goes on ascending to the very portal of infinity; and at the uppermost point of existences is the monad, which, in itself contains the reason of all things, which has produced them from nothing, given to them their representative force, and distributed them into their proper categories, establishing among them a sort of parallelism of perception, will, action, and motion, in such a manner that, without any one communicating any thing to another, they all move on in most perfect conformity, in ineffable harmony. This is grand, beautiful, and wonderful; a colossal hypothesis which the genius of Leibnitz alone could ever have conceived.

108. Having paid this tribute of admiration to the eminent author of the *Monadology*, we observe that its gigantic conception is only an hypothesis which all the talent of its inventor could never base upon a single fact capable of giving to it an appearance of probability. Omitting the very serious difficulties, which this system, doubtless against the will of its author, opposes to the explanation of free will, we shall confine ourselves to the examination of the bearings of this system upon the question now before us.

In the first place, the representation of the monads, being a mere hypothesis, can serve to explain nothing, unless philosophy is to be made the sport of ingenious combination. The *me* is a monad, that is, an indivisible unity; of this there can be no doubt. The *me* is a monad representative of the universe: this is an absolutely gratuitous assertion, and until it is proved in some way or other, we have the right to ignore it.

109. Now, suppose the representative force, as understood by Leibnitz, to exist in the *me*; this hypothesis does not impugn what has been said against the primitive origin of transcendental science. On close inspection, the hypothesis of Leibnitz will be found to explain the origin of ideas, but not their connection. Make the soul a mirror, in which, by an effect of the creative will, every thing is represented; still it does not explain the order of these representations, show how one of them springs from another, or assign to them any other bond than the unity of consciousness. This system then is quite out of the question: we are not disputing on the manner in which representations exist in the soul, nor on their origin; but we are examining the opinion which pretends to found all science upon a single fact, and to unfold all ideas as simple modifications of that fact. This Leibnitz never said, nor can any thing be found in any of his works to indicate such a thought. Moreover, the difference between this system of *Monadology* and that of the German Philosophers, which we impugn, is too palpable to escape any one.

I. So far is Leibnitz from advocating universal identity, that he establishes an infinite plurality and multiplicity: his monads are beings really different and distinct among themselves.

II. The whole universe, composed of monads, proceeded, according to Leibnitz, from one infinite monad; and this procession was not by emanation, but by creation.

III. In the infinite monad, in God, Leibnitz places the sufficient reason of every thing.

IV. Knowledge has been freely given by God himself to the monads.

V. This knowledge, and the consciousness of it, belong to the monads individually, and Leibnitz never even remotely took into consideration this foundation of all things, which by its transformation ascends from nature to consciousness, or descends from the region of consciousness and is converted into nature.

110. These differences so marked need no comments; they show most evidently that the philosophers of modern Germany cannot shield themselves under the name of Leibnitz; although, in truth, these philosophers have no failing of that kind: far from seeking guides, they all aspire to originality, and this is one principal cause of their extravagance, Hegel, Schelling, and Fichte, all pretend to be founders of a philosophy; and Kant was so governed by the same ambition, that he made very important alterations in the second edition of his *Critic of Pure Reason*, lest he should be taken for a plagiarist from Berkeley's idealism.(10)

CHAPTER XI
PROBLEM OF REPRESENTATION EXAMINED

111. All our knowledge is by representation, without which it would be inconceivable; and yet what is representation in itself considered? We cannot say: it enlightens us as to other objects, but not as to itself.

It is obvious that we do not attempt to conceal the very grave difficulties which the solution of this problem offers: on the contrary, we point them out with all clearness, in order to avoid that vain presumption which is as fatal to science as to every thing else. But let it not be supposed that we intend to banish this question from the arena of philosophy: for many and serious as are its difficulties, we are yet of opinion that they allow of sufficiently probable conjectures.

112. The representative force may emanate from any one of these three sources: identity, causality, or ideality. We will explain ourselves. A thing may represent itself; and this we call representation of identity. A cause may represent its effect; and this is what we understand by representation of causality. A being, whether substance or accident, may represent another distinct from itself, which is not its effect; and this we call representation of ideality.

We do not see how it is possible to assign any other source of representation: holding, therefore, the division to be complete, we will examine its three points; and we beg to call the attention of the reader more especially to this matter, because it is one of the most important in philosophy.

113. That which represents must have some relation to the thing represented: whether essential or accidental, inherent or communicated, this relation must exist. Two beings, having absolutely no relation, one of which nevertheless represents the other, are a monstrosity. There is nothing without a sufficient reason; and there being no relation between the thing representing, and that represented, there is no sufficient reason of the representation.

It is here to be borne in mind that, for the present, we abstract the nature of this relation; we do not assert it to be either real or ideal; we only say that, between the thing representing and that represented, there must be some link, whatever that link may be. Its mysteries, its incomprehensibility, do not destroy its existence. Philosophy perhaps may be unable to explain the enigma; but it can demonstrate the existence of the link. Thus, abstracting all experience, it is possible to demonstrate *a priori*, that there is a relation between the *me* and other beings, by the mere fact of their representation existing in the *me*.

The incessant communication of intelligences with each other, and with the universe, proves that there is a point of union for them all. Representation, alone, is a convincing proof of this: so many beings, apparently dispersed and unconnected, are intimately united in some centre, so that the simple phenomenon of intelligence leads us to affirm the common link, the unity in which plurality is joined. This unity, with pantheists, is universal identity; with us, it is God.

114. Here observe that this relation between the thing representing and that represented, is not necessarily direct or immediate; it suffices that it be with a third object: thus, they who explain representation by identity, and they who account for it by intermediate ideas, must equally admit it; for, on the present matter, there is no difference between those who hold these ideas to be produced by the action of objects upon our mind, and those who make them proceed immediately from God.

115. Whatever represents any thing, contains in some sense the thing represented; for an object cannot be represented unless it is in some manner or other in the representation. It may be the object itself, or its image; but this image cannot represent the object, unless it is known to be its image. Every idea then involves the relation of objectivity; otherwise it could not represent the object, but only itself. The act of intelligence is immanent, but in such a manner, that the intellect does not need to go out of itself to attain its object. When we think of a star a million leagues distant, our mind certainly does not go to the point where the star is; but by means of the idea, it destroys in an instant this immense distance, and unites itself with the star. What it perceives is not the idea, but its object: if this idea did not involve a relation to the object, it would cease to be an idea to the mind, and would represent nothing except itself.

116. There is then, in every perception, a connection of the being that perceives with the thing perceived. When this perception is not immediate, the medium must be such as to contain a necessary relation to the object; it must conceal itself in order to offer to the eye of the mind only the thing represented. From the instant that it presents itself, and is seen, or even noticed, it ceases to be an idea and becomes an object. The idea is a mirror,

which is most perfect when it creates the most perfect illusion. It must necessarily present only the objects, and project them at the proper distance, without allowing the eye to see the crystalline plane which reflects them.

117. This union of the thing representing, with that represented, of the intellect with its objects, may, in some instances, be explained by identity. In general, no contradiction is discovered in any thing representing itself to the eye of the understanding, if we suppose them to be united in some way or other. In case then that the thing known is itself intelligent, we see no difficulty in its being its own representation, and consequently none in confounding ideality and reality in the same being. If an idea can represent an object, why may it not represent itself? If an intelligent being can know an object through the medium of an idea, why may it not know that object immediately? The union of the thing known with the intellect is to us a mystery, it is true; but is the union effected by the medium of an idea less so? To the idea may be objected all that can be brought against the thing itself; and it is even more inexplicable how one thing represents another, than how it represents itself. The thing representing and that represented, have between them a sort of relation of containing and contained. It is easily conceived that the identical contains itself, since identity expresses much more than to contain; but it is not so easily conceived how the accident can contain the substance, the transitory the permanent, the ideal the real. Identity is then a true principle of representation.

118. We would here make the following remarks necessary to avoid equivocations.

I. We do not assert a necessary relation between identity and representation; for this would make every being representative, since every being is identical with itself. We establish this proposition: identity may be the origin of representation; but we deny the two following: identity is the necessary origin of representation; representation is a sign of identity.

II. We determine nothing as to the application of the relations between representation and identity, so far as finite beings are concerned.

III. We abstract the duality which results from supposing only subject and object, and enter into no question on the nature of this duality.

119. These ideas being fixed, we may observe that we have an incontestable proof that there is no intrinsic repugnance between identity and representation in two dogmas of the Catholic religion: the beatific vision and the divine intelligence. The dogma of the beatific vision teaches us that the human soul in the mansion of the blessed is intimately united to God, and sees him face to face in his very essence. No one ever said that this vision was made by the medium of an idea, but theologians, and among

them St. Thomas, expressly teach the contrary. We have then identity united with representation, that is, the divine essence representing, or rather presenting, itself to the eyes of the human mind. The dogma of divine intelligence teaches that God is infinitely intelligent. God does not need to go out of himself, nor employ distinct ideas in order to understand; he sees himself in his essence. Here, too, identity is united with representation, and the intelligent being identified with the thing understood.(11)

CHAPTER XII
IMMEDIATE INTELLIGIBILITY

120. Neither active nor passive representation can be predicated of all things; we mean to say, that there are some beings which are not endowed with intellectual activity, and cannot be even passively the object of the acts of the intellect.

As regards the power of active representation, which is at bottom only the faculty of intelligence, it is evident that many beings are destitute of it. There may be greater difficulty with regard to passive representation, or the fitness to be the immediate object of the intellect.

121. An object cannot be known immediately, that is, without the mediation of an idea, if it do not itself perform the functions of this idea, and unite itself to the intellect which is to know it. This alone takes from all material objects the character of being *immediately intelligible*: so that if a mind be imagined having no idea of the corporeal universe, it could know nothing of it, although for all eternity in the midst of it.

Hence it follows that matter neither is, nor can be, intelligent or intelligible: the ideas which we have of it come from another source; without them we might be united to matter, and never know or even suspect its existence.

122. An opportunity is here presented of explaining an exceedingly curious doctrine of St. Thomas. This eminent metaphysician was of opinion that it required greater perfection to be immediately intelligible than to be intelligent; so that the human mind, although endowed with intelligence, does not possess intelligibility.

In his *Summa Theologica*,[6] the holy Doctor asks if the soul knows itself by its essence, and answers that it does not, and thus defends his position:

"Things are intelligible accordingly as they act, and not as they have the power to act, as is said in the ninth book of Metaphysics (tex. 20 tr. 3). For any thing that comes under knowledge is being, is the true, in so far as it is in act, and this is manifestly apparent in sensible things. Thus the sight does not perceive that which may be colored, but that only which actually is colored. And in the same manner as is manifest, the intellect, in so far as it knows material things, knows that only which is in act.... Hence, also, in immaterial substances, each one is intelligible by its essence, accordingly as it is in act by its essence. Therefore, the essence of God, which is a pure and perfect act, is absolutely and perfectly intelligible by itself; thus God knows, by his essence, not only himself but also all other things. But the essence of the angel belongs to the class of intelligible beings as an act, but not as a pure and complete act, wherefore his understanding is not completed by his essence. For, although the angel knows himself by his essence, he cannot know all things by his essence, but knows those distinct from himself only by their images. But the human intellect in the class of intelligible beings is only a possible being.... Therefore, considered in its essence, it is an intelligent power; hence of itself it has the faculty of understanding, but not of being understood, except inasmuch as it acts. On this account the Platonists placed the order of intelligible beings above the order of intellect; because the intellect understands only by participation of the intelligible; but according to them, that which participates is beneath that of which it participates. If, then, the human intellect places itself in act by the participation of separate intelligible forms, as the Platonists held, it would know itself by this participation of incorporeal things. But as it is natural to our intellect in the present life to look to material and sensible things, it follows that our intellect knows itself only as it is placed in act by the species (ideas) abstracted from sensible things by the light of the intellect acting, which is the act of the intelligible things themselves.... Therefore our intellect does not know itself by its essence but by its acts."

Such is the doctrine of St. Thomas. Cardinal Cajetan, one of the most penetrating and subtle minds that ever existed, has a commentary on this passage, worthy of the text. These are his words: "Two things expressly follow, from what is said in the text. The first is, that our intellect has of itself the faculty of understanding. The second is, that our intellect has not of itself the faculty of being understood. Hence the order of intellect is below the order of intelligible beings. For if the perfection, which our intellect has of itself, is sufficient to understand, but not to be understood, it necessarily follows that greater perfection is required in a thing to be understood than to understand. And because St. Thomas saw this consequence, which at first sight does not seem true, and might even be objected to him, he excludes this apprehension, by showing that this must be admitted to be true not only by the Peripatetics, from whose doctrine it results, but also by the Platonists."

But afterwards, in answer to an objection brought by Scotus, called the Subtle Doctor, he adds: "But because in order to understand an intellect and an intelligible object are required, and the relation of the intellect to the intelligible, is the relation of the perfectible to its perfection, since the intellect in act consists in its being itself the intelligible thing, as is evident from what has been said above; it follows that immaterial beings are divided into two orders, intellects, and things intelligible. And as the intelligible consists in perfective immateriality, it follows that any thing is intelligible inasmuch as it is immaterially perfective. That intelligibility requires immateriality is shown by this, that no material thing is intelligible, unless, inasmuch as it is abstracted from matter.... It has already been shown that any thing is intelligible by this, that not only itself, but others, also, are in the intelligible order, either in act or in potentiality; it is thus nothing more than to be perfected or perfectible by the intelligible."

123. This theory may be more or less solid, but it is in either case something more than ingenious; it raises a new problem in philosophy of the highest importance: to assign the conditions of intelligibility. It has moreover the advantage of being in accordance with a fact attested by experience; this fact is the difficulty experienced by the mind in knowing itself. If it is immediately intelligible, why does it not know itself? What condition is wanting? Its intimate presence? It has not only presence but identity. Perhaps the effort to know itself? But the greater part of philosophy has no other end than this knowledge. By denying immediate intelligibility to the soul, we can explain why so great a difficulty is involved in ideological and psychological investigations, by showing the reason of the obscurity experienced in passing from direct to reflex acts.

124. The opinion of St. Thomas is not a mere conjecture: we may, in order to establish it in some manner upon fact, assign a reason which seems to us greatly to strengthen it, and which may be regarded as merely an extension of the one already given.

A thing to be intelligible must have two qualities: immateriality, and the activity necessary to operate upon the intelligent being. This activity is indispensable, for in the act of intelligence, the intellect is in some sense passive. When the idea is present, the intellect cannot but know it: when it is wanting, it is impossible for the intellect to know it. The idea, therefore, enables the intellect to act; without it the intellect can do nothing. Consequently, if we admit that any being can serve as idea to the intellect, we must concede that being an activity to excite intellectual action; and so far we make it superior to the intellect excited.

Thus we explain why our intellect, in this life at least, does not know itself by itself. Experience shows that its activity needs to be excited. Left to itself it is like one asleep; and this want of activity in our mind, in the absence of exciting influences, is one of the most constant of psychological facts.

This is not, however, to say that we have no spontaneity, and that no action is possible without an external determining cause; but only that this same spontaneous development would not exist, if we had not previously been subjected to the influence of causes which brought out our activity. We may learn things not taught us; but we could learn nothing, if teaching had not presided over the first development of our mind. There are, it is true, many ideas in our mind, which are not sensations, and which cannot have emanated from them; but it is equally true that a man, deprived of all his senses, could not think, because his mind would want the exciting cause.

125. We have dwelt thus long upon the explanation of the problem of intelligibility, because we consider it of scarcely less importance than that of intelligence, although we do not find it treated in philosophical works as it merits. We will now reduce this doctrine to clear and simple propositions, so that the reader may form a more complete conception of it; and also, in order to deduce some consequences which have been only slightly indicated in our exposition:

I. A thing must be immaterial in order to be immediately intelligible.

II. Matter cannot be intelligible by itself.

III. The relations of spirits to bodies, or the representation of the latter in the former, cannot be purely objective.

IV. Some other class of relations must necessarily be admitted to explain the representative union of the world of intelligences with the corporeal world.

V. Immediate objective representation supposes activity in the object.

VI. The power of an object to represent itself to the eyes of an intelligence, supposes in it a faculty of acting on that intelligence.

VII. This faculty necessarily produces an effect, and consequently involves a kind of superiority of the object over the intelligence.

VIII. An intelligent being is not necessarily immediately intelligible.

IX. Immediate intelligibility seems to require greater perfection than intelligence.

X. Although not every intelligent being is intelligible, yet every intelligible being is intelligent.

XI. God, who is in every sense infinite activity, is infinitely intelligent and infinitely intelligible by himself.

XII. God is intelligible by all created intellects, provided it be his will to present himself immediately to them, and strengthen and elevate them as may be necessary.

XIII. There is no repugnance in immediate intelligibility being communicated to some beings, which are consequently intelligible by themselves.

XIV. Our soul, while united to our body, is not immediately intelligible, and we know it only by its acts.

XV. In this want of immediate intelligibility is found the reason of the difficulty of ideological and psychological studies, and the obscurity which we experience in passing from direct to reflex knowledge.

XVI. Therefore, the philosophy of the *me*, or that which seeks to explain the internal and external world by starting from the *me*, is impossible; it commences by denying one of the fundamental facts of psychology.

XVII. Therefore, the doctrine of universal identity is also absurd, since it gives both intelligence and immediate intelligibility to matter, which can have neither.

XVIII. Spiritualism, therefore, is a truth which springs as well from subjective as from objective philosophy, from intelligence as from intelligibility.

XIX. We must, therefore, go beyond ourselves, and even rise above the universe to find the origin of either subjective or objective representation.

XX. Therefore, we must ascend to a primitive, infinite activity, which places intelligences in communication among themselves and with the corporeal world.

XXI. Therefore, purely ideological and psychological philosophy leads us to God.

XXII. Therefore, philosophy cannot commence by a single fact, the origin of all other facts, but must, and does end with this supreme fact, the infinite existence, which is God.(12)

CHAPTER XIII
REPRESENTATION OF
CAUSALITY AND IDEALITY

126. Besides the representation of identity, there is what I have called the representation of causality. A being may represent itself, a cause its effect. Productive activity is inconceivable, if the principle of the productive act does not in some manner contain the thing produced. Therefore we say that God, the universal cause of all that does or can exist, contains in his essence all real and possible beings in a virtual or eminent manner. A being can just as well present whatever it contains in itself, as it can represent itself; causality, therefore, under the conditions above explained, may be an origin of representation.

127. And here we would remark how profound a philosopher St. Thomas shows himself to be, when he explains the manner in which God knows his creatures. In his *Summa Theologica*,[7] he asks if God knows things distinct from himself, and answers in the affirmative; not that he regards the divine essence as a mirror, but that by recourse to a more profound consideration he seeks the origin of this knowledge in causality. This is his doctrine in a few words: It is manifest that God knows himself perfectly; therefore he knows all his power, and consequently all the things to which it extends. Another reason, or rather enlargement of the same reason, is, that the being of the first cause is its intellect: all effects pre-exist in God as in their cause; they must, therefore, be in him in an intelligible manner, since they are his intellect itself. God then sees himself by his essence; but he sees other things not in themselves, but in his essence, inasmuch as his essence contains the similitude of everything.

The same doctrine is found in another place,[8] where he asks if they who see the divine essence see all things in God.

128. Representation of ideality is that which neither proceeds from the identity of the thing representing with that represented, nor from the relation of cause and effect. Our ideas are of this class, for they are neither identical with their objects nor do they cause them. It is impossible for us to know whether, besides this representative force which we experience

in our ideas, there are finite substances capable of representing things distinct from, and not caused by, themselves. Leibnitz maintains that there are such substances; but, as we have seen, his system of monads must be regarded as merely hypothetical. It is better to say nothing than to make conjectures which lead to no result; we shall therefore content ourselves with establishing the following propositions:

I. If any being represent another which is not its effect, it has not this representative force of itself, but has received it from another.

II. The communication of intelligences can only be explained by recurring to a first intelligence, which, being the cause of the others, can give them the force to act upon one another, and consequently to produce representation.

129. Causality may be a principle, but is not a sufficient reason, of representation.

In the first place, a cause cannot represent its effect unless intelligible in itself. Thus, although we attribute to matter an activity of its own, we cannot concede it the power to represent its effects, for want of the indispensable condition of immediate intelligibility.

130. In order that effects may be intelligible in their cause, it must of necessity possess the character of cause in its fulness, by uniting all the conditions and determinations requisite to the production of the effect. Free causes do not represent their effects, because these effects with relation to their causes are found only in the sphere of possibility. The production may be realized, but is not necessary; and thus the possible, but not the real, is seen in the cause. God knows future contingencies, which depend upon the human will, not precisely because he knows the activity of man, but because he sees in himself, without succession of time, not only all that may, but all that will happen; since nothing can exist in the present or in the future without his will or permission. He also knows future contingencies dependent solely on his own will, because he knows from all eternity what he has resolved, and his decrees are indefectible and immutable.

131. Even if we refer to the necessary order of nature, and suppose one or more second causes to be known, it is not possible to see in them all their effects with entire security, unless the cause act in isolation, or all the others are known together with it. As experience shows us that all the parts of nature are in intimate and reciprocal communication, we cannot suppose the above isolation, and consequently the action of every second cause is subjected to the combinations of others, which may either impede or modify its effect. Hence the difficulty of establishing general, and at the same time, perfectly safe laws in all that concerns nature.

132. The preceding considerations, it is to be observed, demonstrate anew the impossibility of transcendental science based upon a fact from which all other facts proceed. Intellectual representation is not explained by substituting necessary emanation for free creation. Even supposing the variety of the universe to be purely phenomenal, and at bottom only a being always one, identical, and absolute, it cannot be denied that the phenomena are governed by certain laws, and subject to various conditions. Either the human intellect can see the absolute in such a way as to discern by a simple intuition whatever is contained in it, all that it is or can be, under all possible forms; or else it is condemned to follow the unfolding of the unconditioned, the absolute, and the permanent, through its conditioned, relative, and variable forms. The former, which is a sort of ridiculous plagiarism from the dogma of beatific vision, is, in treating of the intellect in its present state, so palpable an absurdity, as to merit neither debate nor refutation. The latter subjects the intellect to all the fatigue of investigation, and destroys at one blow all the illusory promises of transcendental science.

133. The understanding is, in its acts, subject to a law of succession, or the idea of time. The same thing obtains in nature, whether it is so verified in reality, or time is considered as a subjective condition which we transfer to objects; be this doctrine of Kant, which we shall in due time examine, as it may, it is certain that succession, at least for us, exists, and that we cannot ignore it. In this hypothesis an infinite evolution can be known to us only in an infinite time. Thus, by a metaphysical necessity, we are unable to know not only the future evolution of the absolute, but also the present and the past. This evolution being absolutely necessary, according to the doctrine to which we have reference, an infinite succession must have preceded us; thus the present organization of the universe must be regarded as one round of an unlimited ladder, which in the past as in the future, has no measure but eternity. We can know the present state of the world solely by observation, and then only to a very limited degree; we must, therefore, of necessity, deduce it from the idea of the absolute, by following it in its infinite evolution. Were this not, however, in itself radically impossible, it would, nevertheless, labor under the inconvenience of being too long a task to be accomplished in the life-time of any one man, or even in that of all men who have ever lived, taken collectively.

134. But let us return to the representation of causality. The ideal representation may be reduced to that of causality; for since a spirit can have no idea of an object not produced by it, unless communicated to it by another spirit, the cause of the thing represented, we infer that all purely ideal representations proceed either directly or indirectly, mediately or immediately, from the cause of the objects known. And since, on the other hand, as we have already seen, the first being knows things distinct from

himself only, as he is their cause; we hold the representation of ideality to be reduced to that of causality, thus in part verifying the principle of Vico, the profound Neapolitan thinker: "the intellect only knows what it does."

135. From this doctrine flow two consequences of which we must take note:

I. There are only two primitive sources of intellectual representation: identity and causality. That of ideality is necessarily derived from that of causality.

II. In the real order, the principle of being is identical with the principle of knowledge. That only which gives being can give knowledge. The first cause can give knowledge only in so far as it gives being: it represents because it causes.

136. The representation of ideality, although connected with that of causality, is yet really distinct from it. The explanation of its nature belongs indeed to the treatise on ideas; but we cannot relinquish, without an illustration, a point so closely connected with the problem of intellectual representation.

Some conceive ideas to be a sort of image or copy of the object; but this is true only with respect to the representations of the imagination, that is, the purely corporeal; and even here it is necessary to suppose the external world to be such as the senses present it, which, however, under many aspects, is not true. To be convinced how illusory is the theory founded on the likeness of sensible things, we have only to ask, what the image of a relation is, or, how causality, substance, and being are portrayed. In the perception of these ideas, there is something more profound than any thing apparent in sensible things, something of an entirely different order. Necessity has led us to compare the understanding to an eye which sees, and the idea to an image present; but this is only a comparison; the reality is something more mysterious, more secret, more intimate: there is an ineffable union between the perception and the idea: man cannot explain it, but he experiences it.

137. Our consciousness attests that there is in us unity of being, that the soul is at all times identical with itself, and that it remains constant notwithstanding the variety of ideas and of acts which pass over it, like waves over the surface of a lake. Ideas are a mode of being of the mind: but what is this mode? In what does it consist? Does the production and reproduction of ideas proceed from a distinct cause which continually acts upon our soul, and produces immediately those modes of being which we call representations, or ideas? Or must we admit that there has been given to the mind an activity to produce these representations, subject, however, to the determination of exciting causes? These are questions which, for the present, we shall only indicate.(13)

CHAPTER XIV
IMPOSSIBILITY OF FINDING THE FIRST PRINCIPLE IN THE IDEAL ORDER

138. We shall in vain seek in the region of ideas for that which we could not find in that of facts, for there is no ideal truth, the origin of all other truths.

Ideal truth only expresses the necessary relation of ideas, abstracting the existence of the objects to which they relate: hence it follows, first of all, that ideal truths are absolutely incapable of producing the knowledge of reality.

No ideal truth can lead to any result in the order of existences, unless there be some fact to which it applies. Otherwise, however fruitful it may be in the order of ideas, it will be absolutely sterile in that of facts. The fact without the ideal truth remains in its isolated individuality, incapable of producing any thing more than cognition of itself: but in return, the ideal truth, apart from the fact, remains purely objective in the logical world, and has no means of descending to that of existences.

139. Let us apply this doctrine to the most certain and most evident ideal principles, to those which contain the most general ideas, and which ought, therefore, to possess the fecundity in question, if, indeed, it be anywhere to be encountered.

"It is impossible for the same thing to be and not be at the same time." This is the famous principle of contradiction, which may undoubtedly claim to be regarded as one source of truth to the human understanding. The ideas contained in it are the clearest and most simple conceivable; in it is affirmed the repugnance of being to not-being, and of not-being to being, at the same time, which is most evident. But what advance can we make with this principle alone? Present it to the most penetrating mind, to the most powerful genius; leave them alone with it, and there will result only a sterile, although pure and most clear intuition. Since it does not affirm that any thing is or is not, nothing can be inferred either for or against any existence: it only offers to the mind this conditional relation: that if any thing does exist, it is repugnant for it not to exist at the same time that it exists, or to exist at the same time that it does not exist. But if the condition of existence or non-existence be not given, *yes* and *no* in the real order are indifferent; nothing is known concerning them, however great the evidence in the ideal order.

To pass from the logical world to that of reality, all that is required is a fact to serve as a bridge. If this fact be offered to the understanding, the two banks are joined, and science commences. I feel, I think, I exist: these are facts of consciousness; combine any one of them with the principle of contradiction, and what before were sterile intuitions become prolific ratiocinations, embracing at once the world of ideas, and that of reality.

140. Even in the purely ideal order, the principle of contradiction is sterile unless joined with particular truths of the same order. In geometry, for example, it is often argued thus: such a quantity is either greater or less than another, or equal to it; for otherwise it would be both greater and less, equal and unequal, at the same time, which is absurd. Here the principle of contradiction is effectively applied, not alone, but together with a particular truth which makes such an application available. Thus, in the above argument, no use could be made of the principle of contradiction, to prove equality or inequality were not the existence or non-existence of one of the two previously proved or supposed: since this neither does nor can result from the principle of contradiction which includes, not a particular idea, but the most general ideas presented to the human mind.

141. General truths, of themselves, even in the purely ideal order, lead to nothing, because of the indeterminateness of the ideas which they contain; and, on the other hand, particular truths of themselves produce no result, because they are limited to what they are, making reasoning, which cannot take one step without the aid of general ideas and propositions, impossible. Light results from the union of one with the other; separated they afford only an abstract and vague intuition, or the contemplation of a particular truth, which, limited to a contracted sphere, can give no knowledge of beings considered under a scientific aspect.

142. We shall see when we come to treat of ideas, that our mind has two very distinct classes of them; the one supposes space, and cannot abstract it, such are all geometrical ideas: the other does not relate to space, and includes all non-geometrical ideas. These two orders of ideas are separated by an impassable abyss, if the two orders are not approximated by a simultaneous use of both. The ideal order is not complete without this approximation; and the real order of the universe is turned into a chaos, or rather disappears, if real and ideal truths are not combined, in both the geometrical and non-

geometrical orders. From all geometrical ideas imaginable, considered in all their ideal purity, nothing would result for the ideal non-geometrical order, for the world of material, much less of immaterial realities; and, on the other hand, from non-geometrical ideas alone we could not get so much as the idea of a right line. This observation shows that there is for us in the ideal order no one truth, the origin of all other truths; for if we take the geometrical order, we are limited to those combinations which do not go out of it; if the non-geometrical order, we lack the idea of space, without which we lose even the possibility of conceiving the corporeal world.(14)

CHAPTER XV
THE INDISPENSABLE CONDITION OF ALL HUMAN KNOWLEDGE.— MEANS OF PERCEIVING TRUTH

143. We have not been able to discover, either in the real or the ideal order, a truth, the origin of all other truths to our intellect while in this life. Therefore it stands proved that transcendental science properly so called is for us a chimera. Our cognitions must, doubtless, have some resting-point, and this we shall now investigate.

For the better understanding of the subject now before us, we will recall the true state of the question. We do not seek a first principle, which of itself alone illumines or produces all truths; but we seek a truth which shall be the indispensable condition of all knowledge; for this reason, we do not call it an origin, but a resting-point. The edifice does not originate in the foundation, but rests upon it. We must consider the principle sought for as a foundation, just as in the preceding chapters, we treated of discovering a seed. These two images *seed* and *foundation*, perfectly express our ideas, and exactly trace the limits of the two questions.

144. Is there a resting-point of all science, and of all knowledge, scientific or not scientific? If there is, what is it? Are there many, or only one? Evidently there must be a resting-point. If asked the reason of an assent, we must at last come to a fact or a proposition, beyond which we cannot go; for we cannot admit the process *ad infinitum*. This is the point where we must of necessity stop, and consequently the resting-point of certainty.

145. Starting with a given assent, we may, perhaps, arrive at different principles, independent one of the other, all equally fundamental, as regards our mind: in this case there will be not only one, but many resting-points.

We do not believe it possible to determine *a priori*, whether there is unity or plurality for our intellect in this matter. That human science must be reduced to a single principle is a proposition that has been asserted, but never yet proved. Since the source of all truth, as has been shown in the preceding chapters, is not in man, it is evident that the principles, on which his knowledge is founded, must be communicated. Who shall assure us that they are not many in number, and of different orders? Nothing then in the present question can be resolved *a priori*, and we must descend to ideological and psychological observations.

146. Our mind acquires truth, or at least the appearance of truth; that is to say, that in one way or another, it performs those acts which we call perception and sensation. Whether the reality does or does not correspond to the acts of our soul, is at present of no consequence, is not what we now seek: we place the question on a ground accessible to the most skeptical; for even they do not deny perception and sensation; although they destroy reality, they admit appearance.

147. The means by which we perceive truth are of different orders; and this is why truths perceived correspond equally to different orders, parallel, so to speak, with the respective means of perception.

Consciousness, evidence, and intellectual instinct or common sense, are the three means; to which correspond truths of consciousness, necessary truths, and common-sense truths. These are distinct, different, and in many cases unconnected with each other; and he, who seeks to acquire complete and accurate ideas upon matters relating to the first principle of human knowledge, must mark out their limits with great care.

148. That means which we have called consciousness, or the intimate sense of that which passes within us, that which we experience, is independent of all the others. Destroy evidence, destroy intellectual instinct, yet consciousness remains. In order to feel, and to be sure that we feel, and what we feel, we need only experience. If we suppose the principle of contradiction to be doubtful, still it will not shake our certainty that we suffer when we suffer, that we rejoice when we rejoice, that we think when we think. The presence of the act, or the impression at the bottom of our soul, is intimate, immediate to us, and of irresistible efficacy to place us above all doubt. Sleeping or waking, sane or insane, the testimony of consciousness is the same; there may be an error in the object, but there can be none in the internal phenomenon. The lunatic who believes that he counts numberless bags of dollars, certainly does not count them, and in this he is deceived; yet he has in his mind the consciousness of what he does, and in this he is infallible. A man who dreams that he has fallen into the hands of robbers, is deceived as to the external object, but not as regards the act by which he believes it.

Consciousness is independent of all extrinsic testimony; its necessity is inevitable, its force irresistible in producing certainty; it is infallible in what concerns only itself; if it exist it must give testimony of itself; if it does not exist it cannot give it. In it reality and appearance are confounded; it cannot be apparent without being real; the appearance alone is already a true consciousness.

149. We include in the testimony of consciousness all that which we experience in our soul, all that which affects what some call the human *me*, ideas, thoughts of every class, acts of the will, sentiments, sensations; in a word, every thing of which we can say: I experience it.

150. Manifestly the truths of consciousness are rather facts to be pointed out, than combinations to be enunciated. This is not to say that they cannot be enunciated, but that in themselves they abstract all intellectual form, are simple elements, in ordering and comparing which the intellect may occupy itself, but which of themselves give no light, *represent* nothing, but only *present* what they are; that they are mere facts, beyond which we cannot go.

151. The habit of reflecting upon consciousness, and of joining purely intellectual operations with facts of simple internal experience, makes it difficult to conceive this isolation, in which every thing purely subjective is by its nature found. We endeavor to abstract reflection, but we reflect upon our very effort to abstract it. Our intellect is a fire, which, extinguished on one side, burns on the other; the very effort to extinguish it ordinarily makes it burn brighter. Hence the difficulty of distinguishing the two characters of purely subjective and purely objective, to mark the dividing line between evidence and consciousness, between the known and the experienced. Nevertheless, the separation of two such different elements may be made easy, by considering that brutes are, in their own way, conscious of what they inwardly experience; not supposing them to be mere machines, we must allow them consciousness, or the intimate presence of their sensations. Without this even sensation is inconceivable, for that can have no sensation which does not perceive that it feels. Brutes reflect not on what passes within themselves; they experience it, but nothing more. Sensations succeed one another in their soul, connected only by the unity of the being experiencing them; but they do not take them for objects and consequently, do not combine or transform them in any manner; they leave them as they are, simple facts. From this we may derive some light for the conception of what the simple facts of consciousness are in us when abandoned to themselves, perfectly isolated, separated from purely intellectual operations, and under no subjection to reflective activity, which, combining them in various ways, and elevating them to the region of the purely ideal, presents them to us in such a manner as to make us forget their primitive purity.

An effort is necessary in order clearly to perceive what the facts of consciousness are, and what its testimony is; for without this it is impossible to advance one step in the investigation of the first principle of human knowledge. Confusion on this point makes us fall into transcendental equivocations. We shall hereafter have occasion to observe this, and we have already encountered lamentable examples of such deviations in the errors of the philosophy of the *me*.

152. Evidence is usually called an intellectual light. This is a very happy metaphor, and even exact; but, like all metaphors, it has the defect of being of but little service to explain the mysteries of philosophy. We also find intellectual light in many acts of consciousness. There is also a sort of clear light in that intimate presence by which an operation or an impression is offered to the mind; it shines upon the eye of the soul, and makes it see what is before it. If, then, we define evidence only by calling it the light of the intellect, we confound it with consciousness, or, at least, by the use of ambiguous language, give others occasion of confounding them.

Let us not be thought to blame those who have used the metaphor of light, or to flatter ourselves with being able to define evidence with all exactness; for who can express in words this phenomenon of our mind? If we are to have any metaphor, that of the intellectual light seems to be the most adequate. For, in truth, when we fix our attention upon evidence, in order to examine its nature and its effects on the mind, it very naturally presents itself under the image of a light, whose splendor illumines the objects, and enables the mind to contemplate them: but this, we repeat, is not enough. We will, then, although we do not undertake exactly to define it, point out a mark to distinguish it from every thing else.

153. Evidence is always accompanied by the necessity, and consequently, by the universality, of the truths which it attests. There is no evidence of the contingent, except in so far as subjected to a necessary principle.

Let us explain this doctrine by comparing examples taken respectively from consciousness and evidence.

That there is in me a being which thinks, I know, not by evidence, but by consciousness. That whatever thinks exists, I know, not by consciousness, but by evidence. In both cases the certainty is absolute, irresistible; but in the first it rests upon a particular, contingent fact; in the second upon a universal and necessary truth. That I think is certain for me, but not necessarily so for others; the disappearance of my thought does not overturn the world of intelligences; if my thought should now cease to exist, truth in itself would suffer no change; other intellects might and would continue to perceive truth; and neither in the real nor in the ideal order would there be less concert and harmony.

I ask myself if I think, and in the bottom of my soul I read that I do think: I ask myself if this thought is necessary, and not only does experience tell me that it is not, but I can find no reason why it should be necessary. Even supposing that my thought ceases to exist, I perceive that I continue to reason in due form. Thus I examine what would have happened if I had not existed, or what may hereafter happen if I cease to exist; and I assent to principles and draw conclusions without transgressing any law of the intellect. The ideal world and the real world are presented to my eyes as a magnificent spectacle at which I indeed assist, but from which I may withdraw without the representation undergoing any change, except that I should leave vacant the imperceptible place which I now occupy. But it is very different with the truths which are the object of evidence. It is not necessary for me to think; but it is so necessary for whatever thinks to exist, that no efforts of mine could suffice to abstract this necessity for one moment. If, taking an absurd position, I suppose the contrary, and imagine for an instant the relation between thought and being to be cut short, I break the chain which supports the order of the entire universe; every thing is reversed, thrown into confusion; and I know not if what I see be chaos or nonentity. What has taken place? The intellect has only suffered a contradiction, at the same time affirming and denying thought, because it affirmed a thought to which it denied existence. It has violated a universal and absolutely necessary law, the violation of which throws every thing into chaos. Not the certainty of the soul's existence, supported by the testimony of consciousness, suffices to prevent the confusion: the intellect by contradicting itself has denied itself; from its insensate words, not being, but nonentity has resulted, not light, but darkness; and this darkness cast over whatever exists or is possible turns back upon it and involves it in eternal night.

154. We have here fixed and defined the conditions of consciousness and evidence. The object of the former is the individual, the contingent; that of the latter the universal and the necessary. Only in God, the source of all truth, the universal and necessary principle of being and of knowledge, is consciousness identified with evidence; and it is not possible to abstract the testimony of his consciousness, without annihilating everything. What would remain in the world were I to disappear? the creature asks itself, and answers: *everything except myself.* Were God to ask himself this question, he would answer: *nothing.*

155. We have given the name of intellectual instinct to the impulse which in many cases produces certainty without the aid of the testimony either of consciousness or of evidence. If you show a man a target, then blindfold his eyes, and turn him around at random several times, and, after

this, place a bow in his hands, and assure him that the arrow will strike the precise centre of the target, he will say that this is impossible; and nothing can induce him to believe so great an absurdity. And why not? Because of the testimony of consciousness? No! For the question is now of external objects. Neither does he depend on evidence; for the objects of evidence are things necessary, and it is not intrinsically impossible for the arrow to hit the mark assigned. On what then rests his profound conviction that this is not possible? If we suppose him to know nothing of theories, of probabilities, and combinations, to have no knowledge of this science, and never to have so much as thought of such things, his certainty is just as great as it would be were he able to base it upon some sort of calculation. All the bystanders, whether rude or cultivated, ignorant or learned, need no reflection to be equally certain; all will say, or think, "this is impossible; it cannot happen." We again ask, what is the foundation of so strong a conviction? Not springing from consciousness, or from either mediate or immediate evidence, it manifestly can have no other origin than that internal force which we call intellectual instinct, and which may be called common sense, or anything else, so long as the fact itself is recognized. It is a precious gift, which the Creator has given to us, to make us reasonable even before we reason, and to enable us rightly to govern our conduct when we lack time to examine motives of prudence.

156. This intellectual instinct embraces many objects of different orders; it is the guide and the shield of reason: the guide, because it precedes and shows the way; the shield, because it defends reason from her own cavils, and because sophistry becomes dumb in its presence.

157. The testimony of human authority, equally necessary to the individual and to society, commands our assent, by means of an intellectual instinct. Man believes man, believes society, even before thinking of the motives of his faith; few examine them at all, and yet this faith is universal.

We do not here inquire if intellectual instinct sometimes deceives, or why, or in what cases it deceives; at present we only seek to establish its existence; and with regard to the errors to which it leads, we shall simply remark, that in a weak being, such as man, the rule is continually changing, and as it is not possible to find a man good, without any admixture of evil, so is it impossible to find truth without some admixture of error.

158. We make sensations objective only by virtue of an irresistible instinct. Nothing is more certain, more evident to the eyes of philosophy, than the subjectivity of all sensations; that is, sensations are immanent phenomena, are within us, and do not go out of us; and yet nothing is more constant than the transition made by the whole human race from

the subjective to the objective, from the internal to the external, from the phenomenon to the reality. On what is this transition grounded? If the most eminent philosophers experienced so much difficulty in finding the bridge, which unites the two opposite banks; if some of them, wearied with investigation, resolutely asserted that it was not possible to discover it, will the commonalty of mankind discover it from their very childhood? Evidently, motives of reasoning do not explain the transition; appeal must be made to the instinct of nature. There is then an instinct, which by itself assures us of a truth demonstrated with difficulty by the most abstruse philosophy.

159. Here I shall notice the errors of those methods which isolate man's faculties, and, in order better to know the mind, disfigure and mutilate it. One of the most constant and fundamental facts of ideological and psychological science, is the multiplicity of acts and faculties of the soul, notwithstanding its simplicity attested by the unity of consciousness. There is in man, and in the universe, an assemblage of laws, the effects of which are simultaneously evolved with harmonious regularity; to separate them, is often equivalent to placing them in contradiction; for, no one of them being capable of producing its effect if isolated, but requiring to be combined with the others, they produce, when made to operate alone, instead of their regular effects, the most hideous monstrosities. If you retain in the world only the law of gravitation not combined with that of projection, every thing will be precipitated towards one centre; instead of that infinity of systems which adorn the firmament, you will have only a rude and indigested mass. If you destroy gravitation, and preserve the force of projection, all bodies will be decomposed into imperceptible atoms, and be dispersed, like most subtle ether, through regions of immensity.(15)

CHAPTER XVI
CONFUSION OF IDEAS IN DISPUTES ON THE FUNDAMENTAL PRINCIPLE

160. There are, in our opinion, various principles, which, with regard to the human intellect, may be called equally fundamental, both because they serve as foundation in the common and scientific orders, and because they do not rest upon any other, since it is impossible to assign any one which enjoys this quality as an exclusive privilege. In seeking the fundamental principle, it is customary in the schools to observe that they do not endeavor to find a truth from which all others emanate, but an axiom the destruction of which draws with it that of all other truths, and the firmness of which sustains them, at least indirectly, in such manner that whoever denies them may be refuted by indirect demonstration, or reduction *ad absurdum*; that is, admitting the above axiom, it may follow that whoever denies the others will be convicted of being in opposition to one which he himself has acknowledged to be true.

161. It has been much disputed whether this or that principle merit the preference. We believe that there is here a confusion of ideas, proceeding in great part from not sufficiently marking the limits of testimonies so distinct as those of consciousness, of evidence, and of common sense.

Descartes' famous principle, *I think, therefore I am*; that of contradiction, *it is impossible for a thing to be and not to be at the same time*; and what is called the principle of the Cartesians, *whatever is contained in the clear and distinct idea of anything, may be affirmed of it with all certainty*; are the three principles that have divided the schools. In favor of each, reasons the most powerful, and even conclusive against the others, considering the ground on which the question was placed, have been brought forward.

If you are not certain that you think, argues the partisan of Descartes, you cannot be certain even of the principle of contradiction, or know the criterion of evidence to be valid; for both, it is necessary to think; whoever affirms or denies anything, thinks; without thought, neither affirmation nor negation is possible. But let us admit thought: we have already a foundation, and one of such a nature that we find it in ourselves, attested by consciousness, irresistibly forcing upon us the certainty of its existence. The foundation once laid, we see how the edifice can be raised; for this we need not go out of our own thought; there is the luminous point to conduct us in the path to truth; let us follow its splendor, and having established an immovable point, let us draw from it the mysterious thread to guide us in the labyrinth of science. Thus our principle is the first, the basis of all others; it has sufficient power to sustain itself, sufficient also to impart firmness to others.

This language is certainly reasonable; but it has this fault, that the conviction which it is intended to produce, is neutralized by the not less reasonable language of those who hold a directly contrary opinion. One who maintains the principle of contradiction may reason thus: if you do not admit it to be impossible for the same thing to be and not be at the same time, it may be possible that you think and do not think at the same time; your assertion, then, *I think*, is of no weight, for its opposite, *I do not think*, may, at the same time, be true. In this case, the conclusion of existence is invalid; for, even admitting the legitimacy of the consequence, *I think, therefore I am*, as we know on the other hand that this other premise, *I do not think*, is possible, the deduction cannot be made. Nor is the other principle: *whatever is contained in the clear and distinct idea of anything, may he affirmed of it with all certainty*, of any more value without the principle of contradiction; because if being and not-being are possible at the same time, an idea may be clear and obscure, distinct and confused; a predicate may be contained and not contained in the subject; we may be certain and uncertain, affirm and deny; therefore it is of no service.

He who argues thus seems quite reasonable; but strangely enough, the advocate of the third principle brings equally strong arguments against his two adversaries. How is it known, he asks, that the principle of contradiction is true? Only because we see in the idea of being the impossibility of its being and not being at the same time, and *vice versa*; therefore, we are sure of the principle of contradiction only from the application of the principle: *whatever is contained in the clear and distinct idea of anything, may he affirmed of it with all certainty*. If nothing can be sustained without relying upon the principle of contradiction, — and this is based upon our principle, — ours is the foundation of them all.

162. They are all three right, and all three wrong. They are right in asserting that the denial of their respective principles is the ruin of the others. They are all wrong in pretending that the denial of the others is not the ruin of their own. Whence then the dispute? From the confusion of ideas, by which they compare principles of very different orders, all indeed very true, but not to be compared with each other for the same reason that we cannot

compare the white and the warm, and dispute whether a thing has more degrees of heat or whiteness. Comparison requires not only opposition in the extremes, but also something in common; if things are totally unlike, comparison is impossible.

Descartes' principle is the enunciation of a simple fact of consciousness; that of contradiction is a truth known by evidence; and that of the Cartesians is an assertion that the criterion of evidence is valid, and that it is a truth of reflection expressing the intellectual impulse by which we are borne to believe the truth of what we know by evidence.

The importance of this question requires a special examination of each of the three principles, which we shall make in the next chapters.(16)

CHAPTER XVII
THOUGHT AND EXISTENCE.–
DESCARTES' PRINCIPLE

163. Am I certain that I exist? Yes. Can I prove it? No. Proof supposes reasoning; there is no solid reasoning without a firm principle on which to rest it; and there is no firm principle unless we suppose the existence of the reasoning being.

In effect, if he who reasons is not certain of his own existence, he cannot be certain of his own reasoning, since there will be no reasoning if there be no one to reason. Therefore there are, unless we suppose this, no principles on which to rest; there is nothing but illusion, or rather there is neither any illusion, for there can be none where there is no one illuded.

Our existence cannot be demonstrated: we have so clear and strong a consciousness of it that it leaves us no uncertainty; but it is impossible to prove it by reasoning.

164. It is a prejudice and a fatal error to believe ourselves able to prove everything by the use of reason; the principles on which it is founded are prior to its use; the existence of reason, and that of the being that reasons, are prior to both.

Not only are not all things demonstrated, but it may even be demonstrated that some things are indemonstrable. Demonstration is a ratiocination in which we infer from evident propositions, a proposition evidently connected with them. If the premises are of themselves evident, they do not admit of demonstration; if we suppose them in their turn demonstrable, we shall have the same difficulty with respect to those on which the new demonstration is founded; therefore we must either stop at an indemonstrable point, or proceed to infinity, which would be never to finish the demonstration.

165. And it is to be remarked that indemonstrability does not belong solely to certain premises; it is found, in some measure, in every argument by its very nature, abstracting the propositions which compose it. We know that the premises A and B are certain; from them we infer the proposition C.

By what right? Because we see that C is connected with A and B. But how do we know this? If by immediate evidence, by intuition, here is something else that cannot be demonstrated, the connection of the conclusion with the premises. If by argument, ratiocination, establishing ourselves on the art of reasoning, there are two considerations, both tending to demonstrate indemonstrability. I. If the principles of the art are indemonstrable, we have at once something indemonstrable; if they are demonstrable, we must make use of others which serve as their basis, and at last either come to one which does not admit of demonstration, or else proceed to infinity. II. How do we know the principles of reasoning to be applicable to this case? By another act of reasoning? Then we shall encounter the same difficulty as in the other case. Is it because we see that it is so? because it is immediately evident? Then here again we have an indemonstrable point. These reflections will clearly show that to demand proof of everything is to demand what is impossible.

166. A being which does not think has no consciousness of itself: the stone exists, but does not know that it exists, neither would man himself in a similar case, were all his intellectual and sensible faculties in complete inaction. We easily conceive the difference of these two states by calling to mind what occurs, when from waking we pass into a profound sleep, and again when we awake from it. The first starting-point of our cognitions is this intimate presence of our internal acts, abstraction made of the questions which may be raised upon their nature. If every thing existed as at present, and there also existed, besides the world which we see, infinite other worlds, not even then would any thing exist for us, had we not those internal acts of which we are speaking. We should be like an insensible body placed in the immensity of space, which would suffer no mutation were every thing around it to disappear, and would perceive no change even if it were itself to sink into the abyss of nothing. On the other hand, if we suppose every thing to be annihilated except this being within us which feels, thinks, and wills, there still remains a point whereon to base the edifice of human cognitions: this being, though alone in immensity, would render itself an account of its own acts to the extent of its ability, and might go into numberless combinations having for their object the possible though not the real.

167. The famous principle of Descartes, *I think, therefore I am*, has been often attacked, and justly and conclusively so, if this philosopher really understood his principle in the sense which the schools are accustomed to give it. If Descartes presented it as a true argument, as an enthymema with an antecedent and a consequent, the argument was clearly defective in its foundation. For when he said, "I am going to prove my existence with this enthymema: I think, therefore I am:" this objection might have been made;

your enthymema is equivalent to a syllogism in this form: whatever thinks, exists; but I think; therefore, I exist. This syllogism, in the supposition of a universal doubt, excluding even the supposition of existence itself, is inadmissable in its propositions and in their connection. In the first place, how do you know that whatever thinks exists? Because nothing can think without existing. How do you know that? Because what does not exist, does not act. But how in its turn do you know this? Supposing every thing to be doubted, nothing to be known, these principles are not known; otherwise we fall short of the supposition of universal doubt, and consequently go out of the question. If any one of these principles must be admitted without proof, it is just as well to admit your own existence and save yourself the trouble of proving it with an enthymema.

In the second place, how do you know that you think? Your argument may be retorted, as dialecticians say, in the following manner: nothing can think without existing; but your existence is doubtful, for you are trying to prove it; therefore you are not sure that you think.

168. Manifestly, then, Descartes' principle, taken as a true argument, cannot be defended; and it is so easy to see its defect, that it seems impossible for so clear and penetrating an intellect to have overlooked it. It is therefore probable that Descartes understood his principle in a very different sense; and we will now briefly show what meaning, in our judgment, the illustrious philosopher must have given to it.

Supposing himself for a moment in universal doubt, without accepting for certain anything that is known, he concentrated himself on himself, and in the depth of his soul sought a point whereon to base the edifice of human cognitions. Although we abstract all around us, we clearly cannot abstract ourselves, our mind, which is present to its own eyes, only the more lucidly, the greater the abstraction in which we place ourselves with respect to eternal objects. Now in this concentration, this collection of himself within himself, this withdrawal from every thing for fear of error, and asking himself if there be any thing certain, if there be any foundation and starting-point in the career of knowledge; first of all is presented to him the consciousness of thought, the very presence of the acts of his mind. If we mistake not, this was Descartes' thought: I wish to doubt of every thing; I refrain from affirming as from denying any thing; I isolate myself from whatever surrounds me, because I know not if it be any thing more than an illusion. But in this very isolation, I meet with the intimate sense of my internal acts, with the presence of my mind; I think, therefore I am; this I feel in a manner that leaves no room for doubt or uncertainty; therefore, I am; that is to say, this sense of my thought makes me know my existence.

169. This explains why Descartes did not present his principle as a mere enthymema, as an ordinary argument, but as determining a fact presented to him and first in the order of facts: even if he inferred existence from thought, it was not by deduction, properly so called, but as one fact contained in another, or rather identified with it.

We say *identified*, because it really is so in Descartes' opinion; and this confirms what we have already advanced, that this philosopher did not offer an argument, but laid down a fact. According to him, the essence of the soul consists in thought; and as other schools of philosophy distinguish between substance and its acts, considering the mind in the first class, and thought in the second, so Descartes held that there was no distinction between mind and thought, that they were the same thing, that thought constituted the essence of the soul. "Although one attribute," he says, "suffices to make us know the substance, there is, nevertheless, in every substance one attribute, which constitutes its nature and its essence, and on which all the others depend. Extension in length, breadth, and depth, constitutes the essence of corporeal substance; and thought constitutes the nature of the substance which thinks."[9] From this it follows that Descartes, in laying down the principle, *I think, therefore I exist*, only declared a fact attested by consciousness; and so simple did he consider it, and so unique, that in evolving his system, he identified thought with the soul, and its essence with its existence. He was conscious of thought, and said: "this thought is my soul; I am." It is not now our purpose to weigh the value of this doctrine, but only to explain in what it consists.(17)

CHAPTER XVIII
THE PRINCIPLE OF DESCARTES, CONTINUED.—HIS METHOD

170. Descartes did not always express himself with, sufficient accuracy when announcing and explaining his principle; and hence his words have been misinterpreted. In the passage where he establishes consciousness of our own thought and existence as the foundation whereon all our cognitions must rest, he uses terms from which it can be inferred that he not only means to declare a fact, but that he also intends to afford a true argument. Nevertheless, if we read his words attentively, and compare them with one another, it will be evident that such was not his idea, although we should not sometimes be wrong in saying that he did not make sufficient account of the difference, which we have just pointed out, between an argument and the simple declaration of a fact; and that, when concentrating himself on himself, he did not have a sufficiently clear *reflex* knowledge of the manner in which he rested upon his fundamental principle. To convince ourselves of this, let us examine his own words: "While we thus reject every thing of which we can have the least doubt, and even *feign* that it is false, we easily suppose that there is no God, no heaven, no earth; that we have not a body: but we cannot in like manner suppose that we are not whilst we doubt the truth of all these things; for we experience so great repugnance to conceive that what thinks is not at the same time that it thinks, that notwithstanding all the most extravagant suppositions, we cannot help believing this conclusion, *I think, therefore I am*, to be true, and consequently the first and most certain to present itself to him who orders well his thoughts."[10]

In this passage we detect a true syllogism: whatever thinks, exists; but I think; therefore I exist. "We have," says Descartes, "so great repugnance to conceive that what thinks is not at the same time that it thinks;" which is the same as to say, whatever thinks, exists; and this, in scholastic terms, is to establish the major. He then says: "notwithstanding all the most extravagant suppositions, we cannot help believing this conclusion, *I think, therefore I am*, to be true;" which is equivalent to proving the minor, and the conclusion of the syllogism. We know that Descartes was somewhat taken up with the idea of proving at the same time that he was engaged in declaring. This was the general tendency of his age, and even the most ardent reformers with difficulty preserved themselves from the surrounding atmosphere. We encounter this same spirit throughout his meditations, admirably joined, however, with the spirit of observation.

But through these obscure or ambiguous explanations, what thought do we discover at the bottom of Descartes' system when we abstract his having, or not having, rendered himself an exact account of what he experienced? This thought: "By an effort of my mind I can doubt the truth of everything; but this effort has a limit in myself. When I turn my attention upon myself, upon the consciousness of my internal acts, upon my existence, doubt is at an end; it cannot extend so far: I find *so great repugnance* that the most extravagant suppositions cannot overcome it." This his very words show: besides declaring this fact, he rises to a general and undoubtedly true proposition; he draws a conclusion also very legitimate; but neither of these was at all necessary to the present case; neither seemed to explain well his opinion, but either served to confuse it.

171. Descartes did nothing more in this point than what all philosophers do; and strange as it may seem, he did not differ from the chiefs of the metaphysical school diametrically opposed to his own, that of Locke and Condillac. That man, in seeking to examine the origin of his cognitions, and the principles on which his certainty is based, encounters the fact of consciousness of his internal acts, that this consciousness produces a firm certainty, and that we can conceive nothing more certain, is a fact on which all ideologists agree, and which all establish, although not in the same words. The more we reflect on these matters, the more we discover in them the realization of a principle confirmed by reason and experience, that many truths are not new, but only presented under a new form, and that many systems are not new, but only expressed in new formulas.

172. Even the universal doubt of Descartes, rightly understood, is practised by every philosopher; whence we see that the basis of his system, opposed by many, is in fact adopted by all. In what does his method consist? It may all be reduced to these two points: I. I wish to doubt of everything: II. When I wish to doubt of myself, I cannot.

Let us examine these points, and we shall see that they are common to all philosophers with Descartes.

Why does Descartes wish to doubt of everything? Because he proposes to examine the origin and certainty of his cognitions, his whole knowledge; and therefore he cannot help supposing nothing to be true. If then he supposes anything, he does not examine the origin and motives of the certainty of everything, since he excepts that which he supposes to be true.

He must suppose nothing to be true, that he knows nothing of anything; otherwise he cannot say that he examines the foundation of everything. Either there is no such philosophical question, although one is found in all books of philosophy, or else Descartes' method must of necessity be followed.

But in what does this doubt consist? Can it, rationally speaking, be a real and true doubt? No! that is absolutely impossible. Man does not, because a philosopher, destroy his nature; and nature is invincibly opposed to this doubt taken in a strict sense.

173. What then is this doubt? Nothing more than a *supposition*, a *fiction*; a supposition and fiction such as we make at every step in all science, and which, in reality, is only non-attention to a conviction of our own. Use is made of this doubt in order to discover the first truth on which our understanding rests; and this only requires a fictitious doubt: there is no necessity of its being positive, for it will evidently make no difference whether we really doubt of everything, admit absolutely nothing, or say: I suppose that I have nothing for certain, know nothing, admit nothing. An example will make this explanation more evident. Whoever knows the rudiments of geometry, knows that in a triangle, the greater angle is opposite to the greater side, and he is absolutely certain of the truth of this theorem; but if he propose to demonstrate it to another, or repeat the demonstration to himself, he abstracts the said certainty, and proceeds as though he had it not, in order to show that it is founded upon something.

In all our studies, at every step, we do the same. Such expressions as these are common: "This is so, it is evident; but *let us suppose* that it is not; what will be the result?" "This demonstration is conclusive, but let us set it aside and suppose that we have it not; how shall we demonstrate what we desire?" Arguments *ad absurdum*, so much in use in every science, more especially in mathematics, consist not only in abstracting what we know, but in supposing something directly contrary. "If the line A," says continually the geometrician, "is not equal to B, it is either greater or less: let us suppose it to be greater, etc." Thus to investigate truth, we frequently abstract what we know, and even suppose the contrary. Apply this system to the investigation of the fundamental principle of our cognitions, and Descartes' universal doubt will follow, in the only sense admissible at the tribunal of reason, and possible to human nature.

It is probable that the illustrious philosopher understood it in the same sense, although we must confess that his words are ambiguous. We cannot conceive what object he could have had in understanding it differently, supposing, as we do, that he had no other purpose than to pave the way for the investigation of truth. By his manner of expressing himself, he gave occasion to disputes, which greater clearness would have prevented.

As he did not express himself with sufficient clearness, so his adversaries did not press him with all the precision and energy possible. To settle this whole matter, it would have sufficed to ask him this question: Do you mean to say that, in commencing our philosophical investigations, there is a moment in which we *really* and *actually* doubt of every thing; or do you deem it sufficient to abstract certainty, and to suppose that we have it not, as is frequently done in other studies?

174. Descartes was like all reformers who are ruled by one idea, and express it so strongly as to seem to admit no other beside it. In their language every thing is absolute, exclusive. They anticipate the combat which they must sustain, perhaps already experience it, and so they concentrate all their strength on the idea whose triumph they propose, and lose sight of every thing else. It cannot be inferred from this that they have no others which notably modify the principal; but to oppose their adversaries, who say, "This is absolutely false," they assert that it is absolutely true. History and experience furnish innumerable examples of such exaggerations.

The dominant idea of Descartes was to demolish the philosophy which at that time reigned in the schools; and he gave it so rude a shock as to make the world tremble. See how he expressed his contempt for many called philosophers: "Experience shows that they who make profession of being philosophers are often less wise and less reasonable than they who never applied themselves to this study."[11]

175. The second part of Descartes' method consists in taking thought for the point of departure, and in declaring that in trying to doubt of every thing man finds a limit in the consciousness of his thought, his existence. This is evidently the phenomenon which remains in the mind of the observer after doubting of every thing else; at least he cannot doubt that he doubts, and consequently that he thinks; for it must be remarked that this is an argument which has always been used against skeptics, which is equivalent to Descartes' method, and establishes as an undeniable phenomenon a certainty superior to all sophisms, the consciousness of one's self.

When Descartes said, *I think*, he meant by this word every internal act, every phenomenon immediately present to the soul; he spoke not of thought taken in a purely intellectual sense, but included in it all that of which we have immediate consciousness. "By the word *thought*," he says, "I understand all that is done within us, in such a manner that we perceive it immediately by ourselves: this is why not only to understand, to will, to imagine, but also to feel, are here the same thing as to think. For if I say that I see, or that I walk, and thence I infer that I am; if I mean to speak of the action performed with my eyes or with my feet, this conclusion is not so infallible that I have no reason to doubt it; because it may be that I think I see, or walk, although I do not open my eyes or stir from my seat; for this sometimes happens when I am asleep, and the same might also happen even if I had no body; but if I mean to speak only of the action of my thought or of the feeling, that is to say, the knowledge that I possess, which makes it seem to me that I see, or that I walk, this same conclusion is so absolutely true that I cannot doubt it; because it relates to the soul, which alone has the faculty of feeling, or of thinking, in any other manner whatever."[12]

176. This passage shows very clearly Descartes' ideas; he destroyed every thing by doubt, excepting one thing which defied all his efforts, the consciousness of himself; and this consciousness he took for the basis, on which, with full certainty, he might build anew the edifice of science. Locke and Condillac did nothing else; they followed, indeed, a different path, but their point of departure was at all times the same. Locke says: "First, I shall inquire into the *original* of those *ideas*, notions, or whatever else you please to call them, which a man observes, and is conscious to himself he has in his mind; and the ways whereby the understanding comes to be furnished by them."[13] "Since the mind, in all its thoughts and reasonings, hath no other immediate object but its own *ideas*, which it alone does or can contemplate, it is evident that our knowledge is only conversant about them."[14] "Whether, to speak metaphorically," says Condillac, "we ascend even to the heavens, or descend into the abysses, we do not go out of ourselves, and it is always our own thought that we perceive."[15]

177. All ideological labors commence then by establishing the fact of consciousness of our ideas; and it cannot be otherwise with respect to their certainty. Man, although he overthrow and destroy every thing, still encounters himself, the one who overthrows and destroys every thing. When he has gone so far as to doubt the existence of God, the world, his fellow-beings, his own body, he still, in the midst of this immense solitude, encounters himself. The effort to conceal himself from his own eyes serves only to render him more visible: he is a spirit to be killed by no blow, and rays of light flow from every wound inflicted on him. If he doubts that he feels, he at least feels that he doubts; if he doubts of this doubt, he feels that he doubts of doubt itself; thus, in doubting of direct acts, he enters into an interminable series of reflex acts, necessarily linked one with the other, and unrolled to the internal view like folds of a scarf which has no end.(18)

CHAPTER XIX
VALUE OF THE PRINCIPLE. I
THINK: ITS—ANALYSIS

178. We have already seen that Descartes' principle, considered as an enthymema, cannot aspire to be fundamental. In every argument there are premises and a consequence; and to be conclusive, the premises must be true, and the consequence legitimate. To say that an argument may be a fundamental principle, is a manifest contradiction.

But if we take Descartes' principle in the sense above explained, that is, not as an argument but as the declaration of a fact, the contradiction ceases, and it is a question, worthy to be examined, whether it merits the title of fundamental principle or not, and in what sense. We have already somewhat illustrated this matter, but not yet sufficiently cleared it up; we have made some preliminary remarks in order to show the state of the question, but have not yet completely solved it.

179. The proposition, *I think*, as we have remarked, expresses something more than merely thought, strictly so called: it embraces acts of the will, sentiments, sensations, acts, and expressions of all kinds which are realized within us; it includes all phenomena immediately present to our mind, and attested by consciousness.

Nothing that distinguishes between various acts and impressions can be a fundamental principle: such a distinction supposes analysis, and analysis requires reflection. We do not reflect without rules and objects already known; consequently, to admit classifications in the first principle, is to divest it of its character and to contradict ourselves.

180. We must not confound what is expressed by the proposition *I think* with the proposition itself. The thing itself and the form are here very different: the nature of the form may make us conceive ambiguous ideas of the thing itself: the thing itself is a most simple fact; the form is a logical combination, and includes very heterogeneous elements. This demands explanation.

The fact of consciousness, in itself considered, abstracts all relations; it is nothing but itself, leads to nothing but itself; it is the presence of the act or impression, or rather it is the act, the impression itself, which is present to the mind. There is no combination of ideas, no analysis of conceptions; when it comes to this latter, it leaves the territory of pure consciousness, and enters the objective regions of intellectual activity. But as language is to express the products of this activity, and as it is cast, so to say, not in the mould of consciousness, but in that of the intellect, it is impossible for us to speak without some logical or ideal combination. Were we seeking an expression of pure consciousness, unmixed with intellectual elements, we should seek it not in language, but in the natural sign of grief, joy, or some other passion; in this alone is it expressed spontaneously and uncombined with foreign elements, that something passes in our mind, that we are conscious of something; but the instant that we speak, we express something more than pure consciousness: the external world indicates the internal, the product of intellectual activity, its conception; and this involves a subject and an object, and therefore pertains to an order far superior to that of consciousness.

181. To demonstrate the truth of what we have just said, let us examine the expression, *I think*. This is a true proposition, and it may, without being in the least changed, be presented under a strictly logical form, *I am thinking*. Here we have a subject, a predicate, and a copula. The subject is *I*; that is to say, we at once find the idea of a being, the subject of acts and impressions, the possessor of an activity expressed in the predicate. This *I* is then presented to us as something far superior to the order of pure consciousness; it is nothing less than the idea of substance. We will analyze more at length what is contained under it.

We have, in the first place, the idea of unity: the *I* has no meaning, if it do not denote that something is one and identical, notwithstanding the plurality and diversity realized in it. The experimental unity of consciousness draws with it, as a rigid consequence, the unity of the being possessing it. This being is the subject; and in it are realized the variations without which it would be impossible to say *I*. We hold then that in so simple an expression the ideas of unity and its relation to plurality, of substance and its relations to accidents, are contained; that is, the idea of the soul, although expressive of a most simple unity, is, under the logical aspect, composite, and contains many things pertaining to the ideal order, and not to be found in pure consciousness. The idea of the soul, strictly speaking, although in a certain sense common to all men, is in itself highly philosophical, for it involves a combination of elements belonging to the intellectual order.

182. The predicate *thinking* is the expression of a general idea, comprehending not only all thought, but also all phenomena which

immediately affect the mind. These phenomena, considered in what they have in common, under the general idea of present to the mind, are expressed in the word thinking.

The relation of the predicate with the subject, or the agreement of *thinking* with the soul, also expresses an analysis worthy of attention. We at once detect a decomposition of the conception of the soul into two ideas; that of the subject of various modifications, and that of thinking. Otherwise the proposition has no meaning, or rather its expression becomes impossible. The idea of subject involves the ideas of unity and substance, and that of thinking involves the idea of activity, or of passivity, so to speak, accompanied by consciousness.

183. To render the proposition possible, we must suppose the decomposition of the ideas to commence at some point, that is, either in the idea of the soul we find that of *thinking*, or in that of *thinking* we find that of the soul. Fixing ourselves in the soul, and abstracting *thinking*, we meet with the idea of subject, or of substance in general; and there, however much we cavil, we shall never find the idea of *thinking*. The soul in itself is not manifested to us; we know it by thought; in thought therefore we must fix the point of departure, not in the soul; wherefore in the above proposition, what is primitively known is rather the predicate than the subject; and of the two conceptions, that of subject has rather the character of a thing contained, than of a thing containing.

The soul by itself, so to speak, springs up with the presence of thought. If the intellectual activity is concentrated in search of its first basis, it finds it, not in the pure subject, but in its acts, that is, in its thoughts. These last are then the first object of reflective intellectual activity, its first element of combination, its first *datum* for the solution of the problem. Fixing its sight on this element, it discovers a unity in the midst of plurality, a being that remains the same through the ebb and flow of the phenomena of consciousness; and this identity is incontestably asserted by consciousness itself. The idea of the soul then is taken from that of thought, and consequently the subject springs from the predicate, rather than the predicate from the subject.

184. The thought from which we derive the idea of the soul is not thought in general, but thought realized, existing in ourselves. But this reality is sterile unless offered to the mind under a general idea; for it is evident that the soul does not come from one single act, since it is unity, the subject of plurality. To arrive at the idea of the soul we require unity of consciousness, and this we know only as we have experienced it, that is, so far as we perceive the relation of the one to the multiple, of a subject to its modifications.

Such elaboration is necessary to the production of so simple an expression as *I think*; and here we see how much reason there is to distinguish between the thing itself and the form, and how inconsiderately they act who confound things so different. Thus, from want of due analysis, they take in philosophy immense strides from one order to another, confound ideas and entangle matters.

185. To completely illustrate this matter, we will examine the relations of existence to thought; a very easy examination, if we bear in mind the observation just made.

It is certain that we conceive existence before thought: nothing can think without existing: existence is an indispensable condition to thought: to think and not to exist is a manifest contradiction. But what is first offered to our mind is not existence, but thought, and this not in the abstract, but determinate, experimental, or as the expression now is, empyrical. The idea of existence is general, includes all beings, and consciousness cannot commence with it. At one time we obtain this idea by abstraction; at another, it is a form pre-existing in our mind, not the first that occurs to us, or to speak more exactly, not the last point to be attained when we follow back the thread of our cognitions in order to discover their starting-point. This consciousness, when made objective, and when the conception which it offers is analyzed, presents to us the idea of existence as contained in itself.

Hence we infer that the *therefore I exist* is not, strictly speaking, a consequence of the *I think*, but the intuition of the idea of existence in that of thought. There are here two propositions *per se notæ*, as the scholastics say: the one general, *the thinking is existing*; the other particular, *I thinking am existing*. The first belongs to the purely ideal order, and is intrinsically evident, independently of all particular consciousness; the second participates of the two orders, the real and the ideal; the real, in so far as it includes the particular fact of consciousness; the ideal, in so far as it includes a combination of the general idea of existence with the particular fact; since thus only is the union of the predicate with the subject conceivable.

186. It will now be very easy to solve all the questions discussed in the schools.

First question. Does the principle *I think* depend on another? We answer with a distinction. If by this principle is meant the simple fact of consciousness, it evidently does not. For our understanding there is nothing prior to ourselves; whatever we know so far forth as known by us, supposes our consciousness; if we suppress it, we destroy every thing, and although we attempt to destroy every thing, it still remains indestructible, since it depends on nothing, presupposes nothing.

If by the principle *I think* is meant a proposition, it can only have proceeded from reasoning or analysis, and so cannot be the fundamental principle of our cognitions.

187. Second question. When the other principles are wanting, is this one also wanting? We must apply the same distinction here: as a simple fact? No! as a proposition? Yes! Deny every thing, even the principle of contradiction, and consciousness still subsists; but deny the principle of contradiction, and every proposition is destroyed, every combination becomes absurd: analysis, and the relation of the predicate with the subject, are unmeaning words.

188. Third question. Admitting the principle *I think*, can he who denies the others be reduced at least indirectly to truth? We again distinguish: you speak of reducing him either by reasoning or by observation; that is, either you wish to convince him by arguments, or else to turn his attention to himself, as is done with a man distracted, or one suffering mental derangement. The second is possible, but not the first. Whoever denies all principles, that of contradiction included, makes all argument impossible; in vain then will you reason with him. Let us see.

You think, one may say to him, at least you so assert, when you admit the principle *I think*. True. Then you must also admit the principle of contradiction. Why so? Because otherwise you could think and not think at the same time. Very well. But then you destroy your own thought. How? Is it not true that you think? Certainly. According to yourself it is possible that at the same time you do not think. I agree with you. Therefore, you destroy your thought; for if you do not think, the *I think* is destroyed, and, as all this is simultaneous, you destroy your own thought.

Not at all. What I object to in your system is that you suppose true the very thing which I deny, and so fall into the sophism named by logicians *petitio principii*. By the very fact of my denying the principle of contradiction, I deny that not-being destroys being, and that being destroys not-being; consequently, I do not admit that the *I do not think* destroys the *I think*. When you argue against me in this way, you suppose the very point in question, and attack me with principles which I do not admit. In your system, in which being destroys not-being, and *vice versa*, it is certain that to think, and not think, are incompatible; but on my principles, it is a very simple thing; since, according to them, it is not impossible for the same thing to be and not be at the same time, when I do not think, I do not cease to think. This is indeed absurd, but not illogical; deny the principle, and the deduction is necessary. And if it be said that in such a case he cannot reason, as he just has reasoned, he may reply that neither can his adversaries reason; or, if you choose, he sees no difficulty in their both reasoning and not reasoning.

Observation is the only means of bringing back one who has thus strayed away; such a one has departed from reason, and cannot be brought back to it by means of reason. Observations directed to him must be more of a call, a sort of alarm to arouse reason, not a combination to re-construct it: he is as a man asleep, or one in a swoon, and we must call him, and shake him, in order to arouse him; we must not dispute with him as with an adversary.(19)

CHAPTER XX
TRUE SENSE OF THE PRINCIPLE OF CONTRADICTION.—KANT'S OPINION

189. Before examining the value of the principle of contradiction as a basis for our cognitions, it will be well to fix its true and exact sense. This renders necessary some considerations upon an opinion of Kant, advanced in his *Critic of Pure Reason*, when treating of the form in which the principle of contradiction has hitherto been enunciated in all schools of philosophy. The German metaphysician grants, that whatever may be the matter of our cognitions, and in whatever manner they may relate to their object, it is a general, although a purely negative, condition of all our judgments, that they should not mutually contradict each other; otherwise, even without reference to their object, they are nothing in themselves. This doctrine established, he observes that what is called the principle of contradiction is the following: "A predicate that is opposed to a subject does not belong to it;" and then goes on to say, that this is a universal, although purely negative criterion of all truth; that it moreover belongs exclusively to logic, since it is of use to pure cognitions as to cognitions in general, without relation to their object, and he declares that the contradiction makes them completely disappear. "But of this celebrated principle, although stripped of all contents, and purely formal," he continues, "there is still a formula containing a synthesis, which has inadvertently, and quite unnecessarily, been mixed up therein. It is this: *It is impossible for the same thing to be and not be at the same time.* Not only has the apodictic certainty (by the word *impossible*) been unnecessarily added, which certainty would have been of itself understood from the proposition; but the proposition is affected by the condition of time, and says, as it were: a thing = A, which is something = B, cannot at the same time be not B, but it can very well be both (B as well as not B) in succession. For example: a man who is young, cannot at the same time be old; but the same person may very well be young at one time, at another not young, that is, old. Now, the principle of contradiction, as a mere logical principle, must not at all restrict its meaning to the relations of time, and consequently, such a formula is quite opposed to its intention. The misapprehension arises simply from this: that we first separate the predicate

of a thing from its conception, and afterwards unite its opposite with this predicate, which never gives a contradiction with the subject, but only with its predicate, which is synthetically joined with that subject, and that only when the first and second predicates are asserted at the same time. If I say a man who is unlearned is not learned, the condition, *at the same time*, must be expressed; for he who is unlearned at one time may very well be learned at another. But if I say no unlearned man is learned, the proposition is analytic, since the sign (the unlearnedness) now constitutes the conception of the subject, and then the negative proposition is evident immediately from the principle of contradiction, without it being necessary for the condition, *at the same time*, to be added. This is also the cause why I have so changed the formula of this principle, that the nature of an analytic proposition might be clearly expressed."[16]

190. The reader will not easily comprehend the meaning of this passage, not very clear of itself, unless he knows what Kant understands by analytic and synthetic propositions. We will explain this. In all affirmative judgments, the relation of a predicate to a subject is possible in two manners: either the predicate belongs to the subject as contained in it, or is completely extraneous to it although joined with it. In the former case, the judgment is analytic; in the latter, it is synthetic. Analytic affirmative judgments are those in which the union of the predicate with the subject is conceived by identity: those are called synthetic in which this union is conceived without identity. Kant illustrates his idea by the following examples: "When I say all bodies are extended, I express an analytic judgment; for I need not go out of the conception of body in order to find that of extension, which I connect with it, but I have only to analyze the conception of body, that is, to become conscious of the diversity which I always think in this conception, in order to find the predicate. It is, therefore, an analytic judgment. But when I say, all bodies are heavy, the predicate heaviness is by no means included in my conception of the subject, that is, of body in general. It is a conception added to the conception of body. The addition in this way of the predicate to the subject gives a synthetic judgment."[17]

It is easy to see the reason of the new nomenclature employed by the German philosopher. He calls those judgments analytical, in which it suffices to decompose the subject to find therein the predicate, without the necessity of adding any thing not already thought, at least obscurely, in the very conception of the subject; and he calls synthetic those in which it is necessary to add something to the conception of subject, since the predicate is not found in this conception however much we decompose it.

191. This division of judgment, into analytic and synthetic, is much used in modern philosophy, above all among the Germans; certainly there

are some who may imagine this to be a discovery made by the author of the *Critic of Pure Reason*; and the very novelty of the name may give occasion to equivocation. Yet, in all the scholastic writers who lie forgotten, and covered with dust, in the recesses of libraries, we find analytic and synthetic judgments, though not under these names. They said there were two kinds of judgments; some, in which the predicate was contained in the idea of subject, and others, in which it was not. They called the propositions which expressed judgments of the former class, *per se notæ*, or known by themselves, because, the meaning of the terms being understood, the predicate was seen to be contained in the idea, or the conception of the subject. They also called them first principles, and the perception of them, *intelligence, intellectus*, to distinguish them from *reason*, which is conversant about the cognitions of mediate evidence, or ratiocination.

See if the following texts of St. Thomas leave any thing to be desired in clearness or precision: "A proposition is known by itself, *per se notæ*, when the predicate is contained in the subject, as; *man is an animal*; for animal is of the essence of man. If, then, it is known to all, what the subject and the predicate are, that proposition will be known by itself to all, as is seen in the first principles of demonstration, which are certain, common things, not unknown to any one, as being and not-being, the whole, the part, and others similar."[18]

"Any proposition the predicate of which is of the essence of the subject, is known by itself, although such a proposition is not known by itself for any one who is ignorant of the definition of the subject. Thus this proposition, *man is rational*, is by its nature known by itself, because *whoever says man, says rational*."[19]

192. By these, and many other examples, which it would be easy to adduce, it is seen that the distinction between analytic and synthetic judgments was common in the schools centuries before Kant flourished. Analytic judgments were all those formed by immediate evidence; and synthetic, those resulting from mediate evidence, whether of the purely ideal order, or in some sense depending on experience. It was well known that there were conceptions of the subject, in which the predicate was thought, at least confusedly; and thus union, or identity, was explained by saying that the propositions, in which it was found, were *per se notæ ex terminis*. In analytic judgments, the predicate is in the subject; nothing is added, according to Kant, it is only unfolded. *Whoever says man says rational*, are the words of St. Thomas: the idea is the same as that of the German philosopher.

193. But let us see if it is necessary to change the formula by which the principle of contradiction has hitherto been expressed.

The first observation of Kant refers to the word *impossible*, which he considers unnecessarily added, since the apodictic certainty, which we wish to express, should be contained in the proposition itself. Kant's formula of the principle is this: "a predicate which is *opposed* to a subject, does not belong to it." What is the meaning of the word *impossible*? "Possible and impossible absolutely, are said in relation to the terms. Possible, because the predicate is not opposed to the subject; impossible, because the predicate is opposed to the subject;" says St. Thomas,[20] and with him agree all the schools. Therefore, impossibility is the opposition of the predicate to the subject, and to be repugnant is the same thing as to be impossible, and Kant uses the very language which he blames in others. The common formula might be expressed in this manner: "there is opposition in the same thing being and not-being at the same time," or, "being is opposed to not-being," or, "being excludes not-being," or, "every thing is equal to itself;" and Kant expresses nothing more when he says: "a predicate which is opposed to a subject does not belong to it."

194. As a universal criterion, there is more exactness in the common formula than in that of Kant. The latter restricts the principle to the relation of predicate and subject, and consequently to the purely ideal order, making it of no value for the real, unless by a sort of enlargement. This enlargement, although legitimate and easy, is not needed in the common formula: by saying being excludes not-being, we embrace the ideal and the real, and present to the mind the impossibility, not only of contradictory judgments, but also of contradictory things.

Kant admits that the principle is the condition *sine qua non* of the truth of our cognitions, so that we must take care not to place ourselves in contradiction with it, under pain of annihilating all cognition. Let us put this to the proof. Give a man, unacquainted with these matters, although not ignorant of what is meant by predicate and subject, these two formulas; which will appear to him the best for all uses in the external as in the internal? Certainly not that of Kant. He sees in an instant, in all its generality, that a thing cannot both be and not be at the same time; and he applies the principle to all uses as well in the real as in the ideal order. Treating of an external object, he says, this cannot both be and not be at the same time; treating of contradictory judgments, of ideas which exclude one another, he says, without any difficulty, this cannot be, because it is impossible for the same thing to be and not be at the same time. But it is not so easily and so readily seen how transition is made from the ideal to the real order, or how the purely logical ideas of predicate and subject can be used in the order of facts. The common formula, then, besides being fully as exact as that of Kant, is more simple, more intelligible, and more easy of application. Are there any qualities more desirable than these in a universal criterion, in the condition *sine qua non* of the truth of our cognitions?

195. We have thus far supposed Kant's formula really to express the principle of contradiction; but this supposition is far from being exact. Undoubtedly there would be a contradiction, were a predicate opposed to a subject, and yet to belong to it; and in this sense it may be said that the principle of contradiction is in some manner expressed in Kant's formula. But this is not enough; for we should then be obliged to say that every axiom expresses the principle of contradiction, since no axiom can be denied without a contradiction. The formula of the principle must *directly* express reciprocal exclusion, opposition between being and not-being; this is what was intended, and nothing else was ever meant by the principle of contradiction. Kant, in his new formula, does not directly express this exclusion: what he expresses is, that when the predicate is excluded from the idea of the subject, it does not belong to it. So far from expressing the principle of contradiction, it is the famous principle of the Cartesians: "whatever is contained in the clear and distinct idea of any thing may be affirmed of it with all certainty." In substance the two formulas express the same thing, and are only distinguished by these purely accidental differences: first, that Kant's formula is the more concise; second, that it is negative, and that of the Cartesians affirmative.

196. Kant says: "whatever is *excluded* from the clear and distinct idea of any thing, may be denied of it." A *predicate which is opposed* to a subject "is the same thing as that which is *excluded* from the idea of any thing;" "does not belong to it" is the same as "may be denied of it." And as, on the other hand, the principle of the Cartesians must be understood in both senses, the affirmative and the negative, because when they say that whatever is contained in the clear and distinct idea of any thing may be affirmed of it, they mean also that when any thing is excluded, it may be denied; it follows that Kant says the same thing as the Cartesians; and thus, in attempting to correct all the schools, he has fallen into an equivocation not of a nature to acquire him any great credit for perspicacity.

It is clear that Kant's formula implies this: the predicate contained in the idea of a subject belongs to it. This condition is equally the condition *sine qua non* of all analytic affirmative judgments; for these disappear if that does not belong to the subject which is contained in its idea. In this case there is not even an apparent difference between Kant's formula and that of the Cartesians; the only difference is in terms; the propositions are exactly the same. Hence we see that instead of affirming that the schools expressed themselves inaccurately in the clearest and most fundamental point of human knowledge, we ought to proceed with great circumspection; witness the originality of Kant's formula.

197. The author of the *Critic of Pure Reason* was not more fortunate in censuring the condition, *at the same time*, which is generally added to the formula of the principle of contradiction. Since he took the liberty of believing that no philosopher before himself had expressed this formula in the proper manner, we beg to say that he did not himself well understand what the others intended to express, and we do not, in saying this, deem ourselves guilty of a philosophical profanation. If Kant is an oracle for certain persons, all philosophers together and all mankind are also oracles to be heard and respected.

According to Kant, the principle of contradiction is the condition *sine qua non* of all human cognitions. If, then, this condition is to serve as their object, it must be so expressed as to be applicable to all cases. Our cognitions are not composed solely of necessary elements, but admit, to a great extent, ideas connected with the contingent; since, as we have seen, purely ideal truths lead to nothing positive, unless brought down to the ground of reality. Contingent beings are subject to the condition of time, and all cognitions relating to them must always depend on this condition. Their existence is limited to a determinate space of time; and it is necessary to think and speak of it conformably to this determination. Even their essential properties are in some manner affected by the condition of time; because if abstracted from it, and considered in general, they are not as they are when realized; that is, when they cease to be a pure abstraction, and become something positive. Here, then, is the reason, and a very profound and cogent reason, why all the schools joined the idea of time to the formula of the principle of contradiction: the reason, we repeat, is very profound, and it is strange how it escaped the German philosopher's penetration.

198. The importance of this subject requires still further explanation. What is essential to the principle of contradiction, is the exclusion of being by not-being, and of not-being by being. The formula must express this fact, this truth, which is presented by immediate evidence, and is contemplated by the intellect in a most clear intuition, admitting neither doubt nor obscurity of any kind.

The word *being* may be taken in two senses: *substantively*, inasmuch as it signifies existence; and *copulatively*, as it expresses the relation of predicate to subject. Peter *is*: here the verb *is* signifies the existence of Peter, and is equivalent to this: Peter exists. The equilateral triangle is equiangular: here the verb *is* is taken copulatively, since it is not affirmed that any equilateral triangle exists; merely the relation of equality of angles to equality of sides is established absolutely, abstraction made from the existence of either.

The principle of contradiction must extend to the cases in which *being* is copulative, and to those in which it is substantive; for when we say it is impossible for the same thing to be and not be, we speak not only of the ideal order, or of the relations between predicates and subjects, but also of the real order. Were no reference made to this last, we should hold the entire world of existences to be deprived of this indispensable condition of all cognitions. Moreover this condition is not only necessary to every cognition, but also to every being in itself, abstracting its being known, or being intelligent. What would a being be that could both be and not be? What is the meaning of a contradiction realized? The principle must extend to the word being, not only as copulative, but also as substantive. All finite existences, our own included, are measured by a successive duration; therefore, if the formula of the principle of contradiction is to be applicable to whatever we know in the universe, it must be accompanied by the condition of time. All finite things, which now exist, at one time did not exist, and it may again be true that they do not exist. Of no one can it be truly said that its non-existence is impossible; this impossibility springs from existence in a given time, and can only be asserted with respect to that time. Therefore, the condition of time is absolutely necessary in the formula of the principle of contradiction, if this formula is to serve for the existent, that is, for that which is the real object of our cognitions.

199. Let us now see what happens in the purely ideal order, where the word *being* is taken copulatively. Propositions of the purely ideal order are of two classes; in the first, the subject is a generic idea, which, by the union of the specific difference, becomes a determinate species; in the second, the subject is this determinate species, or the generic idea joined with the difference. The word *angle* expresses the generic idea comprehending all angles, which, united with the corresponding difference, constitutes the species of acute, obtuse, or right angle. At every step we modify the generic idea in various ways, and as a succession, in which are represented to us distinct conceptions, all having for their basis the generic idea, necessarily enters into it, it follows that we consider this idea as a being which is successively transformed. To express this succession, which is purely intellectual, we employ the idea of time; and here is one of the reasons which justify the use of this condition even in the purely ideal order. Thus we say, an angle cannot at the same time be both a right angle and a not-right angle; for the idea of angle may be successively determined by the difference which constitutes it a right angle, and a not-right angle; but these determinations cannot co-exist even in our conception, for which reason we do not assert the union of the difference with the genus to be absolutely impossible, but limit the impossibility to the condition of simultaneousness.

In this proposition, a right angle cannot be obtuse; the subject is not the generic idea alone, but is united with the difference expressed by the word *right*. In the conception formed of these two ideas, right and angle, we see the impossibility of uniting the idea *obtuse* with them. This is without any condition of time, and here there is none expressed. We frequently say, an angle cannot be at the same time right and obtuse; but we never say, a right angle can never *at the same time* be obtuse, but, absolutely, a right angle cannot be obtuse.

200. Kant observes that the equivocation proceeds from commencing by separating the predicate of a thing from the conception of this thing, and afterwards joining to this same predicate its opposite, which never makes a contradiction to the subject, but to the predicate, which is synthetically united with it; a contradiction which happens only when the first and second predicates are supposed at the same time. This observation of Kant is at bottom very true, but it has its defects: first, it pretends to be original, when it only says things already well known; and secondly, it is used to combat an equivocation existing only in the mind of the philosopher who wants to free others from it. The two propositions analyzed in the last paragraph confirm what we have just said. An angle cannot be both right and not right. Here the condition of time is necessary, because the opposition is not between the predicate and the subject, but between the two predicates. The angle may be right or not right, only at different times. A right angle cannot be obtuse; here the condition of time must not be expressed, because the idea *right* entering into the conception of the subject, entirely excludes the idea obtuse.

201. If the principle of contradiction were to serve only for analytic judgments, that is, for those in which the predicate is contained in the idea of the subject, the condition of time should never be expressed; but as this principle is to guide us in all other judgments, it follows that, in the general formula, we cannot abstract a condition absolutely indispensable in most cases. In the present state of our understanding, while we are in this life, non abstraction of time is the rule, abstraction the exception; and would you have a general formula conform to the exception and neglect the rule?

202. We cannot conceive what reason Kant had to illustrate this subject with the examples above cited. Nothing can be more common and inopportune than what he adds in illustration of this matter by examples. "If I say a man who is unlearned is not learned, the condition *at the same time* must be understood; for he who is unlearned at one time, may very well be learned at another." This is not only very common and inopportune, but it is exceedingly inexact. If the proposition were: a man cannot be ignorant and instructed; then the condition *at the same time* should be added, because not giving preference to either predicate over the other indicates the manner

of the opposition, which is of predicate to predicate, and not of predicate to subject. But in the example adduced by Kant, "the man that is ignorant is not instructed." The subject is not man alone, but an ignorant man; the predicate *instructed* devolves on man modified by the predicate *ignorant*, and, consequently, the expression of time is not necessary, nor is it used in ordinary language.

There is a great difference between these two propositions: a man that is ignorant *is not* instructed; and a man that is ignorant *cannot be* instructed. The condition of time must not be expressed in the former, for the reason already given; it must be in the latter, because speaking of the impossibility in an absolute manner, we should deny the ignorant man even the *power* to be instructed.

203. Kant's other example is the following: "But if I say no unlearned man is learned, the proposition is analytical, since the sign of unlearnedness now constitutes the conception of the subject, and then the negative proposition is immediately evident from the principle of contradiction, without it being necessary for the condition *at the same time* to be added." We cannot see why Kant makes so great difference between these two propositions: a man who is unlearned is not learned, and no unlearned man is learned; in both, the predicate relates not only to man, but to an unlearned man; and it is the same to say, a man that is unlearned, as, an unlearned man. If, then, the expression of time is not necessary in the one, neither is it in the other.

If the idea of unlearned affects the subject, the predicate is necessarily excluded, because the ideas, learned and unlearned, are contradictory; and we encounter the rule of logic, that in necessary matters, an indefinite is equivalent to a universal proposition.

The principle of contradiction must, therefore, be preserved as it is; the condition of time must not be suppressed, for this would render the formula, in many cases, inapplicable.(20)

CHAPTER XXI
DOES THE PRINCIPLE OF CONTRADICTION MERIT THE TITLE OF FUNDAMENTAL; AND IF SO, IN WHAT SENSE?

204. Having cleared up the true sense of the principle of contradiction, let us now see whether it merits to be called fundamental, whether it possesses all the characteristics requisite to such a dignity. These characteristics are three in number: first, that it depend on no other principle; secondly, that its fall involve the ruin of all others; thirdly, that it may, while it remains firm, be conclusively urged against all who deny the others, and be of avail to bring them back to the truth by a demonstration at least indirect.

205. In order completely to solve all questions depending on the principle of contradiction, we shall state a few propositions, and accompany them with their proper demonstrations:

FIRST PROPOSITION.

If the principle of contradiction be denied, all certainty, all truth, and all knowledge are at an end.

Demonstration.—If a thing may be and not be at the same time, we may be certain and not certain, know and not know, exist and not exist; affirmation may be joined with negation, contradictory things united, distinct things identified, and identical things distinguished: the intellect is a chaos to the full extent of the word; reason is overturned; language is absurd; subject and object clash in the midst of frightful darkness, and all intellectual light is for ever extinguished. All principles are involved in the universal wreck, and consciousness itself would totter, were it not, when this absurd supposition is made, upheld by the invincible hand of nature. Consciousness, indeed, in this absurd hypothesis, does not perish, for this is impossible, but it sees itself carried away by this violent whirlwind, which precipitates it and every thing else into chaotic darkness. In vain does it strive to save its ideas; they all vanish before the force of contradiction: in vain does it generate new ideas to be substituted for those it loses; these also disappear: in vain does it seek new objects, for they, too, disappear in like manner, and it endures only to feel the radical impossibility of all thought, and see contradiction lording it over the intellect, and destroying, with irresistible might, whatever would germinate there.

SECOND PROPOSITION.

206. It is not enough not to suppose the principle of contradiction false; we must suppose it to be true, if we would not have all certainty, all knowledge, all truth to perish.

Demonstration.—The reasons given for the first proposition avail also to prove this. In the one case the principle of contradiction is supposed to be denied; in the other, it is neither supposed true nor false; but this evidently is not enough, for, until the principle of contradiction is placed beyond all doubt, we remain in darkness, and must doubt of every thing. We do not mean to say that it is impossible for us to have certainty of any thing, if we do not think explicitly of this principle; but that it must be so firmly established, that we cannot raise the least doubt concerning it, and that, when we see any thing connected with it, we must, of necessity, consider that thing as founded upon an immovable basis: the least vacillation, the least doubt of this principle utterly destroys it; the possibility of an absurdity is itself an absurdity.

THIRD PROPOSITION.

207. The certainty of the principle of contradiction rests upon no other principle.

Demonstration.—It is, as we have seen, necessary in every cognition to suppose the truth of the principle of contradiction; therefore, no one can avail to demonstrate it. Every argument, made to demonstrate this, necessarily involves a vicious circle; the principle of contradiction is proved by another principle, which, in its turn, supposes that of contradiction; and so we shall have a superstructure resting upon a foundation, which foundation rests upon the superstructure itself.

FOURTH PROPOSITION.

208. Whoever denies the principle of contradiction can neither directly nor indirectly be refuted by any other.

Demonstration.—It would be amusing to hear the arguments directed against a man who admits both affirmation and negation to be at the same time possible; although forced to admit the affirmative, he will still hold the negative, and *vice versa*. It is impossible not only to argue, but even to speak, or to think on such a supposition.

FIFTH PROPOSITION.

209. It is not exact to say, as is generally said, that by the principle of contradiction, we may argue conclusively against whoever denies the others.

Here take notice that we only say *it is not exact*, for we believe it at bottom to be true, although not free from inexactness. To show this, let us examine the weight of the demonstration ordinarily given. The reasons, arguments, and replies may be presented most clearly and strongly in the form of a dialogue. Let us suppose some one to deny this axiom: the whole is greater than its part.

If you deny this, you admit that the same thing may both be and not be at the same time. This is what you have to prove. With you the whole is the whole and not the whole, and the part the part and not the part. Why so? First, it is the whole by supposition. Admitted. And at the same time it is not. Denied. It is not the whole because it is not greater than its part. An excellent way of arguing! This is a *petitio principii*. I commence by asserting that the whole is not greater than its part, and you argue on the contrary supposition; for you tell me the whole would not be the whole were it not greater than its part. If I had conceded that the whole is greater than its part, and then denied this property, I should indeed fall into a contradiction, making that a whole, which, according to my principles, is not a whole; but as I now deny that the whole must be greater than its part, I must also deny that it ceases to be a whole by not being greater than its part.

210. What will you reply to one reasoning thus. Certainly nothing in the form of an argument: all that you can do is to call his attention to the absurdity of his position; but this is to be done not by argument, but by exactly determining the meaning of the words and analyzing the conceptions which they express. This is all that can or should be done. The contradiction exists; this is certain; but what is wanted is, that he see that he has fallen into it; and if the explanation of the terms, and the analysis of the conceptions do not suffice, nothing else will.

Let us see how this may be done in the same example. The whole is greater than its part. What is the whole? The collection of the parts, the parts themselves united. The idea of the parts then enters into the idea of the whole. What is the meaning of greater? One thing is said to be greater than another, when, besides containing an equal quantity, it also contains something else. Seven is greater than five, because, besides the same five, it contains also two. The whole contains one part and also the other parts; therefore, the idea of *greater than its part* enters into the idea of whole. Thus it is that we must refute whoever denies this principle; and this method, better than that of argumentation, may be said to explain the terms and analyze the conceptions, for it clearly does nothing but define the former and decompose the latter.

SIXTH PROPOSITION.

211. The principle of contradiction is known only by immediate evidence.

Demonstration.—Two things are here to be proved: that the knowledge is by evidence, and that the evidence is immediate. As regards the former we will remark that the principle of contradiction is not a simple fact of consciousness, but a purely ideal truth. Every fact of consciousness involves reality, and cannot be expressed without the assertion of some existence: the principle of contradiction neither affirms nor denies any thing positive; that is, it does not say that any thing exists or does not exist; it only expresses the opposition of being to not-being, and of not-being to being, abstraction made from our taking the word being copulatively or substantively.

212. Every fact of consciousness is not only something existent, but something determinate; it is not a thought in the abstract, but is this or that thought. The principle of contradiction contains nothing determinate; it abstracts not only the existence, but also the essence of things, since it relates not only to existing things, but also to things possible: it distinguishes no species among them, but embraces them all in their greatest generality. When we say, "it is impossible for the same thing to be and not be," the word *thing* does not at all restrict the meaning; it expresses being in general, in its greatest indeterminateness. In the *to be* or *not be*, the word *be* expresses not only existence, but also every class of essences in their most complete indeterminateness. Thus the principle is equally applicable in these two propositions: it is impossible for the moon to be and not be; it is impossible for a circle to be and not be a circle; although the first is in the real order, and there the word *be* expresses existence, and the second is in the ideal order, and the word *be* expresses only the relation of predicate to subject.

213. Every fact of consciousness is individual; the principle of contradiction is the most universal imaginable: every fact of consciousness is contingent; the principle of contradiction is absolutely necessary, a necessity which is a mark of truths known by evidence.

214. The principle of contradiction is a law of all intelligence; it is of absolute necessity for the finite as for the infinite; not even the infinite intelligence is beyond this necessity, for infinite perfection cannot be an absurdity. Every fact of consciousness as purely individual, relates only to the being that experiences it; neither the order of intelligences, nor that of truth suffers any mutation from my existence or non-existence.

215. The principle of contradiction, besides the marks of necessity and universality, which distinguish truths of evidence, possesses also that of being seen with that immediate, intellectual clearness, of which we have already treated. In the idea of being we see most clearly the exclusion of not-being.

Hence the proof of the second part of the proposition: because there is immediate evidence of the relation of the predicate to the subject, when the sole idea of the subject, without the necessity of combination with other ideas, enables us to perceive this relation: this is so in the present case, for not only no combination is needed, but all combinations are impossible if the truth of this principle be not supposed.(21)

CHAPTER XXII
THE PRINCIPLE OF EVIDENCE

216. Among the principles which, by their pretensions to the title of fundamental, have most figured in the schools, is one called the principle of the Cartesians: "whatever is contained in the clear and distinct idea of any thing, may be affirmed of it with all certainty." We have already seen Kant resuscitate this principle, although in other words, equivocally taking it as synonymous with that of contradiction. Upon close examination we shall easily perceive that the formula of the Cartesians, like that of Kant, only expresses the legitimacy of the criterion of evidence. Both may be simplified to this: evidence is a criterion of truth; or, whatever is evident is true. As we shall hereafter use this transformation to distinguish ideas which we consider very confused, we will show the reason of the equality of the two expressions.

217. To say that any thing is contained in the clear and distinct idea of another thing, is the same as to say that there is evidence that a predicate belongs to a subject; the words have, and can have, no other meaning. To be contained in a clear and distinct idea, is equivalent to seeing one thing in another by that intellectual light which we call evidence; therefore, this expression, "whatever is contained in the clear and distinct idea of any thing," is exactly equivalent to this, "whatever is evident."

To say, that any thing may be affirmed of another with all certainty, is the same as to say, "this thing is true, and we may be perfectly certain of it." It is the truth that is affirmed, and the truth only; therefore, this expression, "may be affirmed of it with all certainty," is exactly equivalent to this, "it is true."

Thus the expression of the Cartesians may be transformed into this: "Whatever is evident is true," or its equivalent, "evidence is a sure criterion of truth."

218. "A predicate that is opposed to a subject does not belong to it," is Kant's formula. The opposition here meant is that founded on ideas, when the predicate is necessarily excluded by intrinsic *opposition* from the idea of the subject. The expression, then, "a predicate that is opposed to a subject,"

is equivalent to this: "when the predicate is clearly seen excluded from the idea of the subject," which last is in its turn equivalent to this: "the exclusion, or the opposition between the subject and the predicate, is evident."

"Does not belong to it," means the same as, "it is true that it does not belong to it;" and since these formulas have two values, one for affirmative, another for negative cases, if we say the predicate that is opposed to a subject does not belong to it, we may with equal reason say, the predicate contained in the idea of a subject belongs to it; wherefore, Kant's formula exactly coincides with this: "whatever is evident is true."

219. This transformation gives us greater simplicity and generality; simplicity by the very expression, and generality, because affirmative as well as negative cases are included. The words, "whatever is evident," embrace affirmations as well as negations, for the inclusion of a predicate in a subject may be just as evident as their mutual opposition. Thus, we may see one thing contained in the idea of another, just as we may see it excluded from that idea. Under all conceptions the formula, "whatever is evident is true," is preferable; and if we would express it not as a principle, but as a rule to be applied, it may be converted into this: "evidence is a sure criterion of truth."

220. This transformation must not be supposed to be the only object of the preceding analysis; although in these matters clearness and precision should be carried to the highest possible point, we should nevertheless have abstained from these considerations, had we only proposed to make an innovation, and one perhaps of little practical consequence; the same thing is expressed in both formulas, and he who does not understand the first will not understand the second. Our principal object was not, however, to make this innovation, but to show into what a confusion of ideas those fall who inquire whether the principle involving the legitimacy of the criterion of evidence ought, or ought not, to be considered as fundamental, and be preferred to the principle of contradiction, as also to that of Descartes.

221. We begin by establishing a proposition which may seem a most strange paradox, but is far from being so: *the principle of evidence is not evident.*

Demonstration.—This principle in its simplest form is this: the evident is true. This proposition, we say, is not evident. When is a proposition evident? When we see the predicate in the idea of the subject; and here this does not occur. *Evident* is the same thing as *clearly seen,* as offered to the intellect in a most lucid manner. *True* is the same as conformity of the idea with the object. We now ask, can you, however much you analyze this idea, "seen with clearness," ever find this other, "conformed to the object?" No. This is an immense leap: we pass from subjectiveness to objectiveness; we affirm subjective to be the reflex of objective conditions; we go from the idea to its object, and this transition is the most transcendental, difficult, and obscure problem of philosophy. Let the reader now decide if we had not ground to assert that the proposition, "the principle of evidence is not evident," was not a paradox.

222. What, then, shall we say of this proposition: "Whatever is evident is true?" It is not an axiom, for the predicate is not contained in the idea of the subject; it is not a demonstrable proposition, for all demonstration rests on evident principles, and consists in deducing from them a consequence evidently connected with them; this cannot take place unless we presuppose the legitimacy of evidence, that is to say, that which is the object of the demonstration. At the commencement of the argument, it might be asked, how do you know the principle on which your argument is based? How do you know it to be true? By evidence. But recollect you are proving that whatever is evident is true, and, therefore, you beg the question. The truth of the laws of logic, to which every argument must conform, is known only by evidence; therefore if we do not suppose whatever is evident to be true, we cannot argue at all.

223. We hold then that the principle of evidence can be based on no other principle, and that, consequently, it has the first mark of the fundamental principle. If it fails, all other principles,—that of contradiction, known like the others only by evidence, included,—fail with it; this is another mark of the fundamental principle. Let us see if it has the third, by aid of which, whoever denies the rest may be refuted.

Rarely does any one deny the principle of contradiction, and admit that of evidence; yet, making this extravagant supposition, this principle alone would be of avail, because the question would be reduced to this: does he admit the principles to be evident? If he does not, his intellect is unlike that of other men; if he does, the argument brought against him is conclusive. You admit that whatever is evident is true; such or such a principle is evident for you, therefore it is true. The premises are evident of themselves; the legitimacy of the consequence is also evident; and he must consequently admit it, since he admits the criterion of evidence to be a general rule.

224. Whence then the singularity we have noticed in this principle? It is neither evident, nor demonstrable; it is necessary to all others, and whoever denies them is refuted by it. Whence, then, such a singularity? It has a very simple cause; it is, that the principle of evidence expresses no objective truth, and therefore is not demonstrable: it is not a simple fact of consciousness, for it expresses the relation of the subject to the object, for which reason it cannot be limited to the purely subjective; it is a proposition

known by a reflex act, and it expresses the primary law of all our objective cognitions. These are founded on evidence; this we experience: but when the mind asks why we trust evidence, we can make no other answer than that whatever is evident is true. What is the foundation of this proposition? Ordinarily it has none; we conform to it without ever thinking of it; but if we take the pains to reflect, we find three motives for assenting to it: the first is an irresistible instinct of nature; the second is the destruction of all our cognitions and the impossibility of thought, if we do not admit the legitimacy of the criterion; the third is the perceiving that, admitting this criterion, every thing is co-ordinated in the intellect, that an ideal universe admirably harmonized, takes the place of chaos, and that we feel possessed of the means necessary to reason and to construct a scientific edifice in the real universe, the knowledge of which we have from experience.(22)

CHAPTER XXIII
THE CRITERION OF CONSCIOUSNESS

225. Having established the worth of the principles of consciousness, of evidence, and of contradiction, in relation to the dignity of fundamental, we will now examine the intrinsic value of the different criteria. And here the doctrine of the preceding chapters, of which the following are the development and complement, furnishes much light. We will begin with consciousness, or the internal sense.

The testimony of consciousness includes all phenomena, either actively or passively, realized in our soul. It is by its nature purely subjective; so that in itself considered, apart from the intellectual instinct and the light of evidence, it testifies nothing with respect to objects. By it we know what we experience, not what is; we perceive the phenomenon, not the reality; what authorizes us to say: such a thing appears to me; but not, such a thing is.

The transition from subject to object, from the idea representing to the thing represented, from the impression to the cause impressing, belongs to other criteria: consciousness is limited to the interior, or rather, to itself, which is nothing but an act of our soul.

226. We must distinguish between direct and reflex consciousness: the former accompanies every internal phenomenon; the latter does not: the former is natural; the latter philosophical: the former abstracts the act of reason; the latter is one of these acts.

Direct consciousness is the presence of the phenomenon to the mind, whether that phenomenon be a sensation or an idea, an act or an impression, in the intellectual or the moral order.

This distinction shows that direct consciousness accompanies every exercise, whether active or passive, of the faculties of our soul. It is a contradiction to say that these phenomena exist in the soul, and are not present to it.

These phenomena are not modifications like those which occur in insensible things; we here treat of living modifications, so to speak, in a living being; in the idea of these modifications is contained their presence to the mind.

It is impossible for us to have a sensation without experiencing it; for whoever says he has a sensation, says that he experiences a sensation: this experience is its presence; an experienced sensation is a present sensation.

Thought is by its essence, a representation that can neither exist nor be conceived without presence; the name itself shows this, and the idea which we join with it confirms the meaning of the word. When we speak of representation, we understand that there is some real or imaginary object, which mediately or immediately offers itself to the subject. There is then presence in every representation, and consequently in every thought.

If, from what is passive, like sensations and representations, we pass to the active, that is, to the phenomena when the soul freely evolves its force in the intellectual or moral order, *in combining or willing*, this presence is, if possible, yet more evident. The being that thus acts, does not obey a natural impulse, but motives which it proposes to itself, and to which it may or may not attend. To make intellectual combinations and to exercise acts of the will, without either being present to the soul, are contradictory assertions.

227. Reflex consciousness, called by the French *aperception*, from the verb *s'apercevoir*, and denoting perception of the perception, is the act whereby the mind explicitly knows any phenomenon which is realized in it. Thus, I hear a noise: the simple sensation, present to and affecting my mind, constitutes what we have called direct consciousness; but if besides hearing, I also *aperceive*, to use a Gallicism, that I hear; then I not only hear, but also think that I hear: this we call reflex consciousness.

228. It is clear from this example, that direct and reflex consciousness are not only distinct but separable. I may hear without thinking that I hear; and this is very often the case.

229. Most men have little reflex consciousness, and the greatest intellectual force operates directly. This ideological fact is connected with moral truths of the utmost importance. The human mind was not born to contemplate itself, to think that it thinks: its affections were not given as an object of reflection, but as impulses which elevate it to what it is called to: the principal object of its intelligence and love is, in this life as in the other, the infinite being. The worship of itself is an aberration of pride; its punishment is darkness.

230. All great scientific discoveries lie in the objective, not in the subjective order. The exact sciences, natural as well as moral, have emanated not from reflexion of the subject upon itself, but from knowledge of objects and their relations. Even the metaphysical sciences, in all that is most solid in them, ontology, cosmology, and theology, are purely objective: ideology and psychology which consider the subject, are full of the obscurity

inherent in all that is subjective; ideology scarcely does more than merely observe internal phenomena,—an observation, we may remark, generally very defective, poorly made, and bewildered with vain cavils; and what has psychology itself, truly demonstrated, except the simplicity of the soul, the necessary consequence of the unity of consciousness? In all else it resembles ideology, and to a certain point, is confounded with it; it observes phenomena, and afterwards defines and classifies them better or worse, but fails to explain their mysterious nature.

231. Consciousness is the foundation of the other criteria, not as a proposition which serves as their basis, but as a fact which is a necessary condition of them all.

232. Consciousness tells us that we see the idea of one thing contained in the idea of another: thus far there is nothing but appearance; the formula, to express its testimony would be: *it appears to me*; which denotes a purely subjective phenomenon. But this phenomenon is accompanied by an intellectual instinct, an irresistible impulse of nature, which makes us assent to the truth of the relation, not only so far as it is in us, but as it is formed without us, in the purely objective order, whether in the sphere of reality or possibility. Thus it is explained how evidence is founded on consciousness, not as identified with it, but as resting upon it as a fact from which it cannot be abstracted, and as also containing the intellectual instinct which makes us believe whatever is evident to be true.

233. Sensation, in itself considered, is a fact of pure consciousness, since it is immanent in us: so far is it from being an act whereby the mind passes beyond itself, translates itself to the object, that it ought rather to be regarded as a passion than an action, and this accords with the common mode of speaking, which ascribes it to a passive rather than to an active faculty. Nevertheless on this mere fact of consciousness is in some sense founded what is called the testimony of the senses, and consequently all knowledge of the external world, its properties, and relations.

In the sensation whereby we see the sun, there are two things: the sensation itself, that is, the representation which I experience in myself, and which I call sight; and the correspondence of this sensation to the external object which I call the sun. Evidently, these are two very distinct things, and yet we always unite them. Consciousness is certainly the first basis of the formation of judgment; but alone it does not suffice, for it only testifies that the sensation is, not what it is. How is the judgment completed? By means of a natural instinct which makes us render sensations objective, that is, makes us believe in an external object corresponding to the internal phenomena. Thus the testimony of the senses is in some manner founded on consciousness; it does not, however, proceed from consciousness alone, but requires the natural instinct, by means of which we form our judgments in perfect security.

234. We must here remark that evidence has nothing to do with the testimony of the senses, even in their intellectual part, wherein we judge that an external object corresponds to the sensation. The idea of the existence or possibility of an external object does not enter into the idea of the sensation as purely subjective, and without this indispensable condition there can be no evidence. Not only is this clear of itself, but it is confirmed by daily experience. We continually have the representation of the external subjectively considered, as a pure phenomenon in our soul, although no real object corresponds to it; more or less clear when we are awake, but most vivid, even so as to produce a perfect illusion, when we are asleep.

235. With this exposition, the value and extent of consciousness may be exactly determined: this we shall see in the following propositions, in all of which, we would observe, we treat only of direct consciousness.

FIRST PROPOSITION.

The testimony of consciousness extends to all the phenomena that are realized in our soul, regarded as an intellectual and sensitive being.

SECOND PROPOSITION.

236. If there exist in our soul phenomena of a different order, that is to say, if it may in some sense be modified in non-representative faculties, the testimony of consciousness does not extend to such phenomena.

We do not advance this proposition without a solid reason. It is probable, and even very probable, that our soul has active faculties, of the exercise of which it is not conscious; otherwise how explain the mysteries of organic life? The soul is united to the body, and is for it the vital principle, the separation from which causes death, manifested in complete disorganization and decomposition. This activity is exercised without consciousness, either of the mode or of the fact of its existence.

It may be said that there is here a series of those confused perceptions of which Leibnitz speaks in his *Monadologie*; or that these perceptions are so slight, so wan, as to leave no trace in the memory, nor be an object of reflection: but these are only conjectures. It is hard to persuade one's self that the foetus in the mother's womb has any consciousness of the activity exercised for the development of its organization: it is also hard to persuade one's self that even in adults there is any consciousness of that same activity producing circulation of the blood, nutrition, and other phenomena which constitute life. If these phenomena are produced, as they certainly are, by the soul, there is in it, an exercise of activity of which it either has no consciousness, or one so weak and confused that it is as if it were not.

THIRD PROPOSITION.

237. The testimony of consciousness, in itself considered, is so limited to the purely internal, that it is *of itself* worth nothing in the external order, either for the criterion of evidence or that of the senses.

FOURTH PROPOSITION.

The testimony of consciousness is the foundation of the other criteria, inasmuch as it is a fact which they all require, and without which they are impossible.

FIFTH PROPOSITION.

238. From the combination of consciousness with intellectual instinct arise all the other criteria.(23)

CHAPTER XXIV
THE CRITERION OF EVIDENCE

239. There are two species of evidence, mediate and immediate. We call immediate evidence that which requires only understanding of the terms; and mediate evidence that which requires reasoning. That the whole is greater than its part is evident by immediate evidence; that the square of the hypothenuse is equal to the sum of the squares of the other two sides, is known by mediate evidence, that is, by demonstrative reasoning.

240. We have said that one of the distinctive characteristics of evidence is the necessity and universality of its object. This is a characteristic as well of mediate as of immediate evidence.

Besides this characteristic there is another, called with more reason essential, notwithstanding some doubt as to whether it extends to mediate evidence or not; it is that the idea of the predicate is found contained in that of the subject. This is the most complete essential notion of the criterion of immediate evidence, by which it is distinguished from the criteria of consciousness and common sense.

We have said there is some doubt as to this characteristic extending to mediate evidence; by this we mean that also in mediate evidence the idea of the predicate may be contained in that of the subject. In this it is not our intention to ignore the difference between theorems and axioms, but to call the reader's attention to a doctrine which we propose to develop, while treating of mediate evidence. In the present chapter we shall only treat of evidence in general, or of immediate evidence alone.

241. Evidence involves relation, for it implies comparison. When the understanding does not compare, it has no evidence, but only a perception, which is a pure fact of consciousness; and this evidence does not refer to perception alone, but always supposes or produces a judgment.

We find two things in every act where there is evidence: the pure intuition of the idea, and the decomposition of this idea into various conceptions accompanied with the perception of their mutual relations. This we will explain by an example from geometry. The triangle has three sides: this is an evident proposition, for in the very idea of triangle, we find the three sides; and in conceiving the triangle, we in some sense conceive the three sides. Had we limited ourselves to the contemplation of the simple idea of triangle, we should have had intuition of the idea, but not evidence, which begins only when we find, in decomposing the conception of triangle, and considering in it the idea of figure in general, of side, and of the number three, these all contained in the primitive conception. Evidence consists in the clear conception of this.

So true is this that the very nature of things makes common language philosophical. We do not say, an idea is evident, but a judgment is: no one calls a term evident, but a proposition only. And why? Because the term simply expresses the idea without any relation, or decomposition into its partial conceptions; whereas the proposition expresses the judgment, that is, affirms or denies that one conception is contained in another, which, in the present matter, supposes decomposition of the entire conception.

242. Immediate evidence is the perception of identity between various conceptions, separated by the analytical power of the intellect. Thus identity combined in a certain way with diversity is not a contradiction, as it might at first sight seem, but something very natural, if we observe one of the most constant facts of our intellect, the faculty of analyzing the most simple conceptions, and of seeing relations between identical things.

What are all axioms? What are all propositions *per se notæ*? Nothing but expressions, in which it is affirmed that a predicate belongs to the essence of the subject, or is contained in its idea. The mere conception of the subject includes the predicate: the term which denotes the first also denotes the second; yet the intellect, with a mysterious power of analysis, distinguishes between identical things, and then compares them in order to make them again identical. Whoever says triangle, expresses a figure composed of three sides and three angles; but the intellect may take this idea and consider in it the ideas of the number three, side, and angle, and compare them with the primitive conception. In this distinction there is no deception; there is only the exercise of the faculty, which regards the thing under different aspects, in order to arrive at the intuition and affirmation of the identity of the very things it had before distinguished.

243. Evidence is a sort of calculation of the intellect, whereby it finds in the conception analyzed whatever was placed in the principle or was contained in it. Hence the necessity and universality of the object of evidence, inasmuch as, and in the manner, in which it is expressed by the idea. To this there are no exceptions. Either a predicate is or is not placed in a primitive principle: if it is, it is there, according to the principle of contradiction. Either it was or was not excluded from the conception; if the

conception itself excludes or denies it, this it does by virtue of the principle of contradiction.

Thus the more fundamental of the two characteristics of evidence given above is, that the idea of the predicate is contained in the idea of the subject. Hence the necessity and universality; since, in verifying this condition, it is impossible for the predicate not to belong *necessarily to all the subjects.*

244. Thus far we have encountered no difficulty, because we have treated only of evidence subjectively considered, that is, as relating to pure conceptions; but the intellect does not stop with the conception, but extends to the object, and says not only that it sees the thing, but that the thing is as it sees it. Thus the principle of contradiction, considered in the purely subjective order, means that the conception of being is opposed to that of not-being, which destroys it, just as the conception of being destroys that of not-being; it means, that in endeavoring to conceive jointly these two things, and to make them co-exist, a sort of struggle of thoughts, reciprocally annihilating each other, takes place in the depths of our soul, — a struggle which the understanding is condemned to witness without hope of establishing peace between the combatants. If we confine ourselves to this phenomenon, no objection can be made. We experience it, and there is no further question about it; but in announcing the principle, we would announce something more than the incompatibility of the conceptions; we would transfer this incompatibility to the things themselves, and assert that not only our own conceptions, but also all real and possible beings are subjected to this law. Whatever be the object of which we treat, whatever the conditions under which we suppose it existent or possible, we say that while it is, it cannot not be; and while it is not it cannot be. We affirm, then, the law of contradiction, not only for our own conceptions, but also for things themselves; the intellect applies to every thing the law which it finds necessary to itself.

By what right? An incontestible right, for it is the law of necessity. With what reason? With none, for we are now at the foundation of reason; this is the *ne plus ultra* of the human understanding; philosophy can go no farther. Let us not, however, be thought to abandon the field to skeptics, or to entrench ourselves in necessity, contented with pointing out a fact of our nature. The question is susceptible of different solutions, which may not, indeed, go beyond the *ne plus ultra* of our mind, but which yet leaves the cause of skepticism in great straits.

245. To ask why the criterion of evidence is legitimate, is to ask why this proposition is true: "whatever is evident is true;" it is to raise the question of the objectiveness of ideas. The fundamental difference between dogmatists

and skeptics, is not that the latter deny the facts of consciousness,—the most refined skepticism has not come to this, and both agree in recognizing the purely subjective appearance of phenomena; but it is that dogmatists found science on consciousness, and skeptics maintain that this is an illegitimate transition, and that we must despair of science, and confine ourselves to mere consciousness.

According to this doctrine, ideas are empty forms of the understanding, mean nothing, and can lead to nothing; although they entertain the understanding, and offer to it an immense field for combinations, the world they present to it is purely illusory, and can serve for nothing in the real order. In contemplating these entirely empty forms, the intellect is the sport of fantastic visions, from the union of which results the spectacle which seems now to belong to reality, and now to possibility; either it is a mere nonentity, or something, and if so, it can never make us sure of the reality it possesses.

246. It is difficult to fight skepticism when it takes this ground: situated beyond the domains of reason, the decisions of reason cannot reach it. It will appeal from them all, for it begins by denying the competency of the judge. But as these skeptics admit consciousness, it is right that they should defend it against whoever attempts to deprive them of it. We believe that if the objectiveness of ideas be denied, not only all science, but also all consciousness is annihilated; and here skeptics are guilty of an inconsequence; for, while they deny the objectiveness of some ideas, they admit that of others. No consciousness, properly so called, can exist, if this objectiveness be absolutely destroyed. We beg the reader to follow us in a brief, but severe analysis of the facts of consciousness, in their relations with the objectiveness of ideas.(24)

CHAPTER XXV
THE OBJECTIVE VALUE OF IDEAS

247. The transition from subject to object, from subjective appearance to objective reality, is a problem which vexes fundamental philosophy. Consciousness will not permit us to doubt that certain things *appear* to us in such a manner; but *are* they in reality what they appear to us? How are we to know this? What shall assure us of this conformity of the idea with the object?

The question does not relate solely to sensations; it also extends to purely intellectual ideas, even to those inundated with that internal light which we call evidence. "What I evidently see in the idea of a thing, is as I see it," philosophers have said, and all mankind with them. No one doubts what is presented to him as evidently true. But how prove that evidence is a legitimate criterion of truth?

248. "God is truthful," says Descartes, "and could not have deceived us; He could not have taken pleasure in making us the victims of perpetual illusions." All this is true. But the skeptic will ask how we know that God is truthful, or even that he exists. If we found the veracity of God on the idea of an infinitely perfect being, as Descartes does, there is still the same difficulty with respect to the correspondence of the idea with the object. If we draw the demonstration of the veracity and existence of God from the ideas of necessary and contingent beings, of effect and cause, of order and intelligence, we again meet the same obstacle, and are still unable to pass from the idea to the object.

No matter how much we cavil, we shall never get out of this circle, we shall always return to the same point. The mind cannot think out of itself; what it knows, it knows by means of its ideas; if these deceive, it has nothing left to set it right. All rectification, all proof must employ these ideas, and these, in their turn, require new proof and rectification.

249. Many books of philosophy exaggerate the illusions of the senses, and the difficulty of assuring ourselves of the sensible reality, when they solve this question: "I perceive it to be so; but is it as I perceive?" These same books immediately afterwards speak of the order of ideas with security equal

to their mistrust in the sensible order. This does not seem very logical, for phenomena relating to the senses, may be examined by the light of reason, and it may be seen how far they agree with it: but what touch-stone have we for the phenomena of reason itself? If there be difficulty in the sensible, there is likewise in the intellectual, and the more serious, since it affects the very basis of all cognitions, even those which relate to sensations.

If we doubt the existence of the external world which the senses present to us, we may appeal to the connection of the sensations with causes not in us; and so deduce by demonstration the relations of the appearances with the reality: but this requires the ideas of cause and effect; we must have some truth, some general principles, as for example, that nothing can produce itself, and others similar, without which we cannot take one step.

250. We do not believe any satisfactory reason can be given for the veracity of the criterion of evidence, although it is impossible not to yield to it. The connection, therefore, of evidence with reality, and consequently, the transition from the idea to the object, are primitive facts of our nature, a necessary law of our understanding, the foundation of all that it contains, —a foundation which in its turn rests, and can rest only on God, the Creator of our soul.

251. We must observe the contradiction into which those philosophers fall who say: I cannot doubt what is subjective, what affects myself, what I feel within myself; but I have no right to go out of myself, and affirm that what I think is in reality as I think. Do you know that you feel, that you think, that you have within you such or such an appearance? Can you prove it? Evidently you cannot. You yield to a fact, to an internal necessity which forces you to *believe* that you think, that you feel, or that such a thing appears to you; but then there is equal necessity in the connection of the object with the idea, an equal necessity forces you to *believe* that what *appears* to you to be in such or such a condition is as it appears. Neither case admits of demonstration; in both there is an indeclinable necessity: where, then, is philosophy, when it is attempted to establish so great a difference between things which admit of none?

Fichte says: "It is impossible to explain in a precise manner how a philosopher can get beyond the *me*:"[21] and we may with equal reason say, that we cannot conceive how he has been able to raise a system upon the *me*. To what does he appeal? To a fact of consciousness, that is, to a necessity. And is not the assent to evidence, the certainty to which the reality apparently corresponds, also a necessity? On what does Fichte found his system of the *me* and the *not-me*? We have only to read his works to see that he only founds it on considerations which suppose a value in certain ideas, a truth in certain judgments. Otherwise it is impossible to speak or to think: and this even he himself admits when, in commencing his investigations on the principle of our cognitions, he utters the words we have just quoted. He then confesses that we cannot take one step without trusting all the laws of general logic, which are *not always demonstrated, but are supposed tacitly admitted*. And what are these laws, without objective truths? What are they without the value of ideas, without correspondence with objects? Fichte says rightly, it is a circle; but he can no more get out of it than other philosophers.

252. To take from ideas their objective value, to reduce them to mere subjective phenomena, to resist that internal necessity which obliges us to admit the correspondence of the soul to objects, is to destroy the very consciousness of the soul. This must have been seen, and this we think we can most evidently demonstrate.

253. We have consciousness of ourselves. We now abstract what we feel, what we are; but we know that we feel and that we are. This experience is so clear, so vivid, that we cannot resist the truth of what it attests to us. But this *me* is not only the *me* of the present instant, it is also the *me* of yesterday, and of all prior time of which we have consciousness. We are the same that we were yesterday, the being in which this succession is verified, to which this variety of appearances is presented. The consciousness of the *me* then includes the identity of a being at distinct times, in various situations, with different ideas, and diverse affections,—the identity of a being which *endures* and is the same throughout the changes succeeding in it. If this duration of identity be broken, if I be not sure that I am the same *me* that I was previously, the consciousness of the *me* is destroyed. There would exist a series of unconnected facts, isolated acts of consciousness, but not that intimate consciousness I now experience. This cannot be doubted; every man feels it in himself; it admits neither discussion nor proof in any one, it requires them of no one. The moment this consciousness of identity fails, we are in our own eyes annihilated; whatever we may be in reality, for ourselves we are nothing. What is the consciousness of a being, formed from a series of acts of consciousness, without connection or mutual relation? It is a being revealed successively to itself, yet not as itself, but as a new being, a being which is born and dies, and dies and is born before its eyes, without its knowing that what is born is what died, or that what died is what was born: it is a light which burns and is extinguished, and again burns and is again extinguished, without its knowing that it is the same light.

254. This consciousness is completely destroyed by those who deny the connection between the idea and object.

Demonstration.—In the instant A, I have no other subjective presence of my acts than the very act I am at that moment performing: I cannot therefore be certain that I have had any previously, if they be not represented in the present idea; there is therefore a connection between this idea and its object. Attending then simply to the phenomena of consciousness, to the mere consciousness of the subject, we find that we do, by an irresistible necessity, attribute an objective value to ideas, an objective truth to judgments.

255. Without this objective truth, all certain recollection even of internal phenomena, and by a legitimate consequence, all reasoning, judgment, and thought, are impossible.

Recollection is of past acts. When we recollect them, they already are not; for, if they were, we should not have recollection, but present consciousness of them. Even when in the act of recollecting them we have other similar acts, these are not the same, for something of past time always enters into the idea of recollection. Therefore, we can have no certainty of them, but by their connection with the present act, their correspondence with the idea presenting them to us.

256. We have said that if, in internal phenomena, the certainty of the objective truth fail, all reasoning is impossible. In fact, all reasoning supposes a *succession* of acts; when one of them exists in the mind, the other does not exist; therefore, continued minute recollections are required, lest the chain be broken; and thus, without this chain, there is no reasoning; without recollection this chain is not; without objective truth, there is no certain recollection; therefore, without objective truth there is no reasoning.

257. All judgments also seem impossible. Judgments are of two classes: some require demonstration, others do not. Those that require demonstration would be impossible, for there can be no demonstration without reasoning, and reasoning in this case is impossible. As to those that do not need demonstration, because they shine with immediate evidence; all of them, not relating to the present act of the soul, in the very instant when the judgment is pronounced, would be impossible. Therefore, there could be no judgment but that of the present act, that is, the consciousness of the present without relation to the preceding. But it is remarkable that even with respect to the acts of consciousness, this judgment would be little less than impossible; for when we form a judgment upon an act of consciousness, this we do not by this act, but by a reflex act. This reflection requires succession, and succession cannot be known with certainty if there be no objective truth.

It is even very doubtful if the judgments of immediate evidence would be possible. They suppose, as we explained in the preceding chapter, relation of the partial conceptions into which the whole is decomposed; and how can there be decomposition without succession? If there is succession, there is recollection; if there is recollection, there is no immediate presence of the thing recollected.

258. Such consequences are astounding, but they are inevitable. If we destroy objective truth, all rational thought disappears. Such thought includes a certain continuity of acts corresponding to different instants; if this continuity be broken, the human thought ceases to be what it is, ceases to exist as *reason*. It is a series of acts which have no sort of connection, and which lead to nothing. In such a case, all expression, all words fail; nothing has a fixed value; every thing is ingulfed in obscurity. Thus it is in the intellectual and moral order as in the material; and man has not even the comfort of possessing himself; he vanishes from himself like an empty shadow.

259. Sensations may also exist as an unconnected series, but there will be no certain recollection of them, since the objective truth is wanting; past sensations exist only as past, and, consequently, as simple objects. All intellectual reflection upon them will be impossible, for reflection is not sensation; sensation is an object of reflection, not reflection itself. Thus, the ignorant man has the same sensation as the philosopher, but not the same reflection upon it. A thousand times we have sensations without reflecting that we have them. Sensible is very different from intellectual consciousness; the former is the simple presence of the sensation, or the sensation itself; the latter is the act of the intellect occupied with the sensation.

260. This distinction is also found in all purely intellectual acts: the reflection upon the act is not the act itself. One is the object of the other; they are not identical, and are often found separated. If, then, there were no objective truth, reflection would be impossible.

261. It is likewise difficult to comprehend how any act of the consciousness of the *me*, even as present, can be possible. We have already seen the *me* disappear when the series of recollections is broken, and without objective truth it is not even possible to conceive the *me* for one instant. The *me* thinking knows the *me* thought only as object. Whether it *perceive* or *know* it, to account to itself for itself, it must reflect upon itself, and take itself for its own object; and there being no objective truth, it is inconceivable how an object can have any value.

It follows from this, that they who oppose objectiveness, attack a fundamental law of our mind, destroy thought, even consciousness, and every thing subjective which could serve as its basis.

262. In their arguments against objective certainty, its opponents are accustomed to depend upon the errors into which it leads us. The madman believes he sees objects, which do not exist; the lunatic believes firmly in his disconnected thoughts; and why may not that which deceives us in one instance, also deceive us in another, and all cases? Can that be a certain criterion which sometimes fails? Why not stop with the purely subjective? The madman, the lunatic, are deceived in the object, not in the subject; although what they think is not true, it is still very true and certain that they think it.

This is a specious objection; but it does not remove the difficulties under which the system, in favor of which it is adduced, labors; and it may, on the other hand, be solved in so far as it tends to weaken objective truth.

The madman, the lunatic, have also recollections of things that never existed. These recollections do not relate solely to external, but likewise to their internal acts. The madman who calls himself king, acts in accordance with his thought, with what he felt when crowned, when dethroned; and yet, these intellectual phenomena never existed. And, however this may be, he himself may have produced these recollections. We hold, then, that the criterion with respect to memory is wrong in this case, and can be of avail in no case. Therefore, even, although we had not shown that without objective truth there is no recollection even of the internal, the arguments of our adversaries would have sufficed. This objection, if it prove any thing, confirms all that we have advanced in demonstrating that without objectiveness there is no consciousness properly so called, and this even our opponents do not admit.

263. Moreover, we at once see what weight an argument based on craziness should have at the tribunal of reason. It all, at the most, only proves the weakness of our nature, that in some unfortunate individuals the established order of humanity is reversed; that the rule of truth, as it exists in so weak a creature, admits of some exceptions; but these exceptions are known, for their characters are marked. The exception does not destroy, it only confirms the rule.(25)

CHAPTER XXVI
CAN ALL COGNITIONS BE REDUCED
TO THE PERCEPTION OF IDENTITY?

264. Immediate evidence has for its objects those truths which the intellect sees with all clearness, and to which it assents without the intervention of any *medium*, as its name denotes. These truths are enunciated in propositions called *per se notæ*, first principles, or axioms, in which it is sufficient to know the meaning of the terms to see that the predicate is contained in the idea of the subject. Propositions of this class are few in all sciences; the greater part of our cognitions are the fruit of reasoning which proceeds by mediate evidence. In geometry the number of truths that do not require demonstration, but only explanation, is very limited. The body of geometrical science, with its present colossal dimensions, has proceeded from reasoning: even in the most comprehensive works the axioms occupy but a few pages; the rest is composed of theorems, propositions not of themselves evident, but requiring demonstration. The same is true of all other sciences.

265. Since in axioms the intellect perceives the identity of the subject with the predicate, intuitively seeing that the idea of the latter is contained in that of the former, there arises a very grave philosophical question which may prove very difficult, and cause strange controversies, if care be not taken to place it upon its true ground. Is every human cognition reduced to the simple perception of identity? and can its general formula be this: A is A, or: a thing is itself? Some philosophers of note maintain the affirmative; others the contrary. We think there is a confusion of ideas not so much as to the question itself as to its state. Clear and exact ideas of what judgment is, and of the relation affirmed or denied by it, will greatly facilitate the accurate solution of the question.

266. There is in every judgment perception of identity or non-identity, accordingly as it is affirmative or negative. The verb *is* does not express the union, but the identity of the predicate with the subject; and when accompanied with the negation *not*, it simply expresses non-identity, abstracting union or separation. This is so true and so exact, that in things

really united an affirmative judgment is impossible, because they have no identity. We must, then, in such cases, if we would be enabled to make an affirmation, express the predicate in the concrete, that is, in some sense involving the idea of the subject itself in it; for the same property affirmed in the concrete cannot be in the abstract, but must rather be denied. Thus we may say, man is rational; but not, man is rationality: a body is extended; but not, a body is extension: paper is white; but not, paper is whiteness. Why is this? Is it that rationality is not in man, extension is not united to body, nor whiteness to paper? Certainly not; but if rationality be in man, extension in body, and whiteness in paper, we have only not to perceive identity between the predicates and subjects, to render affirmation impossible; on the contrary, despite the union, we have negation: thus we may say, man is not rationality; a body is not extension; paper is not whiteness.

We have said that, in order to save the expression of identity, we used the concrete instead of the abstract term, and involved in the former the idea of the subject. It cannot be said that paper is whiteness, but it may be said that paper is white; for this last proposition means that paper is a white thing; that is, we make the general idea of a *thing*, or the idea of a modifiable subject, enter into the predicate while in the concrete; and this subject is identical with the paper modified by whiteness.

267. Thus it is easy to see, that the expression, *union of the predicate with the subject*, is, at the best, inexact. Every affirmative proposition expresses the identity of the predicate with the subject. Use authorizes these modes of speaking, which still produce some confusion when we endeavor perfectly to understand these matters. And it must be observed, that ordinary language here, as often elsewhere, is admirably exact and appropriate. Nobody says, paper is whiteness, but, paper is white. It is only when we would greatly heighten the degree, to which a subject possesses a quality, that we express it in the abstract, and then we join with it the pronoun *itself*. Thus, speaking hyperbolically, we say a thing is beauty itself, whiteness itself, goodness itself.

268. Even what in mathematics is called equality, also means identity. Thus in this class of judgments, besides what we have observed of general in them all, to wit: the identity saved by expressing the predicate in the concrete, the very relation of equality denotes identity. This needs explanation.

Whoever says $6+3=9$, expresses the same as he who says $6+3$ are identical with 9. Clearly in the affirmation of equality, no attention is paid to the form in which the quantities are expressed, but to the quantities themselves alone; otherwise we should be unable to affirm not only identity, but also equality; for it is evident that $6+3$, as to their form, neither written, spoken, nor thought, are identical with, or equal to, 9. The equality is in the values expressed, and these are not only equal but identical; 6+3 are the same as 9. The whole is not distinguished from its united part; 9 is the whole, 6+3 its united parts.

The different manner of conceiving 6+3 and 9 does not exclude the identity. The difference is in the intellectual form, and occurs not only here but also in the perceptions of the simplest things; there is nothing which we do not conceive under different aspects, and whose conception we may not decompose in various ways; but we do not therefore say that the thing ceases to be simple and identical with itself.

What we have said of an arithmetical equation may be extended to algebraical and geometrical equations. If we have an equation whereof the first member is very simple, as Z, and the second very complicated, as the development of a series, we cannot say that the first expression is equal to the second; the equality is not in the expression but in the thing expressed, in the value designated by the letters; in this sense it is true, in the former it is evidently false.

Two circumferences having the same radius are equal. Here we seem to treat solely of equality, since there are two distinct objects, the two circumferences, which may be traced on paper or represented in the imagination; yet not even in this case is the distinction true, it is only apparent, for here, as in algebraical and arithmetical equations, there is distinction and even diversity in form with identity at bottom. The principal argument, on which the distinction is founded, may be combatted by observing that the circumferences which may be traced or represented, are only forms of the idea, not the idea itself. Whether traced or represented they have a determinate size and a certain position on the planes seen or imagined; in the idea, and in the proposition containing it, there is nothing of this; we abstract all size, all position, and speak in a general and absolute sense. True, the representations may be infinite either externally or in the imagination; but this, so far from proving them identical, shows their diversity, since the idea is one and they are infinite; the idea is constant, they are variable; the idea is independent of them, they are dependent on the idea, and have the character and denomination of circumferences, inasmuch as they approach it by representing what it contains.

What, then, is expressed in the proposition: two circumferences, having the same radius, are equal? The fundamental idea is, that the value of the circumference depends upon the radius, and the proposition here enunciated is simply an application of this property to the case of the equality of radii. The circumferences, then, conceived by us as distinct, are only examples which we inwardly consider in order to render the truth of the application apparent; but in what is purely intellectual, we find only the decomposition of the idea of circumference, or its relation to the radius applied to the case of equality. Then there are not two circumferences in the purely ideal order, but one only, whose properties we know under different conceptions, and express in various ways.

If in all judgments there is affirmation of identity, or non-identity, and all our cognitions either begin or end in a judgment, it would seem that they all ought to be reduced to a simple perception of identity. The general formula of our cognitions will then be: *A is A*, or, *a thing is itself.* This result strikes one as an extravagant paradox, and is so, or not, according to the sense in which it is understood; but if rightly explained, it may be admitted as a truth, and a very simple one. From what has been said in the preceding paragraphs, the meaning of this opinion may be discerned: but the importance of the present matter requires still further explanation.

CHAPTER XXVII
CONTINUATION OF THE SAME SUBJECT

269. It is even ridiculous to say that the cognitions of the sublimest philosophers may be reduced to this equation: A is A. This, absolutely speaking, is not only false, but contrary to common sense; but it is neither contrary to common sense nor false to say that all cognitions of mathematicians are perceptions of identity, which, presented under different conceptions, undergoes infinite variations of form, and so fecundates the intellect and constitutes science. For the sake of greater clearness we will take an example, and follow one idea through all its transformations.

270. The equation circle = circle (1) is very true, but not very lucid, since it serves no purpose, because there is identity not only of ideas but likewise of conceptions and expression. To have a true progress in science we must not only change the expression, but also vary in some way the conception under which the identical thing is presented. Thus, if we abbreviate the above equation in this form: C = circle (2), we make no progress, unless with respect to the purely material expression. The only possible advantage of this is to assist the memory, as instead of expressing the circle by a word, we express it by its initial letter, C. Why is this? Because the variety is in the expression, not in the conception. If, instead of considering the identity in all its simplicity in both members of the equation, we give the value of the circle with reference to the circumference, we shall have C = circumference × 1/2 R (3), that is, the value of the circle is equal to the circumference multiplied by one-half the radius. In the equation (3) there is identity as in (1) and (2), because it is affirmed in it that the value expressed by C is the same as that expressed by circumference × 1/2 R; just as in the other two it is expressed that the value of the circle is the value of the circle. But is this equation different from the other two? It is very different. What is the difference? The first two simply express the identity conceived under the same point of view; the circle expressed in the second member excites no idea not already excited by the first; but in the last, the second member expresses the same circle indeed, but in its relations with the circumference and radius; and, consequently, besides containing a sort of analysis of the circle, it records the analysis previously made of the idea of the circumference in relation to the

idea of radius. The difference is not, then, solely in the material expression, but in the variety of conceptions under which the same thing is presented.

Calling the value of the relation of the circumference with the diameter N, and the circle C, the equation becomes: $C = NR2$ (4). Here, also, there is identity of value; but we discover a notable progress in the expression of the second member, in which the value of the circle is given, freed from its relations with the value of the circumference, and dependent solely on a numerical value, N, and a right line, which is the radius. Without losing the identity, and only by a succession of perceptions of identity, we have advanced in science, and starting from so sterile a proposition as circle = circle, we have obtained another, by means of which we may at once determine the value of any circle from its radius.

Leaving elemental geometry, and considering the circle as a curve referred to two axes, with respect to which its points are determined, we shall have $Z = 2Bx-x2(5)$; Z expressing the value of the ordinate; B the constant part of the axis of abscissas; and x the abscissa corresponding to Z. We have here a still more notable progress of ideas: in both members we now express the value, not of the circle, but of lines, by which we may determine all points of the curve; and we easily conceive that this curve, which was contained in the figure whose properties we determined in elemental geometry, may be conceived under such a form as belongs to a genus of curves, whereof it constitutes a species by the particular relations of the quantities 2x and B; thus modifying the expression by adding a new quantity, combined in this or that manner, we may obtain a curve of another species. If, therefore, we would determine the value of the surface contained in this circle, we may consider it, not solely with respect to the radius, but to the areas comprised between the various perpendiculars the extremities of which determine points of the curve and are called ordinates. It results from this, that the same value of the circle may be determined under various conceptions, although this value is at all times identical; the transition from one conception to another is the succession of the perceptions of identity presented under different forms.

Let us now consider the value of the circle dependent on the radius: this will give us $C = $ function x (6). This equation enables us to conceive the circle under the general idea of a function of its radius, or of x, and consequently authorizes us to subject it to all the laws to which a function is subject, and leads us to the properties of their differentials, limits, and relations. By this equation we enter into infinitesimal calculus, the expressions of which present identity under a form which records a series of conceptions of long and profound analysis. Thus, expressing the differential of the circle by dc, and its integral by S. dc, we shall have $C = S. dc$, (7), an equation in which are expressed the same values as in circle = circle, but with this difference, that the equation (7) records immense analytical labors: it results from a long succession of conceptions of integral calculus, of differentials, and limits of the differentials of the functions, of the application of algebra to geometry, and of a multitude of elementary geometrical notions, algebraical rules and combinations, and of whatever else was needed to arrive at this result. Therefore, when we find the integral of the differential, and obtain by integration the value of the circle, it would clearly be most extravagant to affirm that the integral equation is nothing more than the equation circle = circle; but it is not so to say that at bottom there is identity, and that the diversity of expression to which we have come, is the result of a succession of perceptions of the same identity presented under different aspects. Supposing the conceptions, through which it has been necessary to pass, to be A, B, C, D, E, M, the law of their scientific connection may be thus expressed: A = B, B = C, C = D, D = E, E = M; therefore A = M.

271. What we have just explained cannot be well understood unless we recall some characteristics of our intellect, in which is found the reason of so great anomalies. Our intellect is so weak as to perceive things only successively: only after much study does it see what is contained in the clearest ideas. Hence a necessity, to which corresponds with admirable harmony a faculty that satisfies it: the necessity is of conceiving under various, and different, as well as distinct, forms, even the simplest things: the faculty is that of decomposing the conception into many parts, and multiplying in the order of ideas what in that of reality is only one. This faculty of decomposition would be useless were not the intellect, in passing through the succession of conceptions, to find means of connecting and retaining them: otherwise it would continually lose the fruit of its labors; it would slip from its hands as fast as it grasped it. Happily it has this means in signs either written, spoken, or thought; those mysterious expressions which at times not only designate an idea, but also are the compendium of the labors of a whole life, and perhaps of a long series of ages. When the sign is presented to us, we do not see certainly and with full clearness all that it expresses, nor why the expression is legitimate; but we know confusedly the meaning therein contained; we know that in case of necessity, it is enough for us to follow the thread of the perceptions through which we have passed, thus going back even to the simplest elements of science. In making calculations, the most eminent mathematician does not clearly see the meaning of the expressions he uses, except as they relate to the object before him; but he is certain that they do not deceive him, that the rules by which he is guided are sure; because he knows that at another time he established them by incontestible demonstrations. The progress of a science may be

compared to a series of posts on which the distances of a road are marked: he who marked the numbers on the posts uses them without necessity of recalling the operations which led him to mark the quantity before him; he is satisfied with knowing that the operations were well made, and that he wrote the result correctly.

272. The proof of this necessity of decomposition, besides being fully established by the above example, is found in the elements of all instruction, where, under a form of demonstration, it is necessary to explain propositions which express simply the definitions or axioms that have been before established. For example: we find in the elementary works on geometry this theorem: all the diameters of a circle are equal; and we must, if we would have beginners understand it, give a demonstrative form to that which neither is nor can be any thing more than an explanation, and is almost a repetition of the idea of the circle. When we describe a circle, we fix a point around which we revolve a line called the radius; since then the diameter is nothing more than the sum of two radii continued in the same right line, the mere enunciation of the theorem would seem sufficient to show that it is evidently contained in the idea of the circle, and is as a sort of repetition of the postulate, on which the construction of the curve is founded: still it is not so, and it must be explained as if it were a proof; we must show the diameter to be equal to two radii, these radii to be equal, and at times repeat that this is supposed in its construction: in a word, it is necessary to employ many conceptions to show a truth, which ought to have been known by the simple intuition of one alone, as is the case when the geometrical powers of the intellect have acquired a certain strength and robustness.

273. We may now appreciate at its just value, the opinion of Dugald Stewart, who, in his *Elements of the Philosophy of the Human Mind*, says: "It may be fairly questioned, too, whether it can, with strict correctness, be said of the simple arithmetical equation, 2 plus 2 = 4, that it may be represented by the formula A = A. The one is a proposition asserting the equivalence of two different expressions; to ascertain which equivalence may, in numberless cases, be an object of the highest importance. The other is altogether unmeaning and nugatory, and cannot, by any possible supposition, admit of the slightest application of a practical nature. What opinion then shall we form of the proposition A = A, when considered as the representative of such a formula as the binomial theorem of Sir Isaac Newton? When applied to the equation 2 plus 2 = 4, (which in its extreme simplicity and familiarity is apt to be regarded in the light of an axiom:) the paradox does not appear to be so manifestly extravagant; but, in the other case, it seems quite impossible to annex to it any meaning whatever."[22] This philosopher does not observe that the pretended extravagance arises from his wrong interpretation of his

adversaries' opinion. No one ever thought of denying the importance of the discoveries which prove different expressions equivalent: no one doubts that Newton's formula of the binomial is a great advance upon the formula A = A: but the question consists not in this, but in seeing whether Newton's formula of the binomial is any thing more than the expression of identical things; and whether even the merit of the expression is or is not the fruit of a series of perceptions of identity. Were the question presented under Dugald Stewart's point of view, it would be unworthy of discussion: for philosophy should not dispute upon things that are ridiculous as well as absurd.

CHAPTER XXVIII
CONTINUATION OF THE SAME SUBJECT

274. We will now explain how the doctrine of identity is applied in general to all reasoning, whether upon mathematical objects or not: with this view we will examine some of the dialectical forms in which the art of reasoning is taught.

Every A is B; M is A: therefore M is B. In the major of this syllogism we find the identity of every A with B; and in the minor, the identity of M with B. In each of these propositions there is affirmation, and, consequently, perception of identity. Let us now see what takes place in the connection which constitutes the force of the argument.

Why do we say that M is B? Because M is A, and every A is B. M is one of the As, expressed in the words *every A*; therefore, when we say, M is A, we say only what we had before said by *every A*. What difference, then, is there? There is this difference, that in the expression *every A*, no attention is paid to one of A's contents, M, of which we had nevertheless affirmed that it was B, in affirming that every A is B. If, in the expression *every A*, we have distinctly seen M, the syllogism would not have been necessary, because, in saying every A is B, we had already understood that M is B.

This observation is so true and exact, that in treating of very clear relations we suppress the syllogism, and replace it with the enthymema, which is, it is true, an abbreviation of the syllogism; but we must see in this abbreviation besides a saving of words, a saving of conceptions, for the intellect sees one intuitively in the other, without necessity of decomposition. He is a man, therefore he is rational; we omit the major, and do not even think of it, for we intuitively see, in the idea of man, and its application to an individual, the idea of rational without any gradation of ideas or succession of conceptions.

Let us suppose that we have to demonstrate that the perimeter of a polygon inscribed in a circle is less than the circumference, and that we make the following syllogism: The sum of all the right lines inscribed in their respective curves is less than the sum of those curves; but the perimeter of the polygon is the sum of the right lines, and the circumference is the sum of the arcs or curves; therefore the inscribed perimeter is less than the circumference. We now ask, will any one who knows that the sum of the right lines is less than the sum of the curves, fail to see with equal facility that the perimeter is less than the circumscribed circumference, provided he understands the meaning of the words? It is evident that he will not. What necessity, then, of repeating the general principle? Is it to add any thing to the particular conception? Certainly not; because nothing can be clearer than the following propositions: the perimeter of the polygon is a sum of right lines; the circumference is a sum of arcs or curves; what the general principle does, is to call attention to a phase of the particular conception, so that what otherwise could not be seen in it may be seen on reflection. The certainty of the conclusion does not depend on the general principle; because, from thinking on the relations of greater and less only with respect to the right lines of the perimeter and the arcs, the sum of which forms the circumference, any one would have inferred the same thing.

This example also tends to prove that the enthymema is not a mere abbreviation of words; and it shows why we employ it in reasoning upon matters familiar to the understanding. In any one of the conceptions we see all that is necessary for the consequence; and, therefore, one premise suffices, as in it the other is included rather than understood. A beginner may say: the arc is greater than the chord, because the curve is greater than the right line; but when familiarized with geometrical ideas, he will simply say, the arc is greater than the chord; he will see the idea of the curve in that of the arc, and the idea of the right line in that of the chord, without need of decomposition. If the arc is greater than its chord, this is not because every curve is greater than the corresponding right line. Did the abstract idea of curve not exist, and were this particular arc of a circle the only curve thought of; did the abstract idea of right line not exist, and were this particular chord the only right line thought of, it would still, as at present, be true that the arc is greater than the chord.

275. When treating of the *necessary* relations of things, the general principles, the middle terms, and all the auxiliaries to reasoning furnished by logic, are only inventions of art to make us reflect upon the conception of the thing, and see in it what otherwise we should not see. Hence our judgments on necessary objects are in some sense analytical; and Kant equivocates, when he says there are synthetic judgments not dependent on experience. Without experience we have only the conception of the thing. We do not pretend that all propositions express such a relation between the subject and the predicate, that the conception of the former will always give that of the latter; but we do hold, that the reason of this insufficiency is the incompleteness of the conception, either in itself, or in relation to our

comprehension. But if we suppose the conception complete in itself, and a due capacity in our intellect to understand whatever it contains, we shall find in the conception all that can be the object of science.

276. An example from mathematics will make this clearer. Large works on geometry are filled with explanations, demonstrations, and applications of the properties of the triangle. The conceptions of right lines, and the angles formed by them, enter into the conception of the triangle. We ask, can all the explanations and demonstrations of the properties of triangles in general ever go beyond the ideas of right lines and angles? No. For the new elements introduced would be foreign to the triangle, and would consequently change its nature. Necessary relations neither admit of more nor of less, neither additions nor subtractions of any sort; what is, is, and nothing more. In passing from the triangle in general to its different species, such as equilateral, isosceles, right angled, scalene, it is to be observed that the demonstration must rigorously attend to what is contained in the general conception, modified by the determining properties of the species, that is, the equality of the three sides, of two, the inequality of all, the supposition of a right angle, and others.

277. What we are now explaining is clearly seen in the application of algebra to geometry. A curve is expressed by a formula containing the conception of the curve, or its essence. The geometrician, to demonstrate the properties of the curve, does not need to go out of this formula; it is a touchstone in his hand, and he finds in it all that he wants. He inscribes triangles, or other figures in the curve, draws right lines from it to points without, but never goes out of the conception expressed in the formula; he decomposes it, and finds in it what before he had not discovered.

In this equation $z2 = (e2/E2)(2Ex-x2)$, we find the expression of the relations which constitute the ellipse; E expresses the greater semi-axis, e the lesser, z the ordinates, and x the abscissas. With this equation variously developed and transformed, the properties of the curve are determined; it shows, with the help of constructions, that the new property is contained in the conception, and to find it, we have only to analyze it.

If we suppose an intelligence capable of conceiving the essence of the curve, by an immediate intuition of the law governing the inflection of points, without the necessity of referring it to any line, whether one axis instead of two suffices, or in any other manner not even imaginable by us; this intelligence will not need to follow all the evolutions which we have made in demonstrating the properties of the curve; for it will perceive them to be clearly contained in the very conception of the curve. This supposition is not arbitrary; we see it realized every day, though on a smaller scale.

An ordinary geometrician conceives a curve as also does Pascal; but while Pascal at a glance sees the most recondite properties of the curve in this conception, an ordinary geometrician sees only after long study its most common properties. Kant made no account of this doctrine, and therefore could not solve the problem of pure synthetic judgments: had he examined the subject more profoundly he would have seen that, strictly speaking, there are no such judgments; and instead of wearing out his genius in attempting to solve an insolvable problem, he would have abstained from raising it.(26)

CHAPTER XXIX
ARE THERE TRUE SYNTHETIC JUDGMENTS
A PRIORI IN THE SENSE OF KANT?

278. The great importance attributed by the German philosopher to his imaginary discovery, requires us to examine it at length. This importance may be estimated from what he himself says: "If any of the ancients had only had the idea of proposing the present question, it would have been a mighty barrier against all the systems of pure reason down to our days, and would have saved many vain attempts which *were blindly made without knowing what was treated of.*"[23] This passage is quite modest and naturally excites our curiosity to know what is the problem which needed only to be proposed in order to avoid all the aberrations of pure reason.

Here are his words: "All empirical judgments, as such, are synthetic. For it would be absurd to ground an analytic judgment on experience, since I am not obliged to go out of the conception itself in order to form the judgment, and therefore can have no need of the testimony of experience. That a body is extended, is a proposition which stands firm *a priori*. It is no empirical judgment; for, prior to experience, I have all the conditions of forming it in the conception of body, from which I deduce the predicate, extension, according to the principle of contradiction, by which I at once become conscious of its necessity, which I could not learn from experience. But, on the other hand, I do not include, in the primitive conception of body in general, the predicate, heaviness; yet this conception of body in general indicates, through experience of a part of it, an object of experience, to which I may add from experience other parts also belonging to it. I can attain to the conception of body beforehand, analytically, through its characteristics extension, impenetrability, form, etc., all of which are included in the primary conception of body. But I now *extend* my cognition, and, as I recur to experience, from which I have obtained the conception of body in general, I find along with these characteristics the conception of heaviness. I therefore add this, as a predicate, to the conception of body. The possibility of this synthesis therefore rests on experience; for both conceptions, although one does not contain the other, yet belong as parts to a whole, that is to say, to experience, which is itself a union of synthetic, though contingent intuitions.

But in the case of synthetic judgments *a priori* we have not this assistance. Here we have not the advantage of returning and supporting ourselves on experience. If I must go out of the conception A in order to find another conception B, which is to be joined to it, on what am I to rely? and by what means does the synthesis become possible?"[24]

279. The reason of this synthesis is found in the faculty of our mind of forming total conceptions, in which the *relation* of the partial conceptions composing it is discovered; and the legitimacy of the same synthesis is founded on the principles on which the criterion of evidence is based.

The synthesis of the schoolmen consists in the union of conceptions, and does not refuse to admit as analytical the total conceptions, from the decomposition of which results the knowledge of the relations of the partial conceptions.

If Kant had stopped with the judgments of experience, there would be no objection to his doctrine. But extended to the purely intellectual order, it is either inadmissible, or at least expressed without much exactness.

260. Kant says all mathematical judgments are analytic, and that this truth which in his opinion "is certainly incontestible and important on account of its consequences, seems to have hitherto escaped the sagacity of the analysts of human reason, causing very contrary opinions." We think it is the sagacity of his Aristarchus, and not that of the analysts, that is at fault.

"One would certainly think at first sight that the proposition, $7 + 5 = 12$, is a purely analytic proposition, which follows from the conception of a sum of seven and five, according to the principle of contradiction. But if we examine it more closely, we find that the conception of the sum of seven and five contains nothing farther than the union of both numbers in one, from which it cannot by any means be inferred what this other number is which contains them both."[25]

Were we to say that whoever hears seven plus five, does not always think of twelve, because he does not see clearly enough that one conception is the same as the other, although it is under a different form, it would be true. But from this it does not follow that the conception is not purely analytic. The mere explanation of both suffices to show their identity.

That this may be better understood, we will invert the equation thus: $12 = 7 + 5$. It is evident that if any one does not know that $7 + 5 = 12$, he will not know that $12 = 7 + 5$. Now, in examining the conception 12, we certainly see $7 + 5$ contained in it. Therefore, the conception of 12 is identical with the conception of $7 + 5$; and just as, because he who hears 12, does not always think of $7 + 5$, we cannot thence infer that 12 does not contain $7 + 5$; so, also, we cannot, because he who hears 7 + 5, does not always think of 12, thence infer that the first conception does not contain the second.

The cause of the equivocation is, that the two identical conceptions are presented to the intellect under different forms; and until we have the form, and look to what is under it, we shall not discover the identity. This is not, strictly speaking, *reasoning* but *explanation*.

What Kant adds concerning the necessity of recurring, in this case, to an intuition, with respect to one of the numbers, adding five to seven on the fingers, is exceedingly futile. First, in whatever way he adds the five, there will never be anything but the five that is added, and it will neither give more nor less than 7 + 5. Secondly, the successive addition on the *fingers* is equivalent to saying 1 + 1 + 1 + 1 + 1 = 5. This transforms the expression, 7 + 5 = 12, into this other, 7 + 1 + 1 + 1 + 1 + 1 = 12; but the conception, 1 + 1 + 1 + 1 + 1, has the same relation to 5, as 7 + 5 to 12; therefore, if 7 + 5 are not contained in 12, neither are 7 + 1 + 1 + 1 + 1 + 1 contained in it. It may be replied that Kant does not speak of identity, but of intuitions. This intuition, however, is not the sensation, but the idea; and if the idea, it is only the conception explained. Thirdly, we know this method of intuition not to be even necessary for children. Fourthly, this method is impossible in the case of large numbers.

281. Kant adds that this proposition, "a right line is the shortest distance between two points," is not purely analytic, because the idea of *shortest distance* is not contained in the idea of *right line*. Waiving the demonstrations which some authors give, or pretend to give, of this proposition, we shall confine ourselves to Kant's reasons. He forgets that here the right line is not taken *alone*, but *compared* with other lines. The idea of right line alone neither does nor can contain the ideas of *more* or *less*; for these ideas suppose a comparison. But from the moment the right line and the curve are compared, with respect to *length*, the relation of superiority of the curve over the right line is seen. The proposition is then the result of the comparison of two purely analytic conceptions with a third, which is *length*.

282. If Kant's reasoning were good, even this judgment, "the whole is greater than its part," would not be analytic; for the idea of *greater* enters not into the conception of the *whole* until the *whole* is compared with its *part*. Thus, the judgment, four is greater than three, would not be analytic, because the idea of four until compared with three does not include the conception of greater.

The axiom: "things which are equal to the same thing are equal to each other," would not be analytic, because the conception, *equal to each other*, does not enter into the conception of *things which are equal to the same thing*, until we reflect that the equality of the middle term implies the equality of the extremes.

The x, of which Kant speaks, would be found in almost all judgments, if we could not form total conceptions involving comparison of partial conceptions: in this case we should have no analytic judgments except such as are wholly identical, or directly contained in this formula, A is A.

283. The comparison of two conceptions with a third, does not take from the result the character of analytic judgment, as a predicate cannot be seen in the idea of the subject, without the aid of this comparison. This comparison is often necessary, because we only confusedly think of what is contained in the conception which we already have; and sometimes it even happens that we do not think at all of it. One often says a thing and then contradicts himself, not observing that what he adds is opposed to what he had already said. We often ask, in conversation, do you not see that you suppose the contrary of what you just said; that the conditions you have just established imply the contrary of what you now assert?

284. A conception includes not only all that is expressly thought in it, but all that can be thought. If, on decomposing it, we find in it other things, it cannot be said that we add them, but that we find them. It is not a synthesis, but an analysis. Otherwise we must admit no analytic conceptions, or only such as are purely identical. Except in this last case, of which the general formula is, A is A, there is always in the predicate something not thought in the subject, if not in substance at least in form. The circle is a curve; this undoubtedly is one of the simplest analytical propositions imaginable; still the predicate expresses the general conception of curve, which may be contained in the subject, in a confused manner, with relation to a particular species of curve. Following a gradation in geometrical propositions, we may observe that there is nothing in one proposition not in the preceding, except the greater or less difficulty of decomposing the conception, so as to see in it what before we had not seen.

If we say, the circle is a conic section, evidently any one ignorant of the terms, or who has not reflected on their true sense, will not think of the attribute in the subject. No addition is made to the conception of the circle; only a property not before known is discovered, and this discovery results from comparison with the cone. Is there any synthesis here? No. There is only an analysis of the two conceptions, the circle and the cone, compared. As this error destroys the foundation of Kant's doctrine on this point, we will develop it and place it on a more solid foundation.

285. Synthesis, properly so called, requires something to be added to the conception, which in nowise belongs to it, as the example brought by Kant shows. The conception, extension, is contained in the conception, body; but heaviness is an entirely foreign idea, which we can unite to the

conception, body, only because experience authorizes it. Only with this addition is there properly synthesis. The union of ideas which results from the conception of the thing, although comparison may be necessary in order to fecundate them, does not make a synthesis. The conceptions are not wholly absolute, they contain relations, and the discovery of these relations does not give a synthesis, but a more complete analysis. If it be said that in this case there is something more than the primitive conception, we answer that the same thing happens in all not purely identical. We may also add that by the comparison a new total conception is formed resulting from the primitive conceptions; and the properties of the relations are then seen, not by synthesis, but by the analysis of the total conception.

According to Kant, true synthesis requires the union of things so different from one another, that the bond uniting them is a sort of mystery, an x, whose determination is a great philosophical problem. If this x is found in the essential relation of the partial conceptions constituting the total conception, the problem is resolved by a simple analysis, or, to speak more exactly, it is shown that the problem did not exist, because the x was a known quantity.

We know of no judgment more analytical than that in which we see the parts in the whole, since the whole is only the parts united. If we say, one and one are two, or, two is equal to one plus one; it cannot be denied that we have a total conception, two, in the decomposition of which, we find one plus one. If this be not an analytic conception, that is to say, if the predicate be not here contained in the idea of the subject, it will be hard to tell what is. But even here there are different conceptions, one plus one; unite them, and they form the total conception. The relation, although most simple, exists; and whether it be more or less, simple or complicated, and, consequently, seen with more or less facility, does not alter the character of the judgments, or from synthetic convert them into analytic.

286. We will complete this explanation with an example from elementary geometry. "The surface of a rhomboid is equal to the surface of a rectangle having the same base and altitude." First: in the idea of the rhomboid, we do not see the idea of its equality with the rectangle; and this we cannot see, because the relation does not exist when there is no other term to which it may relate. The idea of the parallelogram does not contain that of the rectangle, and consequently not that of equality. Second: the relation results from the comparison of the rhomboid with the rectangle; and, consequently, it must be found in a total conception containing them both. It cannot, therefore, be said that we add any thing to the conception of the parallelogram which does not belong to it. On the contrary, we see this equality flow from the conception of the rhomboid and that of the rectangle,

as partial conceptions of the total conception, formed by the combination of them both. The analysis of this total conception opens to us the relation we are now in quest of; for it must be observed that when the simple union of the conceptions compared does not suffice, we make use of another including them, and also something more; and from the new conception, duly analyzed, we deduce the relation of the parts compared.

287. In the geometrical construction, that serves for the demonstration of the above theorem, which we have used as an example, may be seen what we have just explained with regard to total conceptions containing other conceptions besides those compared. If we place the rectangle and the rhomboid upon the same base, we at once see that there is something common to both, namely, the triangle formed by the base, a part of one side of the rhomboid, and a part of one side of the rectangle. Neither synthesis nor analysis is here required, because there is perfect coincidence, and this in geometry is equivalent to perfect equality. The difficulty is in the two remaining parts, that is, in the trapezoids to which the parallelograms are reduced by the subtraction of the common triangle. The mere sight of the figures teaches nothing concerning the equivalence of the two surfaces; we see only that the two sides of the rhomboidal surface go on extending, but including a less distance in proportion as the angle becomes more oblique, under these two conditions: length of sides, and diminution of distances between two limits, of which one is infinity, and the other the rectangle. The relation of the equivalence of the surfaces may be demonstrated by prolonging the parallel opposite the base, and thus forming a quadrilateral of which the trapezoids are parts; to discover the equality of these trapezoids, it is only necessary to decompose the quadrilateral, attending to the equality of two triangles, each respectively formed by one of the trapezoids and a common triangle. Is any thing here added to the conception of each trapezoid? No. We only compare them. They could not be compared directly, and therefore we included them in a total conception, the mere analysis of which enabled us to discover the relation sought for. The conception does not give this relation; it only shows it; for if the conception of the two figures compared were more perfect, so that we might intuitively behold the relation existing between the increment of the sides and the decrement of their distance from each other, we should see that there is here a constant law, which supplies on one side what is lost on the other; and consequently we should discover, in the very conception of the rhomboid, the fundamental reason of the equality, that is, the permanent value of the surface, notwithstanding the greater or less obliquity of the angles; thus obtaining what we deduced from the above comparison, and generalize with reference to two constant lineal values, base and altitude. The same would happen with respect to

the equivalence of all variable quantities differently expressed, could we reduce their conceptions to such clear and simple formulas as those of apparent functions; for example, nx/mx, from which, whatever the value of the variable, there always results the same value of the expression, which is constant, to wit, n/m.

288. Let not these investigations be imagined useless. In this, as in many other questions, it happens that most important truths are the result of a philosophical problem which, in appearance, is merely speculative. Thus, in the present case, we observe Kant explaining the principle of causality, in an inexact, and, as we understand him, in an altogether false sense; but, perhaps, the origin of his equivocation lies in his considering the principle of causality as synthetic, although *a priori*, whereas it must be regarded as analytic, as we shall show when treating of the idea of cause.

In consideration of the great importance of clear and distinct ideas on the present subject, we will in a few words, sum up the doctrine we have explained concerning mediate and immediate evidence.

There is immediate evidence when, in the conception of the subject, we see its agreement or disagreement with the predicate, without requiring any other means than mere reflection on the meaning of the terms. Judgments of this class are with propriety called analytic, because we have only to analyze the conception of the subject to find therein its agreement or disagreement with the predicate.

There is mediate evidence when, in the conception of the subject, we do not immediately see its agreement or disagreement with the predicate, and therefore have to call in a middle term to make it manifest.

290. Here arises the question whether judgments of mediate evidence are analytic. It is clear that if we mean by analytic only those in which we have solely to understand the meaning of the terms in order to see the agreement or disagreement of the predicate, the judgments of mediate evidence cannot be called analytic; but if by analytic judgment we mean a judgment in which it is only necessary to *decompose* the conception of the subject in order to find therein its agreement or disagreement with the predicate, we must say that the judgments of mediate evidence are analytic, and the means employed is only the formation of a total conception containing the partial conceptions, the relation of which we seek to discover. In the union of these partial conceptions there is a synthesis, it is true; but there is none in the discovery of their relation, for this is done by analysis.

A judgment is not the less analytic because formed by the union of different conceptions; for then no judgment would be analytic. When we say, man is rational, the two conceptions of *animal* and *rational* enter into the conception of *man*, but do not take from it its analytical character; for this, as its very name imports, consists in the analysis of a conception, being sufficient to show certain predicates in it, without reference to the manner of this conception's formation, whether two or more conceptions are united in it, or not.

291. This clearly shows in what mediate evidence consists. The predicate is indeed contained in the idea of the subject; but, owing to the limitation of our intellect, either these ideas are incomplete, or we do not see them in all their extension, or else we do not well distinguish what we in a confused manner perceive in them; and hence, to know the meaning of the terms does not enable us immediately to see that the predicate is contained in the idea of the subject. Moreover, the objects, even such as are purely ideal, are presented to us separately; and hence, not knowing the sum of them all, we pass successively from one to another, discovering their mutual relations in proportion as we approach them.

292. It may, from what we have said, be inferred that all judgments in the purely ideal order are analytic, since every cognition of this order is obtained by the intuition of whatever is more or less complicated in the conception, and there is no more synthesis than is necessary to bring the objects together, by uniting their conceptions in one total conception, which serves for the discovery of the relation of the partial conceptions.

293. The x, therefore, of which Kant speaks, and the removal of which is one of the most important problems of philosophy, is nothing more than the faculty possessed by the soul to unite the conceptions of different things in one total conception, and to discover in it their mutual relations. This faculty is no new discovery, for the schools have all recognized it under one name or another. No one ever denied to the intellect the faculty of comparing; and comparison is the act whereby the intellect places two or more objects before its sight so as to perceive their mutual relations. In this act the intellect forms a total conception, of which the conceptions compared are a part. Thus we have seen that in geometry to verify the mutual relation of certain figures, we construct a new figure which includes them all, and is a sort of field whereon the comparison is made.

This exposition of analytic and synthetic judgments will suffice for the present; as we proposed to treat of them here only in general, and as related to certainty; consequently we will not descend to their particular application to various ideas, the analysis of which belongs to other parts of this work.

CHAPTER XXX
VICO'S CRITERION

294. The doctrine of Vico on the criterion of truth is connected with the matter of the preceding chapters on immediate and mediate evidence. This philosopher thinks that the criterion consists in having made the truth which is known; that our cognitions then only are completely certain, and that they lose their certainty in proportion as the intellect loses its character of cause with respect to its objects. God, the cause of all, knows every thing perfectly: creatures, whose causality is very limited, are very limited in their cognitions; and if in any thing they may be likened to the infinite, it is in that ideal world which they construct for themselves, and extend at pleasure, stopped by no impassable limits.

Let the author speak for himself. "The terms *verum* and *factum*, *the true* and *the made*, are used one for the other, in the Latin language, or, as the schoolmen say, are convertible. *Intelligere*, to understand, is the same as to read with clearness and to know with evidence. They used *cogitare* in the sense of the Italian *pensare e andar raccogliendo*; *ratio* with them meant a collection of numerical elements, and also the gift by which man is distinguished from, and made superior to, the brute. They defined man to be an animal participating of reason; *animal rationis particeps*: and consequently not absolutely possessed of it. As words are the signs of ideas, so also are ideas the signs and representations of things. Thus, as to read, *legere*, is to unite the elements of writing, which form the words; so to understand, *intelligere*, is to unite all the elements which constitute the perfect idea of anything. Hence we infer that the doctrine of the ancient Italians concerning truth was as follows: Truth is the same as fact; and consequently God is the first truth, because he is the first maker, *factor*; the infinite truth, because he made all things; the absolute truth, because he represents all the elements of things, both internal and external, for he contains them. To know is to unite the elements of things: hence it follows that thought, *cogitatio*, is a property of the human mind; and intelligence a property of the divine mind, because God contains all the internal and all the external elements of things, and therefore he unites them, and he it is that disposes them; whereas the human mind limited as it is, and separated from all that is not itself, may bring together extreme points, but cannot unite them; it may think of things, but cannot understand them; and this is why it is said to participate of reason, but not to possess it. Let us explain these ideas by a comparison. Divine truth is a solid image of things, a sort of plastic figure; human truth is an image on a plane, it has no depth, but is a sort of painting. Divine truth is true, because God knows in the same act by which he disposes and produces; human truth is in relation to things which man in like manner disposes and creates. Science is the cognition of the mode in which the thing is made; a cognition in which the mind makes its object, since it recomposes its elements. For God, who understands every thing, the object is a solid; but it is a surface for man who understands only the exterior. These points being settled, in order that we may more easily make them harmonize with our religion, let us observe that the ancient philosophers of Italy identified truth and fact, for they believed the world to be eternal. Thus the pagan philosophers adored a God who always operated *ad extra*, a point rejected by our theology. Wherefore in our religion, in which we profess that the world was created in time, and out of nothing, it is necessary to distinguish, and identify created truth with what is made, and uncreated truth with what is begotten, *genito*. Thus the Sacred Scriptures, with an elegance truly divine, give the name of *the Word* to the wisdom of God, which contains in itself the ideas of all things and the elements of these ideas. In the Word, truth is the comprehension of all the elements of this universe, and it might produce infinite worlds. From these elements, known and contained in the divine omnipotence, is formed the Word real and absolute, known by the Father from all eternity and begotten by him also from all eternity."[26]

295. From these principles Vico deduces some very transcendental consequences, among others, the explanation of the reason why our sciences are divided into many branches, and that of the different grades of certainty by which they are distinguished. Mathematics is the most certain, because a kind of creation of the intellect, which, starting with the unity of a point, constructs a world of forms and numbers by prolonging lines, and multiplying unity even to infinity. Thus it knows what it produces itself, and hence it is that the theorems commonly held to be objects of pure contemplation depend upon action just as the problems do. Mechanics is a less certain science than either geometry or arithemetic, because it considers motions as realized by machines; and physics is even less certain yet, because it does not, like mechanics, consider the external motion of circumferences, but the internal motion of their centres. There is still less certainty in sciences of the moral order, because these do not consider the motions of bodies arising from one certain and common origin, which is nature, but the motions of the soul, often most profound, often also capricious.

"Human science," he says, "owes its origin to a defect of the human mind; it is beyond all things in its extreme limitation, contains nothing of what it seeks to know, and is consequently unable to make the truth to which it aspires. The most perfect sciences are those which have expiated the vice of their origin, and are assimilated, as a creation, to divine science, that is, those in which the truth and the fact are mutually convertible.

"From what proceeds, we may infer that the criterion of truth, and the rule to recognize it, is *to have made it*: consequently, the clear and distinct idea of our mind which we have, is not a criterion of the truth, nor is it even a criterion of our mind; because the soul does not, by knowing itself, make itself; and not making itself, it knows not in what way it knows itself. Since human science takes abstraction for its basis, sciences are so much the more uncertain, as they more nearly approach corporal matter....

"In a word, the true and the good are convertible, if what is known as true derives its being from the mind which knows it; as human science imitates divine science, wherein God, by knowing the true, begets it *internally* in eternity, and makes it *externally* in time. The communication of goodness to the objects of his thought is to God the criterion of the true: *vidit Deus quod essent bona*; to men it is *to have made the truth which they know*."[27]

296. Vico's system undeniably shows him to have been a profound thinker, and to have carefully meditated the problems of intelligence. His line dividing the certainty of sciences is exceedingly interesting. At first sight, nothing is more specious than the difference marked between mathematical, natural, and moral sciences. Mathematics is absolutely certain, because the work of the understanding, it is as the understanding, which constructed them, sees them to be. On the other hand, the natural and moral sciences regard objects independent of reason, having by themselves an existence of their own; wherefore, the understanding knows little of them, and even in this little it is the more liable to err as it penetrates deeper into a sphere where it cannot construct. We call this system specious, because when examined, it is found to be destitute of all solid foundation. We recognize, however, a profound thought in its author; for one he must have had to consider science under such a point of view.

297. The understanding knows only what it makes. This proposition sums up Vico's whole system; and it must have some foundation, or he cannot advance one step without begging his question. Why does the understanding know only what it makes? Why can the problem of representation have no possible solution out of causality? We think we have shown another origin besides this in identity, also in ideality duly connected with causality.

298. To understand is not to cause. There may be, and there really is, a productive intelligence; but the act of understanding and that of causing, in general, offer distinct ideas. Intelligence supposes an activity; otherwise that intimate life which distinguishes the intelligent being is inconceivable: but this activity does not produce the objects known; it operates in an immanent manner on these objects, presupposed to be either mediately or immediately in union with the intellect.

299. If the intellect be condemned to know nothing not made by itself, it is difficult to conceive how the act of understanding can commence. If we place ourselves in the initial moment, we shall not know how to explain the development of this activity; for, if it can only know what it has made, what is it to understand in the first moment before it has made any thing? In the system before us, the intellect has no object but what it has itself produced; but to understand, without an object understood, is a contradiction, so that not having in its initial moment yet produced any thing, there can be nothing understood; and, consequently, intelligence is inexplicable. We cannot suppose its activity to be blindly exercised: nothing is done blindly when there is question of representation, and the productive activity essentially relates to things represented as represented. So far as the problem of intelligence is concerned, it makes no difference that these are produced externally, with an existence distinct from the intellectual representation. As Vico himself explains, human reason knows what it constructs in a purely ideal world; and God knows the Word which he begets, although the Word is not without the divine essence, but is identified with it.

300. The Neapolitan philosopher, not satisfied with applying his system to human reason, makes it applicable to all intelligences, not excepting the divine; although with a praiseworthy regard for religion, he endeavors to reconcile his ideological doctrine with the dogmas of Christianity. Truly, the problems of intelligence cannot be completely solved without greatly cumulating them. To trace the footsteps of human reason does not suffice to make us know the human understanding; we must, moreover, propose the general problem of intelligence itself, now limited, like our own, to faint glimmerings, now dilating itself in a sea of light over the regions of infinity. The sublime words, with which St. John commences his Gospel, besides the august truth taught by divine inspiration, involve transcendental doctrines of an importance higher than can be found in the words of any man, even if considered under a merely philosophical point of view.

When Vico identifies truth with the made, he is aware that he must, according to a dogma of our religion, distinguish between what is created and what is uncreated. What is created is made; what is uncreated, begotten. He admires the divine elegance of the Holy Scriptures in calling the wisdom of God, in which the ideas of all things are contained, and the elements of ideas themselves, his Word: but when he would explain the conception of the Word, his expressions are very inexact; he would have us understand, so it would seem, that the Word only results from the elements known and contained in the divine omnipotence. "In this Word," he says, "the true is the comprehension of all the elements of this universe; and it might form infinite worlds: from these elements, known and contained in the divine omnipotence, is formed the Word real and absolute, known by the Father from all eternity, and by him begotten also from all eternity."[28]

If the author means that the Word is conceived by the mere knowledge of what is contained in the divine omnipotence, his assertion is false; if he does not, his mode of speaking is inexact.

St. Thomas asks whether any relation to creature be contained in the name of the Word: "*utrum in nomine Verbi importetur respectus ad creaturam;*" and he resolves the question with admirable laconism and solidity. "I reply that in the Word relation to creature is contained. For God, by knowing himself, knows every creature. The Word, therefore, conceived in the mind, is representative of all actually understood by it. Wherefore there are in us different words according to the different things we understand. But because God by one act understands both himself and all things, his only Word is expressive not only of the Father, but also of creatures. And as the science of God is, with respect to himself, cognition, but with respect to creatures, cognition and cause; so the Word of God is expressive only of what is in God the Father, but both expressive and productive of creatures; and this is why it is said in the Thirty-second Psalm: "He said, and they were made;" because the productive reason of those things, which the Father makes, is contained in the Word."[29]

We see by this passage, that, according to St. Thomas, the Word also expresses creatures, and that it is conceived not only by the cognition of them, but, and this too, primarily, by the cognition of the divine essence. Elsewhere, the Holy Doctor says: "The Father, by understanding himself, the Son, and the Holy Ghost, and all other things included in His science, conceives the Word, in such a manner that the whole Trinity is expressed in the *Word*, and also all creatures."[30]

301. Another doctrine of St. Thomas is also opposed to this system of Vico, according to whom, the intellect knows what it makes, and that only, and because it makes it; and the made being the sole criterion of the true, the true and the made are convertible. Vico applies this doctrine to the divine intelligence, only substituting *begotten* for *made*; but this inverts the order of ideas, since, according to our mode of conceiving, God does not understand

because he begets, but begets because he understands: intelligence must be conceived before the Word can be conceived. "In whoever understands," says St. Thomas, "*by the very fact of understanding*, something proceeds within him, which is the conception of the thing understood coming from the intellective power, and proceeding from its knowledge."[31]

This doctrine of St. Thomas confirms the opinion, expressed above, concerning the impossibility of explaining the intellectual act solely by production. To produce in the intellectual order, it is evidently necessary to understand; and consequently in the initial moment of every intelligence, the productive act cannot be performed without intuition of the object. St. Thomas speaks in this same sense of divine things, as much as one can so speak; he does not found the divine intelligence on the generation of the Word, but rather the generation of the Word on the divine intelligence. God, according to St. Thomas, begets the Word because he understands, but does not understand because he begets. St. Thomas comprises in the Word the expression of every thing contained in God; for he presupposes the divine intelligence, by which he makes it possible to speak or utter the Word. This, then, is the order of conceptions; understanding, object understood, word proceeding from the act of understanding, whereby the intelligent being expresses, or says to itself, the thing understood. These ideas applied to God, are: God the Father understanding; divine essence and all that it contains understood; Word or Son generated by this intellectual act, expressive of all that is contained in the generative act.

302. We have no disposition to blame Vico; we have only endeavored to mark the inexactness of his words, doing him, at the same time, the justice to believe that he understood things differently from what he explained them, which, indeed, he has not succeeded in doing with due clearness. Let us now consider his system under less subtle points of view.

If the made be admitted as the only criterion of the true, the understanding is obviously excluded from communication with all that it has not itself produced. And not having made itself, it cannot know itself. "The soul," says Vico, "knowing itself does not make itself, and therefore knows not in what manner it knows." Thus abstracting the problem of intelligibility proposed in our twelfth chapter, Vico denies to our soul a criterion of itself, for the sole reason that it is not its own cause. Identity, therefore, far from being an origin of representation, as was proved in our eleventh chapter, is incompatible with it; nothing can know itself, because nothing has made itself.

Hence results a very grave error; for it may be inferred that not even God can know himself, since he is not his own cause. It is not enough to say that he knows himself in the Word, since the Word is impossible if intelligence be not supposed.

303. The whole world of reality, distinct from that of intellectual being, will forever remain unknown in Vico's system, which, for this reason, leads to the most rigid skepticism. What does he admit? The cognition by the mind of the mind's own work; and in this are comprised the acts of consciousness and all the purely ideal objects which we create in it. This, also, is admitted by the skeptics, no one of whom would deny that we have consciousness, and that there is an ideal world the work of this consciousness, or at least attested by it.

If, then, we admit no criterion of truth but the made, we open the door to skepticism, and abandon the world of reality to fix ourselves in that of appearance. Nevertheless, so strange are human opinions, Vico thought directly the contrary; he believed that only with his system was it possible to refute skepticism. It is curious to hear him say with perfect seriousness: "The only means of destroying skepticism is to take this for the criterion of truth, that every one is certain of the truth which he makes."

But what is the foundation of so odd an opinion? Let us listen to the philosopher himself, who says, indeed, many good things, but does not show how they may tend to the overthrow of skepticism: "Skeptics are always repeating that things *seem* to them, but that they do not know what they really *are*. They confess effects, and consequently concede causes to them; but they assert that they do not know these causes, because they do not know the genus or form according to which things are made. Admit these propositions, and retort them thus: the comprehension of causes which contains all the genera and all the forms under which effects are produced, and the appearances of which the skeptic confessedly sees, although he denies that he knows their real essence, is found in the first truth which comprises all, and in which all, even to the last, are contained. And since this truth comprises all truths, it is infinite, it excludes none, and it has a superiority over every body, which is only an effect. This truth is consequently something spiritual; in other words, it is God, the God of the Christian. By this we must measure human truth; for human truth is that truth, the elements of which we have co-ordinated within us, and which, by means of certain postulates, we may extend and follow to infinity. By co-ordinating these truths we know and make them at one and the same time; and this is why, in this case, we have the genus and the form according to which we make."[32] We discover nothing in this refutation of skepticism calculated to destroy it. Even supposing all to admit the principle of causality, which all do not admit, what aid can he draw from this principle, when he makes the work of that very understanding, which must make use of it, the only criterion? If causality be the only criterion of truth, the understanding is isolated, and cannot, in the order of effects, take one step beyond what it has itself produced; and, in the order of causes, it cannot ascend higher than itself; for, were it so to ascend, it would know things not made by itself, would know its own cause. With this supposition the skeptics must triumph; cognition is confined to the internal world, to simple appearances; and when one would go out of these, he stumbles against the only criterion which opposes the cognition of all *not made* by the understanding itself. We do then see reality, but are separated from it by an impassable abyss. The world in itself may be any thing we choose to suppose it; but with respect to us, it will be nothing. This law applies to every intelligence, so that vitality can only be known by the first cause.

These consequences, inadmissible as they are, if we would not throw ourselves unreservedly into the tide of skepticism, are nevertheless inevitable in Vico's system. An original way truly of combatting skepticism, thus to throw open its widest gates!

CHAPTER XXXI
CONTINUATION OF THE SAME SUBJECT

304. If the Neapolitan philosopher's criterion be anywhere admissible, it can only be in ideal truths; for as these are absolutely cut off from existence, we may well suppose them to be known even by an understanding which has not in reality produced them. So far as known by the understanding they involve no reality, and consequently no condition that exacts any productive force not referable to a purely ideal order. In this order the human reason seems really to produce. If we, for example, take geometry, we shall readily perceive that, even in its profoundest parts and in its greatest complications, it is only a kind of intellectual construction, wherein that only is to be found which reason has placed there.

Reason it is which by force of perseverance has succeeded in uniting elements and so disposing them as to attain that wonderful result, of which it may say with truth: *this is my work.*

If we carefully observe the development of the science of geometry, we shall perceive that the extended series of axioms, theorems, problems, demonstrations and solutions, begins with a few postulates, and that it goes on with the aid of the same, or others discovered by reason according to the demands of necessity or utility.

What is a line? A series of points. The line, then, is an intellectual construction, and involves only the successive fluxions of a point. What is a triangle? An intellectual construction wherein the extremities of three lines are united. What is a circle? Also an intellectual construction; the space enclosed by a circumference formed by the extremity of a line revolved around a point. What are all other curves? Lines described by the movement of a point governed by a certain law of inflexion. What is a surface? Is not its idea generated by the motion of a line, just as that of a solid is generated by the motion of a surface? And what are all the objects of geometry but lines, surfaces, and solids of various kinds, combined in various ways? Universal arithmetic, whether arithmetic properly so called, or algebra, is a creation of the understanding. Number is a collection of units, and it is the understanding that collects them. Two is only one and one, and three only two and one; and thus with all numerical values. The ideas expressing these values consequently contain a creation of our mind, are its work, and include nothing not placed there by it.

We have already observed that algebra is a kind of language. Its rules are partly conventional, and its most complicated formulas may be reduced to a conventional principle. Take one of the simplest: $a^0 = 1$: but why is it? Because $a^0 = a^{n-n}$; why? Because there is a conventional usage to mark division by the remainder of the exponents; and consequently a^n/a^n, which is evidently equal to one, may be expressed $a^n/a^n = a^{n-n} = 1$.

305. These observations seem to prove Vico's system to be really true, so far as pure mathematics, that is, science of the purely ideal order, is concerned. Possibly also the same may be said of it in relation to other science, as for example, metaphysics; but we shall not follow it farther, since it is not easy to find a ground free from conflicting opinions. Moreover, having shown how far Vico's system is admissible in mathematics, we have thereby given a solution to difficulties to which it is subject in its other branches.

306. That in a purely ideal order the understanding constructs is undeniable, and the schools agree in this. There is no doubt that reason supposes, combines, compares, deduces; operations which are inconceivable without some kind of intellectual construction. The understanding in this case knows what it makes, because its work is present to it: when it combines it knows that it combines; when it compares or deduces, it knows that it compares or deduces; when it builds upon certain suppositions, which it has itself established, it knows in what they consist, since it rests upon them.

307. The understanding knows what it makes; but this is not all that it knows; for it has truths which neither are nor can be its works, since they are the basis of all its works, as, for example, the principle of contradiction. Can the impossibility of a thing being and not being at the same time be said to be the work of our reason? Assuredly not. Reason itself is impossible if this principle be not supposed; the understanding finds it in itself as an absolutely necessary law, as a condition *sine qua non* of all its acts. Here, then, Vico's criterion fails: "the understanding knows only the truth it makes:" and yet the understanding knows but does not make the truth of the principle of contradiction.

308. Facts of consciousness are known by reason, although they are not its production. These facts are not only present to consciousness, but are also objects of the combinations of reason: here, then, Vico's criterion again fails.

309. Although in those things that are a purely intellectual work, the understanding knows what it makes, it does not make whatever it chooses; for then we should have to say that science is perfectly arbitrary: instead of the geometrical results we now have, we might have others as numerous as the individuals who deal in lines, surfaces, and solids. This shows reason to be subject to certain laws, its constructions to be connected with conditions which it cannot abstract. One of these conditions is the principle of contradiction, which would, were it to fail, annihilate all knowledge. True, by a series of intellectual constructions one may ascertain the size of a sphere; but can two understandings obtain two different values of it? They cannot, for that would be an absurdity: they may choose different ways, or express their demonstrations and conclusions in different terms; but the value is the same: if there be any discrepancy, it is because one or the other has fallen into an error.

310. If we thoroughly examine this matter, we shall perceive that the intellectual construction, of which Vico speaks, is a fact generally admitted. There are in this philosopher's system two new things, the one good, the other bad; the good, is to have indicated one reason of the certainty of mathematics; the bad, is to have exaggerated the value of his criterion.

We have said that his system expressed a fact generally recognized, but exaggerated by him. The understanding undoubtedly creates, in some sense, ideal sciences; but in what sense? Solely by taking postulates, and combining its data in various ways. Here ends its creative power, for in these postulates and combinations it discovers truths not placed there by itself.

What is the triangle in the purely ideal order? A creation of the understanding, which disposes the lines in a triangular form, and, preserving this form, modifies it in a thousand ways. Thus far there is only one postulate and different combinations of it: but the properties of the triangle flow by absolute necessity from the conditions of the postulate: the understanding, however, does not make these properties, it discovers them. The example of the triangle is applicable to all geometry. The understanding takes a postulate; this is its free work, but it must not come in conflict with the principle of contradiction. From this postulate flow absolutely necessary consequences, independent of intellectual action, and involving an absolute truth known by the understanding itself. Consequently it is false to say of them that it makes them. Suppose a man so to place a body, that, left to itself, it will fall to the ground: is it the man who gives it the force to fall? Certainly not, but nature. The man only supplies the condition necessary for the force of gravity to produce its effect: when once the condition is performed, the fall is inevitable. Here, then, is a simile which shows clearly and exactly what happens in the purely ideal order. The understanding performs the conditions; from them flow other truths, *not made*, but known, by the understanding. This truth is absolute, is as the force of gravity in the order of ideas. Hence we see what is admissible, and what inadmissible in Vico's system. The power of combination, a generally recognized fact, is admissible; the exaggeration of this fact extended to all truths, when it only comprises postulates in their various combinations, is inadmissible.

The rules of algebra are conventional inasmuch as they relate to the *expression*, for this might evidently have been different. Supposing, however, the expression, the development of the rules, is not conventional, but necessary. In the expression an/an the number of times the quantity has entered as factor might clearly have been expressed in infinite ways; but supposing the present to have been adopted, the rule is not conventional, but absolutely necessary; since whatever the expression, it is always certain that the division of a quantity by itself, with distinct exponents, gives for result the diminution of the number of times it has entered as factor: this is denoted by the remainder of the exponents; and consequently if the number of times be equal in the dividend and the divisor, the result will be = 0. Thus we see that even in algebra, what the understanding has to do, is to perform the conditions, and express them as seems to it best: but here its free work ends, for necessary truths result from these conditions; and these it does not make, but only knows.

311. Vico's merit in this point consists in having expressed a very clear idea of the cause of the greater certainty of the purely ideal sciences. In these the understanding itself performs the conditions upon which it has to build its edifice; it chooses the ground, forms the plan, and raises the construction conformably to it. In the real order this ground is already designated, just as are the plan of the edifice and the materials for its construction. In both cases it is subject to the general laws of reason, but with this difference, that in the purely ideal order, it has to regard these laws and nothing else; but in the real order, it cannot abstract the objects considered in themselves, and is condemned to submit to all the inconveniences they are of a nature to cause. We will explain these ideas by an example. If we would determine the relation of the sides of a triangle under certain conditions, we have only to suppose the conditions and attend to them. The ideal triangle is in our understanding a perfectly exact, and also a fixed, thing. If we suppose it to be an isosceles triangle with the relation of the sides to the base as seven to five, this ratio is absolute, immutable, so long as the supposition remains unchanged. In all our operations upon these data, we are liable to mistakes of calculation, but no error can arise from inexactness of data. The understanding knows, indeed, for what it knows is its own work. If

the triangle be not purely ideal, but realized upon paper, or on the ground, the understanding vacillates because those conditions, which, in the purely ideal order, it fixes with all exactness, cannot be transferred in like manner to the real order; and even were they transferred, the understanding would have no means of appreciating them. Therefore, Vico says, with great truth, that our cognitions lose in certainty in the same proportion as they are removed from the ideal order and swallowed up in the reality of things.

312. Dugald Stewart probably had in view this doctrine of Vico when he explained the cause of the greater certainty of mathematical sciences. It does not, he says, depend upon axioms, but upon definitions; that is, he adopts, with a slight modification, the system of the Neapolitan philosopher, that the mathematical are the most certain, because they are an intellectual construction founded upon certain conditions placed by the understanding and expressed by the definition.

This difference between the purely ideal and the real order did not escape the scholastics. They were accustomed to say that there was no science of contingent and particular, but only of necessary and universal things. In the place of *contingent* substitute *reality*, since all finite reality is contingent; and instead of *universal* put *ideal*, since the purely ideal is all universal; and you will have the same doctrine enunciated in distinct words. It is not easy to show exactly how far modern philosophers have availed themselves of the scholastic doctrine, in so far as the distinction between pure and empirical cognitions is concerned; but it is certain that some very clear passages upon these questions are to be found in the works of the scholastics. It would not be strange if some moderns, particularly Germans, whose laboriousness is proverbial, especially in matters of erudition, had read them.(27)

CHAPTER XXXII
THE CRITERION OF COMMON SENSE

313. *Common sense* is an exceedingly vague expression. It should, like all expressions which contain many and different ideas, be considered under two aspects: that of its etymological, and that of its real value. These two values are not always the same; they are sometimes greatly discrepant; but even in their discrepancy, they usually preserve intimate relations. We must not, in order duly to appreciate the meaning of such expressions, confine ourselves to their philosophical, and contemn their vulgar meaning. In the latter there is often a profound philosophy; for, in such cases, the vulgar sense is a kind of precious sediment left by the flow of reason upon the word during many ages. It thus happens that in measure, as the vulgar sense is understood and analyzed, the philosophical question is determined, and the most intricate questions solved with the greatest facility.

314. It is remarkable, that besides the corporal senses there should be another, called *common sense*. *Sense*: This word excludes reflection, all reasoning, all combination; nothing of this kind enters into the meaning of the word *to sense*. When we sense, the mind is rather passive than active; it does nothing of itself; it does not give, it receives; it suffers, but does not perform, an action. This analysis leads us to a very important result, and this is, the separation from common sense of all that upon which the mind exercises its activity; and the determination of one character of this criterion, which is, with respect to common sense; the understanding has nothing to do but submit itself to a law *perceived*, to an instinctive and unavoidable necessity.

315. *Common*: This word excludes all individuality, and shows the object of common sense to be general to all men.

The simple facts of consciousness are facts of sense, but not of common sense; the mind feels them when it abstracts objectiveness and generality; what it experiences within itself is an experience exclusively its own, and one which has no connection with others.

The word *common* shows the objects of this criterion to be common to all men, and consequently referable to the objective order, since the purely subjective, as such, is limited to the individual, and in no wise affects what is general. So exact is this observation, that in ordinary language no internal phenomenon, however extravagant, is ever said to be opposed to common sense, provided it be expressed simply with abstraction from its relation to the object. If a man says: I experience such or such a sensation, I seem to see such or such a thing, common sense is not against him; but if he says, such or such a thing is in such a manner, and the assertion is extravagant, it is against him, for this is contrary to common sense.

316. I believe the expression *common sense* to denote a law of our mind, apparently differing according to the different cases to which it applies, but in reality and apart from its modifications, only one, always the same, consisting in a natural inclination of our mind to give its assent to some truths not attested by consciousness nor demonstrated by reason, necessary to all men in order to satisfy the wants of sensitive, intellectual, and moral life.

If the fact be agreed on, the name is of little moment: whether *common sense* be or be not the most adequate to signify it, is a philological, not a philosophical, question. What we have to do, is to inquire if this inclination of which we have spoken, really exists, under what forms it is presented, to what cases it is applicable, and how far, and to what degree it may be considered a criterion of truth.

Evidently this inclination cannot, in the complication of the acts and faculties of our soul, and in the multitude and diversity of the objects offered to it, always be presented with the same character; it must undergo various modifications capable of causing it to be considered as a distinct fact, although in reality still the same, transformed in a suitable manner. The best means of avoiding a confusion of ideas, will be to designate the various cases in which the exercise of this inclination occurs.

317. We at once detect it in the case of truths immediately evident. The understanding neither does nor can prove them, and yet it must assent to them, or perish like a flame that has nothing to feed upon. The possession of one or more of these primitive truths is an indispensable condition to intellectual life; without them intelligence is an absurdity. Here, then, we find all that is comprised in the definition of common sense: the impossibility of proof; an intellectual necessity, which must be satisfied by assent; and an irresistible and universal inclination to give this assent.

Is there any objection to calling this inclination common sense? For myself, I shall not dispute upon words; I mark the fact, and this is all I need do in philosophy. I grant that the inclination to assent is not, in treating of immediate evidence, usually called common sense, and this not without a reason. In order that the word sense may be properly applied to it, the understanding ought to feel rather than know: but in immediate evidence it knows rather than feels. However this may be, I repeat that the name is of no account; yet, it would not be difficult to find this criterion of truth called by grave authors *common sense*. What I wish is to establish this law of our nature inclining us to give our assent to certain truths, independently of consciousness and ratiocination.

318. Not immediate evidence alone has this irresistible inclination in its favor; mediate evidence also has it. Our understanding necessarily assents, not only to first principles, but also to all propositions clearly connected with them.

The natural inclination to assent is not limited to the subjective value of ideas; it also extends to their objective value. We have already seen that this objectiveness is not directly demonstrable *a priori*, and yet we stand in need of it. If our understanding is not to be limited to a purely ideal and subjective world, we must know not only that things *seem* to us, as they do with mediate or immediate evidence, but also that they really *are* such as they seem to be. It is then necessary to assent to the objectiveness of ideas, and we find within ourselves an irresistible and universal inclination to such an assent.

319. What we have said of immediate and mediate evidence relatively to the objective value of ideas, is true, not only in the purely intellectual, but also in the moral order. The soul, endowed as it is with free will, needs rules for its direction: if first intellectual principles are necessary in order to know, moral principles are not less so in order to will and work. What truth and error are to the understanding, good and evil are to the will. Besides the life of the understanding, there is a life of the will; the one, without principles on which to rest, is annihilated; the other, as a moral being, perishes, or becomes an inconceivable absurdity, if it have no rule, the observation or violation of which constitutes its perfection or imperfection. Here is another necessity for the assent to certain moral truths, and another reason of this irresistible and universal inclination to assent.

I would here remark, that as it is not enough in the intellectual order to know, but it is also necessary to act, and one of the principles of action is perception by the senses; so moral truths are not only known but felt. When they are offered to the mind the understanding assents to them as unshaken, and the heart embraces them with enthusiasm and love.

320. Sensations considered as purely subjective do not meet the wants of sensitive life. We must be sure that our sensations correspond to an external world, real and true, not phenomenal. Men do not ordinarily possess either

the capacity or the time requisite to investigate the philosophical questions of the existence of bodies, and to decide for or against Berkeley and his followers. What is necessary is perfect certainty that bodies do exist, that sensations have an external object in reality. All men have this certainty when they assent with an irresistible force to the objectiveness of ideas, that is, to the existence of bodies.

321. Faith in human authority furnishes us with another case of this wonderful instinct. Both the individual and society require faith: without it society and family would be impossible; the individual would be condemned to isolation, and, therefore, to death. The speech of man, the human race itself, would disappear were it not for faith. This belief has distinct grades according to different circumstances, but it always exists; man is inclined, by a natural instinct, to believe his fellow man. When many men speak, and none raise their voices against them, the force of this inclination increases in the same proportion as the number of witness, until it becomes irresistible. Who doubts the existence of Rome? And yet, the greater part of us only know it upon the authority of other men.

What foundation has faith in human authority? Most men are ignorant of the philosophical reasons which may be assigned; but their faith is not therefore less lively than that of philosophers. But why is this so? Because there is a necessity, and at its side an instinct to be satisfied. Man must believe in man, and he believes. And here note well, that the greater the necessity, the greater the faith. The very ignorant and imbecile believe all that is told them; they make other men their guide, and blindly follow them. The tender child, knowing nothing, abandons itself to the absolute belief of the greatest marvels: the word of those around is to it an invaluable criterion of truth.

322. Besides the cases of first intellectual and moral principles, the objectiveness of ideas and sensations, the weight of human authority, man must give his instantaneous assent to certain truths, which, although he might, had he the time, demonstrate, he cannot now, because so suddenly are they presented to him, that they exact an immediate formation of judgment, and, sometimes, also action. In all these cases, there is a natural inclination impelling us to assent.

Hence it is that we instinctively judge it impossible, or little less than impossible, to cause a determinate effect, by a fortuitous combination; as, for example, to form a page of Virgil by a chance mixture of types, or to hit the bull's eye of a target without taking aim, and other similar things. In this there is assuredly a philosophical reason, but one not known to common people. There is evidence of this reason in the theory of probabilities:

it is a distinct application of the principle of causality, and of the natural opposition of our understanding to supposing an effect without a cause, and order where there is no ordering intelligence.

323. Arguments of analogy, are in human life necessary in infinite cases. How do we know that the sun will rise to-morrow? By the laws of nature. How do we know that these will continue in force? Evidently, we must finally recur to analogy. The sun will rise to-morrow, because it has risen to-day; it rose yesterday, and it has never failed to rise. How do we know that spring will again bring flowers, and autumn fruits? Because it has so happened in former years. Men ordinarily do not know the reasons which might be given for founding the argument from analogy on the constancy of the laws of nature, and on the relation between certain physical causes and determinate effects; but their assent is required and given.

324. In all the cases cited, excepting, perhaps, that of immediate evidence, the inclination to assent may be, and really is, called *common sense*. The reason of this exception is, that in this case, although there is no demonstration, the predicate is nevertheless most clearly seen contained in the idea of the subject; but in the other cases there is neither demonstration nor this vision. Man assents by a natural impulse; and if any thing is objected to his belief, he does not call attention to his conception, as in immediate evidence, but is completely disconcerted, and knows not what to answer; he then applies to the objection, not the name of error, nor of absurdity, but that of extravagance, of something contrary to common sense.

Suppose, for example, a little grain of sand to be mixed with a great heap, and some one to come and say: I will put my hand into the heap, and instantly draw out the one grain hidden there. What will you object to such a one? What will the beholders reply? Nothing; or, looking at each other in perfect surprise, they will exclaim: "What extravagance! He has no common sense!" Or suppose some one to say, that all we see is nothing, that there is no external world, that we have no body, or that all told us of the existence of a city called London is untrue. Whoever hears such madness, knows not what to answer; but he repels it by a natural impulse, and the mind feels that this is nonsense without stopping to examine.

325. We shall now inquire whether common sense be a certain criterion of truth, whether it be so in all, or in what cases, and what characters it must have in order to be an infallible criterion.

Man cannot lay aside his nature: when it speaks, reason will not allow it to be ignored. A natural inclination, simply because it is natural, is in the eyes of philosophy something highly respectable: it is the province of reason and free will not to allow it to go astray. What is natural to man is not always so perfectly fixed as it is in brutes, where instinct is blind as it must be, where there is neither reason nor free will. The exercise of man's natural inclinations is subordinate to his reason and free will, and, consequently, when these are called instincts, the word has a very different meaning from what it has when applied to brutes. What happens in the moral order is also verified in the intellectual. We have not only our heart to watch, but also our understanding; both are subject to the law of perfectibility; the objects which they offer to us are good and evil, truth and error. Nature herself shows us which one we ought to choose, but does not force our choice; life and death are before us, we may select the one we please.

326. There is in man, independently of the action of free will, a quality which oftentimes has the effect of turning his natural inclinations from their object; it is weakness. Hence, it is nothing extraordinary for these inclinations to be so distorted as to lead to error instead of truth, and this renders it necessary to determine what characters *common sense* should have, in order to be an absolutely infallible criterion.

327. We will point out the conditions, such as we conceive them to be, of true and never-erring common sense.

First Condition. — That the inclination be every way irresistible, so that one cannot, even by the aid of reflection, resist or avoid it.

Second Condition. — That every truth of common sense be absolutely certain to the whole human race. This condition follows from the first.

Third Condition. — That every truth of common sense stand the test of reason.

Fourth Condition. — That every truth of common sense have for its object the satisfaction of some great necessity of sensitive, intellectual, or moral life.

328. When possessed of all these characters, the criterion of common sense is absolutely infallible, and may defy skeptics to assign a case wherein it has failed. The higher the degree in which the conditions are satisfied, the more certain will the criterion be. We will explain this by a few examples.

There is no doubt that ordinary men make their sensations so far objective as to transfer what passes within themselves to the exterior, without distinguishing between the subjective and the objective. Thus, when they consider colors to be in things themselves, they do not take the green, for example, to be the sensation of the green, but a thing certain, a quality, or whatever else it may be called, inherent in the object. But in reality this certainly is not so. The cause of the sensation is in the external object; such a disposition of facts also as to produce through the medium of light the impression called *green*. Common sense here deceives; for philosophical analysis convicts it of error. But here common sense has not the requisite conditions. In the first place, it ought to stand the test of reason; so soon as we reflect upon the case, we discover an illusion as fair as innocent. Moreover, it is not irresistible, for our assent is withheld the instant we are convinced of the illusion. Neither is the assent universal, for not all philosophers have it. Nor is it indispensable to the satisfaction of some great necessity of life. It therefore has no one of the conditions just laid down. What we have said of sight is applicable to the other senses. What is the value of the testimony of common sense inasmuch as it leads us to make sensations objective? We will answer this question.

A certainty that sensations correspond to external objects is necessary to the wants of life. Upon this all men without exception are agreed. Reflection cannot despoil us of our natural inclination; and although reason, when most it cavils, may shake the foundations of this belief, it never succeeds in convicting it of error. Even they who give the most weight to such cavils, cannot prove that bodies do not exist: they can only say that we do not know that they exist.

The natural inclination then possesses upon this point all the characteristics necessary to elevate it to the rank of an infallible criterion: it is irresistible, universal, satisfies a great necessity of life, and stands the test of reason.

As to qualities, the direct objects of sensation, it is not necessary for us that they exist in bodies themselves; it is enough that these bodies have something which produces in us, in some way or other, a corresponding impression. It is of little moment whether a green, or orange color be, or be not, a quality of objects, so long as they have some quality which produces in us the sensation of green, or orange color, as the case may be. The ordinary wants of life are not at all affected by this question; and man's relations with the sensible world would not be disturbed by the generalization of philosophical analysis. There is, perhaps, a kind of disenchantment of nature, since, despoiled of sensations, it is not nearly so beautiful; but the enchantment still continues with most men; and philosophy itself, except in brief moments of reflection, is subject to it; and even in these moments it experiences an enchantment of a different kind, as it considers how much of the beauty attributed to objects, belong to man in his own right, and that the simple exercise of a sensible being's harmonious faculties suffices to make the whole universe glow with splendor and glory.(28)

CHAPTER XXXIII
ERROR OF LAMENNAIS ON COMMON CONSENT

329. The instinctive faith in human authority, of which we have just treated, is a fact attested by experience, and one which no philosopher has presumed to call in doubt. This faith, duly directed by reason, constitutes one criterion of truth. The errors to which it may sometimes lead are inherent in human weakness, and are amply compensated for by the advantages derived from it by society and individuals.

A celebrated writer undertook to include all criteria in that of human authority, resolutely affirming "common consent, *sensus communis*, to be to us the only seal of truth."[33] His system, as strange as erroneous, in which words as unlike as *sensus* and *consensus* are confounded, is defended with that eloquent exaggeration characteristic of its eminent author; but profound philosophy does not always accompany eloquence. The sad fate of this genius, as brilliant as erring, shows the results of such a doctrine; it opens an abyss which swallows up all truth, and the author himself was the first to fall into it. To appeal to the authority of others in all things, and for all things, is to despoil the individual of every criterion, to annihilate them all, not excepting the very one he attempts to establish. It is inconceivable how such a system could have found favor with so gifted an intellect. We feel, when reading the eloquent pages of its development, an undefinable pain to see such brilliant passages squandered on the repetition of all the common-places of skepticism, ending in a most glaring paradox, and the least philosophical system imaginable.

Lamennais calls common sense the only criterion; nevertheless, we have only to glance at the others to be convinced that this new criterion is sterile, and could not produce them.

330. The testimony of consciousness, in the first place, cannot rest in any sense upon the authority of others. Formed as it is by a series of acts intimately present to our own mind, and, as without it, it is not possible for us even to conceive individual thought, it must evidently exist prior to the application of any criterion, since no criterion is possible to him who does not think.

Under a scientific aspect nothing can be weaker than his pretended refutation of Descartes' principle. "When, trying to rise from his methodical doubt, Descartes establishes this proposition, *I think, therefore I am*, he passes an immense abyss, and lays in the clouds the corner-stone of the edifice he is about to raise; for, strictly speaking, we cannot say *I think*, we cannot say *I am*, we cannot say *therefore*, or affirm anything as a consequence."[34]

Descartes' principle merited a more careful examination from whoever would invent a system. To oppose to it that we cannot say *therefore*, is to repeat the worn-out argument of the schools; and to affirm that we cannot say *I think*, is to contradict a fact of consciousness not denied even by skeptics. In place of this, we will explain at due length what is, or at least, what ought to be, the sense of Descartes' principle.

If, according to Lamennais, we cannot say *I think*, still less can we say that others think; and as his system recognizes one only criterion, common consent, which absolutely needs the thought of others, it follows that Lamennais has laid his corner-stone higher in the clouds than he who founded philosophy upon a fact of consciousness.

331. A criterion, especially when it pretends to be the only one, ought to have these two conditions: to apply to all cases, and not to suppose another. Now the criterion of common consent is precisely that which is farthest from possessing these conditions: prior to it is the testimony of consciousness; prior also to it is the testimony of the senses, for we cannot know the consent of others if sight or hearing do not make us certain of it.

332. In many cases this criterion is impossible; in many others it is exceedingly difficult if not wholly impossible. To what point is common consent needed? If the word *common* refers to the whole human race, how are the suffrages of all mankind to be recognized? If the consent need not be unanimous, to what point does the contradiction, or the simple non-assent of some, destroy the legitimacy of the criterion?

333. Lamennais' error consists in taking the effect for the cause, and the cause for the effect. We detect certain truths, upon which all men are agreed, and we say: the guaranty that each one is right is the consent of all. If we analyze this well, we shall perceive that the reason of each individual's certainty is not the consent of others; but on the contrary the reason why all agree is that each one for himself feels obliged to give his assent. In this universal voting of the human race, each one gives his own vote, impelled in a certain sense by nature herself; and as all experience the same impulse, all vote alike. Lamennais says every one votes in the same way, because all vote so; but he does not observe that then the voting could never begin nor end. This comparison is not an accidental satire, but a strictly philosophical

argument, to which there can be no reply; it suffices to show the system of Lamennais to be unfounded and contradictory; just as, on the other hand, it indicates the origin of the equivocation, the taking the effect for the cause.

334. Lamennais, in order to prove his criterion to be the only one, appeals to the testimony of consciousness. In our opinion this testimony establishes directly the contrary. Who ever waited for the authority of others to be certain of the existence of bodies? Do we not see even brutes, by force of a natural impulse, making, in their own way, their sensations objective? Had we not in giving our assent to the words of men some other criterion than common consent, we could never believe any one, for the simple reason that it would be impossible to be certain of what others say or think without beginning by believing some one. Does the child refer to the authority of others before giving faith to what its mother recounts? Does it not rather obey the natural instinct communicated to it by the beneficent hand of the Creator? It does not believe because all believe; but all children believe because each one of them believes: their individual belief does not spring from a general belief, but rather the general belief is formed from the assemblage of individual beliefs; it is not natural because universal, but universal because natural.

335. Lamennais' chief argument consists in this: that in certain cases in order to make sure of the truth relatively to the other criteria, we appeal to that of common consent, and that folly itself is only the deviation from this consent. If you tell a man that his eyes deceive him as to an object which he sees, he instinctively turns to other men, and asks them if they do not see it in the same way. If all agree that he is wrong, and he is satisfied they are in earnest, he will experience a momentary vacillation of his faith in the testimony of sight; he will approach the object, will take a different position, or adopt whatever other means may seem to him best suited to make sure that he is right. If he still sees the object in the same way, and the same persons and others who arrive persist in assuring him that the thing is not as he sees it, he will distrust the testimony of sight, and believe himself subject to some infirmity affecting his sight. To this is the argument of Lamennais reduced. What results from it? Nothing to support the system of common consent. True, the other criteria are, in exceptional circumstances, liable to error; in certain cases when a doubt arises an appeal is taken to the testimony of others: but why? Simply, in order to make sure that one has not labored under one of those derangements to which human misery is subject. We know that what is natural is general; and he who doubts inquires of others, that he may ascertain if he has by some accident been out of his ordinary natural state. Who sees not the unreasonableness of raising an exceptional means to the rank of sole and general criterion? Who sees not the

extravagance of asserting that we are assured of the testimony of the senses by the authority of other men, solely because, in extreme cases fearing some derangement of our organs, we ask others if something appears to them as it does to us?

336. Greater exaggeration we cannot have than that of Lamennais, when he affirms "that the exact sciences are also founded on common consent; that in this they enjoy no privilege, and that the very term *exact*, is one of those empty titles under which man seeks to conceal his weakness; that geometry itself only exists by virtue of a tacit convention, a convention which may be thus expressed: *we are obliged to hold such principles to be certain, and we pronounce every one a rebel to common sense, that is, to the authority of the number, who shall demand a demonstration of them.*" This is an intolerable exaggeration. The arguments which he adduces in his notes to prove the intrinsic uncertainty of mathematics are exceedingly feeble; and some of them might make us suspect the author of the *Essai sur l'Indifférence* to be a less profound philosopher than eloquent writer.

I am not ignorant of what has been advanced against the certainty of the exact sciences, nor of the difficulties they present when called before the tribunal of metaphysics. In the first volume of *Protestantism compared with Catholicity*, I consecrated a chapter to what I call *instinct of faith*; and this instinct, I there maintained, also exercises its influence upon the exact sciences. These I do not place above moral sciences; I esteem these latter the more; but I must avoid an exaggeration that would destroy them all.

CHAPTER XXXIV
SUMMARY AND CONCLUSION

337. In concluding this book, I wish to give a summary of my views on certainty, wherein I shall show the connection between the doctrines exposed in the different chapters.

When philosophy meets a necessary fact its duty is to accept it. Such a fact is certainty. To dispute its existence, is to dispute the splendor of the sun at mid-day. Mankind are certain of many things; philosophers, skeptics not excluded, are equally so. Absolute skepticism is impossible.

Setting aside the question of certainty, philosophy is free from extravagance, and is established in the domain of reason; it can there examine how we acquire certainty, and upon what it is based.

The human race is endowed with certainty as a quality annexed to life, a spontaneous result of the development of the soul's faculties. Certainty is natural; consequently it precedes all philosophy, and is independent of the opinions of men. For the same reason the question of certainty, although important to the knowledge of the laws to which our mind is subject, is, and always will be, unproductive of practical results. It is a dividing line fixed by reason lest at any time something should descend from the realm of abstraction prejudicial to society or individuals. Thus from its first investigations, philosophy forms a kind of alliance with good sense; they mutually promise never to be hostile to each other.

When we examine the foundations of certainty a question arises upon the first principle of human cognitions: does it exist, and what is it?

This question may have a double meaning. It may either mean a primitive truth containing all others, as the seed does plants and fruits; or simply a resting-point. The former gives rise to the question of transcendental science; the latter is the cause of the disputes in the schools on the preference of different truths in relation to the dignity of first principle.

If truth exists, there must be means of knowing it, hence the question of the value of criteria.

There is in the order of being one truth, the origin of all truths, God, who is also in the absolute intellectual order the origin of all truths. In the human intellectual order there is no one truth, the origin of all others; neither is there in the real, nor in the ideal order. The philosophy of the *me* can be of no account in establishing transcendental science. The doctrine of absolute identity is an absurdity; besides, it explains nothing.

The problem of representation is here proposed. The representation may be of identity, causality, or ideality. The last is founded on the preceding, but is distinct from it.

Besides the problem of representation we examined that of immediate intelligibility, a difficult problem, but one of the greatest importance to a perfect knowledge of the world of intelligences.

The disputes on the value of different principles, as to which has the right to be called fundamental, originate in a confusion of ideas. We attempt to compare things of very diverse orders, whereas this is impossible. Descartes' principle is the enunciation of a simple fact of consciousness; that of contradiction, an objective truth, the indispensable condition of every cognition: that of the Cartesians is the expression of a law of our mind. The three, each in its own way and sphere, are necessary; no one of them is totally independent of the others; the ruin of any one destroys our intelligence.

We have various criteria; but they may all be reduced to three: consciousness, or internal sense, evidence, and intellectual instinct, or common sense. Consciousness embraces all facts intimately present to our soul as purely subjective; evidence extends to all objective truths, upon which our reason is exercised; intellectual instinct is the natural inclination to assent in cases which lie without the domain of consciousness and evidence.

The intellectual instinct obliges us to give an objective value to ideas; in this case it mingles with the truths of evidence, and is, in ordinary language, confounded with evidence.

When the intellectual instinct operates upon non-evident objects and inclines us to assent, it is called *common sense.*

Consciousness and the intellectual instinct constitute the other criteria.

The criterion of evidence includes two things: the appearance of ideas, which belongs to consciousness; the objective value, existing or possible, which belongs to the intellectual instinct.

The testimony of the senses also has two parts: sensation as purely subjective, and this pertains to consciousness; and the belief in the objectiveness of sensations, and this pertains to the intellectual instinct.

The testimony of human authority is composed of that of the senses, which place us in relation with our fellow-men, and that of the intellectual instinct, which induces us to believe them.

Not everything is susceptible of proof; but every criterion stands the test of reason. The criterion of consciousness is a primitive fact of our nature; in that of evidence we discover the indispensable condition of the existence of reason itself; in that of the intellectual instinct by which we make our ideas objective, is found a law of our nature likewise indispensable to the very existence of reason; in that of common sense, properly so called, is the instinctive assent to truths, which, when examined, are seen to be perfectly reasonable; in that of the senses, and in that of human authority, we discover the same thing as in the other cases of common sense, which is a means of satisfying the necessities of sensation, intellectual, and moral life.

The criteria do not conflict with, but mutually aid and confirm each other. Neither is reason at war with nature, nor nature with reason; both are necessary to us; both direct us with certainty, although they are both liable to err, since they belong to a limited and very feeble being.

338. The philosophy which considers man only under a single aspect is incomplete, and in danger of becoming false. So far as certainty is concerned, we must bear in mind this last observation: to become excessively exclusive is to place one's self on the brink of error. We may analyze if we will the sources of truth; but we must not lose sight of their connection when examining them separately. To begin by conceiving a system, and then making everything conform to its demands, is to place truth in the bed of Procrustes. Unity is a great good; but we must be satisfied with the measure imposed upon us by nature. We must seek truth by human means, and in proportion to our capacity. The faculties of our soul are subject to certain laws, which we cannot abstract.

One of the most constant laws of our being is the necessity of a simultaneous exercise of our faculties, not only in order to become certain of truth, but even to discover it. Man joins the greatest multiplicity with simplicity: his soul is one, is endowed with various faculties, and united to a body of such variety and complication as to be called with much reason a little world. His faculties are in intimate and mutual relation; they exert a continuous influence upon each other. To isolate them is to mutilate, and sometimes to extinguish them. This remark is important, for it indicates the radical vice of all exclusive philosophy.

If a man have no sensations, his understanding has no materials, nor has it that stimulus, without which it remains dormant. When God united our soul and body, it was that one might aid the other; wherefore he established that admirable correspondence between the impressions of the body and the affections of the soul, which, therefore, needs the body as a medium, as an instrument, whether the action of the body upon it be supposed to be a true action, or only a simple occasion of causality of a higher order.

If a man, having no sensations, were to think, he would only think as a pure spirit; he would not be in relation with the external world, nor would he be a man in the sense in which we use this word. In such a case the body is superfluous, and there is no reason why it should be united to the soul.

If we admit sensations, and abstract reason, man is converted into a brute. He feels, but does not think: he experiences impressions, but does not combine them, for he is incapable of reflecting. Every thing succeeds in him as a series of necessary, isolated phenomena, which indicate nothing, lead to nothing, and are nothing but affections of a particular being who does not comprehend them, nor render to himself an account of them. It is even difficult to say of what kind are his relations with the external world. Arguing from appearances and analogy, it is probable that brutes also make their sensations objective; but ordinarily, their objectiveness differs from ours. Let us take sleep for example. If brutes sleep, and they probably do sleep, as certain appearances seem to indicate, it would not be strange should they not distinguish as we do between waking and sleeping.

This supposes some reflection upon acts, some comparison between the order and constancy of some, and the disorder and inconstancy of others; a reflection which man makes even in infancy, and continues to make all his life without adverting to it. When we awake from a deep sleep, we sometimes remain for several moments in doubt if we are asleep or awake: this doubt alone supposes a comparative reflection of the two states. What do we do in order to resolve this doubt? We examine the place where we are; and the fact that we are abed, in the silence and darkness of night, indicates that the previous vision had no connection with our situation, and therefore that we were asleep. Without this reflection, the sensations of sleeping and waking would be connected, and all confounded in one and the same class.

The instinct conceded to brutes, but denied to men, shows that reason was given to us in order to appreciate sensations.

There are, then, in man no criteria of truth absolutely isolated. They are all in relation with each other, they mutually affirm and complete each other; for we must note that those truths, of which all men are certain, do in some sense rest upon all the criteria.

Sensations instinctively lead us to believe in the existence of an external world; and if this belief be submitted to the examination of reason, it confirms the same truth, resting upon the general ideas of cause and effect. The pure understanding knows certain principles, and assents to them as to necessary truths. The senses, if these principles be submitted to their experience, confirm them as much as their own perfection, or that of the instruments which they use, permit. "All the radii of a circle are equal." This is a necessary truth. The senses perceive no perfect circle, but they see that the more perfect the instrument is with which they construct it, so much more nearly equal are the radii. "There is no change without a cause to produce it." The senses cannot prove the proposition in all its universality, for they are by nature limited to a determinate number of particular cases; but, so far as their experience goes, they discover the order of such a dependence in the succession of phenomena.

The senses mutually aid each other. The sensation of one sense is compared with those of the others, when there arises a doubt as to its correspondence with its object. We seem to hear the whistling of the wind; but our hearing has more than once deceived us: to make sure of the truth we look at trees or other objects. We see a figure, but there is not light sufficient to distinguish it from a shadow, we approach and touch it.

The intellectual and moral faculties also exercise a salutary influence upon each other. Ideas rectify sentiments, and sentiments ideas. The value of the ideas of one order is verified by those of another order; and the same with sentiments. Pity for one suffering punishment inspires the pardon of all criminals; the indignation inspired at seeing the victims of crime, induces to the application of punishment; both sentiments involve something that is good; but the one would engender impunity, the other cruelty; it is to temper them that the ideas of justice exist. But this justice in its turn might pronounce excessively absolute sentences; justice is one, and the circumstances of peoples very different. Justice only considers the culpability, and consequently pronounces such sentences. A sentence may not be proper; for here come in other moral ideas of a distinct order, the amendment of the guilty joined with reparation made to the injured party; ideas also of public convenience which are not repugnant to sound morals, and which may direct their application.

Complete truth, like perfect good, exists only with harmony. This is a necessary law, and to it man is subject. Since we do not intuitively see the infinite truth in which all truths are one, and all good is one; and as we are in relation with a world of finite, and consequently multiple beings, we need different powers to place us in contact, so to speak, with this variety of truths and finite goods; but as they, in their turn, spring from *one* same principle, and are directed to *one* same end, they are submitted to harmony, which is the unity of multiplicity.

339. With these doctrines we believe philosophy without skepticism to be possible. Examination is not excluded; on the contrary, it is extended and completed. This method has another advantage; it does not make philosophy extravagant, and philosophers exceptional. Philosophy cannot

be so generalized as to become popular; human nature is opposed to this; but there is not on the other hand any necessity of condemning it to a misanthropic isolation by force of extravagant professions. In such a case philosophy degenerates into philosophism. Exposition of facts, conscientious examination, clear language; such we conceive sound philosophy to be. This does not require it to cease to be profound, unless by profoundness be meant darkness. The rays of the sun light up the remotest depths of space.

340. I am aware that some philosophers of our age think otherwise, that they deem it necessary, when they examine the fundamental questions of philosophy, to shake the foundations of the world; and yet I have never been able to persuade myself that it was necessary to destroy in order to examine, or that in order to become philosophers we ought to become madmen. We may render the unreasonableness and extravagance of these masters of humanity sensible by an allegory, although the simplicity of my language may somewhat mortify their philosophical profoundness. The reader needs some solace and rest, now that he has followed me through such abstruse treatises, which all the power of the writer does not suffice to illustrate, and still less to render attractive.

A noble, rich, and numerous family preserves in magnificent archives the records of its nobility, alliances, and possessions. Some of these documents are hardly legible, either on account of the handwriting, their great antiquity, or the wear and tear of years. There is also a suspicion that many of these documents are apocryphal; although it is certain that many must be authentic, since the nobility and other rights of the family, so universally recognized, must be founded on some of them, and it is known that no other exists. Such is the state of things. Some curious person enters the archives, and casting a glance upon the shelves, recesses, and drawers, says: "This is all confusion; to distinguish what is authentic from the apocryphal, and put all in good order, we must light a fire at the four corners of the archives, and then examine the ashes."

What shall we think of such a proceeding? This curious person is the philosopher who, to distinguish the true and the false in our cognitions, begins by denying all truth, all certainty, all reason.

We may be told that there is no question of denying, but of doubting; but whoever doubts all truth, destroys it; whoever doubts all certainty denies it; whoever doubts all reason annihilates it. Prudence and common sense in small things are based upon the same principles as wisdom in great things. Let us go on with our allegory, and see what common sense would indicate ought to be done in this case.

To take an inventory of whatever now exists, without forgetting any thing, however contemptible it may appear; to make such temporary classifications as are deemed most proper to facilitate the examination, reserving the final classification to the close; to note carefully dates, characters, references, and thus to distinguish priority and posteriority; to see if there may be found some primitive documents, referring to others anterior, which certify the origin of the family; to establish clear rules for the distinguishing that which is primitive from what is only secondary; and not to insist on referring all documents to one alone, exacting a unity which, perhaps, they have not; for it may have happened that there were several primitive and mutually independent documents. It would even be advisable in distinguishing the authentic from the apocryphal not to burn any thing, for the apocryphal sometimes aids in the interpretation of what is authentic, and it may be desirable to ascertain who were the falsifiers, and what their motives. Moreover, who knows but what he judges a document to be apocryphal, which seems to him so to be solely because he does not understand it? Care, then, is to be taken to make a due separation, and if the apocryphal is of no use in establishing titles, or in defending them, it may serve for the history of the archives, which is no trifling reason for distinguishing the apocryphal from the authentic.

The human mind does not examine itself until well developed; then, at the first glance, it sees in itself a connection of sensations, ideas, judgments, and affections of a thousand kinds, the whole interwoven in an inextricable manner. To increase the complication, it is not alone, but in intimate relation with its like, in mutual communication of sensations, ideas, and sentiments; and all in their turn in contact with, and under the influence of, dissimilar beings of amazing variety, the union of which forms the universe. Shall it begin by throwing it all down? Shall it reduce all to ashes, and hope to rise like the phenix from the pyre? Shall it arbitrarily invent a fact, a principle, and say: "I must have a resting-point, I will take this, and upon it I will found science!" Shall we, before examining, before analyzing, say: "all this is one; there is nothing if there be not absolute unity; in it I place myself, and all that I do not see from my point of view I reject?" No! what we have to do, is first to ascertain what is in our mind, and then to examine, classify it, and give to it its true value; not commence by mad and impotent efforts against nature, but to lend an attentive ear to her inspirations.

There is no philosophy without a philosopher; no reason without a rational being; the existence of the subject is then a necessary supposition. No reason is possible if the contradiction of being and not-being be possible; all reason, then, supposes the principle of contradiction to be true. When we examine reason it is reason that examines; it needs rules, light; all examination, then, supposes this light, the evidence and the legitimacy of its criterion. Man does not make himself, he finds himself already made; it is not he who imposes the conditions of his being; he finds them already imposed. These conditions are the laws of his being, and why contend against them? "Besides factitious prejudices," says Schelling, "man has others *primordial*, placed in him not by education, but by *nature herself*, which in *all* men hold the place of principles of cognition, and are a *shoal* to the free-thinker." For my own part I do not seek to be more than *all* men; if I cannot be a philosopher without ceasing to be a man, I renounce philosophy and adhere to humanity.

BOOK SECOND
ON SENSATION

CHAPTER I
SENSATION IN ITSELF

1. Sensation considered in itself is simply an internal affection; but it is almost always accompanied by a judgment. This judgment may be more or less explicit and more or less noticed by the subject of the sensation.

Suppose I see two architectural ornaments at a proper distance, and I discover no difference between them. In this sensation there are two things to be considered.

I. The internal affection which we call *seeing*. On this point all doubt is impossible. Whether I am asleep or awake, raving or in my sober senses, whether the ornaments are alike or unlike, whether, in fine, they exist or not, there still exists in my soul the representation which I call *seeing the ornaments*.

II. I also at the same time form a judgment that, besides the internal affection which I experience, the ornaments exist, that they are in relief, and that they are before my eyes. In this judgment I may be deceived; for I may be asleep or in a delirium; it may be that the ornaments are behind me, and that I only see their reflection in a mirror; it may be that what I see is only a paper placed in such a manner behind a glass, as to make upon the retina of my eyes the same impression as the ornaments would if they were really present; or, finally, it may all be the work of a skilful painter who has given this illusory appearance to his canvas.

From this we see that, admitting the existence of the internal fact of sensation, it is possible:

I. That there is no external object.

II. That the objects exists, but not in the position supposed.

III. That the object is not the architectural ornaments.

IV. That both are plane surfaces; or, that one is in relief, and the other a plane.

This brings us to the evident conclusion that mere sensation has no necessary relation to an external object; for it not only can, but it not unfrequently does, exist without any such object.

This correspondence of the internal to the external belongs to the judgment which accompanies sensation, not to sensation itself.

If brutes refer their sensations to objects, as they probably do, instinct must supply in them the want of judgment, as in the child who has not acquired the use of the intellectual faculties.

Sensation, therefore, in itself considered, affirms nothing. It is a mere affection of our being, an effect produced in our soul, and does not determine whether there is any action of an external object upon our senses, nor whether the object is what it seems to be.

2. Let us imagine an animal reduced to the one sense of touch, and that not developed as in us, but confined to a few rude impressions like those of heat and cold, warmth and dryness; and let us compare it with human sensibility. What an immense distance between the two! Sensibility in such an animal borders on insensibility, whilst in man it approaches intelligence, the representations of his senses are so varied and so extended as to produce within him a whole world, and they might produce infinite others. Man is at the highest round of the ladder, so far as our observation goes, but who can tell how much higher it may be possible to go?

3. However developed and perfected we suppose sensibility, it falls far short of intelligence, from which it must ever remain separated, as from a faculty of a different order. Though we suppose the sensitive faculties capable of indefinite perfectibility, they can never reach the sphere of intelligence, properly so called. This perfectibility would lie in a different order, eternally distinct from that of intellectual beings. If we suppose a color infinitely perfected, it will never become a sound, a sound a taste, a taste a sound, nor a sound a color; because perfectibility is confined to its own order. Therefore, however it may be perfected, sensibility can never become intelligence.

This observation will serve to guard against one of the most fatal errors of our age, which consists in regarding the universe as the result of a mysterious force, which, developing itself by a continual movement, at once spontaneous and necessary, goes on giving birth to beings and elevating species by a perpetual transformation. Thus the greater perfection of the vegetable organization would produce the animal faculties; these being perfected would become sensitive, and in measure as they progressed in the order of sensation they would approach the realm of intelligence, and would finally attain it. There is not a little analogy between this system and that which makes thought a transformed sensation; it effaces the dividing line between intelligent and non-intelligent beings; the sensations of an oyster may, according to it, be so perfected as to be converted into an intelligence superior to that of Bossuet or of Leibnitz; and the development of the faculties of the man-statue would be an emblem of the development of the universe.

4. It may have been already remarked that we are now speaking of the sensitive faculty in itself considered, abstracting from its relations to external objects; and that we therefore comprehend in the word *sensation*, all affections of the senses, whether actually produced, recollected, or imagined; that is, all affections in all degrees from the first direct consciousness of them, or when they are presented to the being which experiences them, until they reach the limit where intelligence, strictly so called, commences.

It is impossible here to draw the dividing line between the sensible and the intelligible; this requires profound and extensive studies upon sensations compared with ideas, which does not belong to this place: but it will be well to have pointed out the existence of this line, in order to avoid confusion in a most subtle matter, in which every error is attended with the most serious consequences.

5. In what does sensation consist? What is its internal nature? We only know that it is a modification of our being, and that we cannot explain it. No words suffice to convey an idea of a sensation to one who has never experienced it. The man born blind may listen to all that philosophers have said and written on light and colors, but can never imagine what light and colors are.

Experience is the only teacher here; and thus, if we suppose a man's senses to be changed so that green appears to him purple, and purple green, notwithstanding his constant communication with other men, he will never be freed from his error, and he will never suspect that during his whole life he has made use of the words green and purple in a different sense from other men.

6. Analogy and nature incline us to believe that brutes are not mere machines, but that they also have sensations. The vast scale over which irrational beings are distributed, shows that the faculty of feeling is spread over the universe in different degrees, and with a wonderful profusion.

Our experience is confined to the globe in which we live; but are the limits of sensitive life the same as those of our experience? Even on this globe our observation is confined to what the imperfection of our senses, and the instruments which we use, permit; but how far is the chain of life prolonged? Where is its term? Is there not some participation of this mysterious faculty in those beings which we hold to be inanimate? Is the universe, as Leibnitz pretends, composed of a collection of monads endowed with a certain perception? This is indeed an unfounded hypothesis; but since our means of observation are so limited, we should be cautious how we assign boundaries to the realm of life.

7. We ordinarily speak of the faculty of sensation as of something belonging to a very inferior order; so it is, in fact, if compared with intellectual faculties; but this does not prevent it, in itself considered, from being a wonderful phenomenon, of a nature to astonish and confound all who meditate upon it.

Sensation! With this word alone we pass an immense gap in the scale of beings. What is the non-sensible compared with the sensible? The insensible is, but experiences not that it is; there is nothing in it but itself: the sensible experiences that it is; and there is in it something besides itself, all that it feels, all that is represented in it. The insensible, although surrounded with beings, is in complete isolation,—in solitude; the sensible, although alone, may be in a world of infinitely varied representations.

8. The idea of the *me* is in some sense applicable to every sensitive being; for sensation is inconceivable without a *permanent* being, which experiences what is *transitory*; that is, without a being which is *one* in the midst of *multiplicity*. Every sensible being, were it capable of reflection, might, in its own way, say *I*; for it is true of all of them that it is *one same* being that experiences the *variety* of sensations. Without this bond, this unity, there is no *one* sensible being, but a *succession* of sensations as unconnected phenomena of the whole.

9. There is no sensation without direct consciousness; for, as this is nothing but the very presence of the phenomenon to the being experiencing it, it would be contradictory to say that it feels without consciousness. A sensation experienced, is a sensation present; a sensation not present, that is, not experienced, is inconceivable, is an absurdity.[35]

10. Every sensation involves presence, or direct consciousness, but not representation. I think this distinction important. The sensations of smell, taste, and hearing, are not representative; they remain in themselves, and in their object. The being experiencing them might believe himself enclosed in himself, in an absolute solitude, with no relation to other beings; but touch, and, above all, sight, are by their nature representative; they involve relation to objects; and they imply relation to other beings, not as to mere *causes* of the internal affection, but as the *originals* represented in the sensation.

The class of sensible beings endowed with the faculty of representation seems to be of an order very superior to the others; these beings not only have consciousness, but also a mysterious power whereby they see within themselves an entire world.

11. What is the most perfect degree of sensitive life? What the most imperfect? These questions we cannot answer, for we cannot judge of these things otherwise than by experience and analogy. But viewing the immensity of the scale, experience shows us we may infer that nature is far richer than we imagine. Let us not disturb its profound secrets, but be content to suspect that they exist.

CHAPTER II
MATTER IS INCAPABLE OF SENSATION

12. The phenomenon of sensibility reveals to us the existence of an order of beings distinct from matter. However perfect we may suppose material organization, it cannot rise to sensation; matter is wholly incapable of sensation; and the absurd system of materialism can neither explain the phenomena of intelligence, nor even of sensation.

It is of little consequence to us that we do not know the intrinsical nature of sensitive being, or of matter; it is enough to know their essential properties, in order to infer with certainty that they belong to distinct orders. It is not true that the principal idea of the essence of things is necessary, in order to demonstrate their absolute contradiction; thousands of times we consider two geometrical figures whose essential property we do not know; yet not, therefore, do we fail to see that they are different, and that one cannot possibly be the other.

Matter, whatever opinion may be entertained of its essential property, is necessarily a composite being; matter without parts, is not matter. A composite being, although called *one*, inasmuch as its parts are united together, and conspire to the same end, is always a collection of many beings; for the parts though united are still distinct If sensation could be predicated of a composite being, the sensitive would not be a single being, but a collection of beings; but sensation essentially belongs to a being which is *one*, and if divided is destroyed; therefore, no composite being, however well organized, is capable of sensation.

If we observe what takes place in us, and reason from analogy, to other sensitive beings, we shall discover amid the variety of sensations a single being which perceives them; it is one and the same being that hears, sees, touches, smells, and tastes; that remembers sensations after they have disappeared; that seeks them when agreeable, and avoids them when unpleasant, enjoys the former and suffers in the latter. All this enters into the idea of sensitive being; if brutes had not this *common* subject of all sensations; were they not *one* in the midst of multiplicity, *identical* in diversity, and *permanent* under succession, they would not be sensitive beings, such as we conceive them to be; they would have no sensation, properly so called; for there is no sensation, in the sense in which we here understand it, without a being affected by it, a being which perceives it.

If we imagine a flow and ebb of sensations without any connection, without a constant being to experience them, the result will not be a sensitive being, but a collection of phenomena, each one of which by itself alone offers the same difficulty as all united, the necessity of a being to experience it.

13. Let us take a being composed of two parts, A and B, and see if it can acquire, for instance, the sensation of sound. If both parts perceive, either both perceive the whole sound, or each a portion of it. If both perceive it entire, one of them is superfluous, for we are only seeking to explain the realization of the phenomenon, which would thus be verified in one alone. If each part hear the sound, not entire, but only a portion of it, we shall have a divided sound; and what is the division of a sound?

But even such an imaginary division does not serve to explain the phenomenon; for the part of the sound perceived by A will not be perceived by B; never, therefore, will there result a complete sensation.

Shall we suppose A and B to be in relation, and to mutually communicate their corresponding parts? But then A perceives all its own part and also what B communicates to it: of what use, then, is B, if A perceives the whole? Why not place the whole primitive sensation in A? We here see that such a communication is an absurd hypothesis, since it would make a successive and mutual communication of the parts, and a perception by each of its own part, and also of that transmitted to it by the others, indispensable to the formation of an entire sensation. Thus we should have not one sensation only, but as many as there are parts; not one sensitive being only, but as many such beings as there are parts.

This hypothesis of communication of the parts paves the way for our system, since it recognizes the necessity of unity to constitute sensation. Why do the parts mutually communicate what they have respectively perceived? Because an entire sensation could not otherwise be formed, and so each part must receive what it has not of itself. The object of this is, that each one may perceive the whole; the sensation, therefore, must be wholly in only one subject; therefore, at the very time that unity is denied, it is acknowledged to be necessary.

14. These parts, A and B, either are simple or they are not; if they are simple, why persist in advocating materialism, when we must finally return to simple beings? It is a manifest contradiction to say that sensation is an effect of organization, and yet place it in a simple being, for the simple cannot be organized; there is no organization where there are no parts organized.

If we admit the simple being, and place the sensation in it, the organization will then be, if you choose, a medium, a conduit, an indispensable condition to the realization of the phenomenon; then not it, but the simple being will be the subject. If these parts are not simple, they are composed of others; and of these we may argue the same as of the former; for we must come to simple beings, or else proceed to infinity. If we admit such a process, the sensible being will not be one, but infinite; the difficulties encountered with only two parts, A and B, will be multiplied even to infinity, and so the sensible being will be not one but infinite, and every sensation infinite.

15. Here we find a very serious difficulty. If matter be incapable of perceiving, the soul of brutes is not material; if immaterial, it is a spirit, which cannot be admitted.

Let us determine well the meaning of the words, and this difficulty will vanish. An immaterial being is not the same as a spirit; every spirit is immaterial, but not every thing immaterial is a spirit. *Immaterial* denotes negation of matter; spirit implies more than this; for we understand by it a simple being endowed with understanding and free-will. The soul of brutes is then immaterial, but not a spirit.

Some one may say, that what is not body is spirit, that between these two classes of beings there is no medium. But why? Whence such certainty? If it be said that there is no medium between the material and the immaterial, this is true; for there is, in truth, no medium between yes and no; every thing either is or is not; but there enters into the idea of spirit much more than the simple negation of matter; there is the idea of an active, intelligent, and free principle.

16. It may then be asked: wherein consists the nature of the soul of brutes? And we ask, wherein consists the nature of the greater part of the things which we perceive? Do we know this nature in itself or in its acts? Do we see our own soul intuitively? Or do we, perchance, know it by the acts of which we are conscious? If so, we know in like manner the sensitive soul by its acts, that is, by perception of the senses; we know that it is not matter, for matter is incapable of sensation; and the reasons which show us that our soul is a simple being, an active principle endowed with understanding and free-will enable us to say that the soul of brutes is a simple being endowed with the faculty of feeling, and with instincts and appetites of the sensible order.

We know not what this active principle in itself considered is, but its acts show it to be a force superior to bodies, one of the many activities which are the life of nature. We encounter this living force in a portion of matter admirably organized; the end of this organization is the harmonious exercise of the faculties of that living being which we call animal. Not to know what this force in itself is, does not prevent us from affirming its existence, for phenomena reveal it to us in an indisputable manner.

17. What, then, will be the fate of these souls, or living forces, if the organization which gives them life be destroyed? Will they be reduced to non-existence, since, not being composed of parts, they cannot be decomposed? Will they continue to exist until their turn shall come to preside over a new organization? It will be well to separate these various questions, and examine them apart.

If the soul of brutes be not composed of parts, it cannot perish by disorganization; what has no organizable parts is not organized, and what is not organized cannot be disorganized. Hence we infer that the soul of brutes cannot perish by corruption, properly so called; for no being not composed of matter can. We see not what difficulty can arise from this view; but the question is only resolved in its negative part, for thus far we know only that the soul of brutes cannot die, or be corrupted by decomposition; we must know what is done with it. Is it annihilated? Does it continue to exist? And if so, in what way? These are different questions.

First of all we must observe, that we have here only conjectures, and these rather as to the possibility than as to the reality. Philosophy may indeed enable us to see what may be, but not what is, for we can know the reality only by experience, which in the present case we cannot have. When sound philosophy, examining this point, is asked what is, its best reply is, that it knows not; if it is asked what may be, it enters into an argumentation founded on general principles, and more especially upon analogy.

18. It is usually said that nothing is annihilated; but this needs some explanation. What is the meaning of *annihilation?* To cease to be, so that nothing, which before was, remains. If a body be disorganized, it ceases to be as an organized body; but the matter remains, and there is no annihilation. Is it true that nothing is annihilated? Some say we must distinguish between substances and accidents; for, as these latter are a kind of incomplete beings, there is no reason why they should not cease to exist, and nothing of them remain; but in this disappearance there is no annihilation, strictly so called; thus we see things continually transformed, and undergoing a succession of accidents which cease to exist whenever the thing ceases to be modified by them. As to substances, there would indeed be true annihilation should they cease to exist, but this they do not, because no substance is annihilated. Thus some think; we know not how true this system may be, for we know not upon what solid foundation it rests. If a substance be destined to an

end, why may it not be annihilated when this end no longer exists? A created being incessantly needs the conservatory action of the Creator, for which reason conservation is said to be a continued creation; when, then, the end to which the created substance was destined ceases, why may it not be annihilated? We see nothing in its being annihilated repugnant to the wisdom or goodness of God. The artificer abandons a tool no longer serviceable; this, in God, would be equivalent to the withdrawal of his conservatory act, and in the creature, to the reduction to non-existence. If it be not repugnant to the wisdom and goodness of God for an organized being to be disorganized, or cease to exist as an organized being, why may he not allow a substance which has accomplished the object for which it was created to cease to exist? From this we infer that it would not be against sound philosophy to maintain that the souls of brutes are reduced to non-existence.

19. But supposing there is no question of annihilation, is there any reason against their continuing to exist? If there be, we know not what it is.

We know not of what use they would be; but we may conjecture that absorbed anew into the bosom of nature they would not be useless. Neither do we know the use of many other beings, and yet we cannot therefore deny their existence, or doubt their utility. Who says that the vital principle residing in brutes can have no object if the organization which it animates be destroyed? Does the destruction of a plant involve, perchance, the extinction of all the vital principles residing in it? Do these principles, by not operating upon the organized being just destroyed, therefore cease to be of any use in the wonderful laboratory of nature? Who will say that a vital principle cannot be useful if it does not act upon an object within our observation? Who will assert that vital principles do not in the recesses of nature act in many and different ways, and that the effects of their activity are not presented very differently according to circumstances, yet always in conformity to laws established by infinite wisdom? Do not the magnificent profusion of radical materials, the gems without number which we everywhere discover, the immense amount of matter susceptible of transformation and assimilation by the living being, the mysteries of generation in the animal and vegetable kingdoms, all indicate to us that there are scattered over the universe an infinite number of vital principles, which exercise their activity in very different ways, and over a scale of astonishing extent? Who shall assure us that the same vital principle may not present very diverse phenomena, according to the conditions which determine its action? Does not the same principle reside in the acorn, as in the gnarled old oak that for ages has defied the fury of the tempest? Did experience not show it to be so, who would ever have suspected the vital principle of a shapeless and filthy caterpillar to be the same as that of a beautiful butterfly? It is not then contrary either to reason or to experience to suppose the soul of brutes, the vital principle residing in them, to continue after the organization of the body is destroyed, and, absorbed anew in the treasures of nature, to be there preserved, not as a useless thing, but in the exercise of its faculties in different ways, according to the conditions to which it is subjected.(29)

CHAPTER III
SLEEP AND WAKING

20. The fact of sensation is connected with many others, and from this connection results a great part of our knowledge. It has been said in a tone of great confidence, that it was not possible to demonstrate by sensations the existence of bodies; for as sensations are something purely internal, they cannot enable us to infer the existence of any thing external, and there is no reason for not regarding all our sensations as a collection of individual phenomena, inclosed in our soul. At first view it seems impossible to solve the difficulty; nevertheless, if we examine it thoroughly, we shall see that too great importance has been attached to it.

21. The first objection ordinarily made to the testimony of the senses, is the difficulty of distinguishing with certainty between the state of sleep and that of waking. We receive when asleep impressions similar to those we receive when awake: how shall we know that the illusion is not perpetual? Lamennais, with characteristic exaggeration, says: "He who shall show that all life is not a sleep, an indefinable chimera, will do more than all philosophers have thus far been able to do."

There are here, no doubt, grave difficulties; but we cannot persuade ourselves that they are insolvable. First of all we shall examine if sleep and waking be different, not only in the eyes of common sense, but also in those of reason. Lamennais pretends that only at the tribunal of common consent can a satisfactory and definitive sentence be obtained: we are convinced that very close reasoning can arrive at the same result to which consciousness, common sense, common consent, or, in other words, the testimony of our own being and that of our fellow mortals, conjointly conduce.

22. Man finds in himself a perfectly satisfactory certainty of the difference between sleep and waking: we need no testimony of others to know that we are awake.

The difference between these states must not be solely sought in the clearness and vividness of sensations, and the certainty which they generate. Undoubtedly images are sometimes presented to us in sleep with as much clearness as if we were awake, and our certainty for the instant is complete.

Who has not in sleep experienced great joy, or terrible anguish? Sometimes, but very rarely, we have, when we awake, the reminiscence of having in the very act of sleep doubted if we were asleep; but this seldom happens, and it is in general true, that even our dreams are not accompanied by this twilight of reflex reason which warns us of our state and of the illusion that we are under. Ordinarily, while we dream, we have no thought that we are asleep, and we embrace a friend with the same effusion of tenderness, or weep disconsolately over his tomb, with the same affections as we should were all real.

23. The difference is not in momentary uncertainty, for we usually have, on the contrary, complete certainty. Whence, then, is this? How does reason explain it? How does philosophy come to the support of consciousness and common sense? This is the matter we now purpose to examine.

If we abstract sensations having or not having relation to external objects, and also the sufficiency of their testimony in any particular case, and consider them solely as phenomena of our soul, we shall find two orders of facts completely distinguished by marked characters, sleep and waking. In our soul these two orders are totally distinct; even in the system of the idealist this distinction must be recognized.

If we reflect upon what we have experienced since first we had consciousness of what passes within us, we shall observe in our being, two classes of phenomena. Periodically and constantly we experience two series of sensations; some more or less clear, more or less vivid, are confined simply to their object, without the concurrence of many of our faculties, and above all, without reflection upon them; others are always clear, always vivid, accompanied by acts of all our faculties, our reflection upon them, and their difference from those that went before, is entirely subject to our free will in all that is relative; we vary and modify them in a thousand different ways, or suppress and reproduce them.

I see the paper upon which I write; I reflect upon this sight; I abandon and resume it at pleasure; and if I choose, I connect this sensation with others, with a thousand thoughts or different caprices. What takes place in this act, always has happened to me, and always will, whenever that same series of phenomena is produced in me while awake. But if I dream that I write, although it happen not, as it ordinarily does, that I cannot hold my pen exactly right, nor see clearly, but only confusedly, I neither feel the simultaneous exercise of all my faculties, nor reflect upon my present state; I do not have that full consciousness of what I am doing, that clear and strong light which is scattered over all my waking actions and their objects. When awake I think upon what I have done, what I am doing, what I shall do; I recollect my dreams and call them illusions, pronounce them unconnected and extravagant appearances, and compare them with the order and connection of phenomena offered to me while awake. Nothing of this kind takes place in dreams; I may, perhaps, have a clear, lively sensation but it is independent of my will, it is an isolated impression, the use of only one faculty without the aid of the others, without fixed and constant comparisons, such as I make when awake; and above all, this phenomenon quickly vanishes, and I either fall into a state of unconsciousness of my being, or enter another state in which the same series of phenomena as before is reproduced; they are clear, lucid, connected; they stand the test of reason, which compares them with each other, and with anterior phenomena. Apart, then, from all idea of the external world, and even of all being outside of ourselves, we are certain of the distinction between the two orders of phenomena, those of sleep and those of waking.

Therefore, they who attack the certainty of our cognitions because of the difficulty of distinguishing between these states, make use of a very weak argument, and rely upon a fact entirely false. So far am I from believing it impossible to distinguish philosophically between sleep and waking, that I deem the difference between these two states one of the clearest and most certain facts of our nature.

Having established this truth, and supposing no one to doubt that the sensations experienced in sleep are not produced by external objects, and that, consequently, they cannot be a means of acquiring truth, I pass to another more difficult and important question.

CHAPTER IV
RELATION OF SENSATIONS TO AN EXTERNAL WORLD

24. Have our sensations any relation to external objects, or are they merely phenomena of our nature? Can we infer the existence of an external world from the existence of that internal world resulting from the union of the scenes presented by sensations?

This question is theoretical, not practical, and depends solely on the force of reasoning, not on the voice of nature,—a voice stronger than all argument, and irresistible. To whatever result the philosophical examination of the relations of the ideal and the real worlds may lead, we must submit to that necessity of our nature which makes us believe in the existence of such relations. The great majority of mankind never have thought, and probably never will think of making such an examination; and yet they have no shadow of doubt that there exists a real world, distinct from us, but in incessant communication with us. Nature precedes philosophy.

We have no wish to show reason to be unable to vindicate the legitimacy of the inference whereby the real is deduced from the ideal, the existence of the external world from that of the internal; we would only point out a landmark to philosophy, which, if it does not illustrate it, may at least inspire it with sobriety in investigating, and with mistrust in its results. Indeed we cannot but see that that science must be erroneous which is opposed to a necessity, and contradicts an evident fact: it merits not to be called philosophy, if it struggles with a law to which all humanity, not even excepting the philosopher who presumes to protest against it, is inevitably subject. All that can be said against this law, may be as specious as you please, but it will only be a vain cavil, a cavil which, if unanswerable by our weak understanding, nature herself will resist until we shall in another life see the depths of these secrets, and how those links are joined whose points of contact reason cannot detect, although nature feels their irresistible union at every moment of her existence.

25. That sensations are something more than mere phenomena of our soul, that they are effects of a cause distinct from ourselves, is seen by

comparing them with each other. We refer some to an external object; others we do not: these two orders of phenomena present very different characters.

I now have within me the representation of the country where I was born and spent my earliest years. I see clearly a vast plain with its fields and prairies, its little hills, now forming only isolated hillocks, now stretching in various directions, sinking to the level of the plain, or gradually rising until incorporated with the mountains, the lofty chain of which surrounds all the plain, and makes it a great amphitheatre, with no outlet except on the south, and here and there a chasm, seemingly torn in the mighty wall reared by nature. All this is very perfectly represented within me, although more than a hundred leagues distant, and this whenever, and as long as I choose. The same spectacle may, perhaps, be offered to me without the concurrence of my will, but I am always free to distract myself from it; I may drop the curtain upon this scene, or raise it anew at my pleasure.

What happens in this case is confirmed by many others; and thus I internally experience a series of phenomena representative of external objects, but am under no necessity to submit to them, for I can abandon or resume them by simple acts of my free will.

But, at the same time, I feel within myself another class of phenomena which are not dependent upon my will, and which I cannot abandon and resume at pleasure; they are subject to certain conditions which I cannot dispense with under pain of not attaining my purpose.

I now experience that a painting is represented to me; or, in ordinary language, I see a painting before me. Let us suppose this to be a purely internal phenomenon, and observe the conditions of its existence, abstracting, however, all external reality, that of my own body included, and that, also, of the organs whereby the sensation is, or seems to be, transmitted to me.

Now I experience the sensation; now I do not. What has intervened? The sensation of a motion that has produced another sensation of sight, and has destroyed the first; or, passing from ideal to real language, I have placed my hand between my eyes and the object. But why can I not during the last, reproduce the first sensation? We see clearly that if external objects do exist, and my sensations are produced by them, my sensations must be subject to the conditions which they impose upon them; but if they are only internal phenomena, there is no way of explaining them. This is only the more incomprehensible as we do not find in the sensations, which we consider as mere phenomena with no immediate relation to an external object, a close dependence of some upon others, but rather, on the contrary, great discordance.

26. Purely internal phenomena, those which we regard as truly such, are, so far as their existence and their modifications are concerned, greatly dependent upon the will. I produce in my imagination, whenever I please, a scene representing the Column of the Place Vendôme at Paris, and I suppress it at my pleasure. The same occurs with respect to all other objects which I recollect to have seen; their presence within me depends upon my will. It is true that sometimes objects which we do not wish are represented to us, and that some effort is necessary to make them disappear. If we see a dying person, his countenance pale and damp with sweat, his wandering eyes, his clenched hands, his distorted mouth and painful breathing, interrupted with piteous groans, remain long after stamped upon our imagination: this sad spectacle will often recur to us in spite of ourselves; but it is very certain that if we go into some complicated calculation, or engage in the solution of some difficult problem, we shall succeed in making it disappear. We see by this, that even in exceptional cases, so long as we are of sane mind, our will always exerts a great influence over purely internal phenomena.

It is otherwise with those which have immediate relation to external objects. We cannot, when in presence of the dying person, avoid seeing and hearing him. If these sensations be only a purely internal phenomenon, this phenomenon is of a very different order from that of the other. The one is wholly independent of our will, not so the other.

Purely internal phenomena have a very different mutual relation from that of external phenomena. The will exerts a great influence upon the former, but not upon the latter. The former also are offered either by a mere act of the will, or by themselves, in isolation, and need no connection with other preceding phenomena. I write at Madrid, and all at once I find myself on the banks of the Thames, with its countless fleet of ships and steamers. But this did not require me to pass through the series of phenomena which represent what are called France and Spain. I can represent the Thames to myself immediately, after a thousand sensations, neither connected among themselves, nor with it; but if I would produce in myself the phenomenon called *seeing*, I must pass through the whole series of phenomena consequent upon a voyage; and this not in any way I may fancy, but so as to feel really and truly all the accompanying pleasures and inconveniences; I must make a true resolution to depart, and arrive punctually at such an hour, at the risk of missing the sensation called, *seeing the stage*, and another, which I call, seeing myself started; in fine, all the disagreeable sensations arising from such a mischance.

When I would represent this series of internal phenomena, or, in common language, adventures of travel, only internally, I dispose all at my pleasure; I stop, or travel faster; I take steps of a hundred leagues, and pass immediately from one point to another, and I experience none of those inconveniences which render the reality fatiguing. I am in a world where I am master. I command, and the coach is ready, the driver on his box, the postilion in his saddle; and I fly as borne on the wings of the wind. Beautiful landscapes, barren lands, gigantic mountains, and plains whose boundaries join the heavens, all pass before my eyes with wonderful rapidity. Tired of the land, I embark upon the lofty deep; I see the angry waves, and hear, amid their roaring and dashing against the ship, the voice of the captain giving his orders. I see the sailors work the ship; I speak with the passengers, and roam through the cabins; and yet perceive no offensive smell, and neither feel the qualms of sea-sickness, nor observe them in others.

27. If purely internal sensations, especially when they proceed from external sensations, be indeed mutually connected, their connection is not such that it may not be modified in a thousand ways. When we think of the Obelisk of the Place de la Concorde, its fountains and statues, are very naturally presented to us; so, also, are the Palace of the Tuileries, and that of the Chamber of Deputies, the Madeleine, and the Champs-Elysées; but we can, by an act of the will, change the scene; and if we choose we may transfer the Obelisk to the Place du Carrousel, and admire the effect it produces there, until, satisfied with the operation, we restore it to its granite base, or think no more of it.

But with sight, or the external phenomenon, we should in vain strive to perform such manœuvres; everything keeps its place, or, at least, seems to; and the sensations are bound together with bands of iron. One comes after the other, and we cannot pass by any. The mere observation, then, of what passes within us reveals the existence of two wholly distinct orders of phenomena: in the one, everything, or almost everything, depends upon our will; in the other, nothing. In the one, the phenomena have certain mutual relations, very variable, however, and to a great extent subject to our fancy; in the other, they are dependent upon each other, and are produced only under certain conditions. We cannot see, if we do not open the blinds so as to allow the light to enter. Here the phenomena of blinds and sight are necessarily connected; but they are not always so; for we may open them at night, and yet not see; and then we require another auxiliary phenomenon, which is, artificial light. We cannot, if we would, change this law of dependence.

28. What does all this show? Does it not show that the phenomena not dependent upon our will, but subject both as to their existence and accidents to laws which we cannot change, are produced by beings distinct

from ourselves? They are not ourselves, for we often exist without them; they are not caused by our will, for they often occur without its concurrence, often also against it; they are not produced one by the other in the purely internal order, for it very frequently happens that a phenomenon which has a thousand times followed another suddenly ceases, however often the former be reproduced. This leads us to examine an hypothesis which will greatly confirm the doctrine we have laid down.

CHAPTER V
AN IDEALIST HYPOTHESIS

29. The system of the Idealists cannot stand without supposing the connection and dependence which we refer to external objects, to exist only within us, and the causality which we attribute to external objects, to belong solely to our own acts.

I pull a rope in my chamber, and a bell never fails to ring; or in idealist language, the sensation formed from that union of sensations into which enters what we call the *rope and pulling it*, produces or involves that other, which we call *ringing a bell*. Either from habit or some hidden law, that relation of two phenomena will exist, the never interrupted succession of which causes the illusion in us, whereby we transfer to the real order, what is purely imaginary. This is the most irrational explanation possible, and a few observations will show it to be futile.

Today, we pull the rope, and strangely enough, no bell rings: but why not? The causing phenomenon exists; for undoubtedly there passes within us the act called pulling the rope, and yet we pull and pull again, and the bell does not ring. Who has changed the succession of phenomena? Why does not the phenomenon which a little while ago produced another, not produce it now? Nothing new has happened within us, we experience the first phenomenon just as clearly and vividly as before; why, then, is not the second presented? Why is it that formerly we experienced the second whenever we wished, by only exciting the first, and now we cannot? We make the act of our will just as efficaciously as before; who, then, has rendered our will impotent?

Hence we infer: first, that the second phenomenon does not depend upon the first, considered only as a purely internal fact, for this now exists precisely as it did before, and yet produces not the same phenomenon; secondly, that it does not depend upon the act of our will; for this is now as firm and strong as before, and yet produces nothing. We cannot, however, doubt that there is some connection between the two phenomena, for we have innumerable times seen one follow the other, and this cannot be explained by mere chance. Since then, one does not cause the other in the internal order, they must have some dependence in the external order; in other words, still keeping in view the case under examination, although the cause which produced the first phenomenon continues to exist, its connection with that which produced the other phenomenon must be interrupted; and so it was, in fact; for when we pulled the rope no sound followed, for the simple reason that the bell had been removed. This is comprehensible, if there be causes external to what we call sensations; but if there be only simple internal phenomena, no rational explanation can be given.

30. And here it is to be observed, that when we would explain the failure of succession of those phenomena which always have been united, we may recur to many very different ones, such as are internal phenomena, which, as such, have neither relation nor resemblance, and can only have some connection as corresponding to external objects. We may, when seeking the reason why the bell did not ring, in order to explain the cause of the change in the regular order of appearances, think of various causes, which we now consider as mere appearances or internal phenomena; we may have the following sensations: the rope broken, or caught, the bell broken, or removed, or without a tongue. We may attribute the failure of sound to any one of these sensations: but nothing can possibly be more irrational than to attribute it to them, if we regard them as mere internal facts; for as sensations, they nowhere appear. We cannot discourse rationally if we do not make an external object correspond to each of these sensations, of itself alone sufficing to interrupt the connection between pulling the rope and the vibration of the air which produces the sound.

31. Hence we conclude: First, that our sensations considered as purely internal phenomena, are divided into two very different classes; some depend upon our will, others do not; some have no mutual connection, or are variable in their relations, at the pleasure of him who experiences them; others have a certain connection which we can neither change nor destroy. Secondly, we conclude that the existence as well as the modifications of this last class, proceeds from causes not ourselves, independent of our will, and outside of us. That instinct, therefore, which impels us to refer these sensations to external objects, is confirmed by reason: therefore the testimony of the senses, in so far as it assures us of the reality of objects, is admissible at the tribunal of philosophy.

This demonstrates, in a certain manner, the existence of bodies; for we find, in philosophically examining the conception of body, something in it distinct from our own being, the presence of which causes us such and such sensations. We know not the intimate essence of bodies; but even if we did know it, it would not aid our present purpose, for we are not treating of the idea which a philosopher would in such a case form, but of that formed by the generality of men.

CHAPTER VI
IS THE EXTERNAL AND IMMEDIATE CAUSE OF SENSATIONS A FREE CAUSE?

32. A difficulty, at first sight serious, but in reality futile, may be brought against the existence of bodies. Who knows, it may be asked, but what some cause, not at all resembling the idea which we form of bodies, produces in us all the phenomena that we experience? God may, if he pleases, cause one or many sensations in us; and who shall assure us that he does not? Who shall assure us that other beings may not do the same, and so all our imaginations of a corporeal world be a pure illusion?

33. The first and simplest solution that can be given is, that God, being infinitely true, can neither deceive us himself, nor allow other creatures to deceive us constantly and in a way that we cannot resist. But this solution although well founded, just, and reasonable, labors under the inconvenience of establishing the physical by recurring to the moral order; and so it would never satisfy those who desire to see the truth of the testimony of the senses demonstrated by arguments drawn from the nature of things. Such arguments we think we can supply.

34. Our sensations do not proceed *immediately* from a free cause; the being that produces them, as well as that which experiences them, is subject to fixed and necessary laws. To be convinced of this, we have only to reflect that we cannot, if placed in certain conditions, fail to experience a determinate sensation, and that if these conditions be wanting, we cannot experience it. And this proves that we, as well as the being which causes the impression in us, are subject to a necessary order. Were it not thus, we could not produce the sensation even by the means of certain conditions; for as its cause would be subject to no law, but only to its own free will, it might a thousand times happen, that our will would not agree with its will, and so the desired impression would not be produced.

After experiencing a sensation of touch in which it seems that an opaque body covers our eyes, we do not see, and we cannot with all our efforts produce, the sensation called *seeing*; on the other hand, if at a corresponding hour and place this sensation of contact ceases to exist, we cannot possibly fail to experience the sensation of seeing different objects. Here, therefore, we are subject to a necessity; the being, also, that causes the sensations in us, is subject to a like necessity; for if we perform the condition once or a thousand times of closing our eyes, once or a thousand times the sensation will disappear; or if we open them once or a thousand times in a light place, so many times also the sensation will be produced; the same, if we retain everything in the same state, and varied at our pleasure, if we change our situation or the objects around us. There does, therefore, exist without us, subject to necessary laws, a collection of beings which produce our sensations.

35. It is remarkable not only that the influence they exert upon us does not flow from election or spontaneity in them, but that they are not even presented as endowed with an activity of their own. A painting hung upon the wall produces in us the same sensation as often as we look at it; and, saving the deterioration of time, it will continue for ever to produce the same sensation.

It is, moreover, evident that these beings are subject to our action, for we can, by acting upon them differently, make them produce different impressions. We touch a ball, and the continuation of the sensation of a hard, polished, spherical body, assures us that it is one and the same being that produces it for a certain length of time; and yet, in this interval, we may receive many and various sensations from the same object, by presenting it to the light in different ways.

36. The subjection of these beings to necessary laws is not necessarily with respect to sensations, but is rather a mutual connection of their own. The connection of impressions which we receive from them is an effect of the dependence of some of them upon others; so that, in order to produce a determinate impression, we often employ an object which is, in itself considered, of no direct use, but which brings another into action, and so leads to what we desire. To raise a curtain has no connection with a magnificent landscape; and yet, oftentimes, we do nothing else when we wish to obtain a pleasant prospect. The relation in question is not then of sensations, but of their objects; the connection of these is what induces us to make use of one of them in order to obtain another. There is, therefore, outside of us a collection of beings subject to fixed laws, as well with respect to our sensations as to themselves mutually; therefore the external world exists, and the internal world, which represents it to us, is not a pure illusion.

CHAPTER VII
ANALYSIS OF THE OBJECTIVENESS
OF SENSATIONS

37. Is the external world such as we believe it to be? Are the beings, called *bodies*, which cause our sensations in reality what we believe them? May we not, even after having demonstrated the existence of these beings, and their necessary subjection to constant laws, still doubt whether we have demonstrated the existence of bodies? Does it suffice for this to have proved the existence of external beings in relation among themselves and with us by means of laws fixed and independent of them as of ourselves?

38. Thoroughly to understand this question, it will be well to simplify it, and confine it to a single object.

I hold in my hand and see an orange. I am certain, from what has just been demonstrated, that an external object exists in relation with other beings, and with myself, by necessary laws; I am also certain that I may receive different impressions from it; I see its color, size, and shape, perceive its odor, try its taste; feel in my hand its size, weight, and form, its concavities and convexities, and also hear a little noise when I press it with my hand.

The idea of body is composite, and such is that of the orange; for it is that of something external, extended, colored, odorous, and savory. Whenever all these circumstances exist together, whenever I receive from an object these same impressions, I say that I see an orange.

39. Let us now examine how far the object corresponds to the sensations it causes in us.

What do we mean when we say a thing is savory? Simply, that it produces an agreeable impression upon our palate; and the same is true of smell. Therefore, the two words, odorous and savory, express only the *causality* of these sensations resident in the external object. We may say the same of color, for, although we commonly transfer the sensation to the object, and openly contradict the philosophical theory of light and color, this contradiction is less real than apparent; for the judgment well examined is found to consist only in referring the impression to determinate objects;

so that when we for the first time hear professors of physics tell us that colors are not in the object, we easily accustom ourselves to reconcile the philosophical theory with the impression of the sense; especially since this theory does not render it less true that this or that impression comes to us from this or that object, or its different parts.

40. Here, it is not difficult to explain the phenomena of sensation or their correspondence with external objects; for the correspondence is saved if these objects be really the cause (or occasion) of the sensations. The question of extension is more difficult; for this is as the basis of all other sensible properties; and abstracting its constituting or not constituting the essence of bodies, it is certain that we know no body without extension.

41. The following observation will render palpable the difference between extension and other sensible qualities. He who has never thought of the relation of external objects to his sensations is indescribably confused; he in some sense transfers color, odor, taste, and even sound, to objects themselves, and considers confusedly these things to be qualities inherent in them. Thus the child and the uneducated man believe the color green to be really in the foliage, odor in the rose, sound in the bell, taste in the fruit. But this is readily seen to be a confused judgment, of which they render no perfectly clear account to themselves; a judgment which may be changed or even destroyed without changing or destroying the relations of our sensations with their objects. Even at a very tender age we easily accustom ourselves to refer color to light, and even not to fix it definitively, but to regard it as an impression produced upon our sense by the action of that mysterious agent. It costs us no more to consider smell as a sensation produced by the action of the effluvia of bodies upon the organ of smell; we also cease to consider sound as something inherent in the sonorous body, and come to see in it only the impression caused upon the sense by the vibration of the air, excited in its turn by the vibration of the sonorous body.

These philosophical considerations may, at first sight, seem to be in contradiction to our judgment, but they do not change to us the external world; they cause no inversion of our ideas of it; they only make us fix our attention upon some relations which we had imperfectly defined, and do not allow us to attribute to objects what in reality does not belong to them. They make us limit the testimony of the senses to their appropriate sphere, and in some manner rectify our judgments; but the world continues the same that it was before, excepting that we have discovered in the marvels of nature a closer relation with our own being, and have perceived that our organization and our soul play a more important part in them than we had imagined.

42. If we destroy extension, take this quality from external objects, and regard it as only a mere sensation, of which we only know that there is an external object which causes it, the corporeal world at once disappears. The whole system of the universe will be reduced to a collection of beings which cause us different impressions; without the idea of extension we can neither form any idea of body, nor know if all that we have thought of the world be aught else than a pure illusion. I can easily resign my infantile belief that the color I see in my hand is in it, or the noise made when I clap my hands is in them; but I cannot, do what I will, lay aside the idea of extension; I cannot imagine the distance from my wrist to the extremity of my fingers to be only a pure illusion, that there only exists a being which causes it without my knowing whether in reality this distance exists. I can easily separate from the fruit which I find savory the quality of savor; and I may, if I examine it philosophically, admit, without any inconvenience, that it has nothing resembling taste, but that it is only composed so to affect my palate as to produce an agreeable sensation. But I cannot take from the fruit its extension; in no wise can I regard it as something indivisible; I cannot possibly regard the distance from one of its points to another as a mere sensation. My efforts to consider the savory object as in itself indivisible are all in vain; and if, for a single instant, I seem to have overcome the instinct of nature, every thing is overturned. By the same right that I make the fruit something indivisible, I may make the whole universe so; but an indivisible universe is to me no universe; my intellect is confounded, and all around me is annihilated. I am in worse than chaos; for chaos is at least something, although the elements are in horrible confusion and frightful darkness; but now I am worse off, for the corporeal world, such as I have conceived it to be, returns to nothing.

CHAPTER VIII
SENSATION OF EXTENSION

43. Two of our senses perceive extension; sight and touch. Sound, taste, and smell accompany extension, but are something different from it. The sight perceives nothing not extended; extension is every way inseparable from this sensation. We may be so enchanted by the sweet harmony of many instruments as to forget the extension of the instruments, the air, and our organs; but we cannot, in contemplating a painting even in the midst of our most ardent enthusiasm, make its extension vanish. If we withdraw from the *Transfiguration* of Raphael its extension, the marvel disappears; for even considered as a simple phenomenon of our soul, continuity and distance enter of necessity into its very essence.

The same is true of touch, although less generally so. Hardness and softness, roughness and smoothness, squareness and roundness, all involve extension; but it cannot be denied that there are some impressions of touch, in which it is less clearly involved. The acute pain of a puncture, and others felt without any known external cause, are not so clearly referred to extension, but seem to have something of that simplicity which distinguishes the impressions of the other senses. However this may be, it is certain that the perception of extension belongs in a special manner to sight and touch.

44. In order to form a clear idea of extension in its relations to sensation, we will analyze it at some length.

And first of all, it is to be remarked, that extension involves multiplicity. An extended being is of necessity a collection of beings, more or less closely united by a bond which makes them all constitute one whole, but does not prevent them from continuing many. A splendid painting, wherein the unity of the artist's thought dominates, does not cease to be composed of many parts; the *moral* chain which unites, does not identify them; it only connects, co-ordinates them, and makes them conspire to one end. The firm adhesion of the molecules forming the diamond does not prevent these molecules from being distinct: the material chain unites, but does not identify them.

There is then no extension without multiplicity: where there is extension, there is, rigorously speaking, not one only being, but many beings.

45. Multiplicity does not constitute extension, for it may exist without extension. Neither the multiplicity of sounds, of tastes, nor of odors, constitutes extension. We conceive in the material, as in the moral and intellectual orders, multiplicity of beings of different orders, and yet this multiplicity involves no idea of extension. Even if we confine ourselves to the purely mathematical order, we find multiplicity without extension, in arithmetical and algebraic quantities. Therefore multiplicity, although necessary, does not alone suffice to constitute extension.

If we reflect upon the species of multiplicity required to constitute extension, we shall observe that it must be accompanied by continuity. Sensations of touch as well as of sight involve continuity; for it is impossible for us to see or to touch, without receiving the impression of objects continuous, immediately adjoining each other, co-existing in their duration, and at the same time presented as continuous one with another in space. Without this continuity, multiplicity does not constitute extension. If, for example, we take four or more points on the paper on which we now write, and by an abstraction consider them as indivisible, this multiplicity will not constitute extension: we must unite them by lines at least imaginary; and if continuity be wanting to the body in which we suppose them situated, we shall find it necessary to recur to the continuity of space; that is, to regard this space as a collection of points whose continuation connects the first points. No possible efforts can enable us to consider a collection of indivisible points, neither continuous nor united by lines, as extension; this collection will be to us as that of beings having no connection with extension. It is worthy of observation, that if we assign them a determinate position in space, this we do only by connecting them with other points, by means of imaginary lines: for we cannot otherwise conceive either distances or position in space. If we attempt to abstract all this, we either fall into intellectual nothingness, we annihilate all idea of the object, or we pass to another order of beings having no relation either to extension or space. We quit matter and sensations, and mount to the realm of spirits.

46. Multiplicity and continuity are therefore necessary to constitute extension; and we believe that these two conditions suffice; for where they exist, extension exists, and with them alone, we form the idea of extension. The object of geometry is extension; and only multiplicity and continuity constitute it. Lines, surfaces, solids, such as are the object of geometry, are only this continuity considered in its greatest abstraction. Empty space suffices, or rather is requisite for geometry; since, it does not, in making its applications to bodies, find all the exactness of continuity in the abstract.

47. If multiplicity and continuity constitute extension in space, it really exists in the objects which cause our sensations. Basing ourselves upon

the relation of phenomena among themselves and to their causes, we have shown that external objects correspond to sensations: thus it is that this relation also exists with respect to multiplicity and continuity; these two properties are therefore found in nature. The impressions that we receive by sight and touch, are, although we confine ourselves to a single object, multiple, and consequently correspond to many objects: they are continuous, and consequently correspond to continuous objects.

We will explain this reasoning. Looking at a painting, I receive an impression coming from many different points; and this impression, it must be observed, comes uninterruptedly from the whole surface presented. If, as we have shown, the sight of one external point sufficed to convince me of its existence, that of many will make me sure of the existence of many; and the continuity of the impression will also make me certain of the continuity of the impressing points.

If I touch the object seen, my touch will confirm that testimony of sight, in what corresponds to it, that is, the multiplicity and continuity, I experience the same continued succession of sensations; and this shows me the existence and continuity of the objects causing them.

48. In a few words, extension supposes the co-existence of many objects, in such a way, however, that they are one by continuation of others: of both, sensation makes us certain: therefore the testimony of the senses suffices to make us certain that there are external objects, and that they may produce various impressions. These ideas contain every thing included in the idea of body: therefore the testimony of the senses makes us certain of the existence of bodies.

CHAPTER IX
OBJECTIVENESS OF THE
SENSATION OF EXTENSION

49. Having proved the testimony of the senses sufficient to assure us of the existence of bodies, we now come to examine how far the ideas it makes us form are correct. It is not enough to know that we may be sure of the existence of extension; we must inquire if it in reality be such as the senses represent it; and what we say of extension is applicable to the other properties of bodies.

In our opinion, the only sensation that we transfer, and cannot help transferring, to the external, is that of extension; all others relate to objects only as effects to causes, not as copies to originals. Sound, taste, and smell represent nothing resembling the objects causing them, but extension does; we attribute extension to objects, and without it we cannot conceive them. Sound outside of me is not sound, but only a simple vibration of the air, produced by the vibration of a body. Taste outside of me is not taste, but only a body applied to an organ of which it causes a mechanical or chemical modification. The same is true of smell. Even in light and colors, outside of me, there is only a fluid which falls upon a surface, and either directly or reflexly comes, or may come, to my eyes. But extension outside of me, independently of all relation with the senses, is true extension, is something whose existence and nature stand in no need of my senses. When I perceive, or imagine that I perceive it, there is in it, and in my impressions, something besides the relation of an effect to its cause; there is the representation, the internal image of what exists externally.

50. In order that the truth of what we have just advanced may be perfectly understood, and strongly felt, we would offer the reader a picture whence determinate sensations may be successively eliminated, and made to mark the degree of elimination which it is possible to reach, but not pass.

Let us suppose all animals at once to lose the sense of taste, or all bodies to be by nature destitute of the property of causing by their contact with an organ the sensation called taste. The external world, nevertheless, continues to exist as before; the same bodies that caused in us the sensations now lost, continue to exist, and may be applied to the very organ they before affected, and cause in it sensations of touch, as of soft or hard, warm or cold. Either savory bodies, or the organs of animals, have undergone some change, which has interrupted their previous relations; a cause which before produced an effect is now seen to be impotent to produce it. This may be owing to a modification of the bodies without changing their nature, so far as we know it; and it is also possible that they have not been changed, but that this difference arises solely from an alteration of the organs. But in any case, the disappearance of this sensation has not made anything resembling it disappear from the universe; if the change has been only in the organs, external bodies remain untouched; and if it has taken place in bodies, it has made them lose a *causing* property of the sensation, but not a property *represented* by the sensation.

We have taken all taste from food, and the universe exists as before; let us now take away all odors, by changing odoriferous bodies, or the organ of smell. The same follows as in the case of taste. Odoriferous bodies will continue to exist, and even transmit to our organ the effluvia that before produced the sensation of smell; and the only novelty will be the non-existence of that sensation. Either the disposition to receive the necessary impression will be wanting in our organs, or a causality will have disappeared from the universe, but not a thing represented by the sensation. Gardens will not be despoiled of their beauty, nor the fields of their luxuriant verdure; the tree will still display its leafy bower, and the fair fruit hang from its boughs, and be shaken by the wind.

Let us proceed in our destructive march, and now suddenly make all animals deaf. The musician becomes the actor of a silent pantomime; the bell-rope is pulled, and only the mute metal is struck; conversation is reduced to oral gestures, and the howlings of brutes are only the opening and closing of their mouths. But the air vibrates as before; its columns strike as before the drum of the ear; nothing has been changed; nothing has failed in the universe but one sensation. The lightning ploughs the skies, rivers follow their majestic course, torrents dash onwards with the same rapidity, and the proud cascade still leaps from its lofty rocks, and displays its changing hues and foaming waves.

But let us now commit the greatest cruelty; let us make all living creatures blind. The sun still pours out his immense torrents of the fluid we call light; it is reflected from surfaces, and is refracted from the bodies it meets, and passes to the retinas of eyes that formerly saw, but are now converted into insensible membranes, placed behind a crystal; but every thing called color and sensation of light has disappeared. Yet the universe exists as before, and the celestial bodies still follow their immense orbits.

As it is most difficult for us to abstract the sensation of light and colors from objects; or, in other words, as we have a certain propensity to imagine that there really exist without us impressions which are only in us, and to consider the sensation as a representation of the exterior; so it costs us most to conceive all living creatures to be blind, and nothing to remain of what sensations of this kind represented to us, not even a fluid which reflects from certain surfaces, and passes through some bodies, not otherwise than as an invisible fluid. Wherefore, in condescension to the difficulty which some experience in ceasing to externally realize what exists only within them, we will frame our supposition differently; for it will then be all that the demonstration requires, and we may eliminate from objects whatever relates to any sensation excepting that of extension.

We will not then make all animals blind, nor practise the cruelty of Ulysses in the cave of Polyphemus, but spare in our inversion of the world that destructive instinct. It matters little that men and animals are not blind, provided they cannot see. We will then leave those organs untouched, but we will in return, take all light from the universe; quench like faint torches the sun and stars and all the celestial bodies, extinguish their feeblest scintillations upon the earth, the tall tapers which illumine the rich man's dwelling, and the fire kindled in the peasant's cot, the spark struck from the flint, and the pale phosphorescences emitted from the graves of the dead. Every thing is involved in obscurity, and it is as if that darkness which rested upon the face of the abyss before the Creator said: *let there be light,* were restored.

We must bear in mind that we have not, by plunging the world into such frightful obscurity, changed any one of its laws. The gigantic orbs describe as before with astonishing rapidity and admirable precision their immense orbits. Hence we infer that although we destroy smell, taste, sound, light, and colors, the world still exists, and we may without difficulty so conceive it to be. We may even destroy the sensation of touch, for it is easy to suppose that we perceive no impression by this sense. We may substitute some sensations, whose causes lie in bodies like those of heat and cold, hardness and softness, for others, without therefore believing the universe no longer to exist.

51. Let us now make another abstraction, and see what will happen. Let us destroy extension. The world resists not this trial; the stars vanish, and the earth disappears beneath our feet, distances no longer exist, and motion is an absurdity: our own body fades away and the whole universe is tumbled into nothingness, or if it continues somehow to exist, it is totally different from what we now imagine it to be.

And so indeed it is. If we abstract extension, if we do not externally realize that sensation, or idea, or whatever else it may be, which we have of it, if we do not consider it as the representation of what exists without us, every thing is overthrown: we know not what to think either of our sensations, or their relation to the objects causing them; things all go roundabout, and one basis of our cognitions fails: in vain we stretch out our arms to lay hold of some fixed point; and we ask in our trouble, if all that we perceive be only a pure illusion, if Berkeley's extravagances be true.

52. It is worthy of remark that, even if we make extension objective by transferring it to the external, it is not altogether correct to say that it is represented by the sensation. It is better to say that it is a receptacle of certain sensations, a condition necessary to the functions of some of the senses, but not their object. Extension abstracted from the sensations of sight and touch, is, as we have already said, reduced to multiplicity and continuity. The knowledge of it comes to us from the senses, but it is different from what the senses represent it to us. When we take color and light from the sensations, received through the sense of sight, we certainly still retain the idea of a thing extended, but not of a visible thing, nor of an object represented by the sensation. In like manner, if we despoil the sensations received through the sense of touch, of those qualities which affect this sense, the object that caused them is not annihilated, neither is it represented by the impressions it transmits to us.

53. These remarks show that we do not transfer our sensations to the exterior, that they are a medium whereby our soul is informed, but not images wherein it contemplates its objects. All sensations indicate an external cause; but some, like those of sight and touch, in an especial manner denote multiplicity and continuity, or extension.

Hence we also infer that the external world is not a pure illusion, but that it really exists with its great masses, its various motions, its unlimited geometry: but much of its beauty lies rather within ourselves than in it. The Creator of it has in an especial manner, shown his infinite wisdom and omnipotent hand in sensible beings, and above all in intelligences. What would the universe be were there no one to feel and to understand? The beauty, the harmony, the marvels of nature consist in the close relation, the continuous communication of objects and sensible beings. The rarest painting, were there no one to perceive and admire its beauty, would be only a collection of lineaments, a hieroglyphic of unintelligible characters; but so soon as it is seen by a feeling and knowing being, it is animated, is what it ought to be; and in this wonderful communication the object gains in beauty all that it imparts of pleasure.

Suppose a collection of instruments disposed by the proper mechanism to execute with admirable precision the highest conceptions of Bellini or Mozart: to what is it all reduced if there be no sensitive being? To vibrations in the air governed by some law, to mere movements of a fluid, subject to geometrical necessity. Introduce a man, and the geometry is changed into celestial harmony, then there is music, enchantment.

The symmetry of the walks of a garden, the elegance of its shrubbery, the color and beauty of its flowers, the fragrance of its odors, are, without a sensitive being, only geometrical figures, surfaces disposed according to some law, volumes of such or such a kind, columns of fluids springing from them and disappearing in space. Introduce man, and the geometrical figures are adorned with a thousand beauties, the flowers covered with gay colors, and the columns of fluids changed into exquisite perfumes.

CHAPTER X
FORCE OF TOUCH TO MAKE
SENSATIONS OBJECTIVE

54. It has been said that touch is the surest, and perhaps the only witness of the existence of bodies; for without it, all sensations would be nothing more than simple modifications of our being, to which we could attribute no external object. But this I do not believe to be true. We receive by touch an impression, just as we do by the other senses; this impression is in all cases an affection of our being, and not something external. When, from the continuance of these impressions, their order, and their independence of our will, we judge them to proceed from objects without us, our judgment is true not only of impressions of the sense of touch, but also of those of the other senses.

55. One of the reasons whereon it has been attempted to base the superiority of touch to attest the existence of bodies, is that it gives us the idea or sensation of extension; for if we suppose a man to be deprived of all his senses but that of touch, and to pass his hand over the surface of a body, he will experience that continuity of the sensation which involves extension. This observation of those who maintain the supremacy of touch does not prove what they propose. If we pass our sight over various objects, or the different parts of one object, we shall experience the sensation of continuity just as clearly as by touch. We cannot conceive why the sensation of extension must be any clearer when the hand is passed along a balustrade than when it is seen by the eyes.

56. The advocates of this opinion assert that we acquire by the touch of our body a double sensation, which we do not by the other senses. If we pass our hand over our forehead, we feel with both our hand and our forehead, and so verify a continuity of sensations, all originating and terminating in ourselves. Thus we are conscious that both the sensations of our hand and our forehead belong to us.

But this reason, by some deemed conclusive, is nevertheless exceedingly futile; it labors under the sophism called by dialecticians *begging of the question*, for it supposes what was to be proved. The man destitute of all senses but that of touch will, indeed, experience the two sensations and their continuity; but what can he infer from them? Does he even know that he has either hand or forehead? Suppose him not to know, how is he to acquire this knowledge? Both sensations belong to him, and of this he is internally conscious; but whence they came, he knows not. Does the coincidence of the two sensations, perchance, prove something in favor of the existence of his forehead and hand, objects of which we suppose him to have no idea? If this coincidence proved what is pretended, with still greater reason would it prove the combination of some senses with others to elevate us to the knowledge of the existence of bodies, and consequently that this knowledge is not produced exclusively by touch. Whenever I have the sensation of the motion of placing my hand before my eyes, I find that I lose sight of the objects before me, and in their room is presented another always the same, my hand. If, from this coincidence, I infer the existence of external objects, the supremacy of touch is destroyed, for sight, also, acts a part in the formation of such a judgment. I also observe that when I have the sensation of clapping my hands together, I experience the sensation of hearing the noise of their contact; if, therefore, coincidence is of any account, hearing as well as touch comes in. What I say concerning the clapping of my hands, is applicable to what I experience when I pass a hand over any part of my body, for instance my arm, so as to produce some noise. In this case there are two sensations coincident and continuous.

It will, perhaps, be replied, that these examples refer to different senses, and produce sensations of different kinds. This, however, is of no consequence; for, if the being that perceives, infers the existence of objects from the coincidence of various sensations, the supremacy of touch is destroyed, which is what we undertook to demonstrate.

57. The sensation of the hand is not that of the forehead, for the one is warmer or colder, harder or softer than the other, and so the sensation caused by the hand upon the forehead will not be the same as that produced upon the hand by the forehead. It is to be observed, that the less difference we suppose between the two sensations, the less lively will be the perception of their duality, and consequently the less marked the coincidence on which the judgment is founded. Thus by rigorously analyzing this matter we discover that the diversity of sensations contributes in an especial manner to form judgments of the existence of objects, and therefore the combination of two senses will more conduce to this end than two sensations of one sense. Far, then, from its being necessary to consider touch as alone or superior upon this point, it is only to be held as auxiliary to the other senses.

In truth, it is almost beyond doubt that the sense of touch also requires the aid of the other senses, and that the judgments resulting from it are similar to those coming from the other senses. It is probable that only after repeated trials do we refer the sensation of touch to the object that causes it, or even to the part affected. The man who has had his arm amputated, feels pain as if he still preserved it; and this is because a repetition of acts has formed the habit of referring the cerebral impression to the point where the nerves transmitting it terminate. There is, therefore, no necessary relation between the sense of touch and the object; and this sense is, like the others, liable to illusions. Therefore, it is not exact to say that the idea of body springs up under our hand, if this be understood as excluding touch; for the same is true of the other senses, particularly of sight.

CHAPTER XI
INFERIORITY OF TOUCH COMPARED WITH OTHER SENSES

58. That superiority, or rather that exclusive privilege, conceded by Condillac and other philosophers to touch, not only has no foundation, as we have just seen, but seems to be in contradiction to the very nature of this sense. In short, it assigns the first place to the coarsest, the most material of all the senses.

It cannot be known what ideas a man reduced to the one sense of touch would form of things; but it seems to me that far from entering into clear and vivid communication with the external world, and finding a sufficient foundation whereon to base his cognitions, he would grope in the profoundest ignorance, and labor under the most transcendental errors.

59. If we compare touch with sight, or even with hearing and smell, we shall at once perceive a very important difference to its disadvantage. Touch transmits to us only impressions of objects immediately joining our body; whereas, the other three, and especially sight, place us in communication with far distant objects. The fixed stars are separated from us by a distance such as almost to pass our imagination, and yet we see them. Neither smell nor hearing, it is true, go so far; but the former fails not to warn us of the existence of a garden at many paces from us; and the latter gives us notice of a battle fought at many leagues distance, of the electric spark which has cloven the clouds on the confines of the horizon, or of the tempest roaring over the immensity of ocean.

60. The limitation of touch to what is immediate to it involves a scarcity of the ideas originating in it alone, and of necessity places it in a lower grade than the other three senses, particularly sight. Let us in order to form clear ideas upon this point compare the range of sight with that of touch relatively to some object, for example, a building. By means of sight we in a few instants obtain an idea of its front, and other external parts; and in a short time become acquainted with its internal divisions, with the arrangement even of its ornaments and furniture. Can we accomplish all this by touch? Even if we suppose the most delicate sense of touch, and the most tenacious

memory of the impressions communicated, long hours would be necessary to pass the hand over the front of the building, and form some idea of it. How will it be when we come to the whole exterior of the building? the whole interior? We see that it would be necessary to renounce such a task, that the elaborate workmanship of a cornice, a pedestal, a peristyle, the magnificence of a tower, a cupola, the boldness of an arch, a vault, which the eye seizes in an instant, would require the poor being possessed of touch alone to go often on all fours, climb over dangerous scaffoldings, and expose himself to the danger of falling from fearful heights; and yet he would never be able to acquire the millionth part of what the eyes so easily and so quickly perceive.

Apply these observations to a city, to vast countries, to the universe, and see what immense superiority sight has over touch.

61. We do not indeed find so vast a superiority when we compare touch with the other senses; nevertheless, it does exist in a very high degree.

The first difference is the ability to act from a distance. Certainly, touch also may in some manner perceive the presence or absence of the sun, by means of the impressions of heat and cold; and in like manner the presence or absence, and the more or less close proximity of some bodies, etc.; but not only are these impressions far from having the same variety and rapidity as those of hearing, but they would not even give us any idea of distance, if we had not already perceived it otherwise than by touch.

Heat and cold, dryness and moistness, are what the impressions which some bodies, though distant, may make upon touch are reduced to; and these impressions are clearly of a nature to be exposed to many serious errors.

62. If we suppose a man, having only the sense of touch, to know the presence or absence of the sun above the horizon, his only rule being the temperature of the atmosphere, which depends upon a thousand causes having no connection with the orb of day, it will happen that the natural or artificial change of it will lead him into error. The dampness which we perceive around a lake is a sign of the nearness of the water; but do we not a thousand times experience the feeling of dampness from causes operating on the atmosphere, altogether independent of the waters of a lake?

It is certain that the concentration of all sensitive forces upon one sense, the absence of all distraction, and continual attention to only one kind of sensations, might raise the delicacy of touch to a degree of perfection which we probably do not know; just as the habit of connecting ideas with respect to only one order of sensations, and of forming judgments concerning them, produces a precision, exactness, and variety, far superior to all that we can imagine. But however far we might extend our conjectures upon this head, it is certain that there is a limit in the nature of the organ and of its relations to bodies. This organ must be limited to contiguous objects, in order to receive well determined impressions; and with respect to those that are distant, and can act upon it, they can do this by causing on it an impression such as the nature of both permits, heat or cold, dryness or dampness, and if you will, a certain pressure either greater or less. So far as a great many other objects are concerned, we cannot imagine any action. However much the circle of this class of sensations be enlarged, it must ever be very limited. Moreover, we must observe, that the perfectibility of touch by means of its isolation does not belong to it exclusively, but extends likewise to the other senses; for it is founded on the laws of organization, and the generation of our ideas.

63. To comprehend the superiority of hearing to touch in this matter, we have only to consider the relation of distances, the variety of objects, the rapidity of the succession of sensations, the simultaneousness so much greater in hearing than in touch, and their relations to speech.

I. Relation of distances. On this point, hearing is clearly superior to touch, for the latter generally requires contact, the former does not, but for the due appreciation of its object even requires a distance suited to the class of the sound. Of how many distant objects does hearing inform us of which touch can tell us nothing? The gallop of the horse threatening to trample us under foot, the roaring of the torrent which may carry us away in its course, the thunder rumbling from afar, and announcing the tempest, the roar of cannon, telling that a battle has begun, the rattle of carriages in the streets, drums and bells, and clamor of voices which indicate the explosion of popular fury, the noisy music that proclaims the joy caused by happy news, the concert dedicated to the pleasures of the saloon, the song that brings back melancholy recollections, sentiments also of hope and love, the groan that warns us of suffering, the plaint that afflicts us with the idea of misery; all this hearing tells us, but touch can tell us nothing of any of these.

II. Variety of objects. Those distant objects which we know by touch, are of necessity little varied; and for the same reason the ideas resulting from it will be liable to a deplorable confusion and to great uncertainty. Hearing, on the contrary, informs us of infinite and exceedingly different objects, and that, too, with perfect precision and exactness.

III. Rapidity of the succession of impressions. It is evident that hearing has here an incalculable superiority over touch. When touch perceives by juxtaposition, it is under the necessity of successively going over the objects and even their different parts if it would receive varied impressions; and this, however small their number, requires much time. If the objects do not act by juxtaposition, but by some medium, the succession will require much more time, and there will be much less variety. Compare this slowness to the rapidity with which hearing perceives a whole series of sounds in musical combinations, the infinite inflexions of the voice, the countless number of distinct articulations, the infinity of noises of all kinds which we uninterruptedly perceive and classify, and refer to their corresponding objects.

IV. The simultaneousness of sensations so vast in hearing, is extremely limited in touch; for in the latter it can only be in relation to a few objects; but in the other it extends to many very different objects.

V. But what most triumphantly indicates the superiority of hearing to touch, is the facility it affords us of placing ourselves in communication, by means of speech, with the mind of our fellow-mortals,—a facility, resulting from the rapidity of succession already remarked. Undoubtedly, this communication of mind with mind, may be established by touch, if we express our words by characters sufficiently raised to be distinguished: but what an immense difference between these impressions and those of hearing? Even if we suppose habit and a concentration of all the sensitive forces to have produced such a facility in passing the fingers over lines, as far to surpass all that we see in the most dexterous players of musical instruments, what comparison can there be instituted between this velocity and that of hearing? How much time would be requisite only to go over tablets whereon is written a discourse which we hear in a few minutes? Moreover, all men have means of hearing, they need only make use of their organs. But in order to converse by touch, it is necessary to prepare tablets, which can only serve for one object, and cannot be at the same time used by two persons; whereas by means of hearing, one man alone may in brief time communicate an infinity of ideas to thousands of listeners.

CHAPTER XII
CAN SIGHT ALONE GIVE US THE IDEA OF A SURFACE?

64. I have, I believe, made the inferiority of touch to sight and hearing palpable, and have, consequently, shown the extravagance of endeavoring to make it the basis of all cognitions, to found upon it the certainty of the judgments to which our other senses lead us, and to make it a supreme judge to decide in the last appeal upon the doubts that may arise.

I hold it to be manifestly untrue that we cannot make the transition from the internal to the external world, or from the existence of sensations to that of the objects causing them, otherwise than by means of touch; for not only have I combated the principal, or rather the solitary reason upon which it is pretended to found this privilege, but I have also demonstrated the mode of making this transition with respect to all the senses, reasoning from the very nature and connection of internal phenomena.

I have likewise said and proved that the sensation of extension is the only one that is representative, and that in all others there was only a relation of causality, that is, a connection of some sensation or an internal phenomenon with an external object, without our transferring to this any thing resembling what we experienced in that.

65. There are two senses which inform us with certainty of extension, sight and touch. We shall not now inquire if that be a true *sensation* which we have of extension, or if it be an *idea* of a very different order, resulting from the sensation. I propose hereafter to examine this point, but shall now confine myself to comparing sight with touch only as tending to give us the sensation of extension, or, if you will, to furnish us with what is necessary to form an idea of it.

We cannot but see that extension lies within the domain of touch, and that, too, whether it be considered only as a surface, or also as a solid. The same faculty cannot be denied to sight, so far as surfaces are concerned; for it is impossible to see if at least a plane be not presented to the eye. A point without extension cannot be painted upon the retina, but the instant an object is painted, it has painted parts. We can by no effort of our imagination, conceive colors without extension; for what is color without a surface over which it may extend?

66. So hostile was Condillac to the sense of sight that he was unwilling to allow it even the faculty of perceiving extension in surfaces; but as he is of all philosophers the one who has most contributed to the propagation and establishment of this opinion, we will examine his doctrine and its fundamental reasons. We have only to read the chapters in which he explains it, to see that he was not himself very confident of its truth, but that he felt himself contradicted by both experience and reason.

In his *Traité des Sensations*,[36] where he examines the ideas of a man limited to the sense of sight, he says that colors are distinguished by the sight because they seem to form a surface of which the eyes occupy a part, and then asks: "Will our statue, judging itself to be at one time many colors, perceive itself as a sort of colored surface?" We must bear in mind that, according to Condillac, the statue confined to one sense will believe itself the sensation, that is, it will think that it is the odor, the sound, or the taste, according as the sense of smell, hearing, or taste, is the sense in exercise; for which reason, if a surface enter into the sensation of sight, the statue ought to believe itself a colored surface. I shall not examine the correctness of these observations, but shall confine myself to the main point, which is the relation of sight to a surface.

67. According to Condillac, the statue will never believe itself a colored surface, that is, although it may perceive the color, it will not perceive the surface. Let the philosopher himself speak, for his own words will suffice to condemn his opinion, and to show the uncertainty with which he advanced it, or else the obscurity under which it labors: "The idea of extension supposes the perception of many things, *some distinct from others. This perception we cannot deny to the statue*, for it feels that it is repeated outside of itself as many times as there are colors modifying it. When it is the red, it feels itself *outside* of the green; when the green, it feels itself *outside* of the red, and so with other colors." Some may imagine that, conformably to these principles, Condillac goes on to establish that sight gives us the idea of extension, since it makes us perceive things, some *outside* of others, in which, according to him, the idea of extension exactly consists. But he does not; far from following the true road, he miserably loses his way; he not only violates the principle he has just laid down, but notably changes the state of the question. He continues: "But in order to have a distinct and precise idea of magnitude, it is necessary to see how the things perceived, some outside of others, are connected, how they mutually terminate, and how they are all enclosed in the limits which bound them." This, I repeat, is to change

the state of the question; we are not now treating of a distinct and precise idea, but simply of an idea. How far the idea of extension given by sight is perfect, is another question; although it is manifest that if sight can give us an idea of extension, it will come by continual exercise to render this idea more perfect.

68. The statue, in Condillac's opinion, could not perceive itself to be circumscribed by any limit, because it could know nothing beyond itself; but did he not just now tell us that the statue would believe itself different colors; that some of these were outside of others; and that when it would be one, it would perceive itself outside of the others? Does this not imply not only one but many limits?

This difficulty did not altogether escape Condillac; for after having asked if the *me* of the statue, when modified by a blue surface, bordered with white, would not believe itself a limited blue color, he says: "At first sight we were inclined to believe that it would; but the contrary opinion is much more probable." But why? "The statue cannot perceive itself extended by this surface, save inasmuch as each part modifies it in the same way; each part should produce the sensation of blue color; but if it is alike modified by a foot of this surface and by an inch, it cannot perceive itself, in this modification, to be one magnitude rather than another. Therefore it does not perceive itself as magnitude; therefore the sensation of color does not involve the idea of extension." It is easy to see that Condillac either supposes what is in debate, or else says nothing to the point. According to him, the statue is alike modified by a foot of colored surface and by an inch. If by this he means that the two modifications are identical under all aspects, he supposes the very thing he ought to have proved; for this is precisely the point in dispute, whether surfaces differing in magnitude do, or do not, produce different sensations. If he means, as his words seem to indicate, that the sensation as color, and solely as color, is the same in a foot of colored surface as in an inch, he utters, indeed, an incontestable truth, but one not at all to his purpose. Undoubtedly, the sensation of blue, as blue, is the same in different magnitudes, and no one ever thought of denying it. But this is not the question: it is whether, the color remaining one and the same, the sensation of sight is modified differently, according to the variety of magnitude of the colored surface. Condillac denies it, but in an uncertain and hesitating way. We believe his negation to be so groundless that the direct contrary may be proved.

69. I would ask Condillac if he can have color without surface; if an object without extension can be painted upon the retina; if we can even conceive a color without extension. No one of these is possible, sight is therefore necessarily accompanied by extension.

70. Condillac places the idea of extension in some things being presented to us outside of others. This, as he him self confesses, is verified in the sensation of color; therefore the sight of what is colored must produce the idea of extension. Condillac's subterfuge here is an exceedingly weak one. He pretends that it is necessary, in order to have the idea of extension, to have that of its limits. But first of all, we have shown from his own doctrine that these limits are perceived by the senses; besides it is a very strange pretension to attribute to sight the faculty of giving us the idea of unlimited extension, and to deny to it that of producing the idea of limitation; as if there did not by the very fact of our seeing what is extended, rise within us the idea of limitation, if from no other cause, from the very limitation of our organ; or as if an unlimited were not more inconceivable than a limited sensation.

But suppose the limits not be perceived by the senses, does unlimited extension therefore cease to be extension? Is it not rather extension of the highest order? Does the idea of space without end, because unlimited, cease to be an idea of extension?

71. Two colored circles, one an inch, and the other a yard in diameter, are placed before our eyes; will the effect produced upon the retina be the same in both, abstraction made from all sensation of touch? Evidently not; experience shows the contrary, and the reason is founded on the laws of the reflection of light, and on mathematical principles. If the impressions are different, the difference will be perceived; therefore the difference of magnitude can be appreciated.

We will now suppose some one in spite of reason and experience to persist in maintaining that the sensation of the two circles will be the same in order to make the extravagance, even the ridiculousness of this opinion palpable. Let us imagine the two circles to be of a red color, and terminated by a blue line; and now placing the less upon the greater circle so as to bring their centres together, we ask, will not the eye cast upon the figure see the less within the greater circle? Will not the blue line that terminates the circle of an inch in diameter be sure to be contained within the blue line that terminates the other circle of a yard in diameter? But what else is the perception of extension than the perception of some parts beyond others? Is it not to perceive the difference of magnitude, to perceive some greater than others, and containing them? Evidently it is. The sight therefore perceives magnitude; therefore it perceives extension.

72. We may still further confirm this truth. Experience teaches, and did it not exist, reason would still teach that there must be a limit to the field of sight, according to our distance from the object. Thus, when we fix our sight

upon a wall of great extent we do not see it all, but only a part. Now suppose an object of given magnitude to be within the range of sight, but not so great as to cover the surface embraced by the eye. According to Condillac's system, there can be no difference in the perception, provided the color be the same; whence, it will follow, that the sensation will be just the same, whether the object occupy the whole, or only an exceedingly minute part, of the visual field. It will likewise follow, that, if this visual field be, for example, a great white curtain a hundred yards square, and the object a piece of blue cloth a yard square, the sensation will be just the same whether the blue cloth be one inch or ninety yards square.

73. These arguments, which must have occurred at least confusedly to Condillac, made him hesitate in his expressions, and even use contradictory language. We may have already observed this in the passages cited, but we shall see it yet more clearly in the following:—"We have no term to express with exactness the sentiment that the statue modified by many colors at one time has of itself; but in fine, it knows that it exists in many ways, and perceives itself in a certain mode *as a colored point beyond which* are others, in which it turns to find itself; and under this point of view, it may be said, that it *perceives itself extended*." He had before said, that color did not seem extended to the statue, until, sight being instructed by touch, the eye became accustomed to refer the one simple sensation to all the points of the surface: and in the very next line, as we have just seen, he asserts the contrary; the statue now perceives itself to be extended, and the ideologist discovers no way of avoiding the contradiction, but to warn us that the sentiment of extension will be vague because it wants limits. This is a contradiction which we have already made evident. But whence this want of limits? If various figures of different colors, green, red, etc., be supposed to be upon a visual field of a hundred yards square of white surface, the sight will, as is evident, perceive the limits of these figures; where, then, did Condillac discover that illimitation of which he talks?

74. Although it is very true that even if the sensation of color were to involve that of extension, it would not therefore follow that it would produce it in us, because we do not take from sensations all the ideas they contain, but those only which we know. This does not at all affect the present question. We do not treat of what we can take from the sensation, but of what is in it. If Condillac maintains that we may take the idea of extension from the sensation of touch, by what right does he deny the same faculty with respect to sight, supposing the idea of extension to be contained in both sensations?

If I mistake not, this is a tacit confession of the falseness of his opinion. The idea of extension is in the sensation of sight, but we cannot take it thence. Why not? Because it is vague. But then what is to prevent exercise, involving comparison and reflection, from rendering it distinct? The difficulty consists in acquiring it in one way or another; to perfect it is the work of time.

Undoubtedly the first sensations of sight will not have that exactness which they have after much exercise; but the same is true of the sense of touch. This sense is perfected like the others; it like them needs to be educated, so to speak; and those born blind, who, by force of concentration and labor, come to possess it to an astonishing degree of delicacy, offer us a manifest proof of this truth.

CHAPTER XIII
CHESELDEN'S BLIND MAN

75. Cheselden's blind man, of whom Condillac spoke, in confirmation of his opinions, presents no phenomenon upon which they can rest. This blind person was a youth of thirteen or fourteen years of age, upon whom Cheselden, a distinguished London surgeon, performed the operation of removing cataracts, first from one eye, then from the other. He could before the operation tell day and night, and in a very strong light distinguish, white, black, and red. This is an important circumstance, and merits attention. The phenomena the most remarkable, and having the most relation to the question now before us, were the following:

I. When he began to see, he believed that objects touched the external surface of his eye. This would seem to show that sight alone cannot enable us to judge of distances; but, after close examination, we shall clearly see that the argument is not conclusive. No one will pretend that sight, in the first moment of its exercise, can communicate equally clear and distinct ideas to us, as when experience has accustomed us to compare its different impressions. This is the same with touch as with sight. A blind person, from his frequent custom of guiding himself, in many of his movements by sensations of touch alone, comes to know the position and distances of objects with wonderful precision. If we suppose a man deprived of the sense of touch suddenly to acquire it, neither will he at first judge with the same certainty the objects of this sense as after having exercised it. Experience teaches that the sense of touch is capable of a high degree of perfection. We see it in blind persons at its highest point; and probably the lowest point of its perfection, in the first moments of its exercise, would greatly resemble that of sight at the instant of being freed from the cataracts; objects would be presented to it likewise in confusion; and the subject experiencing them could not well appreciate their differences until practice had taught him how to distinguish and classify.

With respect to distance, it is to be observed, that this blind person of Cheselden, so far from having the habit of appreciating it, had false ideas upon it. As he was not totally blind, the light, which he perceived through the cataracts, was sufficient to even enable him to distinguish between white, black, and red, which seemed to him to touch his eye. We may form some idea of this by observing what happens to us if we close our eyes in a very strong light. Hence he ought, when he gained his sight, to have imagined that the new sight was the same as the old, and, consequently, that nothing had happened but a simple change of object. A person totally blind would have better shown the power of sight to appreciate distances; for he would have had no habit either favorable or unfavorable to their knowledge.

II. It cost him much trouble to conceive that there were other objects beyond those he saw; he could not distinguish limits; every thing seemed to him immense. Although he knew by experience that his chamber was smaller than the whole house, he could not conceive how he could see this.

From these facts Condillac draws a confirmation of his system. We are astonished that he should pretend to found an entire philosophy upon such data. We submit the following considerations to the reader:

76. The subject is here a youth of thirteen or fourteen years, and consequently without any habit of observation. He would naturally express very confusedly the impressions he received in so new and strange a situation.

The organ of sight must, when exercised for the first time, be exceedingly weak, and consequently perform its sensitive functions only in a very imperfect way. We ourselves repeatedly experience that we cannot, if we suddenly pass from darkness to light, especially if it be a very strong light, distinguish objects, but we see every thing in great confusion; what then would happen to a poor child, when at the age of thirteen years, he for the first time opens his eyes to the light?

According to Cheselden's own account, objects were presented to him in such confusion that he could not distinguish them, no matter what their size or shape. This confirms what we have just said, that the partial, if not the sole cause of the confusion, was that the organ did not produce impressions well, because if these had been properly produced, he would have been able to distinguish the limits of the different colors; for, in simple sensation, to see is to distinguish.

We are also told that he could not recognize by sight the objects which he knew by touch. But this only proves that not having been able to compare the two orders of sensations, he could not know what corresponded in one to the impressions of the other. By touch he would have known a spherical body; but as he was still ignorant of the impression which a globe makes on the eye, it is clear that if any one should show him a ball which he had handled a thousand times, he would not even have suspected that the object seen was the same which he had touched. This leads me to another observation which I consider very important.

77. The child on whom these experiments were made was obliged to express his sensations in the visual order, in a language which he did not understand. For any one who is deprived of one of the senses must be absolutely ignorant of all the ideas which have their origin in that sensation. Hence it follows that he knows nothing of the language relating to that sense, and the ideas which he joins to the words are entirely different from what those who possess that sense mean to express. The blind man will speak of colors and the impressions produced by sight, because he hears others speak of these things; but for him the word to see does not mean to see, light is not light, nor color color, as we understand them, but they express different ideas which he has formed according to the circumstances, in conformity with the explanations he has heard. What importance then should we attach to what a child may say who, besides the thoughtlessness natural to his age, is placed in a situation new to him, and required to express his ideas in a language which he does not know? He is asked, for example, if he can distinguish a greater object from another which is smaller, without considering that the words greater and smaller as he understood them, inasmuch as they expressed abstract ideas, or were referred to the sensations of touch, were altogether new to him when applied to objects seen, since he had no means of knowing what was meant when referred to a sensation which he experienced for the first time. If within a circle, a number of smaller circles of a different color were described, he would see the smaller circles within the circumference of the greater; but if asked if one appeared greater than the rest, or if he could distinguish the limits which, separated the smaller circles from each other, he could not but give very absurd answers, which the observers might perhaps take as the expression of curious phenomena. They speak to him of figures, lines, extremities, size, position, and distances in relation to sight, and as he is ignorant of this language, yet knows not that he is ignorant of it, he must necessarily talk in a very strange manner. A more attentive and profound observer would have perceived the same misunderstanding as when a deaf man disputes without hearing what was said.

These remarks are further confirmed by the contradiction in the account of Cheselden. The oculist tells us that the child could not distinguish the objects, even those which differed most in form and size: but that he found those most agreeable which were the most regular. He must then have distinguished them; for otherwise, the sensation could not have been more or less pleasing. And here in choosing an alternative in this contradiction, we must hold that he distinguished the objects, since there is a strong argument in its favor. When two objects, the one regular, the other irregular, were presented to him, and he was questioned as to their resemblance and difference, he must have answered so absurdly as to create the suspicion that he could not distinguish them. The reason of this is, that besides the confusion of sensations, to which he was always more or less subject, he was also ignorant of the language, and although he distinguished the objects plainly, still he could not understand what he was asked, nor express what he felt. But when examined as to the nature of the impression and whether it was pleasing or otherwise, he found himself on a field common to all sensations, the ideas of pleasure and displeasure were not new to him, and he could say without confusion, this pleases me; that is displeasing to me.

To sum up what I have said, I believe that the phenomena of Cheselden's blind man, only prove that sight, like all the other senses, needs a certain education, that its first impressions are necessarily confused, that the organ acquires the proper strength and precision only after long practice, and finally, that the judgments formed in consequence, must be very incorrect until comparison, joined with reflection, has taught how to rectify inaccuracies.[37]

CHAPTER XIV
CAN SIGHT GIVE US THE IDEA OF A SOLID?

78. It has been asserted that sight can not give us the idea of size or of a solid, but that this can be obtained only by the help of touch. I believe the contrary may be proved with convincing certainty.

What is a solid? It is the union of three dimensions. If sight can give us the idea of surfaces which consist of two, why not also of solids which consist of three dimensions? This one reflection is enough to show that it has been denied without reason; but I shall not stop with this, but shall prove, by the most rigorous observation, and the analysis of its phenomena, that sight can give us the idea of a solid.

79. I willingly agree, that if we suppose a man deprived of all the other senses, to have his eyes immovably fixed on an immovable object, he would never be able to distinguish between what is solid and what is merely perspective in the object; or, in other words, that all the objects permanently painted on the retina will appear to be projected on a plane. The reason of this is founded on the very laws of the organ of this sense, and of the transmission of its impressions to the brain.

The soul refers the sensation to the extremity of the visual ray; and since in the present instance it has been unable to make any comparisons, it can have no motive for placing these extremities at unequal distances, which constitutes the third dimension.

In order to understand this better, let us suppose the object to be a cube placed so that three of its sides are seen. It is evident that although the three surfaces are equal, they will not appear so to the eye, because their respective positions do not permit them to send their rays equally to it. But as the soul has not had occasion to compare this sensation with any other, it can not calculate the difference produced by the different positions and distances, but must refer all the points to the same plane, regarding the sides of the cube as unequal; though, in reality, they are not so.

Sight, in this case, presents the whole object on a perspective plane; and as it could have no means of calculating the distance of the object from the eye, it would probably believe it joined to the eye, or, more strictly speaking, the sensation would represent only a simple phenomenon, the relations and cause of which we could not explain.

80. It is likewise probable, that if, while the eye remained fixed, we could open and shut the lids, we might form the idea that the object seen was outside of us; so that by this motion alone, we should obtain a point of comparison, by the succession of the alternate disappearance and reproduction of the sensation of the object by the interposition or non-interposition of an obstacle. Then the idea of a greater or less distance would arise, and as this would be in the direction perpendicular to the plane of the object, we should already have the idea of a solid.

Fortunately, nature has been more beneficent to us, and we are not obliged to limit ourselves to a supposition which thus curtails our means of acquiring ideas. Still it will not be useless to have examined the phenomenon on this supposition; for, from this examination, we shall gain light to understand what I propose to demonstrate.

81. In order that sight may originate the idea of a solid, it requires motion. This motion is an indispensable condition, though it may be either in the object or in the eye itself.

Let us suppose an immovable eye, and see how by the motion of the objects, the sensation of sight may present or produce the idea of a solid. The only difficulty is to show how it can add to the two dimensions which constitute the plane, the third which forms the solid.

Let a fixed eye be directed to a point where there is a right rectangular parallelopipedon B, so placed that its two bases are wholly concealed, and let the right line drawn from the centre of the eye to the edge of the parallelopipedon divide the plane angle into two equal parts. Let us also suppose the sides of the parallelopipedon to be of different colors,—white, green, red, and black. In this case, the eye sees the two planes as one, and the edge appears as a right line separating the two parts of the same plane which differ only in color. It is impossible for it to conceive the inclination of the two planes, because as it refers the object to the extremity of the visual ray, and has not been able to compare the varieties which result from difference of position and distance, and from the manner in which the object receives the light, it can only distinguish the different parts of the same plane.

It is well known that perspective can perfectly imitate a solid. For, if instead of the solid B, we suppose two planes exactly representing the two sides seen, the sensation will be the same, the illusion complete. Therefore, there are two distinct ways of producing the same sensation; and consequently, unless there has been a previous comparison, there is no means of distinguishing them apart; but the idea which would naturally result would be the most simple; that is, the idea of a plane.

82. If we suppose the parallelopipedon B to revolve on a vertical axis, it will present the four planes successively to the eye, and they will appear

greater or less according to their inclination to the visual ray, the surface of the plane reaching its maximum when perpendicular to the ray, and its minimum when parallel to it.

The succession and variety of the sensations will immediately produce the idea of motion; for the same planes of the parallelopipedon are seen in different positions. The uniform manner in which these planes succeed one another, will also suggest the idea that the green which appears a few moments after the black, is the same which was seen a few moments before; and so of the other colors. Also, as one is constantly hiding behind the other, this naturally gives rise to the idea of extension in the direction, or continuation of the visual ray; and this is sufficient to produce the idea of size or of a solid. When we see a plane we have the two dimensions which constitute a surface; to form the idea of a solid, we need only the idea of one dimension more; this can not be found in the same plane, but is produced by the motion of the parallelopipedon.

83. This motion which we have supposed to be around a vertical axis, we may equally suppose to take place around a horizontal axis. We shall then see in succession the two opposite sides, and the bases of the parallelopipedon with different appearances, according to their various positions; or, in other words, according to the angle formed by the planes and the visual ray. These appearances will help more and more to form the idea of the third dimension, which is not to be found in the primitive plane, and consequently to supply what was wanted to constitute the idea of a solid.

84. Just as we have supposed the eye fixed and the object movable, we may suppose the eye in motion and the object immovable. The result is the same; for, it is evident that if the eye should move around the parallelopipedon, now vertically, and now horizontally, it would experience the same sensations as when it was quiet, and the parallelopipedon moved. Thus, although we suppose the subject wholly deprived of the sense of touch, so as to be unable to perceive its own motion, it can still form the idea of solid by the impressions of sight alone. True, it could distinguish which moved, the eye or the object, but this does not interfere with the formation of the idea composed of the three dimensions.

CHAPTER XV
SIGHT AND MOTION

85. I said that the observer could not distinguish between his own motion and that of the object; sight alone can not give us a true idea of motion. Thus in a boat, although we are certain that we are moving, the motion seems to us to be in the objects along the shore. Also if the motion of the object and that of the observer are simultaneous, in the same direction, and with the same velocity, all appearance of motion is lost. But if there are two objects, one of which moves in the same direction as ourselves, and the other in the opposite direction, we perceive only the latter. Thus in a canal boat, the horse which walks on the bank in the same direction which the boat follows, seems to move without advancing. Of the two motions of the horse, we perceive only the vertical, the horizontal escapes us.

The reason of this is clear, we can judge the object only by our impressions. When the impression varies, we have the idea of motion; but not otherwise. When the object or the eye is in motion, there is a succession of impressions on the retina, from which the idea of motion arises. But if the motion of the eye accompanies the motion of the object, one cancels the other, the impression on the retina is constant, and the object does not seem to move.

86. In the same manner if the motion of the object and that of the eye are simultaneous, but of unequal velocity, we perceive only the difference; that is to say, if the motion of the eye be represented by 3 and that of the object by 5, the motion of the object will appear as 2, or the difference between 5 and 3. If our motion is more rapid than the motion of the object, although in the same direction, the object will appear to move in the opposite direction, as when we sail down a river faster than the current, the water seems to flow backwards. An immovable object at the same time seems to move in a direction opposite to our own with greater velocity than the current; for, here also, of the two motions we perceive only the difference. The motion of the boat, which is equal to 5, seems transferred to the fixed object, which appears to move in the opposite direction with the velocity represented by 5; and if we suppose the velocity of the current to be equal to 3, it will have the appearance of moving backwards with a velocity of 5-3, or 2.

87. From these considerations it would seem to follow that although sight is sufficient to give us the idea of motion, it is not sufficient to enable us to distinguish our own motion from that of the object, but for this we have need of touch. But this is not so; for by sight alone, we can distinguish the motion of the eye from that of the object, and if in some cases this is impossible, the same is true of touch.

We must observe that in the above examples touch is of much less use than sight in order to preserve us from illusions. How by the aid of touch alone could we perceive the motion of a boat gliding smoothly down a river? Sometimes by the help of sight we observe this motion, especially if we regard the objects along the bank which we pass; but touch is essentially limited to what affects the body immediately, and therefore cannot discover motion when the body is not affected by it.

It is also well to observe that we do not refer the motion perceived by touch to the objects around us until after we have acquired this habit by means of repeated comparisons. When for the first time the hand is passed over an object, we are unable to tell whether the hand moves over the body, or the body under the hand.

The reason of this is that the sensation of motion is essentially a successive sensation, and this succession exists equally whether the hand moves or the object. Let us suppose the hand to pass along an object of a varied surface, we shall experience the variety of sensations corresponding to the surface; suppose now that the hand remains motionless, and the object passes under it with the same velocity, pressure, and friction, the sensations will be the same as before. Every one must have observed that when leaning on a slippery object, it is often difficult to tell whether it is the object which moves, or ourselves. Therefore touch also confirms what we have advanced, that the distinction between the motion of the member and that of the object does not arise from simple sensation.

88. In this respect, therefore, touch does not help sight; let us see if sight alone can enable us to distinguish between the motion of the eye and that of the object. We have already observed that a single sensation with respect to one object only is insufficient, but there is no difficulty in proving that this result may be obtained by the comparison of different sensations.

Let us suppose the eye at a point A, looking at an object B; the object will appear at the extremity of the range of the sight as if projected on a plane. To be more definite we will imagine the object B to be a column in the middle of a large hall, and the point A a corner of the same hall. The column will appear to the eye to be a part of the opposite wall. If the eye changes its position, the column will appear in another part of the wall; so that if the eye should pass around the column, it would appear successively on every part of the wall. The same succession of phenomena would be observed if the eye should remain fixed and the column should move around it; for it is evident that if the observer is placed in the centre of the room, and the column moves around him, the column will appear on all the parts of the opposite wall. From this we infer that only one sensation of sight, with only one object, is not enough to determine whether the eye moves or the object.

But if instead of one object we suppose several moving simultaneously, it is easy to see how the distinction of motions arises. Let us suppose that at the same time that the eye sees the column, it also sees other objects, such as chandeliers, statues, or other columns, placed between the eye and the opposite wall. If the eye moves every time the column changes its position on the opposite wall, the other columns, the chandeliers, statues, everything in the room seems to change its position; whereas, if the column moves and the eye remains fixed, the column alone changes its position, while everything else remains motionless. Therefore sight alone gives us two distinct orders of phenomena of motion:

I. The first, in which all the objects change their position.

II. The second, in which one object only changes its position.

These two orders of phenomena cannot remain unperceived; for by the help of reflection excited and enlightened by the repetition of the phenomena, we must come to the conclusion that when there is an entire and constant change of all the objects, it is not they that move, but the eye; and that when only one or a part of the objects change their position, the rest remaining fixed, it is not the eye that moves, but the objects which change their position. When everything around us changes we infer that it is the eye that moves; when one or two change their position we conclude that they move and not the eye. This is not merely a supposition, it is the reality. The ideas derived from touch are essentially limited, and it is therefore impossible that they should proceed from distant objects which cannot be touched.

89. I believe I have demonstrated that the pretended superiority of touch is without foundation, and that the opinion which makes this the basis of our knowledge of external objects, the touch-stone of the certainty of the sensations transmitted by the other senses, is an error. Without it we can acquire the certainty of the existence of bodies; without it we can form the idea of surfaces and solids; without it we discover motion, and distinguish the motion of the object from that of the organ which receives the impression. The theory of sensation here explained, and the results which are deduced from the relations of the dependence or independence

of the phenomena among themselves, and with our will, may all be applied to the sight as well as to the touch.

90. Summing up all we have said, we have the following results:

I. We distinguish sleep from waking, even abstracting the objectiveness of the sensations.

II. We distinguish two orders of phenomena of sensation;—the one internal, the other external, here also abstracting their objectiveness.

III. The senses give us certainty of the existence of bodies.

IV. Sensations have no type in the external object of what they represent, except *extension* and motion.

V. Touch is not the basis or touch-stone of certainty.

VI. All that we know by means of the senses may be reduced to this; that there are external beings, that is to say, beings placed outside of ourselves, which are extended, subject to necessary laws, and which produce in us the effects which we call sensations.

CHAPTER XVI
POSSIBILITY OF OTHER SENSES

91. Lamennais writes: "Who can say that a sixth sense would not disturb the harmony of the others by a contrary impression? On what foundation could he deny it? If we suppose other senses different from those which nature gave us, might not our sensations and our ideas be different? Perhaps a slight modification in our organs would be sufficient to ruin our whole science. Perhaps there are beings so organized that their sensations are wholly opposed to ours, and what is true for us is false for them, and reciprocally. For, if we examine the matter closely, what necessary connection is there between our sensations and the reality? And if there were such a connection, how could the senses make it known to us?"[38]

The questions which these words raise are of the highest importance and merit a serious examination.

92. Is there any intrinsical impossibility of an organization different from ours, and an order of sensations different from those which we experience? It seems not; and if this impossibility exists, it is unknown to man.

Whatever opinion we adopt as to the manner in which external objects act upon the soul by means of the organs of the body, there is no necessary relation, nor even analogy, between the object and the effect which it produces in us.

A body receives upon its surface rays of the fluid which we call *light*, these rays are reflected upon the retina, which is another surface in communication with the brain. So far all is well, and easily understood. There is a fluid which moves, goes from one surface to another, and may cause this or that purely physical effect on the cerebral matter; but what connection is there between this and the impression of a distinct order which we call *seeing*, an impression which is neither the fluid nor the motion, but an affection of which the living and thinking being, the *me* is intimately conscious?

If, instead of the luminous fluid and its mechanism, we suppose another, as, for example, the air which vibrates upon the tympanum, what *essential* reason is there why this should not produce a sensation similar to that of sight? It must be confessed that it is impossible to assign an *essential* reason. To one who has no idea of our present organization, both phenomena are equally incomprehensible.

93. What has been said of sight and hearing may be applied to the other senses. In all there is a bodily organ affected by a body; we see the surfaces placed one before or under the other, we see motions of one kind or another; but how can we pass over the immense distance which separates these physical phenomena from the phenomenon of sensation? For my part, I see no way to do it; this point is a barrier to the human intellect; all appearances indicate that there is no connection between these two orders of phenomena except what the will of the Creator has *freely* established; if there is any necessary connection, this necessity is a secret to man. Examine the textures which receive the impression of the objects, the material substance which composes the nervous system which is the organ of sensations, and say what relation you can find between the physical phenomena of this matter and the wonderful harmony of sensible phenomena.

94. Still greater will be the difficulty if you consider that, although protected from any injury, the organs cease to produce sensations from the moment they are deprived of communication with the substance of the brain. The phenomena of light are produced in the cavity of the skull amid the most profound darkness; and all the wonderful magic of sensations by which the magnificent spectacle of the universe is presented to our mind, which plunges the soul into raptures at the sound of music, and which produces such varied and delightful sensations of taste and odors, all arises in the brain, a whitish, rude, and unformed substance, from the appearance of which no one could imagine it destined to such noble functions.

95. Why is it that when the nerve A, in communication with the brain is affected, we experience the sensation which we call *seeing*, or if the nerve B is affected, the sensation which we call *hearing*, and so of the other senses? There may be a reason, but, at least, we do not know it; and it is probably no other than the free will of the Creator.

Here, it is true, philosophy confesses its weakness, but, at the same time, it shows its power; for it sees the immense distance which separates these phenomena, between which there can be no point of communication but what is established by the Almighty. When there are second causes, it is the merit of philosophy to discover them; but when there are none, its merit is in rising to the first cause. A confession of its ignorance is sometimes a more sublime act of reason than the impotent effort of an unbounded pride. If the perception of profound truths exalts the intellect, is not the intellect exalted in perceiving its own ignorance, which is sometimes a profound truth?

96. The existence of another sense is, then, possible; at least, we see no impossibility of it. If the deaf man who has no idea of sound, and the blind man who knows not what color is, would be foolish to deny the possibility of those sensations of which they are deprived, can we, with any more show of reason, assert the impossibility of an order of sensations different from what we possess? If we examine the system of sensations by the light of reason, we can discover no essential dependence between the sensations and their respective organs, nor between the organs and the objects and circumstances by which they are affected. Why does the impression of the light upon my eyes cause in me a particular sensation, which cannot result from the same impression on a different part of my body? Why may not the brain receive the same impression in various forms? Why must this fluid which we call *light*, and no other, produce the impression? Why may not this same sensation of *seeing* proceed equally from other affections of the brain? A violent blow on the head produces the sensation of many luminous points, whence the common expression of "seeing stars by daylight." We must confess that philosophy knows nothing of these secrets, that as yet it has not been able to penetrate them, and it can give no answer to these questions. It sees an order of facts, but no necessary connection between them, or rather, judging from its ideas of mind and body, every thing induces it to believe that these phenomena in our life depend solely on the will of our Creator.

97. If an entirely new order of sensations is possible, there may be beings with six or seven senses. The imagination cannot conceive their nature; but reason sees in them no impossibility.

CHAPTER XVII
EXISTENCE OF NEW SENSES

98. Is it certain that we have only five ways of sensation? I have some doubts on this point. In order to present them with the greatest clearness, and solve the questions which they raise, it is well to settle the meaning of the terms.

What is sensation? In the ordinary acceptation of the word, it is the perception of the impression transmitted to us by one of the organs of the five senses. Thus understood it is clearly limited to the action of the organs, but if considered as expressing a certain class of animal phenomena, it is the experiencing of any affection produced by an impression of the organism. Even in common use the word sensation in its broadest signification is not restricted to the impressions of the five senses, and although we make a great difference between *sentiment* and *sensation*; still we are often forced to confound them, and to use the word *sensation* to express things which have nothing whatever to do with the five senses. Thus we say: "The news made a great sensation;" "I cannot resist the force of such strong sensations," etc., in which cases it is evident that there is no reference to seeing, hearing, smelling, tasting, or touching, but to a different order of affections of the soul.

99. I said we were forced to use the word in the broader meaning; it is the truth which forces us. For, to the eyes of philosophy, the phenomenon of sensation consists in the production in the soul of a particular affection determined by an impression on an organ; and of whatever order this affection may be, and whatever organ may be affected, the animal phenomenon is substantially the same. The difference is in the class of affections and of the organ which is their medium, the essence of the phenomenon does not change. And if by sensations we understand such distinct orders of affections as those of sight and of touch, why may we not include other impressions caused by any other organ, whatever that organ may be?

100. Whatever use we may make of the word sensation, it is certain that we experience many affections caused by organic impressions, besides those

of the five senses. What are passions but affections of the soul, springing from organic impressions? Does not the mere presence of an object often excite love, anger, pity, joy, grief, and many other sentiments of the soul?

You may say there is an essential difference between the impressions of the senses and those of the passions, that the former are independent of all previous idea and reflection, which the latter more or less presuppose. Thus, when an object is present to our open eyes, we cannot but see it and always in the same manner; and yet this object will excite in us at one time one passion, at another time another, and sometimes none; and almost always with great difference in the degree of its intensity. Moreover it is not only the mere presence of the object which causes an affection, but certain conditions are necessary, for example; the remembrance of a benefit or of an injury, etc., from which it is easy to see that there is an essential difference between the two classes of impressions.

101. If we reflect well upon this objection we shall find that though it is specious and under many aspects true, it contradicts nothing which I have asserted. I did not deny that the new impressions were subject to very different conditions from those that govern the five senses; but on the contrary I have all along supposed a difference not only in the class of impressions and the diversity of the organ, but also in the manner in which the organ is affected, and the circumstances in which the sensation is produced in the soul. I only contended that the animal phenomenon was substantially the same, that we find in it the three things which constitute its nature; a corporeal object; an organ affected by this object; and an impression produced in the soul. Because this impression cannot exist without the aid of this or that idea, this or that recollection, it does not follow that the phenomenon does not exist, or that it is not the same; it is merely to impose a new condition, and nothing more.

102. But there is no necessity of admitting that some previous idea or reflection is requisite in order that the sight of the object may produce certain impressions in the soul;—daily experience proves the contrary. How is it that the presence of an object charms in an instant a tender and perhaps innocent heart? Whence then arises that sudden fascination which is preceded by no idea, accompanied by no affection, and is scarce voluntary? Not from the thought of gross enjoyments; for perhaps he of whom I speak knows not their existence until he experiences this emotion; he feels for the first time in his breast a trouble unknown before. We must therefore recur to an organic affection similar to that which we find in the other senses. Certain conditions of age and temperament may be requisite, one object may have been necessary, among a thousand, in particular circumstances, of which the soul can give no account to itself though affected by them; yet

it is still true that there is an external object, an affection of the organism, and an impression in the soul, all connected together by a mysterious, but undeniable bond.

It is easy to discover a series of strong impressions in the phenomena relating to reproduction; but although they presuppose the action of some one of the five senses, they nevertheless belong to a different order. No physiological studies are necessary to prove that these affections depend on the organization, and that they are greatly influenced by age, health, temperament, food, climate, and the seasons.

103. There is a difference between sentiments and sensations which, though it does not change the fact physiologically and psychologically considered, still greatly modifies it in its intellectual and moral relations. The passions are commonly excited by an animate and sensible object, whence it would seem that there is more communication between mind and mind, between soul and soul, than there is between one body and another. The sad and mournful appearance not only of a man, but even of an animal, immediately excites in our breast the sentiment of compassion, because it expresses the suffering of a living being. This only proves that nature has mysterious ways by which it transmits to us the knowledge of hidden things; but this transmission is made by the medium of a body which affects in some way our organic constitution. There is here, if you please, a more admirable, more penetrating, and more spiritual a magic than that of the senses alone; but the difference is in the degree, not in the nature of the phenomena.

It is certain that living beings, and those of the same species in particular, are in a constant communication which mutually excites their affections, and that these affections frequently suppose a mysterious correspondence with unknown agencies. Physical nature is full of fluids whose qualities are daily becoming known through scientific observation. The phenomena of electricity and galvanism have revealed secrets of which we had no suspicion before. Who can tell by what means the functions of this vast and complicated system of animal life, spread over the universe, are performed? It is probable that there are profound secrets in the correspondence and relation of organisms and in the way in which they influence one another yet to be discovered; perhaps they will remain forever veiled to the eyes of mortality.

104. Is it true that sensible beings can alone excite the passions? or have not inanimate causes repeatedly affected our organs? Why are we sometimes joyful and sometimes sad, at some times peaceful and at others irritable, when we have had no communication with any living being? It is clear that

this depends on the affections of our organism, and has no relation to the state of other sensible beings.

105. Therefore, besides the impressions caused by the five senses, there are others which proceed from purely corporeal and inanimate objects. Besides the phenomena of ordinary sensations, there are others which differ from them only in the kind of impression and the organ affected; and there is no more difference between these sensations and the former than there is between the impressions of one and those of another of the five senses. Therefore it is not correct to say that there are only five kinds of sensation.

CHAPTER XVIII
SOLUTION OF LAMENNAIS' OBJECTION

106. From the preceding observations we shall now deduce an important consequence,—the solution of the difficulty presented by Lamennais. The existence of new senses would involve new sensations, it is true; but they would not disturb the harmony of those we already have. We have shown that bodies affect our organs in a different manner, and produce impressions different from those of the five senses; but this does not disturb the agreement of our sensations, nor change our ideas. Consequently, the supposition of Lamennais would not involve the disorder which he suspects.

107. Sensations in themselves are mere affections of the soul, and have no external object which corresponds to them except the existence and extension of bodies. Therefore a new order of sensations would only be a new order of affections, which would in nowise alter our ideas.

From what we have hitherto said, it is easy to see that the supposition of Lamennais is already realized; for there are sensations different from those of the five senses; therefore this supposition does not contradict the nature and order of our ideas, nor the certainty of our knowledge.

A musical instrument beautifully fashioned has charms for the ear, the eye, and the touch, none of these impressions destroys the other; if we suppose it placed in new relations with our organs, so as to produce in the soul new impressions, why is it impossible that they should accord? Does the melody of its sound cease because our soul experiences new affections whose nature has no connection with it? Certainly not. Why then fear the overthrow of our knowledge by the introduction of a new order of sensations? Why give such importance to a supposition, the effects of which we can very well calculate, and which, if we examine the phenomena of our present sensations, we find already realized?

108. It is true that we know of no other means of placing ourselves in contact with external objects than the five senses; but it is equally true, that this contact existing, the impressions in the soul correspond mysteriously to the external objects; so that, while we observe the sensations by which the communication is established, it is still impossible for us to explain them.

Let us examine the magical effects of music. They are of two orders; the purely auditive, and the intellectual or moral. The first stop at the ear, the second pass to the brain and to the heart; and one may be admirably organized for the former, yet unable to appreciate the latter. Two persons listen to a sonata, both hear the *material* music, but the intellectual and moral effects are not the same on both. Both perceive the least defect in the time or in the instrument, both admire the art of the composer, both are charmed; but while the heart of one is unmoved, the brain and the heart of the other are bounding with delight, the power of his fancy is multiplied, thoughts and images crowd upon his mind, as though he had caught inspiration from the magic notes of the music. His heart is transported with tenderness, melancholy, hatred, love, anger, generosity, and courage. He is under a magical influence which, moves him in spite of himself; the vibrations of a chord have raised in his heart a mysterious tempest which the might of reason can hardly quiet.

109. From this we must conclude, that besides the ordinary relations between objects and the organs of the senses, there are other relations still more intimate and more delicate between these objects and our organic system, and that these latter are as certain as the former. In them there is greater variety of individuals, and the conditions necessary to produce determinate results are less known, but there can be no doubt of their existence, and this in the eyes of sound philosophy is sufficient to dissipate those absurd suppositions which would pretend to undermine the edifice of our knowledge.

110. Thus, then, the objection is answered, which says: "If we had another sense, what would it tell us?" Nothing which would destroy the certainty of our knowledge, or the nature and order of our ideas. The only new result would be *one more* added to the many ways in which objects now affect us. The same thing would happen to us as to a man who after being deprived of the sense of smell, should suddenly regain it: he would have one sensation more; the same thing would happen to us as to a man who experiences a new sentiment which he had not known before: he has one affection more. New impressions have their own rank, neither interfering with, nor changing those which previously existed.

BOOK THIRD
EXTENSION AND SPACE

CHAPTER I
EXTENSION INSEPARABLE
FROM THE IDEA OF BODY

1. Having seen that among the objects of our sensations, extension alone has any external existence for us as any thing more than a principle of causality, let us now try to understand what extension is.

The idea of extension seems to be inseparable from that of body; at least, I am unable to conceive a body without extension. Take away extension, and the parts disappear, and with them all that has relation with our senses; there is no longer an object, or, if the object remains, it is something altogether different from what is contained in the idea of body. Imagine an apple, for instance, from which you suddenly take away extension. What will remain of it?

I am not now going to examine whether Descartes is right when he says, that the essence of body consists in extension; all that I here assert is that a body cannot be conceived without extension. I do not affirm the identity of two things, but only the inseparability of two ideas in our mind. It is not an opinion, but a fact asserted by consciousness, which is now under discussion.

Abstracting extension, I can conceive, it is true, a substance, or, to speak more generally, a being; but, then, there is no idea of body, unless we confound this idea with, that of substance or of being, in general.

2. All our notions of bodies are obtained through the senses, but without extension no sensation is possible; for without it there can be no color, no sound, no touch, no smell, and no taste; therefore, without extension there remains only something of which we have no idea, a vague notion which cannot enable us to distinguish one object from another, a pure abstraction, and nothing more.

3. To solve the difficulties which attend the separation of the two ideas of extension and of body, it is necessary to determine the essence of body. When we can distinguish the essence of a body from its extension, the difficulty will be overcome, but not until then.

4. In order to understand the reason of this inseparability, it is necessary to remember what was said before, that extension is the basis of all other sensations; it is the *substratum* which is confounded with none, depends on none of them in particular, yet is an indispensable condition of them all.

I look at an apple, and examine the mutual relations of the sensations which it produces.

It is evident that though I abstract the smell, I do not thereby destroy any of the other sensations which it causes. Though it lose its odor, it is still extended, colored, it has a taste, and may produce a sound. I may also, in like manner, abstract its taste, its color, and all that relates to the sight, but I have still an object which is tangible, and consequently extended, figured, and possessed of all its other properties which affect the touch.

If instead of abstracting what relates to the sight, I abstract what belongs immediately to the touch, I may do this without destroying the other sensations; for I can still see the apple, its extension, form, and color.

I may even go farther, and strip the apple of all its sensible qualities, of its taste, smell, color, hardness, and whatever the senses can perceive, still there remains extension, not indeed sensible, but conceivable. Extension exists abstracted from its visibility, since it exists for the blind man: abstracted from its tangibility, since it exists for the sight; abstracted from odor, taste, and sound, since it exists for those who are deprived of these sensations, so long as they have sight or touch.

5. Here a difficulty arises. There seems to be a mistake in what we have said of the existence of extension abstracted from other sensations; for, although in making this abstraction we conceive ourselves to be deprived of these sensations, still we retain the *imagination* of them; thus, when I strip the apple of all light and color, it is still extended; but that is because I still imagine a color, or, if I make a strong effort to destroy the color, it appears to me like a black object, on a ground of greater or less darkness, distinct from the apple. Does not this prove that there is an illusion in such abstractions, and that there is no complete abstraction, since the reality which we abstract is succeeded by the imagination of the same qualities, or of others which supply their place, so as to make the extension perceptible?

This objection is specious, and it would be difficult to give a satisfactory answer if the existence of men deprived of sight did not instantly dissipate it. No such imagination is possible in the case of a blind man, for him there is no color, no shade, no light, no darkness, nor anything which relates to sight, and still he conceives extension.

6. But at least, some one will answer, it must be confessed that the idea of extension is necessarily dependent on the sensations of touch; blind men also possess this sense, and by it they acquire the idea of extension. Therefore the idea of extension is inseparable from the sensations of touch. This argument is no better than the other; for, although we may acquire the idea of extension by the sense of touch, and this sense is all that is required to produce it, it is not true that this idea can only be acquired by touch. I have already proved that sight is sufficient of itself alone to produce the idea of the three dimensions which constitute a solid or extension in its full complement. But here I do not need the idea of a solid, that of a surface is sufficient; the extension of a surface is inseparable from sight. There is no sight without color, or light of some kind or other, and this cannot even be imagined without a surface.

I have another argument. Geometricians, doubtless, conceive extension, and yet they abstract all its relations to sight or touch; therefore, there is no necessary connection between them.

In any object submitted to the sight, what quality relating to the touch is necessary in order to produce the idea of extension? If we examine it closely, we shall find that there is none. Let us take a liquid; is its fluidity the necessary quality? No; for when congealed extension remains. Is it heat or cold? No; for without destroying its extension we may change its temperature as much as we please, no alteration is perceptible. Whatever quality relative to touch we may take, we shall find that it may be varied, modified, or entirely destroyed, without visibly affecting the extension.

It often happens that we have a clear and definite idea of the extension of an object without knowing any thing of its qualities in relation to touch. I see an object at a distance, I distinguish its color and its form, but I know not of what material it is, whether it is of marble, or wood, or wax, nor whether this material is hard or soft, moist or dry, warm or cold. I do not even know if it is tangible, as in the case of figures formed by vapors which are imperceptible to the touch.

7. Without extension there can be neither sight, nor touch, nor any other sensation. As to taste, it is clear that it requires touch, and cannot exist without it. Our assertion is less clear with regard to sound and smell; for, although we cannot separate these sensations from the idea of extension as they always involve this idea in one way or another, we do not know how it would be with a man who was deprived of all the other senses, and

retained only those of smelling and hearing. But without speculating on this hypothesis, it is enough to know:

I. That nothing which is not extended can act upon our organs, unless by means wholly unknown to us, and which would give no idea of what we understand by body.

II. That even supposing the sensations of smelling and hearing to be possible without the idea of extension, they would in that case be only simple phenomena of our being, and would not place us in communication with the external world, as we now perceive it; because, if we should not know that they proceeded from another cause, we could have no more consciousness of them than that which we have of the *me*; and if we should know it, this cause would be represented to us only as an agent influencing us, and not by any means as a being having any thing similar to what we understand by body.

III. That in such a case we should have no idea of our own organization, nor of the universe; for it is clear that every thing being reduced to mere internal phenomena, and their relation to the agents producing them, and the idea of extension wanting, neither the universe nor our own body would be to us what they now are. What would the universe,—what would our body be without extension?

IV. That for the present we limit ourselves to the demonstration of the dependence which in the present system, of things, all sensations have in relation to extension; and this demonstration holds good, even though we suppose the man who possesses only the sense of smelling or that of hearing not to form any idea of extension, and not to need it in order to experience its sensations.

V. That even on this supposition, the proposition before established, that the idea of extension is independent of the other sensations, still remains unassailed.

VI. That the truth which we are principally endeavoring to demonstrate, that for us the idea of extension is inseparable from that of body, also stands firm.

8. This inseparability is so certain, that theologians explaining the august mystery of the Eucharist, distinguish in the extension of bodies the relations of the parts to each other, and their relation to place, *in ordine ad se, et in ordine ad locum*; and they say that the sacred body of our Lord Jesus Christ is in this august Sacrament, by extension *in ordine ad se*, though not by extension *in ordine ad locum*. This proves that the theologians saw that it is not possible for man to lose all idea of extension, without at the same time losing all idea of body; and thus they invented this ingenious distinction, of which I shall speak at greater length in another place.

CHAPTER II
EXTENSION NOT PERCEPTIBLE AS THE DIRECT AND IMMEDIATE OBJECT OF SENSATIONS

9. Extension has the remarkable peculiarity of being perceived by different senses. As regards sight and touch this is evident; it is also true as far as concerns the other senses. We perceive taste in different parts of the palate, and we refer sound and smell to distinct points in space, and this involves the idea of extension.

But what is more strange is, that although extension is the indispensable basis of all sensations and therefore perceived by all the senses, it is, in itself, and separated from every other quality, imperceptible to them all. The eye perceives only light, and the ear sound, the palate taste, the smell odor, and the object of touch is that which is warm or cold, moist or dry, solid or liquid, etc. None of these objects is extension, none *in particular* is necessary for the perception of extension; for we constantly find it separated from each of these qualities, and yet it is still perceptible. No one *in particular* is necessary for the perceptibility of extension, but some one is indispensable; for, unless accompanied by some one of them, it is imperceptible to the senses.

Hence, extension is a necessary condition of our sensations, but is not itself perceived by the senses. Still it is not therefore unknown, and this brings me to some other reflections which take us out of the phenomenal into the transcendental order, and give rise to very serious and difficult questions, which have hitherto been insolvable, and it is to be feared must ever remain so.

10. We have seen that extension in itself is not the direct object of sensation. What, then, is it? What is its nature?

There are two things which may be considered in the idea of extension: that which it is in us, and that which it represents to us; or, in other words, its relation to the subject, and its relation to the object. The first being subject to immediate observation, inasmuch as it exists within us, is difficult but not impossible to explain. The second is more difficult, and almost impossible to explain, because it is a very abstract and transcendental idea, and also requires a series of arguments, the thread of which may be broken without the one who reasons perceiving it.

11. Extension in us is not a sensation, but an idea. Sometimes we imagine it under a sensible form, confounding it with a determinate object; at other times we picture it to ourselves as a vague obscurity in which bodies are placed; but these are only fictions of the imagination. A man born blind can have none of these internal representations, and yet he forms a very good conception of extension. We ourselves in thinking of extension abstract all these forms under which we imagine it.

Two different sensations, those of sight and touch, produce the same idea of extension. This is conclusive proof that extension is rather intelligible than sensible.

Whatever may be the relation of extension to sensation, we cannot deny that it is an idea if we reflect that it is the foundation of the whole science of geometry. Thus, although we form various images of extension, they are only the particular forms with which the mind clothes the idea, if we may use the expression, according to the circumstances of the case. That which is fundamental and essential in the idea, is of a different and higher order, and has nothing in common with the applications which the mind makes in order to explain and apply it. This idea includes dimensions, but not determined or applied; they are mere conceptions which represent nothing in particular.

12. The idea of extension is a primitive fact of our mind. It is not produced by sensations, but precedes them, if not in time, at least in the order of being. There is no ground for asserting that the idea of extension exists in the mind prior to the first impression of the senses, but unless extension serves as their basis these impressions are inconceivable. Whether this idea is innate or developed, or produced in the mind by the impressions, there can be no doubt that it is distinct from them, necessary to them, and independent of any one of them in particular.

It may be that when these impressions are first received extension may not be known as a separate idea; but it is certain that it is afterwards separated and stripped of the corporeal form, and spiritualized, and that this phenomenon may be occasioned but not caused by the sensation.

In sight, abstracting extension, there is color, but we cannot discover in it any thing from which we can produce so fruitful an idea as that of extension. Even at first we see that the color itself is not perceptible without extension, and so far from extension being produced by color, it is on the contrary an indispensable condition without which color cannot be perceived.

Colors as the objects of sensation are only individual phenomena, which have no connection with one another nor with the general idea of extension. What has been said of them will equally apply to all the impressions of touch.

CHAPTER III
SCIENTIFIC FRUITFULNESS OF
THE IDEA OF EXTENSION

13. In order to understand the superiority of the idea of extension over mere sensations; or rather, in order to understand that there is a true idea of extension considered in itself, and that there is no such idea of the direct and immediate objects of sensation, I wish to call attention to the fact that among all the objects of the senses, *extension alone gives origin to a science.*

This is a very important fact;—to explain it as it deserves, I shall establish the following propositions:

FIRST PROPOSITION.

Extension is the basis of geometry.

SECOND PROPOSITION.

Not only is extension the basis of geometry, but all that we know of the nature of bodies may be reduced to the manifestations, applications, and modifications of extension, with the addition of the ideas of number and time.

THIRD PROPOSITION.

Whatever we know of sensations that deserves the name of science is included in the modifications of extension.

FOURTH PROPOSITION.

We can form no fixed idea of corporeal objects, nor make any observation on the sensible world, unless we are guided by the rule of extension.

These four propositions are nothing more than the enunciation of certain facts, the mere exposition of which is a sufficient demonstration.

14. Extension is the basis of geometry. This is evident, since geometry treats only of dimensions, and the idea of dimension is essential to extension.

When geometry treats of figures, it is still extension which it is treating of; for figures are only extension with certain limitations. The quadrilateral contains two triangles. To distinguish them, it is only necessary to draw their limit, which is the diagonal. The idea of figure is merely the idea of limited extension, and the figure is of this or that kind according to the nature of its limits. Consequently, the idea of figure is nothing new superadded to extension; but merely its application.

Moreover, limit or termination is not a positive idea; it is a pure negation. If I have extension and wish to form all the figures possible, I need not conceive any thing new, but only abstract what I have already; I do not add, but take away. Thus in the quadrilateral I obtain the conception of the triangle by abstracting one of the two equal parts into which it is divided by the diagonal. In the same manner I deduce the quadrilateral from a pentagon by abstracting the triangle formed by a line drawn from one of its angles to either of the opposite angles. These observations apply to all geometrical figures.

The idea of extension is like an immense ground on which we have only to *draw limits* in order to obtain whatever we want.

It does not follow from this that the understanding cannot proceed by addition or the synthetic method; for, just as the subtraction of one of the parts of the quadrilateral formed a triangle, so also the addition of two triangles with an equal side will produce a quadrilateral. And in the same way points produce lines, lines surfaces, and surfaces solids. In all these cases the idea of figure is that of limited extension, since the quantities which constitute it are merely extension with certain limitations.

15. An observation here presents itself to my mind, which I think must throw great light upon the question which we are now discussing. If we compare the two methods by which the idea of figure is obtained; the synthetic, or that of composition or addition, and the analytic, or that of subtraction or limitation, we shall find that the second is more natural than the other; because that which the analytic method produces is permanent in the figure and essential to it, whilst the synthetic only seems to constitute it, and as soon as it is thus constituted the marks of its formation are obliterated.

An example will make this clearer. In order to conceive a rectangle I have only to limit indefinite space by four lines in a rectangular position; that is, to *affirm* a part, and *deny* the rest. The lines are nothing in themselves, and represent only the limit beyond which the space included in the rectangle cannot pass. To abstract this limitation or denial of all that is not contained in the surface of the rectangle, would be to destroy the rectangle. Therefore, the denial in which this method consists is always permanent, the manner of the production of the idea is inseparable from the idea itself.

But if, on the other hand, I proceed to form the rectangle by addition or by joining the hypotheneuse of two right-angle triangles, the ideas of the two component parts are not necessary to the idea of the rectangle after its formation. I can conceive the rectangle even abstracting the diagonal.

Thus, then, it is demonstrated that the idea of extension is the only basis of geometry, and that this idea is an immense field on which, by means of limitation or abstraction, we can obtain all the figures which form the object of geometry. Figures are only extension limited, a positive extension accompanied by a negation, and consequently whatever is positive in geometry is extension.

16. We cannot doubt that, whatever we know of the nature of bodies, may be reduced to certain modifications or properties of extension, if we observe that the entire object of the natural sciences is the knowledge of the motion or of the different relations of things in space, which is nothing more than the knowledge of the different kinds of extension.

Statics is occupied in determining the laws of the equilibrium of bodies, but in what way? Does it penetrate into the nature of the causes? No; it only determines the conditions to which the phenomenon is subject, and the only ideas which enter into these conditions are the *direction of the force*, that is to say, a *line* in space, and the velocity, which is the relation of space to time.

The idea of time is the only idea which is here joined with that of extension. In another place I shall prove that time, separated from things, is nothing, and consequently, although this idea is here joined to that of extension, it does not interfere with the truth of what I have established. In statics, all that relates to other sensations is counted as nothing; in order to solve the problems of the composition and decomposition of forces, we abstract all color, smell, and other sensible qualities of bodies in motion. What has been said of statics applies equally to dynamics, hydrostatics, hydraulics, astronomy, and to all sciences which regard motion.

17. Here an objection may be made. That with the ideas of time and space, we seem to combine another which is distinct from them, and necessary, in order to complete the idea of motion, and this is the idea of a body moved. It is not time, nor is it space, for space is not moved, therefore it is distinct from them.

To this I reply, first, that I am speaking of extension, and not of space alone, which it is important to remember, for what I shall afterwards say; and secondly, that science regards the thing moved as a point, and this is sufficient for all its purposes. Thus in the systems of forces there is a point of application for each of the component forces, and another for the resultant. This point is not regarded as having any properties, but is in relation to motion what the centre is in relation to a circle. Every thing is related to it, yet it is nothing in itself, except inasmuch as it occupies a definite position in space. It may change according to the quantity and direction of the forces, it may run over or describe a line in space with greater or less velocity, and the line may be of this or that class, and accompanied by various conditions. If a body be impelled by two forces, B and C, acting upon a point A, science considers in the body only the point through which the resultant of the forces B and C passes, and abstracts all the other points of the body which, being joined to the point A, move with it.

18. When I say that the natural sciences go no farther than the consideration of extension, I only mean to exclude the other sensations, but not ideas; for it is clear that the ideas of time and number are combined with the idea of extension. This is so true in mechanics, in this sense at least, that all its theorems and problems are reduced to geometrical expressions, and even the idea of time is expressed by lines.

In every force there are three things to be considered: the direction, point of application, and intensity. The direction is represented by a line, and the point of application by a point in space. The intensity is represented only in the effect which it can produce, and this is expressed by a line, the length of which expresses the intensity of the force. The effect of the intensity which is represented by a line includes the time also; for the measure of a motion cannot be determined until we know its velocity, which is merely the relation of space to time. Therefore, although the idea of time is combined with that of extension, the result is expressed by lines, that is, by extension.

19. There is another circumstance still which shows the fruitfulness of the idea of extension. It is that in the expression of the laws of nature, it reaches cases which are beyond the idea of number. If we suppose two equal rectangular forces, AB and AC, acting on the point A, the resultant will be AR. Now, if we consider AR to be the hypotheneuse of a right-angled triangle, $AR2 = AB2 + AC2$, extracting the square root $AR = \sqrt{(AB2 + AC2)}$. If we suppose each of the component forces equal to 1, $AR = \sqrt{(12 + 12)} = \sqrt{2}$, a value which can neither be expressed in whole numbers nor in fractions, but which is represented by the hypotheneuse.

20. In the physical sciences, such words as force, cause, agent, etc., are frequently used, but the ideas which these terms express are a part of science only inasmuch as they are represented by effects. This is not because true philosophy confounds the cause with the effect, but as physical science regards only the phenomenon in all that relates to the cause, it limits itself to the abstract idea of causality, which presents nothing determinate, and consequently is not the object of its scientific labors. The system of universal attraction has immortalized the name of Newton, and he begins by confessing his ignorance of the cause of the effect which he explains. When we go beyond the phenomena and the calculations to which they give rise, we enter the field of metaphysics.

21. The natural sciences consider certain qualities of bodies which have no relation to extension, as, for example, heat and light, and this might seem to be a refutation of what we have said of extension. Still this objection disappears when we examine in what manner science takes note of these qualities, and instead of overthrowing our thesis, the result will strengthen, extend, and explain it.

Heat is not measured by the sensation which it produces in us. If we enter a room where the temperature is very high, we experience a strong sensation of heat, which gradually grows weaker, while the temperature remains the same. If we reach our hand to a friend we experience a sensation of heat or cold, in proportion as his hand is warmer or colder than our own.

Heat and cold are measured, not in themselves, nor in relation to our sensations, but in the effect which they produce. These effects are included in the modification of extension; for the thermometer marks the temperature by a greater or less elevation of the mercury in a *line*. Its degrees are expressed by parts of a line, on which they are marked.

I know that what is measured is distinct from extension; but, its measurement is only possible by relation to extension, and by attending to effects which are modifications of extension. Thus, the temperature at which water boils is 212°, and this is discovered by the motion of the water, and has relation to extension. So, also, the rarefaction and condensation of bodies are modifications of extension, since these states consist in the occupation of greater or less space, or in the increase or diminution of their dimensions.

22. All that science teaches us of light and colors relates to the different directions and combinations of the rays of light. Our observation goes no farther than sensation. We know that we can combine the rays in different manners, and direct them, so as to modify our sensation, but this is nothing more than the scientific knowledge of extension in the medium which we make use of, and of the sensation experienced in consequence. All beyond this is entirely unknown.

23. We may say the same of all other sensations, that of touch included. What is that quality of bodies which we call hardness? the resistance which we encounter when we touch them? But abstracting sensation, which only produces the consciousness of itself, what do we find? Impenetrability. And what do we understand by impenetrability? The impossibility of two bodies occupying the same space at the same time. Here, then, we meet with extension. If, by hardness, we mean the cohesion of molecules, in what does cohesion consist? In the juxtaposition of parts in such manner that they cannot, without difficulty, be separated. But, to be separated, is to be made

to occupy a place different from that which was before occupied. Here, too, we find the idea of extension.

Of sound we know nothing scientifically, except as relates to extension and motion. The musical scale is expressed by a series of fractional numbers representing the vibrations of the air.

24. These examples demonstrate the third of the above propositions, that whatever we know of sensations that deserves the name of science, is included in the modifications of extension.

25. It is the same with the fourth proposition, that without the idea of extension, we can have no fixed idea of any thing corporeal, no fixed rule in relation to phenomena, but are like blind men. If, for an instant, we abstract the idea of extension, it is impossible for us to take a step in advance. The examples already adduced in order to demonstrate the second proposition, render further explanation here unnecessary.

26. Although extension is essentially composed of parts, there is in it something fixed, unalterable, and, in some manner, simple. There may be more or less extension, but not different kinds. One right line may be longer or shorter than another, but its length is not of a different species. One surface may be larger than another, a solid of a certain kind greater than another of the same kind, but not in a different manner.

When I say that in the idea of extension objectively considered there is a *certain sort* of simplicity, I do not mean that there is any thing *entirely* simple; for I have just said that its *object* is *essentially* composite. Neither do I abstract its essential elements, which are the three dimensions, nor any idea which it involves, as its limitability, or capacity to be limited in various ways. All I wish to show is that in all the different figures these fundamental notions are sufficient, that they are never modified, but always present the same thing to the mind.

Let us compare a right line with a curve. A right line is a direction which is always constant; the curve a direction which is always varied. A direction always varied is a collection of *right directions infinitely small*. Therefore, the circumference of a circle is considered as a polygon of an infinite number of sides. The curve is therefore formed by the variety of directions reduced to infinitesimal values. This theory which explains the difference of the right line and the curve, is evidently applicable to surfaces and solids.

Let us compare a quadrilateral with a pentagon; all that the second has which the first has not is one side more in perimeter, and in area the space contained in the triangle formed by a line drawn from one of its angles to either of the opposite angles. The lines are of the same kind, the surfaces differ only in the ways in which they terminate. But termination is the same as limitation. Therefore, all that is essential to the idea of extension, that is, direction and limitability, remain always the same and unchangeable.

This intrinsical constancy is indispensable to science. That which is mutable, may be the object of perception, but not of scientific perception.

CHAPTER IV
REALITY OF EXTENSION

27. We now come to more difficult questions. Is extension any thing in itself, abstracted from the idea of it? If any thing, what is it? Is it identified with bodies, or is it confounded with space?

I have proved[39] that extension exists outside of ourselves, that it is not an illusion of the senses; and this solves the first question, whether extension is any thing.

Whatever may be its nature or our ignorance on this point, there is in reality something which corresponds to our idea of extension. Whoever denies this truth must be content to deny every thing except the consciousness of himself, if indeed he does not experience doubts even of this too. Whatever idealists may assert, there is not, nor ever was a man who in his sound judgment seriously doubted the existence of an external world. This conviction is for man a necessity against which it is vain to contend.

This external world is for us inseparable from that which is represented by the idea of extension. It either does not exist, or else it is extended. If we could be persuaded that it is not extended, it would not be difficult to convince us that it does not exist. For my part, I find it just as difficult to imagine the world without extension as without existence, and if I could be made to believe its extension an illusion, I should easily believe its existence also an illusion.

28. It is to be observed that although we confess our ignorance of the internal nature of extension, it is still necessary to admit that we know something of it; its dimensions, namely, and what serves as the basis of geometry. The difficulty is not in knowing what extension is geometrically considered, but what it is in reality. We know the geometrical essence, but what we want to ascertain is, whether this essence realized is something which is confounded with some other real thing, or is only a quality which we know without knowing the being to which it belongs. Without this distinction we should deny the basis of geometry; for, it is evident that if we should not know the essence of extension in the aforesaid manner, we could not be sure that we are not building in the air when we raise upon the idea of extension the whole science of geometry.

29. Thus then under this aspect, we are certain that extension exists outside of us, and that there are true dimensions. This idea is a necessary consequence of the idea of the external world, as we said before. The dimensions in the external world must be subject to the same principles as those which we conceive, or the very idea which we have formed of the external world is reversed. I do not mean by this that a real circle may be a geometrical circle, but only that what is true of the second must be true of the first also, in proportion as it is constructed with greater or less exactness. Beyond what can be formed by the most perfect and exact instruments, I can conceive, without passing from the order of reality, a circle or any other figure, as near as I please to the geometrical idea. The sharpest instrument can never mark an indivisible point, nor draw a line without breadth; but this surface, on which the point is marked, on the line drawn, being infinitely divisible, I can conceive a case in which the reality will come infinitely near to the geometrical idea.

30. Astronomy and all the physical sciences rest on the supposition that real extension is subject to the same principles as ideal extension; and that experience comes closer to theory in proportion as the conditions of the second are more exactly fulfilled in the first. The art of constructing mathematical instruments, which has been brought in our day to a surprising perfection, regards the ideal as the type of the real order; and progress in the latter is the approximation to the models of the former.

Theory directs the operations of practice, and these in their turn confirm by the result the foresight of theory. Therefore, extension exists not only in the ideal order, but also in the real; and it is something, independently of our ideas; and geometry, that vast representation of a world of lines and figures, has a real object in nature.

How far the real corresponds with the ideal, we shall examine in the next chapter.

CHAPTER V
GEOMETRICAL EXACTNESS
REALIZED IN NATURE

31. The disagreement which we discover between the phenomena and the geometrical theory makes us apt to think that reality is rough and coarse, and that purity and exactness are found only in our ideas. This is a mistaken opinion caused by want of reflection. The reality is as geometrical as our ideas; the phenomenon realizes the idea in all its purity and vigor. Be not startled by this seeming paradox; for it will soon appear to you a very true, reasonable, and well-grounded proposition.

We shall first prove that the ideas which are the elements of geometry have their objects in the real world, and that these objects are subject to precisely the same conditions as the ideas. This proved, it clearly follows that geometry in all its strictness exists as well in the real as in the ideal order.

32. Let us begin with a point. In the ideal order, a point is an invisible thing, it is the limit of a line and its generating element, and it occupies a determinate position in space. It is the limit of a line; for when we take away its length, we have a point remaining which we are forced to regard as the limit of the line unless we destroy it entirely so as to have nothing left. The more the line is shortened the nearer it approaches to a point, yet can never be identified with it until its length is wholly suppressed. The point is the generating element of the line; for we form the idea of lineal dimension by considering a point in motion. The occupation of a determinate position in space is another indispensable condition of the idea of a point, if we wish to use it in geometrical figures. The centre of a circle is a point in itself indivisible, it fills no space; but in order that it be of any use as centre, we must be able to refer all the radii to it, and this is impossible unless it occupy a determinate position equidistant from all points of the circumference. As a general rule, geometry acts upon dimensions, and these dimensions require points in which they commence, points through which they pass, and points in which they end, and by which distances, inclinations, and all that relates to the position of lines and planes, are measured. Nothing of all this can be conceived unless the point, although not extended, occupies a determinate position in space.

33. Does there exist in nature anything which corresponds to the geometrical point, and unites all its conditions with as great exactness as science in its purest idealism can desire? I believe there does.

Philosophers have adopted different opinions as to the divisibility of matter. Some maintain that there are unextended points in which the division ends, and that all composite bodies are formed of these. Others assert that it is not possible to arrive at simple elements, but the division may continue *ad infinitum* continually approaching the limit of composition, but never reaching it. The first of these opinions is equivalent to the admission of geometrical points realized in nature; the second, though apparently less favorable to this realization, must come to it at last.

Unextended molecules are the realization of the geometrical point, in all its exactness. They are the limit of dimension, because division ends with them. They are the generative elements of dimension, because they form extension. They occupy a determinate position in space, because bodies with all their conditions and determinations in space are formed of them. Therefore, from this opinion, held by eminent philosophers like Leibnitz and Boscowich, it follows that the geometrical point exists in nature in all the purity and exactness of the scientific order.

The opinion which denies the existence of unextended points, admits, as it necessarily must admit, infinite divisibility. Extension has parts, and therefore is divisible; these parts, in their turn, are either extended or not extended; if unextended, the supposition fails, and the opinion of unextended points is admitted; if extended, they are divisible, and we must either come at last to unextended points, or continue the division *ad infinitum*.

I remarked above that, although less favorable to the real existence of geometrical points, this opinion as well as the other does acknowledge their realization. The parts into which the composite is divided are not created by the division, but exist before the division, and without them the division would be impossible. They do not exist because they may be divided, but they may be divided because they exist. This opinion therefore, does not expressly admit the existence of unextended points, but it admits the possibility of eternally coming nearer to them, and this not only in the ideal, but also in the real order; because the divisibility is not affirmed of the ideas, but of the matter itself.

Although our experience of division is limited, divisibility itself is unlimited. A being endowed with greater powers than we possess, might carry the division further than we are able to do. Our ability to divide is limited, but God, by his infinite power, can push the division *ad infinitum*, and His infinite intelligence sees in an instant all the parts into which the composite may be divided.

Omitting the difficulties which attend an opinion which seems to suppose the existence of what it denies, I will ask if geometry can require more rigorous exactness than is found in the points to which infinite power can come, if we suppose it to exercise its eternal action in dividing the composite; or, in other words, can there be any more strictly geometrical points than those seen by an infinite intelligence in an infinitely divisible being? This not only satisfies our imagination and our ideas of exactness, but goes even beyond. Experience teaches us that to *imagine* an unextended point is not impossible; and to *think* it in the purely intellectual order, is only to conceive the possibility of this infinite divisibility, and to be suddenly placed at the last limit,—a limit which must still be far distant from that to which, not abstraction, but the sight of infinite intelligence can reach.

If the geometrical point exists, the geometrical line also exists; for it is only a series of unextended points; or, if we are unwilling to acknowledge these, a series of extremes to which division infinitely continued at last arrives. A series of geometrical lines forms a surface; and a union of surfaces forms a solid, the ideal order agreeing with reality in its formation as in its nature.

34. This theory of the realization of geometry extends equally to all the natural sciences. It is an error to say, for example, that the reality does not correspond to the theories of mechanics. It should rather be said that it is not the reality that is at fault, but the means of experimenting; the blame should not be imputed to the reality, but rather to the limitation of our experience.

The centre of gravity in a body, is the point where all the forces of gravitation in the body unite. Mechanics supposes this point to be indivisible, and in accordance with this supposition, establishes and demonstrates its theorems, and solves its problems. Here stops the mechanician, and the machinist begins, who can never discover the strict centre of gravity supposed in the theory. Experience disagrees with the principles, and we ought to correct the former by adhering to that which is determined by the latter. Is this because the centre of gravity does not exist in nature with all the exactness which science supposes? No; the centre exists, but the means of finding it are wanting. Nature goes as far as science; neither remains behind; but our means of experience are unable to keep up with them.

The mechanician determines the indivisible point in which the centre of gravity is situated, supposing the surface without thickness, lines without breadth, and the length divided at a determinate point of space, which has no extension. Nature entirely fulfills these conditions. The point exists, and the reality should not be blamed for the limitation of our experience. The point exists in either of the hypotheses mentioned above. The first, which favors unextended points, admits the existence of the centre of gravity in all its scientific purity. The other is not so decided, but it says to us: "Do you see this molecule, this little globe of infinitesimal diameter, the smallness of which the imagination cannot represent? Make it still smaller, by dividing it for all eternity, in decreasing geometrical progression, and you will always be coming nearer the centre of gravity without ever reaching it. Nature will never fail; the limit will ever retire from you; but you will know you are approaching it. Within this molecule is what you seek. Continue to advance, you will never reach it,—but what you want is there." In this case I do not see that the reality falls short of scientific exactness; no mechanical theory imagined or conceived can go farther.

35. These reflections place beyond all doubt that geometry with all its exactness, and theories in all their rigor, exist in nature. If we could follow it in our experience, we should find the real conformed to the ideal order, and we should discover that when experience is opposed to theory, it is not the latter which is wrong, but the limitation of our means makes us lay aside the conditions imposed by the theory. The machinist who constructs a system of indented wheels finds himself obliged to correct the rules of theory, on account of friction, and other circumstances, proceeding from the material which he employs. If he could see with a glance the bosom of nature, he would discover in the friction itself a new system of infinitesimal gearing which would confirm with wonderful exactness those very rules which a rude experience represents to him as opposed to reality.

36. If the universe is admirable in its masses of gigantic immensity, it is not less so in its smallest parts. We are placed between two infinities. Man in his weakness, unable to reach either one or the other, must content himself with feeling them, hoping that a new existence in another world will clear up the secrets which are now veiled in impenetrable darkness.

CHAPTER VI
REMARKS ON EXTENSION

37. If extension is something as we have proved; what is it?

We find extension in bodies and also in space because in both we find that which constitutes its essence, which is dimension. Is the extension of bodies the same as the extension of space?

I see and hold in my hand a pen: it is certainly extended. It moves, and its extension moves with it. The space in which its motion is executed remains immovable. At the instant A the extension of the pen occupies the point A'; at the moment B the same extension of the pen occupies the part B' of space which is distinct from the part A'; therefore neither the part A' of space nor the part B' is identified with the extension of the body.

This seems to have all the force of a demonstration; but to make it more clear and more general, I will put it into the form of a syllogism. Things which are separated or may be separated are distinct; but the extension of bodies may be separated from any part of space; therefore the extension of bodies and the extension of space are distinct. I said that this reasoning seems to have all the force of a demonstration, but it is nevertheless subject to serious difficulties. These difficulties cannot be understood without a profound analysis of the idea of space, and therefore I shall reserve my opinion until this has been treated of in the following chapters.

38. Is the extension of a body the body itself? I cannot conceive a body without extension, but this does not prove that extension is the same thing as the body. My soul has acquired a knowledge of the body by means of the senses. These senses have *awakened* in me the idea of extension; but they have told me nothing of the intrinsic nature of the body perceived.

In those beings which we call bodies we find the power of producing in us impressions very distinct from that of extension. From two bodies of equal extension we receive very different impressions, therefore there is in them something besides extension. If extension was their only quality, this being equal, the effect would be the same; but experience teaches us that it is not so.

Moreover we conceive extension in pure space where there is no body. The idea of body implies the idea of mobility, while space is immovable. It implies the power of producing impressions; the extension of space has not of itself this power.

Therefore the simple idea of extension does not include even in our cognitions the whole idea of a body. We do not know in what the essence of body consists; but we know that in the idea which we have of it there is something more than extension.

39. When it is said that a body is inconceivable without extension it is not meant that extension is the constitutive notion of the essence of body. This essence is unknown to us, and therefore we cannot know what does or does not belong to it. The true meaning of this inseparability of the two ideas of extension and body is this: As we have no knowledge *a priori* of bodies, but whatever we know of them, their existence included, we derive through the senses, all that we think or imagine concerning them must presuppose that which is the basis of our sensations. This basis, as we have already seen, is extension; without it there is no sensation, and consequently without it a body ceases to exist for us, or is reduced to a being which we cannot distinguish from others.

I will explain my ideas. If I strip bodies of extension and leave them only the nature of a being which causes the impressions which I receive; this being is the same, so far as I am concerned, as a spirit which should produce the same impressions. I see this paper, and it causes in me the impression of a white surface. There is no doubt that God could produce in my mind the same sensation without the existence of any body. Then supposing that I knew that no external extended object corresponded to my sensation, which was caused by a being acting upon me, it is evident that there would be two distinct things in my mind. First, the phenomenon of sensation, which under all hypotheses is the same; and secondly, the idea of the being which produced it, which is only the idea of a being distinct from myself, acting upon me, which in relation to the external world, would involve two ideas; those of distinction and causality.

I now take from the paper extension, and what remains? The same as before. 1. An internal phenomenon, made known by consciousness. 2. The idea of a being the cause of this phenomenon.

I do not know whether this must always be a body; but I know that the idea of a body, as I understand it, includes something more than this. I know that being is not in relation to myself distinguishable from other beings, and that if there is any thing in its nature to distinguish it from them, it is something unknown to me.[40]

40. This is the sense in which I say that we cannot separate the idea of extension from the body. But from this it must not be inferred that the things themselves are identified; perhaps, even, a more profound knowledge of matter would show us that instead of being identical, they are entirely distinct. We have seen that it is so with their ideas, and this is a sign that it is so in reality.

41. We have few ideas as clear as that of extension geometrically considered; every attempt to explain it is useless; we know it more perfectly by mere intuition than whole volumes could make it known to us. It is so clear an idea, that on it is founded a whole science, the most extensive and evident which we possess, that of geometry. Therefore there is reason to believe that we know the true essence of extension, since we know its *necessary* properties, and even base a whole science on this knowledge. Yet we do not discover in this idea, either impenetrability or any of the properties of bodies; but rather on the contrary, we find a capacity indifferent to them all. We conceive extension penetrable as easily as impenetrable, empty or full, white or green, with properties by which it can be placed in relation with our organs, as easily as without them. We can conceive extension in a body acting on another body, or in pure space; in the sun which enlightens and warms the world, or in the vague dimensions of an empty immensity.

CHAPTER VII
SPACE.—NOTHING

42. It may have been remarked in the preceding chapters that the idea of extension is always united with that of space, and when we endeavor to determine the *real* nature of the former, we encounter the questions which relate to the latter. It is not possible to explain one, while the other remains in obscurity. It is for this reason that I have concluded to examine carefully the questions concerning space under its ideal as well as under its real aspect; since only in this manner is it possible to determine clearly the nature of extension.

43. Space is one of those profound mysteries which the natural order presents to man's weak understanding. The deeper he examines it the more obscure he finds it; the mind is buried in the darkness which we imagine to exist beyond the bounds of the finite, in the abyss of immensity. We know not if what we behold is an illusion or a reality. For a moment we seem to have found the truth, and then we discover that we have stretched our arms to embrace a shadow. We form arguments which in any other matter would be conclusive, but are not so here, because they are in direct contradiction to others equally conclusive. We seem to have reached the limit which the Creator has put to our investigations; and in endeavoring to pass beyond it, our strength fails, for we find ourselves out of the element which is natural to our life.

When certain philosophers pass rapidly over the questions relating to space, and flatter themselves with explaining them in a few words, we can assure them that either they have not meditated much upon the difficulty which these questions involve, or else they have not understood them. It was not so that Descartes, Malebranche, Newton, or Leibnitz proceeded.

To descend this bottomless abyss is not to lose time in useless discussion; even though we should not find what we seek, we obtain a most precious result, for we reach the limits assigned to our intellect. It is well to know what may be known and what cannot; for from this knowledge philosophy draws high and valuable considerations. Moreover, though we have small hope of success, we cannot pass over without examining an idea that is so closely connected with all our knowledge of corporeal objects, that is to say, extension. There must be a motive of investigation since all philosophers have investigated it, and who can say that after long ages of efforts the truth is not perhaps reserved as the reward of constancy?

44. What then is space? Is it something real or only an idea? If an idea is there any object in the external world which corresponds to it? Is it a pure illusion? And is the word space without meaning?

If we do not know what space is, let us at least fix the meaning of the word, and thus determine in some measure the state of the question. By space we understand the extension in which we imagine bodies to be placed, or the capacity to contain them to which we attribute none of their qualities except extension.

Let us suppose a glass to be hermetically sealed, and the interior to remain empty by the annihilation of what it contained; this cavity or capacity which in our way of understanding it may be occupied by a body is a part of space. Let us imagine the world to be an immense receptacle in which all bodies are contained; let us suddenly make it empty and we have a cavity equal in space to the universe. If we imagine beyond the limits of the world a capacity to contain other bodies, we have an unlimited or imaginary space.

Space appears to us at first sight, if not infinite, at least indefinite. For in whatever part we conceive a body to be placed, we also conceive the possibility of its moving, describing any class of lines, or taking any kind of direction and departing indefinitely from its first position. Therefore we imagine no limit to this capacity, to these dimensions. Therefore space appears to us as indefinite.

45. Is space a pure nothing? Some philosophers maintain that abstracted from the surface of bodies, and considered as a mere interval, it is a pure nothing. At the same time they admit that it is only owing to space that two bodies are really distant from each other, and add that if we suppose the whole world, with the exception of one body only, to be reduced to nothing, this body could move and change its place. I am confident that this opinion involves irreconcilable contradictions. To say *extension-nothing* is a contradiction in terms, and the opinion of these philosophers is reduced to this expression.

46. If every thing in a room be reduced to nothing, it seems impossible for the walls to remain distant from each other; for the idea of distance implies a medium between the two objects; and nothing, being nothing, cannot be the medium required. If the interval is nothing, there is no distance. To attribute properties to nothing, is to destroy all ideas,—to affirm that a thing may be and not be at the same time,—and consequently to overthrow the foundation of human knowledge.

47. To say that if the contents were annihilated, a negative space would remain, is only to play with words without touching the difficulty to be solved. This negative space is either something or nothing; if it is something, the opinion we are opposing is false; if it is nothing, the difficulty remains the same.

48. But, it may be said, although nothing remains between the surfaces, they still retain the capacity of containing something. To this I reply, that this capacity is not in the surfaces themselves, but in their distance from each other; for if it were in the surfaces, they would still preserve it, no matter how they may be placed, which is absurd. We have not therefore advanced a single step. We must explain what this capacity, or this distance, is; and this is still untouched.

49. Perhaps it may be said that annihilating all that is contained between the surfaces, does not destroy the volume which they form, and the idea of this volume implies the idea of capacity. But I reply, that the idea of volume involves that of distance, and there is no distance if this distance is a pure nothing.

50. In our efforts to surmount these difficulties, another seemingly specious solution offers, but if we examine it we shall find it as weak as the others.

Distance, it might be said, is a mere negation of contact, but negation is a pure nothing; therefore this nothing is what we seek. I say this solution is as weak as the others; for, if distance is only the negation of contact, all distances must be equal, because negation cannot be greater or less. The negation of contact is the same whether the surfaces are a million leagues or only the millionth part of an inch distant from each other. This negation, therefore, explains nothing, and the difficulty still remains.

51. Not only is the idea of distance not explained by the idea of contact, but on the contrary, the idea of contact can only be explained by the idea of distance. Contiguity is explained by immediate union of two surfaces; we say that they touch each other because there is nothing between them, or there is no distance. The idea of contact does not involve the qualities which relate to the senses, nor the action which one body may exercise upon another which touches it, as impulse or compression. Contiguity is a negative, and purely geometrical, idea, and implies only the negation of distance. Contiguity cannot be greater or less; it is all that it can be when there is a true negation of distance. Two objects may be more or less distant, but they cannot touch more or less, with respect to the same parts. There may be contact of more points, but not more contact of the same points.

52. If we attribute distance and capacity to space, the argument in favor of its reality becomes still stronger. Let us suppose an empty sphere two feet in diameter. Within there is only space; if space is nothing there is nothing in it.

Is motion possible in this empty sphere? It does not seem that there can be any doubt of this. There is a movable body, an extension greater than the extension of the body, and a distance to be passed over. We may add to this, that if motion were not possible, it would not be possible to make the sphere empty, or after making it empty, to fill it. Neither emptying nor filling the sphere can be done without motion of bodies in the interior of the sphere, and motion of a body in another body is only possible in space, because bodies are impenetrable, and also because, when the sphere is filled after it is empty, the body which enters does not meet another body; and when the sphere is made empty, the body which passes out, moves over the space which it abandons, and in which nothing remains after it has passed out.

Therefore, supposing the sphere empty, there may be motion in it. But if the space contained in the sphere is a pure nothing, the motion also is nothing, and consequently does not exist. Motion can neither exist nor be perceived without a distance passed over. If, therefore, the distance is nothing, there is no motion. If we say that the body has passed over half of the diameter, or one foot, what does this mean? If the space is nothing, it can mean nothing. I see no reply which can be made to these arguments, which are all based on the axiom, that nothing has no properties.

53. However great may be the difficulties opposed to the reality of space, they are not so great as those which are brought against the opinion, which, while granting extension to space, still regards it as a pure nothing. The former, as we shall soon see, are produced by certain inaccuracies in our way of conceiving things, rather than by arguments founded on the nature of things; whilst those objections which we have brought against the opinion denying the reality of space, are founded on the ideas which are the basis of all our knowledge, and on this evident proposition: nothing has no properties. If this proposition is not admitted as an established axiom, the principle of contradiction falls, and all human knowledge is destroyed. For, it would be a plain contradiction, if nothing could have any properties or parts; if any thing could be affirmed of nothing, or could be moved in nothing; if a science like geometry could be founded upon nothing; or if all the calculations which are made on nature are referred to nothing.

CHAPTER VIII
DESCARTES AND LEIBNITZ ON SPACE

54. If space is something, what is it? Here is the difficulty. To overthrow the opinion of our adversaries was easy, but to maintain our position is more difficult.

Can we say that space is only the extension of bodies; that conceived in the abstract it gives us the idea of what we call pure space; and that the different points and positions are mere modifications of extension?

It is easy to see that if space is the extension of bodies, where there is no body there can be no space, and consequently vacuum is impossible. This consequence is unavoidable.

This has been the opinion of celebrated philosophers like Descartes and Leibnitz; but I cannot understand why they both gave the universe an indefinite extension. It is true that by this means they avoid the difficulty of the space which we imagine beyond the limits of the universe; since, if the universe is not limited, there can be nothing beyond its limits, and therefore, whatever we can imagine, must be within the universe. But our object is not to avoid difficulties, but to solve them; and it argues nothing for the soundness of our opinion that it escapes difficulties.

55. According to Descartes, the essence of body is in extension, and as we necessarily conceive extension in space, it follows that space, body, and extension, are three essentially identical things. Vacuum, as it is generally conceived, that is, an extension without a body, is then a contradiction; for it is a body, because it is extension, and it is not a body, because we suppose that there is no body.

Descartes accepts all the consequences of this doctrine. He does not admit the supposition that if God should annihilate all the matter contained in a vessel, this vessel could still retain its form.

"We shall observe," he says, "in opposition to this serious error, that there is no necessary connection between the vessel and the body which fills it; but such is the invincible necessity of the relation between the concave figure of the vessel and the extension contained in this concavity, that it is not more difficult to imagine a mountain without a valley, than to conceive this concavity without the extension contained in it, or this extension without a thing extended. Nothing, as we have often said, cannot be extended. Therefore, if any one should ask, what would happen if God should destroy the matter contained in a vessel, without replacing it, we must say that the sides of the vessel would come so closely together as to touch each other. Two bodies must touch each other, when there is nothing between them. It would be a contradiction to assert that these two bodies were separated; that is to say, that there was a distance between them, if this distance were nothing, or did not exist. Distance is a property of extension, and cannot exist without extension."[41]

56. If Descartes had gone no farther than to maintain that space, because it contains real distances, cannot be a mere nothing, his reasoning would seem conclusive. But when he adds that space is body, because space is extension, and extension constitutes the essence of body, he asserts what he does not prove.

Because we cannot imagine or conceive a body without extension, it only follows that extension is a property of bodies without which we cannot conceive them, —not that it is their essence. To be able to say this, it would be necessary for us to have the idea of body as we have that of extension, in order that we might see if they are identical. But all that we know of bodies is derived through the senses; we are not able to penetrate into their more intimate nature.

Whence arises the inseparability of the ideas of body and extension? It arises from the idea which we have of bodies being a confused idea, since we conceive it to be a substance in certain relations to ourselves, and causing in us the impressions which we call sensations. But since the basis of sensations is extension, as we have demonstrated in a former chapter, this is the only medium by which we are placed in relation with bodies. When we suppress this basis, by abstracting it, we retain nothing of body beyond a general idea of being or substance without any thing to characterize it, or to distinguish it from others. We find all this in the order of our ideas, but we cannot infer from this that bodies have no other reality than extension.

57. The same reasoning destroys the opinion of indefinite or infinite extension. Descartes, explaining his doctrine on the idea of extension, says: "We shall also know that this world, or the extended matter which composes the universe, is without limits; for, no matter how far off we place these limits, we can imagine spaces indefinitely extended beyond them; and we not only imagine these spaces, but we conceive them as really existing such as we imagine them, and containing an indefinitely extended body, as the idea of extension which we conceive in every space is the true idea which we ought to form of a body."[42]

In this passage, besides the error in relation to the essence of bodies, there is a gratuitous transition from a purely ideal or rather, imaginary order, to the real order. It is certain that wherever I may imagine the limits of the universe, if I consider them as an immense arch surrounding it, I still imagine new immensities of space beyond this arch; but to conclude that the reality is as I imagine it, does not seem conformed to the rules of good logic. If it is as clear as Descartes supposes, if it is not only an imagination, but a conception founded on clear and distinct ideas, how happens it that so many philosophers see in all this only a play of the imagination?

58. Leibnitz thinks that space is "a relation, an order, not only between things existing, but also between possible things as if they existed."[43] He also believes vacuum impossible, but not for the reason which Descartes gives. These are his words:

"*Philalethes.*—Those who take matter and extension for the same thing, pretend that the sides of a hollow empty body would touch each other. But the space which is between the two bodies is enough to prevent their mutual contact.

"*Theophilus.*—I am of your opinion; for, although I do not admit a vacuum, I distinguish matter from extension, and concede that although there were a vacuum in a sphere, the opposite poles would not on that account unite. But I do not believe this is a case which the divine perfection would permit."[44]

59. Leibnitz seems to me to commit what logicians call *petitio principii*, or, "begging the question." He says that in the case supposed, the sides would not touch each other, because the space between them would prevent it; but this is what he had to prove,—the real existence of this space. This reality is what Descartes denies.

60. If we compare the opinions of Descartes and Leibnitz, we shall see that both agree in denying to space a reality distinct from bodies, but basing their denial on very different reasons. Descartes places the essence of body in extension; where there is extension there is body; where there is space there is extension; consequently, there neither is nor can be a vacuum. Leibnitz does not believe an empty capacity intrinsically absurd, and that he does not admit it is solely because, in his conception, it is repugnant to the divine perfection. The two illustrious philosophers started from very different principles, but arrived at the same conclusion. Descartes rests upon metaphysical reasons, founded on the essence of things. Leibnitz bases his opinion on the absolute essence of things only in its relations with the divine perfection. Empty capacity is a contradiction in the opinion of Leibnitz, only inasmuch as it is opposed to optimism.

61. It is very remarkable that three so distinguished philosophers as Aristotle, Descartes, and Leibnitz, should agree in denying the existence of this capacity which is called space, considered as a being distinct from bodies, and with the possibility of existing by itself. The difference of their opinions only proves that at the bottom of the question there is a difficulty more serious than some ideologists believe, who explain the idea of space and its generation with the same ease as though they were treating of the simplest matters.

CHAPTER IX
OPINION OF THOSE WHO ATTRIBUTE TO SPACE A NATURE DISTINCT FROM BODIES

62. The preceding considerations seem to me to establish beyond any question, that space and nothing are contradictory terms. If space is a capacity with dimensions that can be really measured, it has real properties, and therefore is distinct from a pure nothing. We have the idea of space, on it is based a certain and evident science, that of geometry; this idea is also necessary for the conception of motion. A pure nothing cannot be the object which corresponds to this idea.

Is space something distinct from the extension of bodies? It is objected to the opinion which maintains this, that space must be either body or spirit, and if not body it must be spirit, which is absurd, since that which is essentially composed of parts, as space is, cannot be a spirit, which is a simple being.

There are strong arguments against the opinion which attributes to space a nature distinct from bodies, but I do not attach much weight to the above objection; for it is only necessary to deny the disjunctive proposition and the whole argument falls to the ground. How can it be proved that there is no medium between body and spirit? We know the essence of neither body nor spirit, and shall we arrogate to ourselves the right to assert that there is nothing in the universe which is not comprised under one of two extremes, the nature of which we know not.

63. It may be replied, that there is no medium between the simple and the composite, any more than between yes and no; and therefore there is no medium between body which is composite, and spirit which is simple. I concede that there is no medium between the simple and the composite, and that whatever exists is one or the other; but I deny that whatever is composite is body, and whatever is simple is spirit.

These two propositions: every composite is a body, and: every body is composite, are not identical. There may, therefore, be composites that are not bodies. Composition, or the possession of parts, is a property of bodies, but does not constitute their essence, or, at least, we do not know that it does. If it were so, we should be obliged to embrace the opinion of Descartes, that extension constitutes the essence of bodies. How do we know that there may not be things which have parts, and yet are not bodies?

64. Even the state of the question makes us suppose space to be a substance, that is, a being subsisting by itself without requiring another being in which to exist. The difficulty once overcome on this supposition, it is solved in its most essential and inaccessible point, and therefore in all others. If we suppose space to be distinct from bodies, and at the same time a true reality, we must consider it as a substance, as it exists in itself without any other being in which it inheres.

65. I said that a simple being is not necessarily a spirit. To explain this, I need only observe, that to say every spirit is simple, is not the same as to say every simple being is a spirit. Simplicity is a necessary attribute of a spirit, but does not constitute its essence. The idea of simplicity expresses only the negation of parts, and the essence of spirit cannot consist in a negation.

66. The argument of those who object to this opinion which attributes to space a nature distinct from bodies, making it an extended substance, that it must also be infinite, is equally inconclusive. For even on this hypothesis, there is no reason why a limit may not be assigned to space. What is there beyond this limit? Nothing. We may, it is true, conceive a vague extension, but imagination is not reality. We also imagine an epoch prior to the Creation; if, then, imagination were an argument in favor of the infinity of the world, it would also be an argument for its eternity.

The arguments with which I have fought against the opinion that space is a pure nothing, are not founded on our imaginations, but on the impossibility of nothing being extended, or having any properties. This is the principal argument which I have used against those who, while they hold space to be a pure nothing, maintain the possibility of the conception or existence of the properties which they attribute to space.

CHAPTER X
OPINION OF THOSE WHO HOLD SPACE TO BE THE IMMENSITY OF GOD

67. Overwhelmed by these difficulties, and unable to reconcile the reality which space offers us with nothing, or to conceive in any thing created the immobility, infinity, and perpetuity which we imagine in space, some philosophers have put forth the opinion that space is the immensity of God. At first sight this seems an extravagant absurdity, but if we wish fairly to prove the falsity of this opinion, we must do justice not only to the right intention of those who have defended it, and the sound explanations which they brought to their assistance, but also to the reasons which forced them to this extremity, and which, though certainly not weighty or solid, are far from being so contemptible as one may imagine.

68. The argument in favor of this opinion may be put in the following form. Space is something. Before God created the world space existed. It is not possible to conceive bodies as existing without space in which they are extended. Before they exist, we conceive this capacity in which they may be placed, as already existing. Therefore, space is eternal. There is no motion without space; and in the first instant of the creation bodies could move and be moved. Though we suppose only one body in the world, it could be moved; and this motion could be infinitely continued. Therefore space is infinite. Annihilate now this body also, and the extension in which it moved will remain; in it new bodies, new worlds may be created. Therefore space is indestructible. But an eternal, infinite, and indestructible being cannot be created. Therefore, space is uncreated. Therefore it is God himself. But it must be God inasmuch as we conceive him in relation to extension; and, therefore, space is the immensity of God. Immensity is the attribute by which God is in every part; it is an attribute which relates to extension. Space is, therefore, the immensity of God. Only by adopting this theory can we reasonably admit that space is eternal, infinite, and indestructible.

69. The objection to this opinion is that it destroys the simplicity of God. If space is a property of God, it is God; for, whatever is in God, is God. Therefore, as space is essentially extended, God too must be extended.

Clarke saw the force of this argument; he was made to feel it by the arguments of his adversary, Leibnitz; but he answers it very weakly. He says that space has parts, but they are not separable. But, however this may be, it is certain that space has parts. True, in the idea of space we distinguish parts without separating them; but we really conceive them in it, and we cannot conceive space without them. Besides, if we should admit this theory, what would become of the proofs of the immateriality of the soul? If the infinite wisdom is extended, why may not the human soul with much more reason be so?

Carried away by his favorite idea, Clarke went so far as to write what we should not have expected from such a man, that: "In questions of this nature, when we speak of parts, we mean parts that are *separable*, composite, and disunited like those of matter, which for this reason is always a compound and never a simple substance. Matter is not one substance, but a composition of substances. This is why, *in my opinion, matter is incapable of thinking*. This incapacity does not proceed from extension, but from the parts being distinct substances, disunited, and independent of each other."[45] This explanation tends to destroy the simplicity of thinking beings; for by simplicity has always been understood the absolute wanting of all parts and not the absence of this or that kind of parts. Inseparability does not destroy the existence of parts; it merely asserts the force of cohesion.

70. It is also to be feared that this doctrine opens the door to pantheism. It was even objected to Clarke that it made God the soul of the world, and although he defended himself from this charge, there still remains an objection which was not proposed to him, and which is a very serious one. If we say that God is space, or that space is a property of God, what hinders our saying that God is the world, or that the world is a property of God? The world is extended; but so is space. If God and space are not contradictory ideas in the same being, why are God and the universe contradictory? Clarke says that bodies are composed of different substances, that they are not one substance; but it is certain that all we know of bodies is that they are extended, and that they cause certain impressions in us. Since, then, extension is not repugnant to God, and much less so the causality of impressions, there can be no reason against saying that what Clarke calls distinct substances, are only the parts, or, if he prefers it, the properties of the infinite substance. Newton went so far as to say that space was the sensorium of God, and even Clarke maintained against Leibnitz that Newton's expression might bear a sound interpretation, as it was intended only as a comparison. But Leibnitz insists so strongly on this charge that it is plain that he had very great objections to this word.

71. Whatever tends to confound God with nature, or to place him in constant communication with it, otherwise than by pure acts of intellect and will, places us on a very slippery declivity, where we can hardly help being precipitated to the bottom, and at this bottom is pantheism, which is but a phasis of atheism.(30)

CHAPTER XI
FENELON'S OPINION

72. Clarke's opinion is very similar to that of Fenelon, who in his *Treatise on the existence and attributes of God*, explains immensity in a very surprising manner. He says: "After considering the eternity and immutability of God, which are the same thing, I ought to examine his immensity. Since he is by himself, he is sovereignly, and since he is sovereignly, he has all being in himself. Since he has all being in himself, he has without doubt extension; extension is a manner of being, of which I have an idea. I have already seen that my ideas upon the essence of things, are real degrees of being, which actually exist in God, and are possible out of him, because he can produce them. Therefore, extension is in him; he can produce it outside of himself, only because it is contained in the fulness of his being."

To a certain extent the words of Fenelon may be explained in a sense which most theologians would not reject. They distinguish two classes of perfections; those which involve no imperfection; such as wisdom, holiness, and justice; and those which involve imperfection, as, for example, all which belong to bodies, extension, form, etc. The former, which are also called perfections *simpliciter*, are in God *formaliter*; that is to say, just as they are, because their nature involves no kind of imperfection, and, therefore, in God, they do not diminish nor tarnish his infinite perfection. Those of the second class, which are called perfections *secundum quid*, are in God not *formaliter*; for the imperfection which they involve is repugnant to his infinite perfection, but *virtualiter* or *eminenter*; that is to say, that all the perfection, all the being which they contain is in God, who is infinite perfection, infinite being; and God can produce them exteriorly by his creative omnipotence. But inasmuch as they pre-exist in an infinite being, they are freed from all limitation and imperfection, and identified with the infinite essence, and have a mode of being far superior to what they are in reality. This is expressed by the term *eminenter*.

Among these perfections *secundum quid*, extension has always been numbered.

73. If the illustrious Archbishop of Cambrai had held to this sense, we should have nothing to say in relation to his doctrine, but the words which

follow seem to show that he inclined to the opinion of those who maintain that space is the immensity of God.

"Whence, then," he adds, "is it that I do not call him extended and corporeal? It is because there is an extreme difference, as I have already remarked, between attributing to God all that is positive in extension, and attributing to him extension with a limit or negation. *He that places extension without limits changes extension into immensity*; he who places extension with limits, makes a corporeal nature." From these words it might be believed that Fenelon did not distinguish the two modes of being of extension as theologians do; but he gives to God all that is positive in extension, though he gives it to him without limit. From this it would seem to follow that God is really extended, although his extension is infinite. With all the respect due to the illustrious shade of one of the greatest ornaments of the Catholic Church, and one of the greatest men of modern times, I must say that such an opinion does not seem to me to be sustainable. A God really extended though with an infinite extension is not God. That which is extended is essentially composite; God is essentially simple. Therefore, God and extension are contradictory.

74. But let us hear the illustrious prelate continue the explanation and defence of his opinion. He says: "From the moment that you place no limit to extension, you take from it figure, divisibility, motion, and impenetrability;— figure, because this is only a mode of limiting by surfaces;—divisibility, because, as we have seen, that which is infinite cannot be diminished, therefore, it cannot be divided, and consequently, it is not *composite* and divisible;—motion, because, if you suppose a whole, which has no parts nor limits, it cannot move beyond its place, because there can be no place beyond the true infinite; neither can it change the arrangement and situation of *its parts*, because it has *no parts* of which it is composed;—impenetrability, in fine, because impenetrability can only be conceived by conceiving two limited bodies, one of which is not the other, and cannot occupy the same space as the other. There are no two such bodies in infinite and indivisible extension; therefore there is no impenetrability in this extension. These principles established, it follows that all that is positive in extension is in God, although God has no figure, is not movable, divisible, or impenetrable, and consequently is not palpable, nor measurable."

From this passage it is very evident that Fenelon was far from imagining a composite God, a God with parts. He expressly denies it more than once in these few lines. Not less was to be looked for from his deep penetration and the purity of his doctrines; but, although this saves the rectitude of his intention, it does not satisfy philosophical exactness. For my part, I honestly confess that if extension is to be taken in its true sense, I cannot conceive how taking away its limits destroys its parts. On the contrary, I should rather say that an infinite extension would have infinite parts. If it is infinite it will have no figure; because figure involves a limit; but if it be true extension, it is a sort of immense field on which all imaginable figures may be traced. It will have no essential figure of its own, but it will be the recipient of all figures, the inexhaustible sea from which they all arise. That which is traced in it, will be in it; the points which terminate the figures must be in it. Is not this to have parts, composition? Infinite extension could have no figure, not because it has no parts, or is simple, but because it has infinite parts, because its composition is infinite.

I agree that an infinite extension would not be divisible, if by dividing, is meant separating; because in that immense fulness everything would be in its position with infinite firmness. So also we imagine space, the place of all motion, with its parts immovable, the field of all separation, with its parts inseparable; but we are treating of division, not of separation. If there is true extension, it is divisible; we conceive space with its parts inseparable, but still divisible; for we measure them, count them, and it is by relation to them that we form an idea of the size, distance, and motion of bodies.

74. Such clear and conclusive reflections could not fail to present themselves to the mind of the illustrious philosopher; but he seems to have preferred inconsequence or obscurity of language to the fatal corollaries of his first proposition. He said plainly and without any restriction, that all that is positive in extension, except the limit, is in God. He had asserted that extension with limits is corporeal, and that to change extension into immensity it was only necessary to take away its limits. He consequently attributed to God a true, although infinite, extension, and then wishing to explain and strengthen his doctrine he tells us that this extension has no parts. What is extension without parts? Who can conceive it? Does not extension necessarily imply an order of things of which some are outside of others. It has been always so understood. To speak of an extension without parts is to speak of an extension improperly so called. When speaking of such extension it is not enough to say it has no limits, it should be added that it is of an entirely different nature, that the word extension is used in another sense. Fenelon seemed to know this, when, notwithstanding the obscurity of his former expressions, elevated on the wings of his religion and his genius, he says: "God is in no place, as in no time; for his absolute and infinite being *has no relation to place or time*, which are but limits and restrictions of being. To ask if he is beyond the universe, if he exceeds its extremities in length, breadth, and depth, is as absurd a question as to ask if he was before the world, and if he will still be when the world is no more. As there is neither past nor future in God, so there is neither hither nor

thither. As his absolute permanence excludes all measure of succession, so also his immensity excludes all measure of extension. He has not been, he will not be, but *he is*. In the same manner, to speak properly, he is not here, he is not there, he is not beyond such a limit, but he is, absolutely. All expressions which place him in relation to any term, or fix him in a certain place, are improper and unbecoming. Where then is he? He is. He is in such a manner that we must not ask where. That which only half is, or with limits, is a certain thing in such a way that it is nothing else. But God is not any particular and restricted thing. He is all; he is being; or better and more simply, *he is*. For the fewer words we use, the more we say. *He is.* Beware of adding any thing to this."

76. While reading these magnificent words, I am carried away by the elevation and grandeur of his ideas of God and of his immensity, and I forget the objections to the first proposition, which, if not false or inexact, is not, to say the least, expressed with all the clearness that could be desired. Still, I do not hesitate to maintain that his opinion coincides with Clarke's; although the illustrious writer, Christian, and poet, seem to merit a pardon for the philosopher.

CHAPTER XII
WHAT SPACE CONSISTS IN

77. Descartes' opinion wholly confounds space and bodies, making the essence of bodies consist in extension, and asserting that wherever there is space, there is body. This opinion we have seen to be void of all reasonable foundation. Perhaps he would come nearer the truth who should say, that in reality space is nothing more than the extension of bodies, without reference to the question whether extension does or does not constitute the essence of bodies, and denying its infinity.

78. Let us examine this last opinion. Analyzing the origin of the idea of space, we find that it is merely the idea of extension taken in the abstract. If I hold before my eyes an orange, I may, by means of abstractions, arrive at the idea of a pure extension, equal to that of the orange. In order to do this, I begin by abstracting its color, taste, smell, and all its qualities which affect the senses. I then have left only an extended being, and if I take from it its mobility, it is reduced to a part of space equal to the size of the orange.

It is plain that the same abstraction is possible in relation to the universe, and the result will be the idea of all the space which the universe occupies.

79. Here I shall answer an objection which might be made to this explanation of the idea of space, and thereby take advantage of this opportunity to throw some light upon the origin of the idea of infinite, or imaginary space.

The difficulty is this. If we form the idea of space by the mere abstraction of the qualities which accompany extension, we can only conceive a space equal to the size of the body from which we have abstracted all its sensible qualities. The abstraction made upon an orange can only give a space equal to the size of the orange, and that made upon the universe can only give a space equal to what we conceive in the universe. Consequently, we can never, by this means, obtain the idea of a space without limits which always presents itself to our mind when we think of space considered in itself.

The solution of this difficulty is in the truth that abstraction rises from the particular to the general. From the idea of gold, by abstracting those properties which constitute gold, and attending only to those which it possesses as metal, I arrive at the much more general idea of *metal*, which belongs not only to gold, but to all other metals. By this abstraction I pass the limit which separates gold from other metals, and form an idea which extends to all, neither specifying, nor excluding any. If from the idea of metal I abstract all that constitutes metal, and attend only to what constitutes *mineral*, I pass another limit, and arrive at a still more general idea. Thus passing successively the idea of inorganic, of body, and of substance, until I come to the idea of being, I thus form the most general idea possible, and which includes every thing.[46]

Thus passing over the limits which distinguish and, as it were, separate objects, abstraction rises to the most general. If we apply this doctrine to the abstractions made upon bodies, we shall discover the reason of the illimitability of the idea of space.

When after the abstractions made upon the orange, I have left only the idea of *its* extension, the abstraction has not reached the highest point possible; for my conception is not that of extension in itself, but only of the extension of the orange; I conceive *its* extension, not *extension* itself. But if I abstract all that makes this extension the extension of the orange, and attend only to extension in itself, then the idea of figure disappears, the extension expands indefinitely, it is impossible for me to assign any term to it, for any limit would make it a determinate, a particular extension, not extension in itself. Then the frontiers of the universe, so to speak, disappear; for however great the universe may be, it is limited, and can give only a particular extension, not extension itself. This is the manner in which the idea of imaginary space seems to be formed.

80. An observation of the phenomena of the imagination will confirm what we have explained by the mere order of intelligence. When I *imagine* the extension of an orange, I imagine it with a limit, with this or that color, and with these or those qualities; since it is not possible for me to imagine a figure without lines which terminate it. This limit in the imagination is distinct both from the extension which it encloses, and from the extension which it excludes. If it were not so distinguished, we could not imagine it as limit, and it would not answer its object, which is to enable us to distinguish that which it encloses. Therefore, the abstraction is not complete. In the imagination there is always something determinate, which is the limit or the lines which constitute the limit. Destroy these limits, and the imagination expands, until it becomes lost in a sort of dark, unbounded abyss, such as we imagine beyond the universe.

A very simple example will make this explanation clearer. Our imagination may be compared to a black board on which a figure is marked with chalk. When we see the white line on the board which forms the figure, we see the figure also; but if we rub out the line, there remains only the uniform figure of the board. If we suppose the lines which terminate the black board to be indefinitely withdrawn, we shall look in vain for a figure; we see only a black surface indefinitely extended. There is a sufficient parity between this and the manner in which the imagination pictures to itself an endless space.

81. The idea of an abstract extension which is limited, is a contradiction. Limit takes from extension generality; and generality destroys the limit. There can, therefore, be no abstract idea of limited extension; but when we form an idea of extension in the abstract, we conceive it as unlimited, and the imagination attempting to follow the understanding, pictures to itself an indefinite space.

82. Summing up this doctrine, and deducing its inevitable consequences, we may say:

I. That space is nothing else than the extension of bodies.

II. That the idea of space is the idea of extension.

III. That the different parts conceived in space are the ideas of particular extensions, from which we have not taken their limits.

IV. That the idea of infinite space is the idea of extension in general, abstracted from all limit.

V. That indefinite space arises necessarily from the imagination, which destroys the limit in attempting to follow the generalizing march of the understanding.

VI. That where there is no body there is no space.

VII. That what is called distance is only the interposition of a body.

VIII. That if every intermediate body be taken away, distance ceases; there is then contiguity, and, consequently, absolute contact.

IX. That if there were only two bodies in existence, it would be metaphysically impossible for them to be distant from each other.

X. That all vacuum, of whatever kind, or however obtained, is absolutely impossible.

83. These are the consequences which follow from the principle explained in this chapter.

If the reader ask me what I think of them and of the principle on which they are based, I frankly confess that, although the principle seems true and the conclusions legitimate, still the strangeness of some of them, and yet more so with regard to others which I shall point out as we come to them, makes me suspect that there is some error concealed in the principle, or else the reasoning which deduces these consequences contains some defect which is not easy to discover. I do not put forth a settled opinion, so much as a series of conjectures, with the arguments in their favor. The reader may see by this what sense I attach to the word *demonstration*, when in the sequel he sees it often employed in treating of the deduction of certain consequences which are exceedingly strange, although, in my opinion, deserving a careful attention. I say this not only to explain what is passing in my own mind, but also to warn the reader against too great confidence on these points, whatever may be the opinion which he adopts. Before commencing these investigations on space, I remarked that the arguments on both sides seemed equally conclusive; which shows that the human reason has reached its bounds, and makes us suspect that this investigation is beyond the sphere to which the mind is restricted by a primary condition of its nature.

However this may be, let us continue to conjecture; and although we cannot pass beyond certain limits, let us exercise the understanding by examining them in their full extent. Thus, if we were placed on a very elevated ground with deep precipices on all sides, we should take pleasure in walking around the circumference, and gazing upon the immense depth under our feet.

I shall now proceed to deduce other results, and to solve as far as possible the difficulties which arise, making some applications, the immense importance of which produces uncertainty and causes fear.

CHAPTER XIII
NEW DIFFICULTIES

84. If space is the extension of bodies, it follows that extension has no recipient, that is to say, no place in which it can be situated. This seems to be in direct contradiction to our most common ideas; for when we conceive any thing to be extended, we conceive the necessity of a place equal to it in which it can be contained and situated.

This difficulty, which seems so serious at first, immediately vanishes if we deny that every extended thing needs a place in which it may be situated. What is this place? It is an extension in which the thing may be contained. Does this extension also require another extension in which it may be placed, or does it not? If it does, then the same question may be asked of this new place in which the other place is contained, and so on *ad infinitum*. This is evidently impossible, and therefore we must admit that it is false that all extension requires another extension in which it may be placed. Just as the extension of space does not require another extension, so the extension of bodies does not require space. There is no disparity between the two cases. Therefore the necessity of a place for every extension is merely imaginary, and is opposed to reason. Extension, therefore, may exist in itself, and there is no reason why the extension of bodies may not also exist in this manner.

85. What in this case would be the meaning of changing place? It would simply mean that bodies change their respective position. This is the explanation of motion.

Suppose three bodies, A, B, and C, to be situated in space. Their respective distances are the bodies which are interposed between them. The change which a new position causes, is motion.

86. Therefore, if there were only one body there could be no motion. For motion is necessarily the passing over a distance, and, there is no distance when there is only one body.

This seems at first absurd, because it is opposed to our way of thinking and imagining; but if we carefully examine this way of thinking and imagining, we shall see that the phenomena of our mind are in accordance with this theory.

Motion has no meaning for us, we do not feel or perceive it, when we cannot refer it to the position of different bodies among themselves. If we sail down a river, shut up in the cabin of the vessel which bears us on, we really move, though we have no perception of this motion. We know that we move when watching the objects on the shore, we see that they are continually changing. Even then, the motion seems to be in the objects around us, not in ourselves, and the phenomena would be absolutely the same with respect to us, if, instead of the objects being at rest, and the vessel in motion, the vessel should be at rest and the objects in motion, supposing the motion of the objects to be properly combined.[47]

Therefore, take away the agitation, which is all that informs us of our own motion, and we are unable to distinguish whether the motion is in us or in the objects; and we are naturally more inclined to refer the motion to them than to ourselves. When the vessel that carries us leaves the port, we know very well that it is not the port which moves, and yet the illusion is complete, the port seems to retire from us.

Hence motion for us is only the change of the respective position of bodies. If we had not experienced this change, we should have no idea of motion. Thus no one denies that the phenomena of diurnal motion are the same, whether the heavens revolve around us from east to west, or the earth turns on its axis from west to east.

Therefore, the motion of only one body is a pure illusion; and there is no proof of the argument founded on it which is brought to oppose our doctrine of space.

Hence, also, the whole universe considered as only one body, is immovable, motion takes place only in its interior.

87. But one of the strangest results of this theory is the *a priori* demonstration that the universe can only be terminated in a certain manner, to the exclusion of a multitude of figures which are essentially repugnant to it.

According to the doctrine which we have put forth, if we suppose only one body to exist, it cannot have any part of its surface so disposed that the shortest line from any one point to another shall pass outside of the body. For, as we suppose only one body, *outside* of it is pure nothing; and can, therefore, contain no distances which can be measured by lines. This excludes a multitude of irregular figures, and thus we find geometrical regularity growing out of a metaphysical idea.

Hence if only one body were in existence, it would be impossible for it to have any angles entering into it. For, its figure requires that the point

A, the vertex of the angle, should be at the distance A D from the point D, the vertex of another angle. This distance cannot exist, for there is no distance where there is no body. Therefore, the distance would exist and not exist at the same time, which is contradictory. It would also be an absurdity, because the capacities marked by the angles would not be filled.

The observation of nature confirms the former result, inasmuch as its tendency is always to terminate every thing with curved lines and surfaces. The orbits of the stars are curves, and the stars themselves terminate in curve surfaces. The great irregularities which are observed in their surfaces might seem to destroy this conclusion, but it must be remembered the limit of the figure is not in these irregularities, but in the atmosphere which surrounds them, and which, being a fluid, can have no irregularities of surface.

88. Another consequence, as strange as the former, is, that we are obliged to admit the existence of a perfect geometrical surface, and this *a priori*.

If, where there is no body, distance is metaphysically impossible, this must be just as true in small as in great things, and even in infinitesimals. This is also a reason of the impossibility of vacuum. It is evident that a surface is not perfect when some of its points go farther out than others, so that the less they go out from the surface the more perfect it becomes. As there are no such points in the last surface of the universe, this surface is the realization of geometrical perfection.

We have demonstrated that it is impossible for the surface to have any angles entering into it; it is equally impossible for it to have any, even the least, prominence. The difference is only in greater or less, which does not affect the metaphysical impossibility. It is, therefore, demonstrated that in the ultimate surface of the universe there is no irregularity, but that its surface is geometrically perfect.

CHAPTER XIV
ANOTHER IMPORTANT CONSEQUENCE

89. I now proceed to deduce the last consequence of the principle explained above. It is of the greatest importance, and seems to deserve the careful attention of all those who unite their metaphysical and physical studies.

The existence of universal gravitation may be demonstrated *a priori*.

Universal gravitation is a law of nature by which some bodies are directed to others. [We abstract here the manner.] This direction is metaphysically necessary, if we suppose that there is no distance where there is no body. For, if this be so, two bodies cannot exist separated. The law of contiguity is a metaphysical necessity, and therefore the incessant approaching of some bodies to others is a continual obedience to this necessity.

The velocity with which they approach must be in the ratio of the velocity with which the medium departs. The limit of the velocity of this motion is the relation of space with an indivisible instant, such as we might suppose if God should suddenly annihilate the intervening body.

As the solid masses which revolve above our heads would in this case be submerged in a fluid, supposing this fluid to be of such nature as easily to change its place, it follows that the stars must be subject to the law of approximation, because the medium which separates them is continually retiring in various directions. If we suppose this fluid to be immovable, the metaphysical necessity of this approximation ceases.

90. This theory seems to lead to the explanation of the mechanism of the universe, by simple geometrical laws, and destroys what some have called occult properties, and others forces.

Although it is easy to explain by metaphysical and geometrical ideas, the fact of gravitation, or the mere tendency of bodies mutually to approach, it is still very difficult to determine by this order of ideas the conditions which govern gravitation.

91. If the motion of approximation depended only on the intervening body, inequality of these bodies would produce unequal motions. It is

impossible to calculate the degree of this inequality in bodies which are not subject to our observation.

92. Besides this difficulty there is another still greater, which is, that bodies which move in a medium have no fixed direction, but vary their motions with the variations of the medium.

If the gravitation of the body A towards the body B, depends only on the motion of the retiring medium, the gravitation will not be in the right line AB, but will follow the undulations described by the medium. This is contrary to experience.

93. From these considerations, it follows that even though the gravitation naturally arises from the position of the bodies, still this necessity would not produce the order which exists, if its results were not subject to certain laws. And, therefore, the phenomena of nature, although founded on a necessity, would still, admitting the existence and position of bodies, be contingent in all that relates to the application of this necessity.

94. Going still deeper into this matter, we find that the tendency to approximation, although necessary, is not sufficient either to produce motion or to preserve it.

Whenever one body moves, it is always necessary that another should follow it, in order to preserve the contiguity; but, there being no vacuum, there is no reason why any body should move, and consequently, no cause of motion.

Therefore, geometrical ideas are not sufficient to explain the origin of motion, but we must look for its cause elsewhere. Contiguity being a metaphysical necessity, if the body A moves in any direction, the contiguous bodies B and C must also move; but if the contiguity already existed, there is no reason why the body A should begin to move, nor, consequently, why the bodies B and C should follow its motion.

At any instant whatever, if we suppose motion, we must suppose contiguity; for the state of the question supposes this condition always present, as being metaphysically necessary. There is then no reason why the motion should at any time be prolonged; for the bodies being at every instant contiguous there is no reason for its continuation. The motion of the body A draws with it the body B; B draws C, and so on. Now, if the motion of the body B has no other origin than its contiguity to A, the motion of C has no other origin than its contiguity to B. The cause of the motion is only not to interrupt the contiguity; this contiguity always existing as is absolutely necessary, there is no reason why the motion should begin, or after it has begun, why it should continue.

95. The laws of nature cannot then be explained by geometrical and metaphysical ideas, although we suppose approximation to be an intrinsical necessity of bodies. Under any supposition it is necessary to seek out of matter a superior cause which impresses, regulates, and continues motion.

CHAPTER XV
ILLUSION OF FIXED POINTS IN SPACE

96. Since space is only the extension of bodies, and there is no space where there are no bodies, it follows that the extension which we conceive distinct from bodies, with fixed points and dimensions, immovable in itself, and the receptacle of all that is movable, is a pure illusion, and there is nothing in reality corresponding to it.

In order to explain this doctrine and at the same time to solve certain objections which may be made, it will not be out of place to analyze the idea which we form of fixedness in relation to space. Because there are certain immovable points in the world in relation to which we conceive directions, we form the idea that these points are fixed, and in relation to them and because of them we imagine fixedness, immobility, as one of the properties which distinguish this ideal receptacle which we call space. The four cardinal points, East, West, North, and South, have had a great influence in producing this idea. Still it is easy to show that there is no such thing and that it is a pure illusion.

97. We shall first destroy the fixedness of East and West. Supposing the earth to have a diurnal motion of rotation on its axis, as astronomers now hold, the points of East and West, so far from being fixed, are continually changing their position. Thus, supposing an observer at the point A of the earth, East to him will be the point B, and West the point C. If the earth revolves on its axis, the East and West of the observer will be successively at the points M, N, P, Q, etc. of the heavenly arch. Although we suppose this arch fixed, East and West have no fixed meaning.

If we deny the rotation of the earth, the appearances will be the same as though this rotation existed; and the most that we can say is that this fixedness is an appearance. Besides, if we suppose the earth to be at rest, and the heavens to move round it, it is still more impossible to determine the fixed points of East and West; for, in this case, the points in the heavens to which we refer them are in continual motion.

We repeat that all this is a mere appearance. If a man who knows not that the earth is spherical, but imagines it to be a plane surface, walks from

West to East, he will believe that these two points are immovable, although they are continually changing. He would still imagine that he was going farther from the place where he started, although, after passing over the whole circumference of the earth, he would find himself where he was at first.

98. North and South seem to present greater difficulty, by reason of their fixedness in relation to us; still it is easy to show that this is not absolute, but only apparent. Let N and S represent the north and south poles. If we imagine the earth and the heavens to turn at the same time from south to north, it is evident that the fixedness of the points N and S would not exist, and yet the observer A would believe that every thing was immovable, because the appearances would be absolutely the same.

To an observer travelling from the equator toward either pole, the pole would rise over the horizon, while to another who remains in the same place, the pole would be at rest.

Even in relation to the same position on the earth the altitude of the pole changes, by the variation of the angle formed by the plane of the ecliptic with the plane of the equator, which variation is according to some calculations 8″ in a century, according to others 0″.521 in a year, or 52′.1″ in a century.

99. It follows from these reflections that the position of bodies is not absolute, but relative; that one body might exist alone, but then it would have no position, as this is entirely a relative idea, and there is no relation in this case, because there is no point of comparison; and that absolutely speaking there is no such thing as *above* or *below*; for although we imagine these to be fixed points, this imagination is only a comparison which we make between two points: below being that point toward which we gravitate, and above the opposite. Thus in the antipodes above is what we call below, and below what we call above.

100. Direction is impossible without points to which it can be referred. Therefore, without the existence of bodies, directions are purely ideal, and if only one body existed, it could have no directions out of its own extension.

101. Here arises a difficulty apparently serious, but in reality of little weight. If only one body existed, could God give it motion? To deny it seems to limit the omnipotence of God; and to concede it is to destroy all that has been said against space distinct from bodies.

This objection derives its seeming importance from a confusion of ideas, which is caused by not understanding the true state of the question. Is this motion *intrinsically impossible*, or is it not? If it is impossible, there is no reason why we should be afraid to say that God cannot produce it:

for omnipotence does not extend to things which are contradictory. If the possibility of this motion is admitted, then we must return to the questions on the nature of space, and examine whether the reasons on which this impossibility is founded are, or are not, valid.

The questions relating to omnipotence are out of place here, and this difficulty can be solved without them. If the impossibility of the motion is demonstrated, it is no limitation of the omnipotence of God to say that he cannot produce it, no more than it is when we say that he cannot make a triangle a circle. If the impossibility is not demonstrated, then the question of omnipotence does not come in at all.

102. Neither does the argument founded on the existence of vacuum destroy the doctrine which we have established. Natural philosophers generally admit vacuum, and suppose it necessary for the explanation of motion, condensation, rarefaction, and other phenomena of nature. But to this I reply as follows:

I. The opinions of Descartes and Leibnitz are of weight in what relates to nature, whether experimental or transcendental, and neither of them admitted a vacuum.

II. No observation can prove its existence, because disseminated vacuum would occupy such small spaces that no instrument could reach them, and also because observation can only be made on those objects which affect our senses, and we know not but what there may be bodies which, on account of their excessive tenuity, are not perceptible by the senses.

III. We can determine nothing certain concerning the internal modifications of matter in motion, condensation, and rarefaction, until we know the elements of which it is composed.

IV. It is not strange that we are unable to comprehend the phenomena which seem incompatible with the denial of matter: for we can neither understand infinite divisibility, nor how extension can be composed of unextended points.

V. The existence of vacuum is a metaphysical question which does not belong to the regions of experience, and is not affected by the system of the sciences of observation.

103. By making the idea of space consist in abstract or generalized extension we reconcile all that is necessary, absolute, and infinite in it with its objective reality. This reality is the extension of bodies, while necessity and infinity are not found in the bodies themselves, but in the abstract idea. Objects themselves are confined to the sphere of reality, and are, therefore, limited and contingent. The objectiveness of the abstract idea includes both the existent and the possible, and has, therefore, no limits, and is not subject to any contingency.

CHAPTER XVI
OBSERVATIONS ON KANT'S OPINION

104. We have already shown that extension considered in us, is something more than a mere sensation, that it is a true idea, the basis of some sensations, and at the same time a pure idea. As far as it relates to sensations, it is the foundation of our sensitive faculties; and in so far as it is an idea, it is the root of geometry. This is an important distinction, and we shall find it useful to enable us rightly to appreciate the value of Kant's opinion of space.

105. All our sensations are, either more or less, connected with extension; although if we consider sensation *a priori* by itself, and independently of all habit, it would seem as though only the sensations of sight and touch were necessarily connected with an extended object. It does not seem to me that the loss of these two senses would necessarily involve the privation of the impressions of hearing or smelling, or, perhaps, even of taste; for although it is true that the sensations of touch, such as hardness or softness, etc., are always united with the sensations of the palate; it is equally certain that those sensations are wholly distinct from the sensation of taste, and we have no reason for asserting that they cannot be separated from it.

106. Extension, considered in us or in its intuition, may be regarded as a necessary condition of our sensitive faculties. Kant saw this, but he exaggerated it when he denied the objective reality of space, asserting that space is only a subjective condition *a priori* without which we cannot receive impressions, the form of phenomena, that is, of appearances, but nothing in reality. I have already said that space, as distinguished from bodies, is nothing, but the object of the idea of space is the extension of bodies; or, rather, this extension is the foundation from which we deduce the general idea of space, and is contained in this idea.

107. To say, as Kant does, that space is the form under which the phenomena are presented to us, and that it is a necessary subjective condition of their perception, is equivalent to saying that the phenomena which are presented as extended, require that the mind should be capable of perceiving extension. This is very true, but it throws no light on the nature

of the idea of space, either in itself or in its object. "Space," says Kant, "is no empirical conception which is derived from external experience. For in order that certain sensations may be referred to something out of me, that is, to something in another part of space than that in which I am, and in order that I may conceive them as outside of and near one another, and, consequently, not only as separated, but also as occupying separate places, the conception of space must be placed as the foundation. Therefore, the conception of space cannot be obtained by experience from the relations of the external phenomenon, but this external experience itself is possible only by this conception."[48]

There is a great confusion of ideas here. What are the conditions which are necessary to the phenomenon of the sensation of the extended? We are not here treating of the appreciation of dimensions, but merely of extension as represented or conceived. I do not see how this phenomenon requires any thing *a prior*, except the sensitive faculty which, in fact, exists *a prior*, that is to say, is a primitive fact of our soul in its relations to the organization of the body which is united to it, and of the other bodies which surround it. Under certain conditions of our organization, and of the bodies which affect it, the soul receives the impressions of sight or touch, and with them the impression of extension. This extension is not presented to the mind in the abstract, or as separated from the other sensation which accompany it, but as united with them. The mind does not reflect, then, upon the position of the objects, but it has an intuition of the arrangement of the parts. So long as the fact is confined to mere sensation, it is common to the learned and the unlearned, to the old and the young, and even to all animals. This requires nothing *a prior* except the sensitive faculty, which simply means that a being, in order to perceive, must have the faculty of perceiving, and should hardly deserve to be announced as a discovery of philosophy.

109. There is no such discovery in Kant's doctrine of space, for on the one side he asserts a well known fact, that the intuition of space is a necessary subjective condition, without which it is impossible for us to perceive things, one *outside* of another; and on the other side he falls into idealism, inasmuch as he denies this extension all reality, and regards things and their position in space as pure *phenomena*, or mere appearances. The fact which he asserts is true at bottom; for it is, in fact, impossible to perceive things as distinct among themselves, and as outside of us, without the intuition of space; but, at the same time, it is not accurately expressed, for the intuition of space is this perception itself; and, consequently, he ought to have said that they are identical, not that one is an indispensable condition of the other.

110. Prior to the impressions, there is no such intuition, and if we regard it as a pure intuition and separated from intellectual conception, we can

only conceive it as accompanied by some representation of one of the five senses. Let us imagine a pure space without any of these representations, without even that mysterious vagueness which we imagine in the most distant regions of the universe. The imagination finds no object; the intuition ceases; there remains only the purely intellectual conceptions which we form of extension, the ideas of an order of possible beings, and the assertion or denial of this order, according to our opinion of the reality or non-reality of space.

111. It is evident that a series of pure sensations cannot produce a general idea. Science requires some other foundation. The phenomena leave traces of the sensible object in the memory, and are so connected with each other, that the representation of one cannot be repeated without exciting the representation of the other, but they produce no general result which could serve as the basis of geometry. A dog sees a man stoop, and make a certain motion, and is immediately struck with a stone, which causes in him a sensation of pain; when the dog sees another man perform the motion, he runs away; because the sensations of the motions are connected in his memory with the sensation of pain, and his natural instinct of avoiding pain inspires him to fly.

112. When these sensations are produced in an intelligent being, they excite other internal phenomena, distinct from the mere sensitive intuition. Whether general ideas already exist in our mind, or are formed by the aid of sensation, it is certain that they are developed in the presence of sensation. Thus, in the present case we not only have the sensitive intuition of extension, but we also perceive something which is common to all extended objects. Extension ceases to be a particular object, and becomes a general form applicable to all extended things. There is then a perception of extension in itself, although there is no intuition of the extended; we then begin to reflect upon the idea and analyze it, and deduce from it those principles, which are the fruitful germs from the infinite development of which is produced the tree of science called geometry.

113. This transition from the sensation to the idea, from the contingent to the necessary, from the particular fact to the general science, presents important considerations on the origin and nature of ideas, and the high character of the human mind.

Kant seems to have confounded the imagination of space with the idea of space, and notwithstanding his attempts at analysis, he is not so profound as he thinks, when he considers space as the receptacle of phenomena. This a very common idea, and all that Kant has done is to destroy its objectiveness, making space a purely subjective condition. According to this philosopher, the world is the sum of the appearances which are presented to our mind; and just as we imagine in the external world an unlimited receptacle which contains every thing, but is distinct from what it contains, so he has placed space within us as a preliminary condition, as a form of the phenomena, as a capacity in which we may distribute and classify them.

114. In this he confounds, I say, the vague imagination with the idea. The limit between the two is strongly marked. When we see an object we have the sensation and intuition of extension. The space perceived or sensed is, in this case, the extension itself perceived. We imagine a multitude of extended objects, and a capacity which contains them all. We imagine this capacity as the immensity of the ethereal regions, a boundless abyss, a dark region beyond the limits of creation. So far there is no idea, there is only an imagination arising from the fact that when we begin to see bodies we do not see the air which surrounds them, and the transparency of the air permits us to see distant objects, and thus from our infancy we are accustomed to imagine an empty capacity in which all bodies are placed, but which is distinct from them.

But this is not the idea of space; it is only an imagination of it, a sort of rude, sensible idea, probably common to man and the beasts. The true idea, and the only one deserving the name, is that which our mind possesses when it conceives extension in itself, without any mixture of sensation, and which is, as it were, the seed of the whole science of geometry.

115. It should be observed that the word representation as applied to purely intellectual ideas must be taken in a purely metaphorical sense, unless we eliminate from its meaning all that relates to the sensible order. We know objects by ideas, but they are not represented to us. Representation, properly speaking, occurs only in the imagination which necessarily relates to sensible things. If I demonstrate the properties of a triangle, it is clear that I must know the triangle, that I must have an idea of it; but this idea is not the natural representation which is presented to me like a figure in a painting. All the world, even irrational animals have this representation, yet we cannot say that brutes have the idea of a triangle. This representation has no degrees of perfection, but is equally perfect in all. Any one who imagines three lines with an area enclosed, possesses the representation of a triangle with as much perfection as Archimedes; but the same cannot be said of the idea of a triangle, which is evidently susceptible of various degrees of perfection.

116. The representation of a triangle is always limited to a certain size and figure. When we imagine a triangle, it is always with such or such extension and with greater or smaller angles. The imagination representing

an obtuse angled triangle sees something very different from an acute or right angled triangle. But the idea of the triangle in itself is not subject to any particular size or figure; it extends to all triangular figures of every size. The general idea of triangle abstracts necessarily all species of triangles, whilst the representation of a triangle is necessarily the representation of a triangle of a determinate species. Therefore the representation and the idea are very different, even in relation to sensible objects.

117. It is the same with space. Its representation is not its idea. The representation is always presented to us as something determinate, with a clearness like that of the air illuminated by the sun, or a blackness like the darkness of night. There is nothing of this sort in the idea, or when we reason upon extension and distances.

The idea of space is one; its representations are many. The idea is common to the blind man and to him who sees. For both it is equally the basis of geometry, but the representation is very different in these two. The latter represents space as a confused reproduction of the sensations of sight; the blind man can only represent it as a confused repetition of the sensations of touch.

The representation of space is only indefinite, and even this progressively. The imagination runs over one space after another, but it cannot at once represent a space without limits; it can no more do this than the sight can take in an endless object. The imagination is a sort of interior sight, it reaches a certain point, but there it finds a limit. It can, it is true, pass beyond this limit, and expand still farther, but only successively, and always with the condition of encountering a new limit. Space is not represented as infinite, but as indefinite, that is to say, that after a given limit there is always more space, but we can never advance so far as to imagine an infinite totality. It is the contrary with the idea; we conceive instantaneously what is meant by infinite space, we dispute on its possibility or impossibility, we distinguish it perfectly from indefinite space, we ask if it has in reality limits or not, calling it in the first case finite, in the latter infinite. We see in the word indefinite the impossibility of finding limits, but at the same time we distinguish between the existence of these limits, and finding them. All this shows that the idea is very different from the representation.

To regard space as a mere condition of sensibility is to confound the two aspects under which extension should be considered, as the basis of sensations, and as idea; as the field of all sensible representations, and as the origin of geometry. I have often insisted on this distinction, and shall never weary of repeating it; because it is the line which divides the sensible from the purely intellectual order, and sensations from ideas.

CHAPTER XVII
INABILITY OF KANT'S DOCTRINE TO SOLVE THE PROBLEM OF THE POSSIBILITY OF EXPERIENCE

118. I think that Kant's *Transcendental Æsthetics*, or theory of sensibility, is not sufficiently transcendental. It is too much confined to the empirical part, and does not rise to the height which we should expect from the title. The problem of the possibility of experience which Kant proposed to solve, either is not at all touched by his doctrine, or else it is solved in a strictly idealist sense. It leaves the problem untouched, if we consider only what relates to observation; for he only repeats what we already knew in establishing the fact of the *exteriority* of things; it solves the problem in a strictly idealist sense, inasmuch as these things are only considered as phenomena or appearances.

119. A purely subjective space either does not explain the problems of the external world, or it denies them in denying all reality. What progress has philosophy made by affirming that space is a purely subjective condition? Before Kant, did we, perchance, not know that we had perception of external phenomena? The difficulty was not in the existence of this perception attested by consciousness; but in its value to prove the existence of an external world, in relation with it. The difficulty was in the objective, not the subjective part of the perception.

120. To say that the perception is nothing more than a condition of the subject, is to cut the knot instead of untying it. It does not explain the manner of the possibility of experience, but denies this possibility.

What is experience if there is only the subject? There will be the *phenomenon* or *appearance* of objectiveness, but nature is then only a mere appearance, and there is nothing in reality which corresponds to our experimental perceptions. We then have experience reduced to the perception of appearances; and as even this purely phenomenal experience is only possible by virtue of a purely subjective condition, the intuition of space; all experience remains purely subjective, and we find ourselves holding the system of Fichte, admitting the *me* as the primitive fact, the development of which constitutes the universe. Thus the system of Fichte follows from Kant's doctrine; the former has only carried out the principles of his master.

121. In order to make the connection between the two doctrines still clearer, we shall make some further reflections on Kant's system. If space is something purely subjective, a condition of the sensibility and of the possibility of experience, it follows that the mind instead of receiving any thing from the object, creates whatever is in the object, or rather, whatever we consider as in it. Things in themselves are not extended; extension is only a form with which the mind clothes them. In the same manner, they are not colored, sonorous, tasteful, or odorous, except inasmuch as we transfer to them that which is in ourselves alone. Every thing being reduced to mere appearances, there is in the external world not even the principle of causality of subjective extension; the mind gives it to objects, does not receive it from them. These objects are pure phenomena; and, consequently, the soul only sees what it contains in itself, it knows no other world than that which is its own creation. Thus, we see the real world spring from the *me*; or, rather, the real world is only the ideal creation of the mind. On this supposition, the laws of nature are only the laws of our own mind, and instead of seeking for the types of our ideas in nature, we ought to regard our ideas as the generative principle of all that exists, or seems to exist; and the laws of the universe are merely the subjective condition of the *me* applied to phenomena.

122. Some of the disciples of Kant show no fear of his idealist tendencies; in fact they accept them without any hesitation, as may be seen by the comparisons which they use in explaining his doctrine. If a seal be applied to a piece of soft wax, it will leave its impression on the wax; if we suppose the seal to be capable of perception, it would see its mark on the wax, and attribute to the object what it had itself given it. If a vase full of water were capable of perception, it would attribute to the water the form, which in reality is only the form of the vase itself, and is communicated from it to the water. In a similar manner the mind constructs the external world, giving to it its impression and form, and then believing it has received from the external world what it has itself communicated to it.

123. Still we must confess that Kant, in the second edition of his *Critic of Pure Reason*, rejects these conclusions, and expressly combats idealism. There is no necessity of examining how far the second edition contradicts the first: it is sufficient for me to inform the reader that this contradiction exists, and that in the first edition there are expressions which so plainly lead to idealism, that it is impossible not to be surprised on finding the same author in the second edition of his work strongly opposing the idealist system. I have pointed out the consequences of the doctrine; if the author understood it in a different sense from that which his words expressed, this is merely a personal, not a philosophical question.(31)

CHAPTER XVIII
THE PROBLEM OF SENSIBLE EXPERIENCE

124. The great problem of philosophy does not consist in the explanation of the possibility of experience; but in establishing the reason of the consciousness of experience, as experience. Experience in itself is a fact of our soul attested by consciousness, but *to know* that this fact is a fact of experience, is something very different from mere experience; for, by knowing this, we pass from the subjective to the objective, referring to the external world what we experience within us.

We refer objects to different points of space, and regard them as outside of, and distinct from, each other: to say that the instinct by which we so regard them is a condition of the subject and of sensible experience is to establish a sterile fact. The difficulty is in knowing why we have this instinct; why the representation of an extension is in our soul; and why this subjective extension in a simple being should be presented to our perception as the image of something external and really extended.

125. Transcendental esthetics may determine the following problems:

I. To explain what is the subjective representation of extension, abstracted from all that is objective.

II. Why this representation is found in our soul.

III. Why a simple being contains in itself the representation of multiplicity, and an unextended being the representation of extension.

IV. Why and how we pass from ideal to real extension.

V. To determine how far we may apply to extension what is true of the other sensations, which are considered as phenomena of our soul, having no external object like them, and no other correspondence with the external world than the relation of effects to their cause.

126. What is the subjective representation of extension, abstracted from all that is objective? It is a fact of our soul; no further explanation is possible; he that has it, knows what it is; he that has it not, does not, except intelligences of a higher order, which know what this representation is, without experiencing it as we do.

127. I do not pretend that it is possible to explain why the representation of extension is found in our soul; we might as well ask why we are intelligent and sensible beings. The only reason *a priori* which we can give, is that God has so created us. This representation may be found in us, and it is so found, for we experience it; but this internal experience is the limit of philosophy; immediate observation can go no farther back. Reason raises us to the knowledge of a cause which created us, but not to a phenomenon which is the source of the phenomena of experience.

128. Why a simple being contains in itself the representation of multiplicity, and an unextended being the representation of extension, is the problem of intelligence, which, because it is intelligence, is one and simple, and capable of perceiving multiplicity and composition.

129. We pass from ideal to real extension by a natural and irresistible impulse, which is confirmed by the assent of reason. This has been demonstrated in the first book, and also in the second when treating of the objectiveness of sensations.

130. Of the five problems the last remains. We must determine how far we may apply to extension what is true of the other sensations, which are considered as phenomena of our soul, having no external object like them, and no other correspondence with the external world than the relation of effects to their cause.

131. The solution of this problem settles the question for or against the idealists. If we may apply to extension what is true of the other sensations, idealism triumphs, and the real world, if it exists, is a being which has no resemblance to the world which we think.

I have proved in treating of sensations[49] that extension is something real, and independent of our sensations, and I have shown[50] that it represents multiplicity and continuity. This is sufficient to overthrow idealism, and also to explain, to a certain extent, what extension consists in; but as the idea of space, which is closely connected with extension, had not then been examined, it was not possible for us to rise above the order of phenomena and regard extension under a transcendental aspect, examining it in itself, abstracted from all its relations with the world of appearances. This is what I propose to do in the following chapters.

132. We come now to a more cragged path; we have to distinguish the reality from appearance; our understanding, which is always accompanied by sensible representations, must now depart from them, and place itself in opposition to a condition to which it is naturally subjected in the exercise of its functions.

CHAPTER XIX
EXTENSION ABSTRACTED FROM PHENOMENA

133. That which is extended is not one being only; it is a collection of beings. Extension necessarily contains parts, some outside of, and consequently distinct from, others. Their union is not identity; for, the very fact that they are united, supposes them distinct, since any thing is not united with itself.

It would seem from this that extension in itself and distinguished from the things extended, is nothing; to imagine extension as a being whose real nature can be investigated is to resign one's self to be the sport of one's fancy.

Extension is not identified in particular with any one of the beings which compose it, but it is the *result* of their union. This is equally true whether we consider extension composed of unextended points, or of points that are extended but infinitely divisible. If we suppose the points unextended, it is evident that they are not extension, because extended and unextended are contradictory. Neither are these points identified with extension, if we suppose them extended; for extension implies a whole, and a whole cannot be identified with any of its parts. If a line be four feet long, there cannot be identity between the whole line and one of its parts a foot long. We may suppose these parts, instead of a foot, to be only an inch in length, and we may divide them *ad infinitum*, but we shall never find any of these parts equal to any of its subdivisions. Therefore, extension is not identical with any of the particular beings which compose it.

134. The idea of multiplicity being involved in the idea of extension, it would seem that extension ought to be considered, not as a being in itself, but as the result of a union of many beings. This result is what we call continuity. We have already seen[51] that multiplicity is not sufficient to constitute extension. It enters into the idea of number, and yet number does not represent any thing extended. We also conceive a union of acts, faculties, activities, substances, and beings of various classes, without conceiving extension, and yet multiplicity is a part of all these conceptions.

135. Therefore continuity is necessary, in order to complete the idea of extension. What, then, is continuity? It is the position of parts outside of, but joined to other parts. But what is the meaning of the terms, *outside of*, and *joined to*? Inside and outside, joined and separated, imply extension, they presuppose that which is to be explained; the thing to be defined enters into the definition in the same sense in which it is to be defined. Exactly; for, to explain the continuity of extension is the same as to show the meaning of the terms inside and outside, joined and separated.

136. We must not forget this observation, unless we wish to accept the explanations which are found in almost all the books on the subject. To define extension by the words *inside* and *outside*, is not to add any thing, under a philosophic aspect; it is merely to express the same thing in different words. Without doubt this language would be the simplest, if all we wanted was to establish the phenomenon only, but philosophy will not be satisfied with it. It is a practical, not a speculative, explanation. The same may be said of the definition of extension by space or places. What is extension?—the occupation of place:—but, what is a place?—a portion of space terminated by certain surfaces:—what is space?—the extension in which bodies are placed, or the capacity to receive them. But even admitting the existence of space as something absolute, what is the capacity of bodies to fill space? Who does not see that this is to define a thing by itself, a vicious circle? The extension of space is explained by the capacity of *receiving*; the extension of bodies by the capacity of *filling*. The idea of extension remains untouched; it is not defined, it is merely expressed in different words, but which mean the same thing.

To suppose the existence of space as something absolute, does not help the question, and is, besides, an entirely gratuitous supposition. To take the extension of space as a term by relation to which we may explain the extension of bodies, is to suppose that to be found which we are looking for.

We run into the same error if we try to explain the words inside and outside, by referring them to distinct points in space, we should define a thing by itself; for, we have the same difficulty with respect to space to determine the meaning of inside and outside, joined and separated, and contiguous and distant. If we presuppose the extension of space as something absolute, and try to explain other extensions by relation to this, we only make the illusion more complete. We have to explain extension in itself, the extension of space must be explained as well as the rest; to presuppose it is to assume the question already solved, not to solve it.

137. Extension in relation to its dimensions seems to be independent of the thing extended in the same place. An extension may remain absolutely

fixed with the same dimensions, notwithstanding the change of place of the thing extended. If we suppose a series of objects to pass over a fixed visual field, the things extended vary incessantly, but the extension remains the same. If we suppose a very large object to pass before a window, it changes continually; for the part which we see at the instant A is not the part which we see at the instant B, but the extension has not varied in its dimensions. This regards surfaces only, but the same doctrine may be applied to solids. A space may be successively filled with a variety of objects, but its capacity remains the same. There is no identity between the object and the extension which contains it; for any number of objects of the same size may occupy the same place; neither is the air, or any surrounding object, identified with the extension; for these, too, may change without affecting the extension in which the object is contained.

138. Though the dimensions remain fixed while the objects vary, it does not follow that extension is purely subjective, even though we suppose that the objects which vary cannot be distinguished. If the contrary were maintained, the change of the dimensions would prove them to be objective; and the argument might be retorted against our adversaries. That the dimensions are fixed shows that different objects may produce similar impressions; and therefore we can form an idea of a determinate dimension or figure, without reference to the particular object to which it does, or may correspond. No one will deny that we have the representation of dimensions, without necessarily referring them to any thing in particular; but what we wish to determine is, whether these dimensions exist in reality, and what is their nature, independently of their relations to us.

139. If we admit that continuity has no external object either in pure space or in bodies, what becomes of the corporeal world? It is indeed to a collection of beings which in one way or another, and in a certain order, act upon our being.

The difficulties against the realization of phenomenal continuity are not destroyed by appealing to the necessities of the corporeal organization of sensible beings. If any one should ask how external beings can act upon us, and affect our organs, if they have not in them the continuity with which they are presented to us; such a one would show that he does not understand the state of the question. For it is evident that if we should take from the external world all real continuity, leaving only the phenomenal, we should at the same time take it from our own organization, which is but a part of the universe. There is here a mutual relation and sort of parallelism of phenomena and realities which mutually complete and explain each other. If the universe is a collection of beings acting upon us in a certain order, our organization is another collection of beings, receiving their influence in the same order. Either both are inexplicable, or else the explanation of one involves the explanation of the other. If that order is fixed and constant, and its correspondence remains the same, nothing is changed, no matter what hypothesis is assumed in order to explain the phenomenon.

140. The object of our searches here, is the reality subject to the condition of explaining the phenomenon, and not contradicting the order of our ideas.

It might be objected to those who take from the external world the phenomenal or apparent qualities of continuity, that they destroy geometry, which is based on the idea of phenomenal continuity. But this objection cannot stand; for it supposes the idea of geometry to be phenomenal, whereas it is transcendental. We have already shown that the idea of extension is not a sensation, but a pure idea, and that the imaginary representations by which it is made sensible are not the idea, but only the forms with which the idea is clothed.

141. All phenomenal extension is presented to us with a certain magnitude; geometry abstracts all magnitude. Its theorems and problems relate to figures in general abstracted absolutely from their size, and when the size is taken into consideration it is only in so far as relative. Of two triangles of equal bases that which has greater altitude has the greater surface. Here the word *greater* relates to size, it is true; but to a relative, not to any absolute size; the question is not of the magnitudes themselves, but of their *relation*. Consequently, the theorem is equally true whether the triangles are immense, or infinitely small. Therefore, geometry abstracts absolutely all magnitudes considered as phenomena, and makes use of them only in order to assist the intellectual perception by the sensible representation.

142. This is an important truth, and I shall explain it further when combating Condillac's system in the treatise on ideas, where I shall show that even the ideas which we have of bodies neither are, nor can be, a transformed sensation. According to these principles, geometry is a science which makes its pure ideas sensible by a phenomenal representation. This representation is necessary so long as geometry is a human science, and man is subject to phenomena; but geometry in itself and in all its purity has no need of such representations.

143. In order that this doctrine may seem less strange, and may be more readily accepted, I will ask, whether pure spirits possess the science of geometry? We must answer in the affirmative; for, otherwise we should be forced to conclude that God, the author of the universe and greatest of geometricians, does not know geometry. Does God, then, have these representations, by the aid of which we imagine extension? No; these representations are a sort of continuation of sensibility which God has not;

they are the exercise of the internal sense, which is not found in God. St. Thomas calls them *phantasmata*, and says they are not found in God, or in pure spirits, nor even in the soul separated from the body. Therefore, the science of geometry is possible, and does really exist without sensible representations, and, consequently, we may distinguish two extensions, the one phenomenal, and the other real, without thereby destroying either the phenomenon or the reality, so long as we admit the correspondence between them; so long as we do not break the thread which unites our being with those around us; so long as the conditions of our being harmonize with those of the external world.(32)

CHAPTER XX
ARE THERE ABSOLUTE MAGNITUDES?

144. The preceding doctrine will seem much more probable if we reflect that all purely intellectual perceptions of extension may be reduced to the knowledge of order and relation. There is nothing absolute in the eyes of science, not even of mathematical science. The absolute, in relation to extension, is an ignorant fancy which the observation of the phenomena is sufficient to dissipate.

In the order of appearances there are no absolute magnitudes; all are relations. We can not even form an idea of a magnitude, unless with reference to another which serves for a measure. The absolute is found only in number, and never in extension; a magnitude is absolute, not in itself, but only by being numbered. A surface two feet square, presents two distinct ideas; the number of its parts, and the kind of parts. The number is a fixed idea, but the kind is purely relative. I will try to make this clearer.

145. When I speak of a surface four feet square, the number four is a simple, fixed, and unchangeable idea; but I can explain a square foot only by relations. If I am asked what is a square foot, I can answer only by comparison with a square rod or a square inch; but if I am again asked what is a square rod or a square inch, I am again forced to recur to other measures which are greater or smaller; I can nowhere find a fixed magnitude.

146. If there were some fixed measure it might be some dimension of the body, my hand, or foot, or arm. But who does not see that the dimensions of my body are not a universal measure, and that the hands, or feet, or arms, of all men are not equal? And even in the same individual they are subject to a thousand changes more or less perceptible. Shall we take for our fixed measure the radius of the earth, or of a heavenly body? But one has no claim to preference before the other. Every one knows that astronomers take sometimes the radius of the earth, and sometimes the radius of its orbit as the unity of measure. If we suppose these radii to be greater or smaller, can we not equally in either case take them as the measure? They are preferred because they do not change.

But even astronomers regard these magnitudes as purely relative, and at one time consider them infinitely large, at another infinitely small, according to the point of view from which they look at them. The radius of the earth's orbit is considered infinite in comparison with a small inequality on the earth's surface, and infinitely small when compared with the distance of the fixed stars.

We can form no idea of these measures except by comparison with those in constant use. What idea should we have of the magnitude of the radius of the earth if we did not know how many million measures it is equal to? What idea should we have in turn of these measures if we had nothing constant to which we could refer them?

147. There is something absolute in magnitudes, it may be objected; for a foot is a certain length which we both see and touch, and cannot be greater or smaller; the surface of a square yard is in like manner something definite which we see and which we touch; and the same may be applied to solids. There is no necessity of going farther to find that which is so clearly presented to us in sensible intuition. This objection supposes that there is something fixed and constant in intuition; this is false. I appeal to experience.

It is probable that men see the same magnitudes very differently according to the disposition of their eyes. No one is ignorant that this happens when the objects are at a distance; for, then, one sees clearly what another cannot even distinguish; to one it is a surface, while to another it is not even so much as a point. We all know what a great variety there is in the size of objects when looked at through differently graduated glasses. From all this we conclude that there is nothing fixed in phenomenal magnitude; but that every thing is subject to continual changes.

When we look through a microscope objects which were before invisible, take large dimensions; and as the microscope may be infinitely perfected, it is not absurd to suppose that there are animals to whom what is invisible to us appears larger than the whole earth. The construction of the eye may also be considered in an inverse sense, and as infinite perfection is also possible in this case, it is possible that magnitudes which to us are immense may be invisible to other beings. To this eye of colossal vision the terrestrial globe would perhaps be an imperceptible atom. This is no more than what happens by the interposition of distance; immense masses in the firmament seem to us to be only small specks of light.

148. It must now be very evident that there is nothing absolute in magnitudes of sight; but that all is relative, and that objects appear to us greater or less, according to habit, the construction of our organs, and other circumstances. The variety of appearances is in accordance with philosophy;

since no necessary relation can be discovered between the size of the organ and the object. What connection is there between a narrow surface like the retina of our eye and the immense surfaces which are painted on it?

149. From sight we may pass to touch, but we find no reason of the fixity of phenomenal magnitude. The sense of touch gives us the ideas of magnitudes by relation to the time it takes to pass over them, and to the velocity of our motion. The ideas of time and velocity are also relative; they refer to the space passed over. When we measure velocity we say that it is the space divided by the time; in measuring time we say that it is the space divided by the velocity; and we measure space by multiplying the velocity by the time. All these ideas are correlative, and are measured by each other, and by their mutual relations. This shows that these ideas have nothing absolute; their whole character is that of a relation which is incomplete, or rather does not exist, if one of the terms is wanting.

150. We shall find it equally impossible to determine these measures by the impressions which the motion causes in us. If for example we propose to measure the degree of velocity, by the agitation which we feel in our body, we shall find that the measure varies with the agitation, but this agitation depends on the degree of force exerted, and still more on the strength of the subject. Thus a little child is obliged to run till he is almost out of breath, to keep up with his father who is walking fast.

The impossibility of any fixed measure by means of impressions will be still more apparent if we compare the motion of a horse with the motion of a microscopic animal. The distance which a horse would pass over almost without any sensible motion, would require the microscopic animal to display its whole activity, and run perhaps a whole day. The horse would scarce believe he had changed his place, whereas the poor animalcule would at night be overcome by fatigue like one who has travelled a long journey. Compare now the motion of the horse with the motion of those fabulous giants who piled up mountains to scale the heavens; a single step of one of those giants would be a long distance for the horse to travel.

151. Art seems to be in accordance with science on this point. In art, size is nothing, the only thing which is regarded is the proportion or relation. A skilful miniature represents a person as clearly as a painting the size of life. The same principle is applied to all the objects embraced by art, the artistic thought never refers directly to the size; proportion, the *relative* is all that is attended to; the absolute counts for nothing. We see the system of relations transferred to the order of appearances, inasmuch as they affect the faculties susceptible of pleasure; reason is thus admirably harmonized with sentiment, in the same manner as we have found intellect harmonized with the senses.

CHAPTER XXI
PURE INTELLIGIBILITY OF THE EXTENDED WORLD

152. Objects in themselves do not change their nature, by the variety of appearances which they produce in us. A polygon turning with rapidity has the appearance of a circle; the stars appear like small points; and considering the various classes of objects, we may observe that there is a great variety of appearances depending on circumstances. The nature of a being does not consist in what it appears, but in what it is. Suppose there were no sensitive being in the world, the present order of sensibility would disappear; for without sensitive beings there would be no representations. What would the world be in that case? This is a great problem of metaphysics.

153. A pure spirit,—the existence of which we must always suppose; for, though all finite beings were annihilated, there would still remain the infinite being which is God,—a pure spirit would know the extended world *just as it is in itself*, and would not have the sensible representations either external or internal, which we have. This is certain, unless we mean to attribute imagination and sensibility to pure spirits, and even to God himself.

On this supposition I ask, what would a pure spirit know of the external world? or, to speak more properly, since the existence of such a spirit is certain and its intelligence infinite, what does this spirit know of the external world?

154. That which this spirit knows of the world is the world, because he cannot be deceived. But this spirit does not know the world under any sensible form. Therefore the world may be known without any of the forms of sensibility, and consequently may be the object of a pure intelligence.

There is no difficulty on this point in what regards sensations. It is only necessary that we should say that the pure spirit knows perfectly the principle of causality which resides in the object, and produces the impressions which we experience. There is no need of attributing to the intelligent spirit any sensation of the thing understood.

This question is more difficult when we come to explain what relates to extension. For, if we say that the spirit only knows the principle of causality of the subjective representation of the extended, it follows that there is no true extension in the objects, because the spirit sees all that there is, and if the spirit does not see it, it is because it is not. We fall into Berkeley's idealism; an external world without extension is not the world of common sense, but the world of the idealists. If, on the other hand, we say that this pure spirit does know extension, we seem to attribute to the spirit sensible representation; because the extension represented seems to involve sensible representation. What is an extension with lines, surfaces, and figures? And these objects, as we understand them, are sensible; if, however, they be taken in another sense, the extension of the world will be of another nature, it will be something of which we have no idea; and here again we fall into idealism.

155. To solve this difficulty, which is really a serious one, it is necessary to recollect the distinction on which I insisted so earnestly between extension as sensation and extension as idea. The former can become subjective only in a sensible being; the second may be, and is, subjective in a purely intellectual being. Extension as sensation is something subjective, it is an appearance; its object exists in reality, but without including in its essence any thing more than is necessary in order to produce the sensation. Extension as idea is also subjective; but it has a real object which corresponds to it, and satisfies all the conditions of the idea.

156. Does not this theory seem to establish two geometries? We must distinguish. The scientific and the pure ideal geometry will remain the same, save the difference of the intelligences which possess it. But notwithstanding this difference, what is true in one is true in the other. Empirical geometry as the representative part of geometry will be different: we have the idea only of our own.

157. In fact we observe two parts in geometry even in ourselves; the one purely scientific, the other of sensible representation. The former includes the connection of ideas; the latter the images and particular cases by means of which we make the ideas sensible: the first is the ground; the second is the form. But although the two are different, we cannot separate them entirely: we cannot have the geometrical idea without the sensible representation, we understand it only *per conversionem ad phantasmata*, as say the scholastics. Thus the two orders of geometry, the sensible and the intellectual, though different, are always joined in us; whether because the pure geometrical idea arises from the sensible, or is excited by it, or because this is perhaps a necessary primitive condition imposed on our mind by its union with the body.

158. This shows how the pure geometry may be separated from the sensible, and how it may exist in pure intellectual beings, without any of the forms which represent the geometrical idea in sensible beings.

159. But what becomes of extension in itself and stripped of all sensible form? When we speak of extension stripped of all sensible form, we do not mean to deprive it of its capacity to be perceived by the senses, we merely abstract the relations of this capacity to sensible beings. Extension is then reduced, not to an imaginary space, nor to an eternal and infinite being, but to an order of beings, to the sum of their constant relations subject to necessary laws. What then are these relations? I know not. But I know that they exist and that these necessary laws exist. That they exist in reality I know by experience, which gives testimony of their existence; that they are possible, I know on the authority of my ideas, the connection of which forces my assent to their intrinsical evidence.

160. That this evidence touches but one aspect of the object, is true; that there are many things in the object which we do not know, is likewise true; but this only proves that our science is incomplete, not that it is illusory or false.

161. It is difficult for us to conceive the pure intelligibility of the sensible world, both because our ideas are always accompanied by representations of the imagination, and because we try to explain it by simple addition and subtraction of parts, as though all the problems of the universe could be reduced to expressions of lines, surfaces, and solids. Geometry plays an important part in all that regards the appreciation of the phenomena of nature; but when we want to penetrate to the essence of things, we must lay aside geometry and take up metaphysics.

There is no more seductive philosophy than that which reduces the world to motions and figures, but at the same time there is none more superficial. A slight reflection on the reality of things shows the insufficiency of such a system. For, though the imagination be satisfied with it, the understanding is not, and it takes a noble revenge on its unfaithful companion, when, forcing the imagination to fix itself upon objects, the understanding sinks it in an ocean of darkness and contradiction. Those who laugh at the forms, the acts, the forces, and other such expressions used with more or less exactness in different schools, ought to reflect that even in the physical world there is something more than is perceived by the senses; and that even sensible phenomena cannot be explained by mere sensible representations. Physical science is not complete until it calls to its aid metaphysics.

The best proof of this will be found in the next chapter, where we shall see the imagination entangled in its own representations.

CHAPTER XXII
INFINITE DIVISIBILITY

162. The divisibility of matter is a question that torments philosophers. Matter is divisible because it is extended, and there is no extension without parts. These parts are extended or are not: if they are, they are again divisible; if they are not, they are simple, and in the division of matter we must come to unextended points.

This last consequence can be avoided only by recourse to the infinite divisibility of matter, and even this is a means of escaping the difficulty rather than a true solution. I intimated elsewhere[52] that infinite divisibility seems to suppose the very thing which it denies. Division does not make the parts, it supposes them; that which is simple cannot be divided; therefore, the parts which may be divided pre-exist in the infinitely divisible composition.

Let us imagine God to exert his infinite power in dividing, will he exhaust divisibility? If you say no, you seem to place limits to his omnipotence; if you say yes, we shall have arrived at simple points, as otherwise the divisibility would not be exhausted.

Even supposing that God does not make this division, his infinite intelligence certainly sees all the parts into which the composite is divisible; these parts must be simple, or else the infinite intelligence would not see the limit of divisibility. If you answer that this limit does not exist, and therefore cannot be seen, I reply that we must then admit an infinite number of parts in each portion of matter; there would, in this case, be no limit of divisibility, because the number of parts would be inexhaustible; but this infinite number would be seen by the infinite intelligence, as it is, and all these parts would be known as they are. The difficulty still remains; these parts are simple or composite; if simple, the opinion which we are opposing does, at least, admit unextended points; if composite, the same argument may be repeated; they are again divisible. We shall then have a new infinite number in each one of the parts of the first infinite number; but as this series of infinities must be always known to the infinite intelligence, we must come to simple points, or else say that the infinite intelligence does not know all that there is in matter.

It does not mend the matter to say that the parts are not actual but only possible. In the first place, possible parts are existing parts, because, if the parts are not real, there must be real simplicity, and consequently, indivisibility. Secondly, if they are possible, they may be made to exist by the intervention of an infinite power; and then what are these parts? they are either extended or unextended, and the matter returns to where it was before.

163. Some say that a mathematical quantity, or a body mathematically considered, is infinitely divisible, but that natural bodies are not, because their natural form requires a determinate quantity. This is the explanation which was given in the schools; but it is very clear that there is no ground for affirming that these natural bodies require a certain quantity, beyond which division is impossible. This cannot be proved either *a prior* nor *a posteriori*: not *a priori*, because we do not know the essence of bodies, and cannot say that there is a point where the natural form requires the limit of divisibility; neither can it be proved *a posteriori*, because the means of observation at our disposal are so coarse, that it is impossible for us to reach the last limit of division and discover a part which cannot be divided. Besides, when we reach this quantity beyond which division cannot go, we have a true quantity, by the supposition; if it is quantity it is extended; if it is extended it has parts; if it has parts it is divisible. Therefore there is no reason for saying that there is any natural form which limits division.

164. The distinction between a natural and a mathematical body is not admissible in what relates to division. This is a result of the nature of extension, which is real in natural bodies, and ideal in mathematical. That the parts in natural bodies are not actual but possible, may be understood in two ways; it may mean that they are not actually separated; or, that they are not distinct. That they are not separated has no bearing on the question; for division may be conceived without separating the parts. But, if they are not distinct, the division is impossible; for it cannot even be conceived where the things are not distinct.

165. This distinction seems to have originated in the attempt to avoid the necessity of admitting infinite divisibility in natural bodies. But the difficulty still remaining with regard to mathematical bodies, the philosophical mystery still subsists. It consists in this, that no limit can be assigned to division so long as there is any thing extended; and, on the other hand, if, in order to assign this limit, we come to simple points, then it is impossible to reconstitute extension. The difficulty arises from the very nature of extended things, whether realized or only conceived; the real order escapes none of the difficulties of the ideal. If ideal extension cannot be constituted out of unextended points, neither can real extension; if ideal extension has no limit to its divisibility until we come to simple points, the same is also true of real extension; for in both it is a result of the essence of extension, and inseparable from it.

CHAPTER XXIII
UNEXTENDED POINTS

166. There are two strong arguments against the existence of unextended points: the first is, that we must suppose them infinite in number, for otherwise it does not seem possible to arrive at the simple, starting from the extended: the second is, that even supposing them infinite in number they are incapable of producing extension. These arguments are so powerful as to excuse all the aberrations of the contrary opinion, which, however strange they may seem, are not more strange than the simple forming extension, and the smallest portion of matter containing an infinite number of parts.

167. It does not seem possible to arrive at unextended points unless by an infinite division. The unextended is zero in the order of extension, and in order to arrive at zero by a decreasing geometrical progression it must be continued *ad infinitum*. Mathematical calculation presents a sensible image of this. When two parts are united they must have a side where they touch, and another where they are not in contact. If we separate the interior side from the exterior we have two new sides, one which touches and another which does not. Continuing the division the same thing happens again; we must, therefore, pass through an infinite series in order to arrive at the unextended, which is equivalent to saying that we shall never arrive there. To continue the division *ad infinitum* we must suppose infinite parts, and consequently the existence of an actual infinite number. From the moment that we suppose this infinite number to exist it seems to become finite, since we already see a limit to the division, and also other numbers greater than it. Let us suppose that this infinite number of parts is found in a cubic inch; there are numbers which are greater than this which we suppose infinite; a cubic foot, for example, will contain 1,728 times the infinite number of parts contained in the cubic inch.

Thus the opinion of unextended points seeking to avoid infinite division, runs into it; just as its adversaries trying to escape from unextended points are forced to acknowledge their existence. The imagination loses itself and the understanding is confused.

168. The other objection is not less unanswerable. Suppose we have arrived at unextended points, how shall we reconstitute extension? The unextended has no dimensions; therefore, no matter how many unextended points we may take, we can never form extension with them. Let us imagine two points to be united, as neither of them alone occupies any place, neither will they both together. We cannot say that they penetrate each other; for penetration cannot exist without extension. We must admit that these parts being zero in the order of extension, their sum can never give extension, no matter how many of them we may add together.

169. It is certain that a sum of zeros can give only zero for the result, but mathematicians admit that there are certain expressions equal to zero, which multiplied by an infinite quantity will give a finite quantity for the product. $0 + 0 + 0 + 0 + N \times 0 = 0$; but if we take $0/M = 0$, and multiply it by the expression $M/0 = 0$, we shall have $(0/M) \times (M/0) = (0 \times M)/(M \times 0) = 0/0$ which is equal to any finite quantity, which we may express by A. This is shown by the principles of elementary algebra only; if we pass to the transcendental we have $dz/dx = 0/0 = B$; B expressing the differential coefficient which may be equal to a finite value. Can these mathematical doctrines serve to explain the generation of the extended from unextended points? I think not.

It is evident that, multiplication being only addition shortened, if an infinite addition of zeros can give only zero; multiplication can give no other result, although the other factor be infinite. Why then do mathematical results say the contrary? This contradiction is not true, but only apparent. In the multiplication of the infinitesimal by the infinite we may obtain a finite quantity for product, because the infinitesimal is not regarded as a true zero, but as a quantity less than all imaginable quantities, but still it is something. If this condition were wanting, all the operations would be absurd, because they would turn upon a pure nothing. Shall we therefore say that the equation, $dz/dx = 0/0$, is only approximate? No; for it expresses the relation of the limit of the decrement, which is equal to B only when the differentials are equal to zero. But as geometricians only consider the limit in itself, they pass over all the intervals of the decrement, and place themselves at once at the point of true exactness. Why then operate on these quantities? Because the operations are a sort of algebraic language, and mark the course that has been followed in the calculations, and recall the connection of the limit with the quantity to which it refers.

170. Unity which is not number produces number; why then cannot points without extension produce extension? There is a great disparity between the two cases. The unextended, as such, involves only the negative idea of extension; but in unity, although number is denied, this negation does not constitute its nature. No one ever defined unity to be the negation

of number, yet we always define the unextended to be that which has no extension. Unity is any being taken in general, without considering its divisibility; number is a collection of unities; therefore the idea of number involves the idea of unity, of an *undivided* being, number being nothing more than the repetition of this unity. It belongs to the essence of all number that it can be resolved into unity; it contains unity in a determinate manner. But the extended can not be resolved into the unextended, unless by proceeding *ad infinitum*, or else by some process of decomposition which we know nothing of.

CHAPTER XXIV
A CONJECTURE ON THE TRANSCENDENTAL NOTION OF EXTENSION

171. The arguments for or against unextended points, for or against the infinite divisibility of matter seem equally conclusive. The understanding is afraid that it has met with contradictory demonstrations; it thinks it discovers absurdities in infinite divisibility, and absurdities in limiting it; absurdities in denying unextended points, and absurdities in admitting them. It is invincible attacking an opinion, but its strength is turned into weakness as soon as it attempts to establish or defend any thing of its own. Yet reason can never contradict itself; two contradictory demonstrations would be the contradiction of reason, and would produce its ruin; the contradiction can, therefore, only be apparent. But who shall flatter himself that he can untie the knot? Excessive confidence on this point is a sure proof that one has not understood the true state of the question, and such vanity would be punished by the conviction of ignorance. With all these reserves I now proceed to make a few observations on this mysterious subject.

172. I am inclined to believe that in all investigations on the first elements of matter, there is an error which renders any result impossible. You wish to know whether extension may be produced from unextended points, and the method which you employ consists in imagining them already approached, and then trying to see if any part of space can be filled by them. This seems to me like trying to make a denial correspond to an affirmation. The unextended point represents nothing determinate to us except the denial of extension; when, therefore, we ask if this point joined with others like it can occupy space, we ask if the unextended can be extended. Our imagination makes us presuppose extension in the very act in which we wish to examine its primitive generation. Space, such as we conceive it, is a true extension; and, as has been shown, is the idea of extension in general; to imagine, therefore, that the unextended can fill space, is to change non-extension into extension. It is true that this is precisely what is required, and in this consists the whole difficulty; but the error is in attempting to solve it by a juxtaposition which makes these points both unextended and extended, an evident contradiction.

173. In order to know how extension is generated, it would be necessary to free ourselves from all sensible representations, and from all ideas which are in the least degree affected by the phenomenon, and to contemplate it with an eye as simple, a look as penetrating, as that of a pure spirit. It would be necessary to take from all geometrical ideas all phenomenal forms, all representations of the imagination, and present them to the imagination purified from all mixture with the sensible order. It would be necessary to know how far extension, real continuity, agrees with the phenomenal. It would, in fine, be necessary to eliminate from the object perceived, all that relates to the subject which perceives it.

174. In extension, as we have already seen, there are two things to be considered; multiplicity, and continuity. As to the first, there is no objection to supposing that it may be the result of unextended points, since number results from various units whether they are simple or composite. But the difficulty is with regard to continuity, which sensible intuition clearly presents to us as the basis of the representations of the imagination, but the nature of which is a puzzle to the understanding. It may perhaps be said that continuity, abstracted from the sensible representation, and considered only in the transcendental order, is, in its reality and as it appears to a pure spirit, nothing more than the constant relation of many beings, which are of a nature to produce in a sensitive being the phenomenon of representation, and to be perceived in the intuition which we call the representation of space.

According to this hypothesis extension in the external world is real, not only as a principle of causality of our impressions, but also as an object subject to the necessary relations which we conceive.

175. But, then, it will be asked, is the external world such as we imagine it? To this we must answer, in accordance with what we have said when treating of sensations, that it is necessary to take from sensations all that is subjective, and which by an innocent illustration we look upon as objective; we may then say that extension really exists outside of us and independent of our sensations; considered in itself, it exists free from all sensible representation, and in the same manner in which a pure spirit may perceive it.

176. We see no objection which can reasonably be made to this theory which affirms the reality of the corporeal world, at the same time that it settles the difficulties of idealism. To give my opinion in a few words, I say: That extension in itself, exists such as God knows it, and in the cognition of God there is no mixture of any of the sensible representations which always accompany man's perception. That which is positive in extension

is multiplicity, together with a certain constant order; continuity is nothing more than this constant order, in so far as sensibly represented in us, it is a purely subjective phenomenon which does not at all affect the reality.

177. We may even assign a reason why sensible intuition has been given to us. Our soul is united to an organized body,—that is to say, a collection of beings bound together by constant relation to each other and to the other bodies of the universe. In order that the harmony might not be interrupted, and that the soul which presides over this organization might rightly exercise its functions, there was need of a continued representation of this collection of the relations of our own and other bodies. This representation must be simultaneous and independent of intellectual combinations; for otherwise the animal faculties could not be exercised with the promptness and perseverance which the satisfaction of the necessities of life demands. Therefore it is that all sensible beings, even those which have not reason, have been endowed with this intuition of extension or space: which is like an unlimited field on which the different parts of the universe are represented.

CHAPTER XXV
HARMONY OF THE REAL, PHENOMENAL, AND IDEAL ORDERS

178. We may consider two natures in the external world, the one real, the other phenomenal; the first is particular and absolute, the second is relative to the being which perceives the phenomenon; by the first the world is, by the second it *appears*. A pure intellectual being knows the world as it *is*; a sensitive being experiences it as it *appears*. We can discover this duality in ourselves; in so far as we are sensitive beings, we experience the phenomenon, but in so far as intelligent, although we do not know the reality, we attempt to reach it by reasoning and conjecture.

179. The external world in its real nature, abstracted from the phenomenal, is not an illusion. Its existence is known to us not by phenomena only, but by principles of pure intelligence which are superior to all that is individual and contingent. These principles, based on the data of experience,—that is, on sensations the existence of which we know from consciousness, assure us that the objectiveness of sensations, or the reality of the external world, is a truth.

180. This distinction between the essential and the accidental, and between the absolute and the relative, was admitted in the schools. Extension was considered not as the essence, but as an accident of bodies; the relations of bodies to our senses are not founded immediately on their essence, but on their accidents. Matter and substantial form united constitute the essence of bodies; the matter receiving the form, and the form actuating the matter. Neither the matter nor the substantial form can be immediately perceived by the senses, because this perception requires the determination of figure and other accidents distinct from the essence of body.

Therefore the scholastics distinguished sensible objects into three classes; particular, common, and accidental, *proprium, commune, et per accidens*. The particular is that which appears immediately to the senses, and is only perceived by one of them, as color, sound, taste, and smell. The common is that which is perceived by more than one sense, as figure, which is the object of sight and of touch. The accidental is that which is not directly perceived by any of the senses, but is hidden under sensible qualities, by means of which it is discovered, as are substances. The sensible *per accidens* is connected with sensible qualities; but they do not present it to the understanding as an image presents the original, but as a sign the signified. Hence they did not consider the sensible *per accidens* as proceeding from the *species* and reducing the sensitive faculty to act: it was intelligible rather than sensible.

181. In the corporeal universe considered *in its essence*, there is no necessity of supposing any thing resembling the sensible representation, but we must suppose the object to correspond to the idea; for otherwise we should have to admit that geometrical truths may be contradicted by experience.

182. Although extension is an order of beings of which we cannot form a perfect conception, because we cannot purify our ideas from all sensible form, still this order must correspond to our ideas, and even to our sensible representations, so far as is necessary to prove the truth of the ideas.

It is evident that although the phenomenal order is distinct from the real, it depends on it, and is connected with it by constant laws. If we suppose that there is no parallel between the reality and the phenomenon, and that the reality has not all the conditions necessary to satisfy the demands of the phenomenon, there can be no reason why the phenomena should be subject to constant laws, and why experience should not suffer continual confusion. Without a fixed and constant correspondence between the reality and the appearance, the world becomes a chaos to us, and all regular and constant experience becomes impossible.

183. Let us examine this at greater length. One of the elementary propositions of geometry says: "When two straight lines intersect each other, the opposite or vertical angles, which they form, are equal." In order to demonstrate this, I must have the internal intuition of two lines intersecting each other. But the geometrical proposition is not confined to any particular intuition, but embraces all that can be imagined, without any limit to their number, or any determination as to the measure of the angles, the length of the lines, or their position in space.

Here the pure idea extends to an infinity of cases, whereas the sensible intuition represents them only one at a time, and isolated if represented successively. The understanding is not limited to the affirmation of this relation between the ideas, but applies it to the reality, and says: Whenever the conditions of this ideal order are realized, that which I see in my ideas is true in reality, and the relation expressed will be more or less exact in proportion to the exactness of the realization of the conditions; the more delicate the real lines are, that is, the more they approach the condition of right lines, the nearer will the relation of the two angles approach to perfect equality. This conviction is founded on the principle of contradiction, which would be false if the proposition were not true; and it is confirmed by experience, so far as it touches the conditions of the ideal order.

184. What is there in reality which corresponds to this proposition? An existing or real line is an order of beings; two lines which intersect each other are two orders of beings with a determinate relation; the angle is the result of this relation, or, rather, it is the relation itself; the equality of the opposite angle is the correspondence of these relations in the ratio of equality by the continuation of the same order in another sense. These relations between the orders and the beings, and the correspondence of these orders to each other, is what corresponds in reality to the pure geometrical idea, or to the idea separated from all sensible representation. Since the relations of the idea have their corresponding objects in the relations of the reality, geometry exists not only in the ideal order, but also in the real. Since the phenomenon or sensible representation is subject to the same conditions as the idea, because the order of phenomena presents certain relations of the same nature as the relations of the idea and the fact; the idea, the phenomenon, and the reality agree, and it is explained why the intellectual order is confirmed by experience, and experience receives with confidence the direction it gives.

185. This harmony must have a cause; we must look for a principle which is the sufficient reason of this wonderful agreement between things so distinct. Here new problems arise which overwhelm the understanding, but at the same time expand and invigorate it by the grandeur of the spectacle presented to its view, and the immensity of the field opened to its investigations.

CHAPTER XXVI
CHARACTER OF THE RELATIONS OF THE REAL ORDER TO THE PHENOMENAL

186. Is the agreement of the idea, the phenomenon, and the reality necessary, is it founded on the essence of things, or has it been freely established by the will of the Creator?

If the world had no other reality than that expressed by the sensible representation, if the appearances were an exact copy of the essence of things, we should have to say that this agreement is unalterable, that things are what they appear, and that if we suppose them to exist, it is absolutely necessary that they should be just what they appear; for nothing can be in contradiction with its constitutive notion. That which now is extended, would be necessarily extended, and could not but be extended in the *same manner* in which it appears to us, and under the *same conditions*; the relation of bodies to each other would be necessarily subject to the same phenomenal laws, and all which does not come under this order would be a contradiction, and beyond the limit of omnipotence.

187. Bodies are presented to us in the sensible intuition with a determinate magnitude, and in a certain fixed relation which we calculate by comparison with an immovable extension, such as we imagine space. By magnitude, bodies occupy a certain space, determinate, though changeable by motion; by the relation of magnitudes they occupy a greater or smaller place, and mutually exclude each other; this exclusion is called impenetrability. The question to be examined here is, whether the determination of magnitudes, and their relation in respect to the occupation of place, are things absolutely necessary, so that their alteration involves a contradiction, or not. I answer that they are not.

188. Relation to place considered as a portion of pure space, means nothing; for I have already shown that this space is only an abstraction of our understanding, and that in itself it has no reality,—it is nothing. Therefore the relation to it must be nothing also, because the relation is destroyed if one of the terms is nothing. Therefore, the relations of bodies to place can only be the relations of bodies to one another.

189. This is the principal thing to be noticed in this question. The understanding gets confused when it begins by supposing space an absolute nature with necessary relation to all bodies. We must remember the doctrine of the chapters,[53] where we explained how the idea of space is generated in us, what object corresponds to this idea in reality, and how; and we shall easily perceive that the absolute and essential relations which we think we discover between bodies and a *vacant and real* capacity, are illusions of our imagination, in consequence of our not sufficiently purifying the ideal order by separating from it all sensible impressions. We cannot understand so much as the meaning of these questions, if we do not make an attempt at this separation as far as is possible to our nature. If this is done, then the questions proposed in the following chapters will appear very philosophical, and their solution will seem probable, if not true; but they must seem absurd, if we confound the pure intellectual order with the sensible. We cannot admit the idealism which destroys the real world; but the empiricism which annihilates the ideal order, is equally objectionable. If we cannot rise above the sensible representations, let us renounce philosophy, give up thinking, and confine ourselves to sensation.

CHAPTER XXVII
WHETHER EVERY THING MUST
BE IN SOME PLACE

190. Is it necessary that whatever exists should be in some place? This question may seem strange, but it is profoundly philosophical. *To be* is not the same as *to be in a place*. To be, whether taken substantively as signifying to exist, or copulatively, as expressing the relation of the predicate to the subject, does not involve the idea of being in a place. The relation of an object to place is not necessary to it; for it is not contained in the notion of object. It is something added to the object, whether it is given to the object with more or less foundation by ourselves, or the object has it in reality by communication from some other.

The imagination can represent nothing which does not occupy a place, but the understanding may conceive things that are not situated in any place. When we reflect on the essence of objects, what position does our mind give them? The intellectual act is always accompanied by sensible representations, which sometimes assist it, and sometimes embarrass and confuse it; but in either case the act of the understanding is always distinct from these representations.

191. There is no reason for saying that every thing must occupy a place. The imagination cannot see how any thing can exist otherwise, but the understanding finds no absurdity in it, and it is in accordance with the principles of philosophy. If place considered in itself is only a part of space terminated by a surface, and space abstracted from bodies is nothing, the relation to place or to points in space must be nothing. We must have bodies in order to have a term of the relation; therefore, if we suppose a being which has no relation to bodies, it is not necessary that it should be in any place.

192. The relation of a being to bodies may be of three kinds: that of commensuration, as is the relation of lines, surfaces, and solids to each other; that of generation, as we conceive the line generated by the point; and that of action in general, as we conceive the relation of pure spirits to matter. The first cannot exist if the object has no dimensions; for then it cannot be

measured; the second can exist only in unextended or infinitesimal points, from which extension is generated; therefore these two relations can only exist between bodies, or their generative elements. Therefore, nothing which is not a body or an element of body, can occupy *place* under either of these aspects. As to the third relation, that of action of a cause upon a body, it may be found in all agents capable of acting upon matter; but it is evident that the position which results from this, is something very different from that which we conceive in bodies or their elements; it is something of a wholly distinct order, and belongs rather to the pure idea of causality than to the intuition of space.

193. We can conceive a being which is not a body, nor an element of body, and which does not exercise any action on bodies; in this case, this being has none of the three relations of which we have spoken, consequently it is not in any place, and to say that it is here, or that it is there, that it is near or distant, would be using words without meaning.

194. Viewed from the point of this doctrine, the following questions are easy to answer:

Where must a pure spirit be which has no relation of causality nor influence of any kind upon the corporeal world? Nowhere. The answer will not seem strange to one who understands that the question is absurd. In the case supposed, there is no *where*, for this involves a relation and there are no relations here.

Where would the pure spirits be if the world did not exist? Nowhere, unless we have a mind to say they would be in themselves. But, the word *to be* does not mean the position of which we are speaking here, but only the existence of the spirit, or its identity with itself.

Where was God before the world was created? *He was*, but he was not in *any place*; for he has no parts.

195. I wish here to expose an error of Kant. This philosopher believed that space was conceived by us as a condition of all existence in general, and on this he founded one of his arguments that space was a purely subjective form. In the second edition of his *Critic of pure Reason*, explaining the subjectiveness of space, he seems to hold, that we do not even conceive things in the pure intellectual order, without referring them to space. He observes that in natural theology, when treating of things which cannot be the object of intuition either for us or for themselves, we are very careful not to attribute to this intuition or manner of perception time and space, which are the conditions of human intuition. "But," he adds, "by what right do we proceed thus, when time and space have already been established as the forms of things in themselves, and conditions of their existence

a prior, subsisting still after all else has been annihilated by thought? As conditions of all existence in general, they must be the conditions of the existence of God. If we do not make space and time the objective forms of *all* things, it *only remains* for us to make them the subjective forms of our mode of intuition, as well internal as external." Kant is right in saying that space and time ought not to be considered as real forms, not susceptible of annihilation, and therefore necessary and eternal; but I do not see the necessity of the disjunctive by which he asserts that if we do not make space and time the objective forms of *all* things, we must make them the subjective forms, and that, otherwise, we should make space and time conditions of the existence of God.

196. We regard space as an actual condition of things, which occupy place, but not of all things. We conceive existence in pure spirits without the necessity of any relation to place, and, consequently, independent of all position in space.

On this point, as on all relating to the pure intellectual order, we find in the theologians doctrines which are highly important, and deserve to be consulted by all who wish to go deeply into philosophical questions. The author of the *Critic of Pure Reason* would have found there some observations which would have cleared up the difficulties which embarrassed him. He would have found how incorrect it is to say that space is a condition of the existence of all things, in the beautiful as well as profound theory by which many of the scholastics explain the presence of God in the corporeal world, and the presence of the angels in different places, their motion from one point to another without passing through the intermediate points, and the manner in which the soul is wholly in the whole body and in every part of the body. In these works, unfortunately so little consulted, the German philosopher would have learned that the presence of a spirit in a place is something different from the presence of a body, and has no relation to the intuition of space, whether regarded as the basis of sensible representations or as a geometrical idea.

197. St. Thomas[54] asks if God is in all things, and answers that he is. In proving this assertion he does not consider the necessity of every thing being in some place, but on the contrary seems rather to forget the idea of space, and regards only causality.

"As God," he says, "is being itself by his essence, created being must be his effect, as to burn is the effect of fire. But God causes this effect in things not only when they begin to be, but as long as they are preserved in being; thus the light is caused in the air by the sun as long as air remains illuminated. As long therefore as things retain their being, God is necessarily present to them, according to the manner in which they have their being. But being is that which is most internal, and most closely inherent in every thing because it is the form of all that is in it, God therefore is in all things internally."

To be situated in space is to be contained in it; so, at least, we conceive whatever we consider situated in space. St. Thomas rejects this meaning as applied to spiritual beings, and says, that although corporeal beings are contained in things, spiritual beings on the contrary contain the things in which they are.

In the second article he asks whether God is in all places (*ubique*); and, he says, that as God is in all things, giving them being and the power of acting, so he is in all places giving them being and capacity (*virtutem locativam*). He states as an objection that incorporeal things are not in any place, and answers in the following philosophical words: "Incorporeal things are not in place by the contact of measurable quantity, like bodies; but by the contact of activity (*virtutis*)." Then explaining how the indivisible can be in different places, he says: "The indivisible is of two kinds; first, it is the limit of the continued, as a point in permanent things, and a moment in successive things. The indivisible in permanent things, cannot be in different parts of place or in different places, because it has a determinate position; and in the same manner the indivisible in action or in motion cannot be in different parts of time, because it has a determinate order in action or motion. But there is another indivisible which is *beyond all kind of continuation*, and in this sense incorporeal substances, as God, the angels, and the soul, are called indivisible. The indivisible in this manner, is not applied to the continued as *any thing which belongs to it*, but only as reaching it by its activity; therefore as its activity may extend to one or many, to the small or to the great, it may be in one place or in many places, in a small place or in a great place."

What can be clearer, relatively to the intuition of space, than that when any thing is in a place it cannot be out of that place? But the holy Doctor, rising above sensible representations, boldly maintains that God may be whole in the whole, and in every part of the whole, as the soul is whole in every part of the body. And why? Because what is called totality in corporeal things relates to quantity, but the totality of incorporeal things relates to essence, and cannot be measured by quantity, and is not confined to any place.

In the *Treatise on the Angels*,[55] he says that the expression to be in place is used equivocally (*æquivoce*),[56] when applied to angels and bodies. Bodies are in place by the contact of measurable quantity, but angels by virtual quantity, that is to say, by the action which they may exercise upon a body. We cannot, therefore, say that an angel has a position in the continued (*quod habeat situm in continuo*). In the *Treatise on the Soul* [57] he maintains that the soul is whole in every part of the body. He distinguishes the totality of essence from the totality of quantity, and makes use of an argument similar to that which he used with respect to the angels. The more we reflect on this doctrine the more profound it appears; those who have made light of it, have shown that they never penetrated beyond the surface in all that concerns the relations of spiritual to corporeal things. It is generally dangerous to laugh at opinions held by great men; for if they are not certain, they have, at least, powerful arguments in their favor. Nothing is more contrary to sensible representations than the possibility of any thing being in different places at the same time, but we shall find nothing more in conformity with the principles of sound philosophy than this possibility, after we have profoundly analyzed the relations of extension with unextended things, and discovered the difference between the position of quantity and the position of causality.

198. From these doctrines it may be concluded, that to be in space is not a general condition of all existences, even according to the manner of existences; for we can conceive existences without relation to any place. Many have confounded imagination with understanding on this point, and believed that what is impossible for the former is equally so for the latter. It is certain that we can *imagine* nothing without referring it to points of space, and even in purely intellectual objects there is always a sensible representation, but the understanding regards these representations as false and does not conform to them. As imagination is a sort of continuation of sensibility, or an internal sense, and the basis of sensations is extension; it is impossible for us to exercise this internal sense, without the presence of space, which, as we have shown, is only the idea of extension in general. Position in space is consequently a general condition of all things, as perceived by the senses, but not as perceived by the intellect.

CHAPTER XXVIII
CONTINGENCY OF CORPOREAL RELATIONS

199. Position in place is the relation of a body to other bodies. Is this relation necessary? I distinguish: conditionally, yes; essentially, no. God has established this relation, and therefore it is necessary; but God might have ordered it otherwise, and can even now change it, without varying the essence of things.

If we admit, as we must, a correspondence between the subjective and the objective, or between the appearance and the reality, we cannot deny that the relations of bodies are constant, and this constancy must proceed from some necessity. But that the existing order is subject to fixed laws, does not prove that these laws have their root in the essence of things, in such a manner that, supposing the existence of objects, their relations could not have been very different from what they actually are.

200. In order to assert that the existing order of the universe is intrinsically necessary, we must know the essence of things; but this is not possible for us, because objects are not immediately present to our understanding, and we see them only under one aspect, that which places them in relation with our sensitive faculties. The best proof of our ignorance of the essence of bodies is the great division of opinion on this subject. Some maintain that the essence of bodies is extension or dimensions; and others that extension is merely an accident, not only distinct, but even separable from corporeal substance.

The great obscurity in which the investigation of the constitutive elements of bodies is involved, proves that their essence is unknown to us, and that we know nothing of them except their relation to our sensibility.

201. It is not necessary that the aspect under which being is presented to us should contain its whole nature. To say that bodies contain nothing besides what we perceive in them, is to make our faculties the type of things in themselves, a ridiculous pretension in a being which finds its activity limited at every step and is almost always passive in its relations to bodies, and which, in order to exercise its faculties externally, is forced to submit to the laws of the external world, or else to encounter obstacles which are absolutely insurmountable.

If we are ignorant of the essence of bodies we can have no certain knowledge of what is intrinsically necessary in them; with the exception of composition, which even the sensible order presents to us, and which we cannot take from bodies without seeming to run into a contradiction. Simplicity and composition in the same object are incompatible and contradictory.

202. Hence, in all that pertains to the relations of bodies we must abstain from judging absolutely, and speak only conditionally. We may say: "This happens now; this must happen according to the order now established;" but we cannot say: "This happens, and it is absolutely necessary that it should happen." The transition from the first proposition to the second, implies the knowledge of what no man can know, that the aspect under which the external world is presented to us is the image of its essence.

203. One of the greatest errors of Descartes was, that he did not make sufficient account of this difference: he placed the essence of bodies in dimensions, which is to confound the real world with the phenomenal, and to take one aspect of things for their nature. It is true that whatever affects us has extension, and that extension is the basis of the relations of our sensibility with the external world; but it does not follow that the essence of this world is nothing more than what is presented to us in its dimensions. We might as well say that the essence of man is the lines which mark his form.

204. The different aspects under which the external world is presented to our senses, ought to prevent us from confounding what is absolute in it with what is relative. A man deprived of one sense would not reason well if he should conclude that the world has no other aspects than those which he perceives. What do we know of the manner in which objects are presented to pure spirits, or of the many other phases which they might offer to our sensibility?

Let us then leave nature its secrets; and let us not limit omnipotence by saying, that the order of the world is so intrinsically necessary that its present relations cannot be changed without contradiction. When we examine the possibility of a new order of relations between the beings which we call bodies, let us not settle the question too quickly, taking for our only type of the possible the vain impotence of our faculties. What should we think of a blind man who should laugh at those who see, if he heard them speak of the relations of objects as seen? Yet we present the same spectacle to a pure spirit when we talk of the impossibility of an order different from what our senses perceive.

205. The principles of physical science are in great part conditional; for they are true only on the supposition of the reality of the data furnished by experience. If position and relation to place are not essential to bodies, distance and motion are conditional facts true only under certain suppositions. All the natural sciences, as we have seen, are reduced to the calculation of extension and motion; they do not reach the essence of things, but are limited to one aspect, that presented by experience. In these sciences there is consequently nothing strictly absolute; in this respect, they are far below metaphysics, which knows things that are absolutely necessary. A further explanation of this doctrine is required, and will be given in the following chapters.

CHAPTER XXIX
SOLUTION OF TWO DIFFICULTIES

206. Must not the theory which supposes the relations of bodies to be variable, put an end to all the natural sciences? Can there be science without a necessary object? and can there be a necessity which is compatible with variability?

The natural sciences have two parts: one physical, and the other geometrical. The first supposes the data furnished by experience; the second forms its calculations relative to these data. Change the relations of external beings, and the data will be different, you will have a new experience producing a new physical science: the calculation will be the same, only new results will be obtained from the new data. The difficulty thus disappears. All the physical sciences are based on observation, all their combinations are made from data furnished by experience; therefore the physical sciences are not wholly absolute, but they have a part which is conditional. The theory of universal gravitation is developed as a body of geometrical science, but it starts from the data furnished by experience. Destroy these data and from a body of physical science it becomes a body of pure geometry. In mechanics, the problems of the composition and decomposition of forces have a physical signification, inasmuch as they presuppose the data of experience; suppress these data and there remains only a composition of lines which mean nothing when we call them forces. Therefore mechanics is only a system of geometrical applications.

207. Here another difficulty arises which is apparently more serious than the other. If the relations of bodies are not essential, but are subject to variation; if our calculations upon them are not founded upon data which are intrinsically necessary, it seems that geometry is destroyed, or limited in such a way to the ideal order, that it cannot be sure that on descending to the field of experience it will not find that false which it regarded as true, and that true which it reputed false. For example, the distances of bodies are calculated by considerations of geometry: if the relation of distance is variable, and a body may be in many places at the same time, geometry turns out false. Such a supposition is no more than the application of the foregoing theory; for, if the relations are variable, this variation may affect

distance, which is only a relation. I said this difficulty was more serious than the other, because it leaves the field of experience, and attacks the order of our ideas, an order which we must hold to be indestructible, unless we wish to give up our reason. What would become of our reason if geometry were contradicted by the reality? what would become of an order of ideas in contradiction to facts? Still I repeat that the force of this difficulty is only apparent, and if analyzed will be found of no more weight than the objection which we have already answered.

A body which is a hundred yards distant from another, cannot be only one yard distant; geometry would be opposed to it. But if the relations of bodies are variable this proposition can mean nothing with respect to the reality. Therefore geometry is false. I admit the consequence; but the principle on which it is based involves a supposition contrary to my theory. If you alter or destroy the relations of bodies, you destroy distance, which is a relation, consequently you cannot have a distance of one hundred yards, nor of one yard, nor any distance at all, and if there is no distance there is no contradiction. If, then, you ask how great is the distance between them, your question is absurd; for it supposes a distance, whereas there is no distance at all.

208. This solution rests on a fundamental principle which we ought never to lose sight of. Geometrical truth is true in reality when the conditions of geometry exist in reality; if these conditions do not exist, there is no real geometry. There is nothing strange in this: in fact, the same occurs in the purely ideal order; even there, geometry rests on certain postulates, without which it is impossible. Two triangles with the same base and altitude are equivalent to each other. This is a true proposition, but only on the supposition that there are those orders of points which are called lines, and that the lines form angles, and are united at three points. If these relations are not presupposed, the geometrical theorem has no meaning.

209. Geometry in itself, or in the purely ideal order, is founded on the principle of contradiction. The truth of this principle being absolutely necessary, that of geometry is equally so. But the principle of contradiction, like all purely ideal principles, abstracts existence, and is applied to nothing in practice, unless we suppose some fact to support it. Yes and no at the same time are impossible; but the principle determines nothing for or against either of the extremes. It only affirms that one excludes the other; if we suppose *yes*, it excludes *no*, and if we suppose *no*, it excludes *yes*; that is to say, it always needs a condition, a datum which only experience can furnish.

It is the same with geometry. All its theorems and problems refer to the ideal field within us, where there are certain conditions which lead to certain results, by virtue of the principle of contradiction: whenever the conditions exist, the results are true; but if the former fail the latter are false. Ideal sciences consider the *connection* of conclusions with principles in the order of possibility, but take no note of facts. If the connection is admitted the science is true.

CHAPTER XXX
PASSIVE SENSIBILITY

210. Active sensibility, or the faculty of perceiving by the senses, has been a subject of great dispute among philosophers. Passive sensibility, or the capacity of an object to be perceived, is a question of not less interest.

Can every thing which exists be perceived by the senses?

Before answering this question, let us remember that to be perceived by the senses may be understood in two ways: First, it may mean, to cause an impression in a sensitive being; and secondly, to be the immediate object of sensible intuition. The first is true of every being capable of producing the impression; the second is true only of those beings which unite the conditions which the intuition supposes.

211. To produce an impression is simply *to cause*; and causality is not repugnant to simple beings. There is, therefore, no absurdity in supposing that pure spirits can produce sensible impressions: were it otherwise God could not act upon our soul, causing an impression in it, without the mediation of bodies. This causality cannot be called passive sensibility; the being which has it is not perceived by the senses. The relation of the sensation to the being which produces it would be only that of an effect to its cause.

212. To be the immediate object of sensible intuition, is to be presented to this intuition as an original to the copy. Under this view, only the extended can be perceived by the senses; that is to say, multiplicity combined with continuity is an absolutely necessary condition of our sensitive faculties in relation to external objects.

213. In this manner, it is a manifest contradiction to say that the simple can be sensible. Instinct and reason force us to suppose a real object of sensible intuition. This intuition is referred to the object as to something essentially composite, belonging to the order which we call continuity. If we make this object simple, it ceases to be sensible; and we both affirm and deny its sensible objectiveness. It is a contradiction to suppose a faculty in act, and at the same time to deprive it of the conditions to which its action is necessarily subject.

214. It may be said, that there is no necessity of transferring to the object the conditions of the subject, and therefore a simple object may be presented to the senses. But this is to elude the question at issue. For, either the sensible intuition is referred to the object, or it is not; if it is, the object cannot be simple; if it is not, we fall into idealism, which we have so often combated in the course of this work.

215. If you answer, that our soul, which is simple, has the representation of the composite, I reply, that the objective representation is not the same thing as the subjective perception of the composite; nor the presentation of the object as multiple the same thing as the perception of the multiple. Our soul perceives the multiple, and for this reason must itself be one, or it could not perceive that which is multiple. So much for the subjective; as to the objective, we must remark, that our sensible representations do not always proceed from real objects; but they always refer to objects which are at least possible; that is to say, the intuition is never entirely void; and when it has no object in reality, it finds one in possibility.

216. The external world, as involving multiplicity, or a collection of many beings, and as susceptible of this order which we call continuity, may be the object of sensible intuition, as we experience in reality. But this passive sensibility is not intrinsically necessary to it: I mean that God could so have disposed the collection of beings constituting the universe as not to be sensible. This is based on the variability of the relations of bodies; for, it is evident that if these relations did not exist, or were not subject to the conditions required by sensible representation, this representation would be impossible, and the world not sensible.

217. Experience confirms this conclusion which is obtained from transcendental philosophy. We find a slight alteration continually changing sensible bodies into insensible, and making sensible those that were insensible. The condensation of the air makes it visible; and its rarefaction invisible. A liquid body is tangible, but it ceases to be so when converted into vapor. The same variety which is caused by the alteration of the object may also proceed from a modification of the organ. A proof of this is found in what happens to the sight when aided by certain instruments. If, then, these transitions from sensible to insensible are now possible, without infringement of the fundamental laws of the relations of bodies, why could there not be a radical change in these relations which should make bodies wholly insensible?

218. By the variation of the relations of the beings which compose the corporeal universe, the sensible might become insensible; and, on the other hand, there are many insensible beings which by a different arrangement

might be made sensible. To a certain extent we have something besides idle conjectures on this matter: facts speak; in proportion as the field of experience is expanded, new phenomena are discovered; thus magnetic attraction, electricity, and galvanism, have been added to experimental science.

In these phenomena there are agents at work which are not perceptible to the senses; why may they not be disposed in such way as to be perceived like other bodies? Where is the limit of these agents? We know not; but reasoning from analogy we may believe that there are many others whose existence is not known to us.

The perfection of a sensitive organ by means of instruments, is an arrangement by which we vary the ordinary system of the relations of our body to those around us. This perfectibility is indefinite, and the farther we advance, the greater do we find its extension. It is therefore probable, that in the universe there are many beings which are imperceptible to our senses, but which a modification of our organs, or a change of some of the laws of nature would render sensible. What a vast field of bold conjectures and sublime meditations!

CHAPTER XXXI
POSSIBILITY OF A GREATER SPHERE IN ACTIVE SENSIBILITY

219. Having treated of passive sensibility in the order of possibles, a similar question naturally arises with respect to the active sensibility of beings subject to different conditions from those of our soul while united to the body.

I speak only of possibility, for, limited to what experience teaches us, we know not what may be in the sphere of beings with which we have no communication. Whatever we know of them is by divine revelation; and the object of revelation is not to teach us philosophy, but virtue.

220. To examine how far active sensibility is possible in an order different from that of our experience, not only raises curious and interesting questions, but it also gives an opportunity to explain by new reflections, the nature of this phenomenon in its relations to bodily organization. There is a special reason why we should seek to investigate this question. It consists in the interest inspired by every thing which relates to a state of existence into which we must soon enter. Short are the moments allotted to man to dwell in this world. We all hasten with astonishing rapidity to the final instant when the fragile organization which envelops our mortal spirit shall dissolve, and crumble into dust,—when the being which feels, thinks, and wills within us, shall pass to a new state, and be separated from the bodily organization. What will then be its faculties? This is a question which we cannot be indifferent to; for it concerns us, and the state of our future existence.

221. If we are asked whether a pure spirit is capable of sensible perception, we must answer negatively; because we are treating of active sensibility, which is not possible without the mediation of a body. I believe that some explanation of the question may be given. But we must first of all determine the meaning of the words. Sometimes we understand by a pure spirit, one which is not united to a body; but, more strictly speaking, the term is confined to a spirit which neither is united to a body, nor destined to this union. Thus the human soul is a spirit, but not a pure spirit; for it is either actually united to a body or is destined to this union.

It might appear at first sight that as we are limiting ourselves to the sphere of possibility, there is no difference between the two acceptations of the term; for, if it is not essentially repugnant to the soul when separated from the body, to have sensible intuition, it will not be so to other spirits. The parity is not certain; still, for the present, when speaking of pure spirits in general, I shall include souls separated from bodies.

222. What do we understand by sensing? This word may mean two things. It may mean the receiving of an impression by means of bodily organs; or it may mean simply the experiencing of the impression, independently of the bodily organ. For example: I see an object. Here is the affection called *seeing*, and the mechanism by which the object transmits light to the retina, and a certain impression to the brain. These are two very different things; the first is a fact of my mind; the second a modification of my body.

223. If by sensing is meant the receiving of the impression of a bodily organ, it is clear that a spirit which has no body cannot sense; but if by it is meant only the subjective affection abstracted from the medium by which it is produced or communicated, then the question is different, and the existence or non-existence of bodies cannot affect its answer either affirmatively or negatively.

224. The question then becomes this: Can a pure spirit have the various affections and representations which we call sensible?

Simplicity is not opposed to the sensitive faculty. Our soul senses, and still it is simple. The body aids it in the exercise of the sensitive faculties; but this aid is instrumental, not, however, in such a manner that the soul senses *by the body*, as an action is performed by means of the instrument. That which senses is the soul itself, and the instrumental action of the body consists in providing certain conditions from which sensation follows, by a physical or occasional influx. Therefore, the simplicity of a pure spirit is no argument against the sensitive faculties. Such an argument would prove too much; consequently, it proves nothing.

225. Hence there would be no *intrinsical* repugnance in God communicating to a pure spirit sensitive faculties; whether representative like those which place us in relation with the corporeal world, or purely subjective, like those of pleasure or pain.

226. Although in the present order these functions depend on certain conditions to which bodies are subject, considered in themselves, inasmuch as they are a modification of the soul, they have no essential relation to the corporeal world. It would therefore seem contrary to the principles of sound philosophy to say, that the soul separated from the body could not experience affections similar to those it has in this life. If this is not repugnant to the soul in its separate existence, why should it be so to other spirits?

The sensitive faculties are a sort of inferior order of perception. We see them in beings united to bodies, but they are not exercised immediately by a bodily organ. So far from contradicting simplicity, they require it; and therefore we have seen[58] that matter is incapable of sensation. Many grave philosophers are of opinion that the causality of bodies with respect to sensations, is only occasional. This opinion is founded on the difficulty of explaining how a composite being can produce affections of any kind in a simple being. Instead of a repugnance between simplicity and the sensitive faculties, there is, on the contrary, a necessary connection. No composite being can be sensitive.

227. Perhaps it may now be thought that there is no longer any doubt of the possibility of sensation independently of the bodily organs; and that to hold the contrary, it would be necessary to maintain that God can not produce immediately that which he produces by means of second causes. The observations which we have made may seem to have exhausted the matter, but if we reflect on it, we shall find that we have scarce entered on it.

It must not be forgotten that we are examining the possibility of sensitive faculties, in relation to one attribute only, that of simplicity. This greatly limits the question, as it leaves it to be solved under one aspect only. Simplicity is a negative property. When we say that any thing is simple, we deny that it has parts, but we affirm none of its properties; we say what it is not, not what it is. Therefore, in maintaining that sensitive faculties are not repugnant to a pure spirit, we ought to restrict the proposition; we should express our meaning more exactly, if instead of saying "sensitive faculties are not repugnant to a pure spirit," we should say, "sensitive faculties are not repugnant to the *simplicity* of a pure spirit."

228. This last observation seems to me to present the question in its true point of view. Any other expression of it seems only to confuse ideas and raise problems which we have not sufficient data to solve. In fact, how do we know but what the repugnance which does not exist between sensibility and simplicity, may exist between sensibility and some attribute which we know nothing about? This argument is not valid for the human soul, because we already know that the soul is capable of sensing; but it is valid for other spirits, whose essence is unknown to us, and the character of whose perceptive faculties experience has not discovered to us.

229. One of the distinctive marks of sensitive perception is the reference to individual objects, not in what concerns their essence, but inasmuch as they are arranged in a certain order, the variations of which do not affect their internal nature. Extension itself, which both instinct and reflection teach us to regard as objective, is rather a result of the relations of the beings

which form the composite extended object, than those beings themselves. The sensitive faculties are the lowest grade in the order of perception. Their sole function is to make known to their possessor a certain arrangement of external objects, but they teach him nothing concerning the nature of those objects. Pure spirits are a grade higher in the scale of perceptive beings, and one of the characteristics of intelligence is, that it penetrates to the inward nature of things. Therefore it might easily happen that the sensible faculties are repugnant to intelligences of a higher order than ours, not by reason of their simplicity, but on account of the different manner of their perception.

230. Reasoning by analogy from what takes place within ourselves, we are confirmed in this opinion. Sensible representations are often powerful auxiliaries to purely intellectual perception; but they just as often embarrass and confuse it. In meditating on very abstract matters sensible representations are a hinderance to the understanding, from which we should be glad to free ourselves. Every one has experienced this to be so. They are like shadows which come between the eye of the intellect and the object: the necessity of continually removing them delays and weakens our perception. Thus, we propose, for example, to think of causality. No sensible representation should find place in this idea in the abstract, yet in spite of all our efforts the representation haunts us. At one time it is the word *causality*, written or spoken; at another, the image of a man doing something, or of any other agent. The sensible representation is always in our way, and we cannot free ourselves from its presence. The understanding is forced to repeat continually to itself, "This is not the idea of causality; it is only an image, a comparison, an expression;" in order to defend itself against illusions, which would make it confound the particular with the universal, the contingent with the necessary, the phenomenal with the real.

231. We must conclude from this that a repugnance of sensitive faculties to the nature of a pure spirit, might proceed from the character of its intelligence, which by reason of its perfection rejects the duality of perception which exists in us. The object of the understanding is the essence of the thing understood, *quidditas*, as the scholastics called it. Sensible representations tell us nothing of this essence. They offer only one aspect of things, and even this is limited to the perception of extension; for as regards the other sensations, they are a subjective fact which instinct and reason teach us to attribute to external causes, rather than a perception of the real disposition of things.

232. This suggests another observation which supports the conjecture that the elevation of intelligence above a certain degree makes it incompatible with sensitive faculties. Sensations would tell us nothing even of this aspect and disposition of things if they did not have extension for

their basis. To what should we reduce the corporeal world if we supposed it unextended? Since extension, as we have shown,[59] although the basis of some sensations, is not the direct and immediate object of sensation; that which in the sensitive faculties makes us perceive something of the reality of objects, is not strictly sensible. Therefore, if it is the character of intellectual perception to know the reality of the object, the more elevated an intelligence is the farther it will be from sensation, and there may be a subject in which intellectual faculties are incompatible with sensitive faculties.

233. We shall better understand the force of this observation by casting a glance at the scale of beings, and noting the difference in them in proportion to their perfection. The isolation of a being is a mark of its imperfection. The lowest idea of an object is that which we form when we conceive it absolutely limited to existence, completely inert, without either internal or external activity. A stone has existence and a determinate form; it is what it was made, and nothing more; it preserves the form which was given to it, but it has no activity to communicate with other beings, no consciousness of what it is; in all its relations it is passive; it receives but cannot give.

234. In proportion as beings rise in the scale of perfection, this isolation ceases; active properties are combined with the passive; such we conceive to be the corporeal agents, which, although they do not reach the category of *living beings*, take an active part in the production of phenomena in the laboratory of nature. In these beings we find besides what they *are*, what they *can do*; their relations with other beings are many and varied; their existence is not confined to the circle of their own existence; but it expands and is communicated in some way to others.

235. In organized beings we find a more expansive nature. Their life is a continual expansion. The living being extends in a measure beyond the limits of its own existence; for it bears within it the germs of its reproduction. Its existence is not for itself alone, but for others also. It is only an imperceptible link in the great chain of nature; but the vibrations of this link are felt in the remotest confines of the universe.

236. Life is still more extended when it becomes sensation. The sensitive being contains in himself, as it were, the universe. By the consciousness of its affections, it places itself in new relations with all that acts upon it. Perception is immanent, that is to say, it remains in the subject, but with the subjective is combined the objective, by which the universe is reflected on a point. Being does not then exist in itself alone, it becomes in some manner other things. There is a profound truth in the expression of the scholastics: "That which knows is the thing known." There is a certain order in sensations; they are more perfect in proportion as they are less subjective; the most

noble are those which place us in communication with objects considered in themselves,—those which are not limited to the experience of what the objects cause in us, but include the knowledge of what the objects are.

237. Extension is the basis of the objectiveness of sensations, but it is not the direct and immediate object of sensation. Although extension teaches us something of the reality of beings as regards a certain arrangement of them among themselves, it is not so much the object of a sensitive faculty as of intelligence. Here sensation ceases and science commences. Science is not satisfied with what the objects appear. It penetrates to the reality; the understanding does not stop with the subjective, but passes to the objective, and when it cannot reach the reality, it wanders in the regions of possibility.

238. Thus we see that the perfection of beings is in proportion to their expansion. Accordingly as they are more perfect, they go farther out of their own sphere, and exercise a more extended activity. Hence the highest degree of perception is the least subjective; the lowest is sensation, which is limited to the experience of the sentient subject. Intelligence which is the highest degree, abstracts experience, and gives its whole attention to reality, its proper object.

239. If we could know the intimate nature of pure spirits, perhaps we should find that the sensitive faculties are altogether incompatible with the elevation of their intelligence, and that the analogy founded on the nature of our perceptions has no value when applied to a more perfect order of intelligence. However this may be, we must admit that the question would have been solved in a very incomplete way, if we had limited it to the single aspect of simplicity. These observations on the nature of intelligence ought to make us very cautious in affirming to be possible, what we should perhaps see to be impossible, if our knowledge of the nature of things were greater.

240. So far we have spoken only of the *intrinsical possibility*; what shall we say of the reality? This is a question of fact which can only be solved on data which our experience is unable to furnish, as we are not in immediate communication either with souls separated from bodies, or with pure spirits.

241. If we wish to look for an argument to prove that pure spirits and souls after they are separated from bodies, have no sensitive faculties, we shall find it in the consideration of the end to which these faculties are destined, better than by attempting to discover the essence of things. The body, to which the soul is united in this life, is an organization subject to the general laws of the corporeal universe. In order that the soul may rightly exercise its functions, it must be in constant communication with its own body and the bodies around it; it must have sensible intuition of the

relations of bodies; it must be notified by pain of any disorder which occurs in its body, and guided by the sentiment of pleasure as by an instinct which, directed and moderated by reason, may point out to it what is profitable or necessary. When the soul is no longer united to the body, there is no reason why it should have these affections, as it does not require to be directed in its acts. As this applies equally to pure spirits, we may form a conjecture as to the cause of the difference which there must be between the state of our soul in this life, and that of spiritual beings which are not united to bodies.

This argument, deduced from the final cause, is not to be considered as a proof; at best it is only a conjecture: for we do not know how far the soul in its separate existence, or pure spirits, may be in relation with bodies; and consequently, we do not know whether these sensible affections would be useful or necessary for ends of which we have no conception. And even supposing that neither the soul nor pure spirits have any relations with bodies, we are far from sure that sensible affections would be useless to them. On the contrary, so far as we can form an opinion on the subject, it seems that to take from the soul its imagination and sensation, would be to deprive it of two of its most beautiful faculties; for they not only assist the understanding, but are often a strong motive of its acts.

242. It is difficult for us to form an idea of pleasure or pain, without sensible affections. In the purely intellectual will, we conceive only *willing* and *not willing*, acts of a most simple relation, which do not have for us the same meaning as a pleasant or unpleasant affection. We often wish a thing in which we experience pain; and as often find pleasure in what we do not wish. Therefore to wish and not to wish do not imply pleasure and displeasure, but are independent of these affections and may exist in opposition to them.

243. It might be said that the cause of this discord is in the disagreement of the sensitive with the intellectual faculties. This is true, but it proves nothing against what I have been saying. The purely intellectual will, in opposition with the sensible affections, does not involve pleasure or exclude pain. The will triumphs, it is true, but it does so by virtue of its freedom. Its triumph is like that of a master obliged to exact obedience by severe punishment, who experiences pain at the very time when he is obtaining the execution of his commands. Who can tell, then, whether the will, after this life, will be accompanied by affections similar to those which it now has, but purified from the grossness of the body which weighs down the soul? I see no intrinsical impossibility in it. If questions of philosophy could be solved by sentiment, I should not hesitate to express my opinion that this fair and noble union of faculties which we call the heart, does not go down to the grave, but flies with the soul to the regions of immortality.

244. As to the imagination,—that mysterious faculty which not only gives life to the real world, but possesses an inexhaustible activity in creating new worlds of its own, displaying before the eyes of the soul rich and splendid panoramas; why should it desert the soul on its separation from the body? Why may not the harmony of nature be perceived in a similar manner hereafter? Let us not advance opinions on secrets of which we are ignorant, but, at the same time, let us beware of setting bounds to the omnipotence of God. Sound philosophy should not multiply opinions beyond measure; but neither should it circumscribe within the limits of human reason the sphere of possibility.

CHAPTER XXXII
POSSIBILITY OF THE PENETRATION OF BODIES

245. The more we meditate on the corporeal world, the more we discover the contingency of many of its relations, and the consequent necessity of recourse to a higher cause which has established them. Even those properties which seem most absolute cease to appear so when submitted to the examination of reason. What more necessary than impenetrability? Yet from the moment it is carefully analyzed, it becomes reduced to a fact of experience not founded on the nature of things, which consequently may exist or cease to exist without any contradiction.

246. Impenetrability is that property of bodies by which two or more cannot be in the same place at the same time. For those who do not make pure space a reality independent of bodies this definition has no meaning; for if place like pure space is nothing, to speak of *the same place* abstracted from bodies, is to speak of nothing. In that case, impenetrability can only be a certain relation either of bodies or of ideas.

247. Above all, we must distinguish the real order from the purely ideal. We may consider two kinds of impenetrability; physical impenetrability, and geometrical impenetrability. The physical is that which we see in nature; the geometrical that which is found in our ideas. Two balls of metal cannot be in the same place: this is physical impenetrability. The ideas of the two balls present two extensions which mutually exclude each other in the sensible representation: this is geometrical impenetrability. If we imagine two balls which perfectly coincide, they are no longer two, but only one; and if we imagine one ball to occupy a part of the other, we have a new figure, or, rather, one is considered as a portion of the other, and is consequently contained in the idea of the other, as a small ball inside of a larger ball. On either supposition the balls are regarded as penetrating each other in whole or in part; but by penetration is here meant only that there are certain parts in one, considered as pure space, which the other, also considered as pure space, occupies. Geometrical impenetrability exists only when the two objects are supposed to be separated, and only inasmuch as they are separated; in which case impenetrability is absolutely necessary, because penetration would be to confound what is by the supposition separated,

and would imply separation and non-separation, which are contradictory. Therefore, geometrical impenetrability is no argument in favor of physical impenetrability; for the former exists only in case it is presupposed or required under pain of contradiction. The same would occur in reality; for if we suppose two bodies separated, they cannot be in the same place whilst they are separated, without a manifest contradiction. On this point, therefore, the ideal teaches us nothing as to the real.

248. Can penetration exist in reality? Can one ball of metal, for example, enter another ball of metal, as we make one geometrical ball enter another? We are not treating of the regular order of things which is repugnant to such suppositions, but of the essence of things. On this supposition, I maintain that there is no contradiction in making bodies penetrable, and that an analysis of this matter proves that the impenetrability of bodies is not essential.

We have seen that the idea of place as pure space is an abstraction. It is therefore an entirely imaginary supposition on which we give to every body a certain extension to fill a certain place, necessarily, and in such a manner that it is impossible for it to admit another body into the same place at the same time. The position of bodies in general is the sum of their relations; the particular extension of each body is only the sum of the relations of its parts among themselves, until we come by an infinite division to unextended or infinitesimal points.

The sum of the relations of indivisible or infinitesimal beings constitutes what we call extension and space, and all that is contained in the vast field of sensible representation. Who can assure us that these relations are not variable? Is our experience, perhaps, the limit of the nature of things? Evidently not. The universe was not planned after our experience, but our experience is obtained from the universe. To say that it contains, and can contain only what our experience sees in it, is to make the *me* the type of the universe; to affirm that its laws are derived from us, that they are emanations from our being. Foolish pride of an imperceptible atom, which appears for an instant on the great theatre of nature, and goes out like a spark of fire; foolish pride for a spirit which, despite its great idea of its own importance, feels that it is unable to withdraw itself from these laws and phenomena, which it pretends to consider as its own creation!

CHAPTER XXXIII
A TRIUMPH OF RELIGION IN THE FIELD OF PHILOSOPHY

249. There are two things in extended objects: multiplicity and continuity. The first is absolutely necessary to extension; it supposes distinct parts, and that which is distinct cannot be identical without evident contradiction. The continuity represented in the sensible impression is not essential to extension, because it is only the result of a union of relations inseparable in the present order of sensibility, but not absolutely necessary in the order of reality. Transcendental philosophy rising above sensible representations, and leaving phenomena to enter on the contemplation of beings in themselves, nowhere discovers the necessity of these relations, and is obliged to consider them as simple facts which might cease to be without any contradiction. In this manner the correspondence of the phenomenon with the reality is saved, and the internal world harmonized with the external, but the subjective conditions of the former are not all transferred to the latter in such a way as to make what is necessary for our representations, absolutely necessary in itself.

250. Arrived at this point of transcendental philosophy, the mind beholds new worlds unfolded to its view. We rejoice to say that this discovers to us a new proof of the divinity of the Catholic religion, and teaches us to distrust that proud philosophy which finds a contradiction in every thing which it cannot understand.

251. There is a mystery which the Church celebrates with august ceremonies, and the Christian adores with faith and with love. The unbeliever sees the holy Tabernacle, and exclaims, in the pride of his ignorance: "Here is a monument of superstition; here man adores an absurdity."

As the present is a work of philosophy, not of theology, I might pass over without answering the objections of infidelity, but the occasion seems so well suited for the solution of some difficulties brought by light and superficial thinkers, that I am unwilling to pass them in silence. The nature of the work requires me to be brief in this discussion, though the subject is too important to be entirely omitted; the more so, as Catholic writers on philosophy have given their explanations on these points in what they considered the most seasonable place, and most frequently when treating of extension.

252. That the mystery of the Eucharist is a supernatural fact incomprehensible to man, and inexplicable by human words, is confessed by Catholics and acknowledged by the Church. We cannot, therefore, give a philosophical reason to explain this secret; no one was ever so vain as to attempt it. We can only examine whether the mystery is absurd and intrinsically contradictory; for if it were, it would not be a truth but an error, because divine omnipotence does not extend to what is absurd. The question is, whether the fact, although beyond the laws of nature, is intrinsically possible; for then it belongs to the field of criticism. If the incredulous man admits God, he must admit his omnipotence; the discussion must then be, not whether God can perform this miracle, but whether he has performed it.

253. The objections brought against the Eucharist may be reduced to the following: a body exists without the conditions to which other bodies are subject; it produces none of the sensible impressions which we receive from other bodies; and is in many places at the same time. To answer these objections, let us first determine our ideas.

254. The doctrines explained in the theory of sensations in this volume, show how false it is to say that the Eucharist is impossible. Under the sacred species is a body which does not affect our senses; here is a miracle, but not an impossible thing. I have shown that there is no necessary relation between bodies and our sensibility. The connection which now exists cannot be explained by any intrinsical property of spirits and bodies; we must, therefore, recur to a higher cause which freely established these relations. The same cause can suspend them. From this point of view the question becomes this: Can the power of God make a body which shall not produce the phenomena of sensibility, and suspend the laws which he was free to establish? Thus presented, the question cannot bear two answers. It must be answered in the affirmative, or the omnipotence of God is denied.

255. Those who attempt to show the impossibility of our dogma, must prove the following propositions:

I. Passive sensibility is so essential to bodies that they cannot lose it without destroying the principle of contradiction.

II. The relations of our organs [to] objects are intrinsically immutable.

III. The transmission of the impressions of the organ to the sensitive faculties of the soul is equally essential, and can fail under no supposition.

If they do not prove the truth of these three propositions, all the objections founded on the phenomena of sensibility fall to the ground. If one only is not proved, all the objections are solved; for it is evident that the phenomena of sensibility may be altered by three causes:

I. By the absence of the dispositions necessary to the body, that it may be the object of sensibility.

II. By the interruption of the ordinary relations between our organs and the body.

III. By the failure of the transmission of the impressions of the organ to the sensitive faculties.

Consequently, if one of the first propositions is false, the doubter is reduced to silence.

256. Whoever should attempt to prove these three propositions, not only would fail, but the attempt would prove his ignorance of the phenomena of sensibility, and that his philosophy on this point is the notions of the vulgar. It is not necessary to be a philosopher, it is sufficient to have acquired a very slight knowledge of philosophy to see that such an attempt would suppose a complete ignorance of the history of philosophy. At any rate, I need not insist on this point; for I have treated these questions at length in the last two books of this volume.

257. The solution there given ought to suffice to answer satisfactorily the objection founded on the particular state of a body without the conditions of extension which we find in others. From the moment that we suppose the correspondence of a body with our senses to be suspended, as these are the only means by which we are informed of what passes in the external world, it is impossible for us to affirm that there is any absurdity in that of which we have no experience. We perceive extension only by sensation, therefore we can say nothing in relation to the extension of an object of which we have no sensation. But although this answer should cut short all objections, I shall not confine myself to this alone.

258. What is extension? In reality it is the sum of the relations of the beings which compose the extended object. These relations, as I have proved, are not intrinsically necessary: therefore God can alter them. Thus this question comes to the same point as the preceding: can the power of God suspend, alter, or entirely take away relations which are not intrinsically necessary? Evidently it can. The difficulty then is not as to what could have been, but as to what is. Again we find ourselves out of the field of philosophy in that of facts, or the examination of the motives of credibility.

259. The other objection founded on the impossibility of body being in several places at the same time, though in appearance more difficult, amounts to the same as the former. To be in a place, as we now understand it, is to have a particular extension, with the ordinary form and relations with respect to the extension of other bodies. If we suppose a body with extension subject to other conditions, without the ordinary relation to the extension of other bodies, we destroy the supposition on which we base the impossibility of a body being at the same time in several places. Therefore, as we have proved that the omnipotence of God can alter and even take away these relations, there is no contradiction in admitting the destruction of the results which proceed from these relations.

260. This is why the distinction of the scholastics between two classes of extension: *in ordine ad se, et in ordine ad locum,* or quantitative and sacramental extension, though to the eyes of a superficial philosophy it might appear to be an empty subtlety, invented for the purpose of avoiding the difficulty, is nevertheless a profound observation, confirmed by the analysis of the reality and the phenomenon in the sensible order. I do not mean by this to say that when this distinction was made in the schools, they understood perfectly all the truth and philosophical nicety which it involves; nor that the distinction was always accompanied by the critical analysis which belongs to it. At present I abstract the merit of the men and regard only the thing. The less philosophical intelligence we suppose in those who used the distinction, the more admirable appears that religion which inspires its defenders with fruitful thoughts which the ages to come might unfold. The philosophical schools disputed warmly on extension, on accidents, and on the sensitive faculties: the Catholic dogma taught a truth which was contrary to all appearances, it stimulated them to examine more profoundly the distance of the phenomenon from the reality, the difference between the contingent and the necessary; the mystery which the Church taught introduced into philosophy questions which without it would probably never have occurred to man's understanding.

261. Bacon expressed a profound truth when he said that a little philosophy carried its possessor from religion, and a great deal of philosophy leads him to it. A careful study of the objections brought against Christianity, lays bare a truth confirmed by the history of eighteen centuries; the most weighty objections against Catholicity, instead of proving any thing against it, involve a proof which confirms it. The secret for discovering this proof, is to go to the bottom of the objection, and examine it under all its aspects. Original sin is a mystery, but it explains the whole world; the Incarnation is a mystery, but it explains the traditions of the human race; faith is full of mysteries, but it satisfies one of the greatest necessities of reason; the history

of the creation is a mystery, but this mystery clears up chaos, throws light on the world, and is the key to the history of mankind; all Christianity is a collection of mysteries, but these mysteries are connected by a secret union with all that is profound, grand, sublime, or beautiful in heaven or earth; they are connected with the individual, with the family, with society, with God, with the understanding, with the heart, with languages, sciences, and art. The investigator who rejects religion and even seeks means to oppose it, finds it at the entrance as at the outlet of the mysterious ways of life; at the cradle of the infant as in the shadow of the tomb; in time as in eternity; explaining every thing by a word; listening unmoved to the wanderings of ignorance and the sarcasms of unbelief, patiently awaiting till the course of ages shall acknowledge its truth, which existed before all ages.

CHAPTER XXXIV
CONCLUSION AND SUMMING UP

262. Before passing to another subject, let us fix our attention for a few moments on the nature and origin of the idea of extension. We shall thus collect the fruit of the preceding investigations, and prepare the way for those which follow.

The scientific fruitfulness of this idea to our mind proves how distant sensible impressions are from intellectual perception. We cannot know whether this idea existed in our mind before the sensible impression; if it did exist we were not conscious of it, and in this respect it is affirming a gratuitous proposition to say that it is an innate idea. What we can safely say, is, that there are two distinct orders of internal phenomena, that sensation could not have produced the idea, that this idea is immeasurably superior to the external impression, or even the internal sensitive intuition, and that if it did not already exist in the mind, it was not produced by sensation as an effect is produced by its cause.

263. Here we make an important transition from the order of sensations, to the order of ideas, and discover in our mind a new class of facts. It matters little whether these facts exist before the impression, or result from its presence. In the first case, we see in the mind a deposit of germs which need only the warmth of life in order to be developed; in the second, we find in the mind a fertility which produces these germs. In either case we find a being of a privileged nature, a sublime being which by a single leap rises above the region of matter, and awakened by the external impression, arises to a new life which this world cannot contain.

264. In this sense there are innate ideas; ideas which sensation could not have produced. In this sense all general and necessary ideas are innate; for sensation could not produce them. Sensation is never any thing more than a phenomenon, a particular and contingent fact, and consequently incapable of producing general ideas, or the ideas of the necessary relations of being. Sight, or the imaginary representation of a triangle, is a contingent phenomenon which tells us nothing of the necessary relations of the sides and angles to each other. In order to perceive these relations, this necessity,

something else is required. This something else, call it innate ideas, force, fecundity, or activity of the mind, or any thing you please, exists, and could not have been produced by sensation, but belongs to a higher order distinct from sensible phenomena.

265. After such long investigations of the phenomena of sensation, we at last find an idea; it is the idea of extension, the foundation of all the mathematical sciences and of their application to the laws of nature.

The human mind, in all its relations with the material world, seems to have one great idea, that of extension, which, modified in infinite ways, is the origin of all the sciences which relate to matter. The whole material world rests on this idea, and all knowledge of material objects proceeds from it. It is a pure idea in its necessary relations and in its necessary branches. It is a light given to the lord of creation that he may know and admire the prodigies of nature.

266. We find the same wonderful simplicity amidst so complicated a multiplicity in another order of ideas. Hence we infer that the whole edifice of the sciences and all human knowledge are founded on a small number of ideas, perhaps on two alone. These ideas are not sensible representations, they are the objects of pure intuitions; they cannot be decomposed, but they may be applied to an infinite variety of things; they are not explained by words, as a union including various conceptions; by them a mind acts on another mind, not to teach it any thing, but to make it concentrate its activity in order to note what it contains within itself, and learn, in a certain measure, what it already knows.

Try to explain extension, the idea by which we perceive this order which we cannot express in words, but on which we found sensible experience and geometrical science, and you can find no expression. Will you define it to be "parts outside of parts?" But what are *parts*, and what does *outside* mean, if you have not the idea of extension? Take any extended thing, make your mind concentrate itself and exercise its activity in generalization. Is this triangle a quadrilateral? No. Are they both extended? Yes. Is this surface a solid? No. Are they both extended? Yes. Are all triangles different from quadrilaterals? Yes. Have all surfaces and solids extension? Yes. How do you pass from one fact to all the facts of the same kind, from the contingent to the necessary? Have you explained what extension is? No. Have you shown what there is common to all these different things? No. All that you have done then is to arouse the activity of your mind, and to make it direct its attention to the general idea of extension, and the mind applies this idea to various things which are different, yet have something in common, it applies the different modifications of this idea to various things which have something in common, and finds them different. You have not taught the truths of geometry to the mind, but have awakened them in it, whether they already existed in it, or the mind had the faculty of producing them.

267. Let us now collect the result of the investigations we have made. I do not give an equal value to all the propositions which follow. I have explained my opinion of each in its proper place, but I consider it well to sum them all up here in order to assist the understanding and help the memory.

I. There is immediate certainty of our relations with beings distinct from us.

II. There is certainty of the existence of an external world.

III. The external world in relation to us, is only an extended being which affects us, and is subject to constant laws which we may determine.

IV. We have the idea of extension.

V. The idea of extension is excited by sensations, but it is not confounded with them.

VI. The idea of extension is the basis of all our cognitions of bodies.

VII. The idea of extension should not be confounded with the imaginary representation of extension.

VIII. An extended space which is nothing real, is an absurdity.

IX. Space is nothing real distinguished from the extension of bodies.

X. Where there are no bodies, there are no distances.

XI. Motion is the change of the positions of bodies among themselves.

XII. There is not and cannot be vacuum of any kind.

XIII. The idea of space is the idea of extension in the abstract.

XIV. The imagination of an unlimited space is only an attempt of the imagination to follow the understanding in the abstraction of extension. It also arises from our habit of seeing through transparent mediums, and moving in fluids whose resistance is not perceptible.

XV. As all that we know of bodies is, that they are extended and affect us, whatever has these two conditions is to us a body.

XVI. But as we do not know the essence of bodies, we do not know whether a body can exist without extension.

XVII. Neither do we know what modifications the extension of one body may be subject to, with respect to others.

XVIII. The elements of which bodies are composed are unknown to us.

XIX. The approximation of some bodies to others, and the gravitation which results from it, seem to be the necessary effect of their present relations.

XX. The necessity of approximation does not suffice to explain the laws of motion, or their beginning, or their continuation.

XXI. The idea of space is not an absolutely necessary condition of sensation.

XXII. The idea of extension has a real objectiveness.

XXIII. The transition from the subjective to the objective in relation to extension is a primitive fact of our nature.

XXIV. Therefore bodily phenomena have a real existence outside of us.

XXV. Therefore a real certainty, scientific as well as phenomenal, arises from the testimony of the senses.

XXVI. Reason justifies the instinct of nature when it examines the relation of subjectiveness with objectiveness in sensations.

XXVII. Geometry considers extension in the abstract; but with the certainty that when the principle exists in the real order, the consequences cannot fail to be produced, and that the consequences will be more or less exact in proportion as the principle is more or less exactly realized.

XXVIII. Notwithstanding our certainty of the existence of the external world we do not know its essence.

XXIX. We do not know what this world is when seen by a pure spirit.

XXX. Sensible intuition, to which our geometry relates, does not constitute the essence of scientific knowledge, and may be separated from it.

XXXI. A change in the relations of corporeal beings among themselves, and with our sensitive faculties, is not intrinsically impossible.

NOTES TO BOOK FIRST

ON CHAPTER I.

(1) We must distinguish between certainty and truth: there are intimate relations between them, yet they are very different things. Truth is the conformity of the intellect with the object. Certainty is a firm assent to a real or apparent truth.

Certainty is not truth, but it must at least have the illusion of truth. We may be certain of what is false, but not unless we believe it to be true.

There is no truth so long as there is no judgment; for without judgment there is only perception, but no comparison of the idea with the thing; and without comparison there can be neither conformity nor discrepancy. If we conceive a mountain a thousand miles high, we conceive a thing that does not exist; but we do not err so long as we do not assert the existence of the mountain. If we affirm it, there is opposition between our judgment and the reality: this constitutes error. The object of the intellect is truth; therefore, we at least require the illusion of truth in order to be certain: our intellect is weak; hence its certainty is liable to error. The first is a law of the intellect, the second a proof of its frailty.

Philosophy, or, rather, man, cannot rest content with appearances, but demands reality; if any one be convinced that he has only the appearance, or if he even doubt of it, he loses his certainty, for it admits appearances only on condition of their being disguised.

ON CHAPTER II.

(2) Even Pyrrho did not doubt of every thing as some pretend; he admitted sensations so far as passive, and resigned himself to the consequences of these impressions, and yielded to the necessity of conforming in practice to what they indicated. No one ever yet denied appearances: it is reality that is disputed; some hold that man must be content with saying *it appears*; others that he can go so far as to say *it is*. It is useful to preserve this distinction, as it prevents confusion of ideas in the history of philosophy, and conduces to render clear the question of certainty. Thus of the three questions: is there certainty? on what is it founded? how is it acquired? the first is resolved alike by all the schools, so far as it relates to a fact of our soul: by only admitting appearances, they admit the certainty of them.

ON CHAPTER III.

(3) In order to form clear ideas of the development of the understanding, and the other faculties of our soul, the reader may refer to what we advanced in our work, entitled *The Criterion*, and particularly to the chapters I., II., III., XII., XIII., XIV., XVIII., and XXII.

ON CHAPTER IV.

(4) We subjoin the passages from St. Thomas on the unity and multiplicity of ideas, to which we referred in the text. We believe the friends of solid and profound metaphysics will read them with great pleasure.

"In omnibus enim substantiis intellectualibus, invenitur virtus intellectiva per influentiam divini luminis. Quod quidem in primo principio est unum et simplex, et quanto magis creaturæ intellectuales distant a primo principio, tanto magis dividitur illud lumen, et diversificatur, sicut accidit in lineis a centro egredientibus. Et inde est quod Deus per suam essentiam omnia intelligit: superiores autem intellectualium substantiarum, etsi per plures formas intelligant, tamen intelligunt per pauciores et magis universales et virtuosiores ad comprehensionem rerum propter efficaciam virtutis intellectivæ, quæ est in eis. In inferioribus autem sunt formæ plures et minus universales, et minus efficaces ad comprehensionem rerum, in quantum deficiunt a virtute intellectiva superiorum. Si ergo inferiores substantiæ haberent formas in illa universalitate, in qua habent superiores, quia non sunt tantæ efficaciæ in intelligendo, non acciperent per eas perfectam cognitionem de rebus, sed in quadam communitate, et confusione, quod aliqualiter apparet in hominibus. Nam qui sunt debilioris intellectus, per universales conceptiones magis intelligentium, non accipiunt perfectam cognitionem, nisi eis singula in speciali explicentur. (P. 1n, Q. 892, A. 1°.)

"Intellectus quanto est altior et perspicacior tanto ex uno potest plura cognoscere. Et quia intellectus divinus est altissimus, per unam simplicem essentiam suam omnia cognoscit; nec est ibi aliqua pluralitas formarum idealium, nisi secundum diversos respectus divinæ essentiæ ad res cognitas; sed in intellectu creato multiplicatur secundum rem quod est unum secundum rem in mente divina, ut non possit omnia per unum cognoscere; ita tamen quod quanto intellectus creatus est altior, tanto pauciores habet formas ad plura cognoscenda efficaces. Et hoc est quod Dio. dicit, 12, cœ. hier. quod superiores ordines habent scientiam magis universalem in inferioribus. Et in lib. de causis dicitur, quod intelligentiæ superiores habent formas magis universales; hoc tamen observato, quod in infimis angelis sunt formæ adhuc universales in tantum, quod per unam formam possunt cognoscere omnia individua unius speciei: ita quod illa species sit propria, uniuscujusque particularium secundum diversos respectus ejus ad particularia, sicut essentia divina efficitur propria similitudo singulorum secundum diversos respectus; sed intellectus humanus qui est ultimus in ordine substantiarum intellectualium habet formas in tantum particulatas quod non potest per unam speciem nisi unum quid cognoscere. Et ideo similitudo speciei existens in intellectu humano non sufficit ad cognoscenda plura singularia; et propter hoc intellectui adjuncti sunt sensus quibus singularia accipiat. (Quodlib. 7, A. 3.)

"Respondeo dicendum, quod ex hoc sunt in rebus aliqua superiora, quod sunt uni primo, quod est Deus, propinquiora et similiora. In Deo autem tota plenitudo intellectualis cognitionis continetur in uno, scilicet in essentia divina, per quam Deus omnia cognoscit. Quæ quidem intelligibilis plentitudo, in intelligibilibus creaturis inferiori modo et minus simpliciter invenitur. Unde oportet, quod ea quæ Deus cognoscit per unam, inferiores intellectus cognoscant per multa; et tanto amplius per plura, quanto amplius intellectus inferior fuit. Sic igitur quanto angelus fuerit superior, tanto per pauciores species universitatem intelligibilium apprehendere poterit, et ideo oportet quod ejus formæ sint universaliores, quasi ad plura se extendentes unaquæque eorum. Et de hoc, exemplum aliqualiter in nobis perspici potest: sunt enim quidam, qui veritatem intelligibilem capere non possunt; nisi eis particulatim per singula explicatur. Et hoc quidem ex debilitate intellectus eorum contingit. Alii vero qui sunt fortioris intellectus, ex paucis multo capere possunt." (P.1a, Q. 55a A. 3°.)

ON CHAPTER V.

(5) Here is the idea of Condillac's man-statue explained by himself: "To gain this object we imagined a statue internally organized like ourselves, and animated with a mind deprived of every sort of ideas. We also supposed its exterior composed wholly of marble, to allow it the use of none of its senses, and we reserved to ourselves the liberty to open them at our pleasure to the different impressions of which they are susceptible.

"We thought we ought to commence with *smell*, because of all the senses this is the one which least contributes to cognitions of the mind. Next we had to examine the others, and after having considered them apart and together, we saw the statue become an animal able to attend to its own preservation.

"The principle that determines the development of its faculties is simple; even sensations contain it; for, all being of necessity either agreeable or the contrary, the statue is interested in enjoying some and shunning others. The reader will now be convinced that this interest suffices to give occasion to the gradations of the will and the understanding. Judgments, reflection, desires, passions, are only sensations variously transformed. This is why it seemed to us useless to suppose the soul to have received immediately from nature all the sensations with which it is endowed. Nature has given us organs which show us by pleasure or pain what we ought to seek or to avoid; but here she stops, and leaves to experience the task of leading us to contract habits, and finish the work she has commenced.

"This object is new, and shows all the simplicity of the ways of the Author of nature. Is it not a thing worthy of our admiration thus to see, from man's sensibility to pleasure or pain, spring up in him ideas, desires, habits, and talents of various kinds?"—*Traite des Sensations. Dessein de l'ouvrage.*

What we admire in Condillac is not his system, but his candor; and we wonder yet more that, for a time, he should have had numerous followers of his so poor and superficial system. The author proposes the difficulty, that as there is in our soul nothing but transformed sensations, it is strange that brutes, which also have sensations, should not be endowed with the same faculties as man. Can the reader imagine what profound reason the French philosopher assigned? We doubt it very much. It is a curious thought: "the organ of *touch* is *less perfect* in brutes, and consequently it cannot be to them an occasional cause of all the operations which we observe in ourselves." He did well to adopt the motto: *nec tamen quasi Pythius Apollo!*

ON CHAPTER VI.

(6) The works of the scholastics are worth reading on these points. Treating of *the object of science*, they are at once exact and profound. It is not easy to think of any thing concerning the classification of truths not explained or indicated by them.

ON CHAPTER VII.

(7) Let us not be thought to judge too severely of the forms adopted by the German philosophers. It is well known how Madame de Staël speaks of them; but happily we can cite in our favor a more competent judge. Schelling, one of the chiefs of German philosophy, says: "The Germans have so long philosophized among themselves, as to gradually depart more and more, in their thoughts and their words, from what is universally intelligible; and the degree of departure therefrom has almost come at last to be the measure of philosophical ability. Examples are not wanting to us. As families which separate from general society, and live wholly among themselves, among other repulsive singularities, come to use expressions intelligible only to themselves, so is it with the Germans in philosophy; and after vain efforts to spread the Kantian philosophy out of Germany, they renounced the attempt

to make themselves intelligible to other nations; they became accustomed to regard themselves as the chosen people of philosophy, forgetting that the primary end of philosophy,—an end often neglected, but not the less to be sought for on that account,—is to gain universal consent, by making themselves universally intelligible. This is not to say that we must judge works of thought like exercises in style; but all philosophy not intelligible to all civilized nations, and accessible in every language, cannot, for this reason alone, be the universal and true philosophy." —*Schelling's Judgment of V. Cousin, and the state of French and German Philosophy in general.* 1834. p. 4.

Schelling flatters himself that German philosophy is about to take a better course with respect to clearness, and adds: "The philosophical writer who, for tens of years past, was unable to depart from the terms and forms of the school, without loss of his scientific reputation, may hereafter emancipate himself from this restraint. He will seek depth of thought; and an absolute incapacity to express himself with clearness, will no longer be regarded as the mark of talent and philosophical inspiration." We have nothing to add to this passage; we would only remind its author that: *mutato nomine, de te fabula narratur.*

ON CHAPTER VIII.

(8) The perusal of Schelling's work on Ideal Transcendentalism leaves no doubt as to his view of this identity, which at bottom neither is nor can be any thing else than pantheism; yet, for the sake of truth, we will allow that Schelling seems to have modified his doctrine, or to have feared its consequences, if we are to consider the indications found in his discourse at the opening of his course of philosophy, at Berlin, the 13th of November, 1841. We there find the following passage, worthy of the attention of all thinking men: "The difficulties and obstacles of all kinds, against which philosophy contends are visible, and in vain would we attempt to dissemble them. Never was there a more powerful reaction against philosophy on the part of real and active life than at this present epoch; and this proves philosophy to have penetrated even to the vital questions of society, those concerning which no one can rest indifferent. So long as a philosophy is only in the first stages of formation, taking the first steps in its march, no one cares for it, except philosophers themselves; other men await the last word of philosophy, since it is important to the general public only in its results.

"We confess that we ought not to take as the practical result of a solid and profoundly meditated philosophy whatever it may please any body to designate as such: were it so, the world would be subjected to doctrines the most repugnant to sound morality, even such as sap its foundation. No! No one judges of philosophy by the practical conclusions drawn by ignorance or presumption. Moreover, lest deception on this point be possible, the public should reject a philosophy which has such results, without examining or even judging it in its principles; it should say that it cannot understand the depth of these questions, or the artificial and intricate march of the arguments; but without pausing here it should promptly decide that a philosophy leading to such conclusions cannot be true in its principles. What the Roman moralist said of the useful: *nihil utile nisi quod honestum*, is equally applicable to the investigation of truth: *no philosophy that respects itself will allow that it leads to irreligion.* Yet actual philosophy is in such a state, that, however much it promises a religious result, no one admits it; for deductions drawn from it convert the dogmas of the Christian religion into a vain phantasmagory.

"As to this, some of its most faithful disciples are openly agreed; be the suspicion well founded or not, its existence suffices, and this opinion is established.

"But active life in the last result is always right; and so philosophy is exposed to great risks. They who war on one philosophy are not far from condemning all philosophy; they say in their heart, there is no longer philosophy in the world. I myself am not exempt from these condemnations, since *it is pretended that it is I, who first gave impulse to this philosophy which is at present so badly judged of, because of its religious results.*

"How shall I defend myself? Certainly I would never attack a philosophy for its last results; but I would judge it in its first principles, as every philosophical mind should. It is moreover well enough known that I have shown myself little satisfied with the philosophy of which I speak.

"The moral and spiritual worlds are so divided that any point of union for an instant should be a motive of satisfaction. Besides to destroy, is a very sad thing when there is nothing wherewith to replace the thing destroyed. 'Do it better yourself,' we say to one who can do nothing but criticize.

"I therefore consecrate myself entirely to the mission with which I am charged; for you I will live; for you I will labor without ceasing while there remains in me the breath of life, and while He permits me, without whose permission not a hair can fall from our head, and yet less a deeply felt word proceed from our mouth. He, without whose inspiration not one lucid idea can shine on our mind, nor one thought of truth and liberty illumine our soul."

This passage shows the embarrassment of the German philosopher's position, and the irreligious consequences attached to his doctrines. It is consoling to see him pay some homage to truth; but it is afflicting to see him still pretend to save its inconsequence.

ON CHAPTER IX.

(9) In these latter days there have not been wanting some to count the illustrious Malebranche among the partisans of pantheism. We cannot conceive how M. Cousin could say; "Malebranche est avec Spinoza le plus grand disciple de Descartes. Comme lui il a tiré des principes de leur commun maître les conséquences que ces principes renfermaient. Malebranche est à la lettre Spinoza chrétien." (*Fragments Philosophiques.* T. 2me. p. 167. Ed. 3ieme.) We repeat that we cannot conceive how any one, who had read ever so little of the great metaphysician's works, should assert such a paradox. The slightest glance at his writings suffices to show in them the most lofty spiritualism united with profound respect for the dogmas of our most holy religion. When we treat of the various philosophical systems of the origin of ideas and the problem of the universe, we shall have other occasions to vindicate the wise and pious author of the *Investigation de la Verité*. Yet we were unwilling to pass by the present occasion without doing him the justice to defend him from imputations, which he would, were he living, repel as intolerable calumnies. Who would have thought when he wrote those works, on every page of which we find, God, the mind, the Christian religion, eternal truth, and original sin, with frequent texts from the sacred Scriptures and St. Augustine, that he would ever be ranked with Spinoza, with the absurd epithet of *Christian Spinoza*? Such is at times the sad lot of great men, thus to be held as chiefs of sects they abhorred. Malebranche styled Spinoza, *l'impie de nos jours*, and M. Cousin dares call Malebranche the *Christian* Spinoza.

ON CHAPTER X.

(10) We are not ignorant of the difficulties to which Leibnitz's systems are subject; but it is necessary to show that in this great man's mind the erroneous doctrines of modern Germans had no place. "Et c'est ainsi," he says, in his Monadologie (No. 38), "que la dernière raison des choses doit être dans une substance necessaire, dans laquelle le détail des changmens ne soit qu'eminemment, comme dans la source, et c'est ce que nous appelons Dieu. Or cette substance étant une raison suffisante de tout ce détail, lequel est aussi lié partout, il n'y a qu'un Dieu, et ce Dieu suffit.

"On peut juger aussi que cette substance suprême qui est unique, universelle, et necessaire, n'ayant rien hors d'elle qui en soit indépendant, et étant une suite simple de l'être possible, doit être incapable de limites et contenir tout autant de realité qu'il est possible.

"D'où il s'ensuit, que Dieu est absolument parfait, la perfection n'étant autre chose, que la grandeur de la réalité positive prise précisément en mettant à part les limites ou bornes dans les choses qui en ont. Et là, où il n'y a point de bornes, c'est-à-dire, en Dieu, la perfection est absolument infinie.

"Il s'ensuit aussi que les créatures ont leur perfections de l'influence de Dieu, mais qu'elles ont leurs imperfections de leur nature propre, incapable d'être sans bornes. Car c'est en cela qu'elles sont distinguées de Dieu.

"Il est vrai aussi, qu'en Dieu est non seulement la source des existences, mais encore celle des essences, en tant que réelles, ou de ce qu'il y a de réel dans la possibilité."

In his dissertation on the Platonic philosophy he combats the pantheistic tendencies of Valentine Weigel, in these words: "Valentinum Weigelium, qui non tantum vitam beatam peculiari libero per Deificationem explicat, sed et passim mortem et quietem hujusmodi commendat, vellem cum aliis Quietistis suspicionem similis sententiæ non dedisse. * * * Spinoza aliter eodem tendebat; ei una substantia est, Deus; creaturæ ejus modificationes, et figuræ in cera continue per motum nascentes et pereuntes. Ita ipsi, perinde ut Almerico, anima non superest, nisi per suum *esse* ideale in Deo ut ibi ab æterno fuit.

"Sed nihil in Platone animadverto, unde colligam, animos propriam sibi substantiam non servare; quod etiam sane philosophanti extra controversiam est, neque intelligi contraria potest sententia, nisi Deum et animam corporea fingas, neque enim aliter ex Deo animas, tanquam particulas divellas; sed talis de Deo atque anima notio, aliunde absurda est." (Leibnitz. Epist. ad Hanschium de Philos. Platon.)

So far was Leibnitz from deeming the tendency to pantheism an elevated philosophy, that, as we have just seen, he considered it the result of a rude imagination. It is very remarkable that under an historical as under a metaphysical aspect Leibnitz agrees with St. Thomas; both express the same ideas in very similar words. The holy doctor asks if the soul is made from the substance of God, and there takes occasion to examine the origin of the error, and says: "Respondeo dicendum, quod dicere animam esse de substantia Dei, manifestam improbabilitatem continet. Ut enim ex dictis patet, anima humana est quandoque intelligens in potentia, et scientiam quodammodo a rebus acquirit, et habet diversas potentias; quæ omnia aliena sunt a Dei natura, qui est actus purus, et nihil ab alio accipiens, et nullam in se diversitatem habens, ut supra probatum est.

"Sed hic error principium habuisse videtur ex duabus positionibus antiquorum. Primi enim, qui naturas rerum considerare inceperunt, imaginationem transcendere non valentes, nihil præter corpora esse posuerunt. Et ideo Deum dicebant esse quoddam corpus, quod aliorum corporum judicabant esse principium. Et quia animam ponebant esse de natura illius corporis, quod dicebant esse principium, ut dicitur in primo de anima, per consequens sequebatur quod anima esset de substantia Dei. Juxta quam positionem etiam Manichæi, Deum esse quamdam lucem corpoream existimantes, quandam partem illius lucis animam esse posuerunt corpori alligatam. Secundo vero processum fuit ad hoc quod aliqui aliquid incorporeum esse apprehenderunt; non tamen a corpore separatum, sed corporis formam. Unde et Varro dixit quod Deus est anima, mundum intuitu, vel motu et ratione gubernans: ut Augu. narrat 7 de Civit. Dei. Sic igitur illius totalis animæ partem, aliqui posuerunt animam hominis: sicut homo est pars totius mundi; non valentes intellectu pertingere ad distinguendos spiritualium substantiarum gradus, nisi secundum distinctiones corporum. Hæc autem sunt omnia impossibilia, ut supra probatum est, unde manifeste falsum est animam esse de substantia Dei." (P. 1a, Q. 90a, A. 1o.)

ON CHAPTER XI.

(11) We often find the intellect identified by the scholastics with the thing known, even when they treat of created intellects; but this identity is limited to the purely ideal order, and denotes only the intimate union of the idea and the intellect. It is well known what importance they attached to matters and forms; and this distinction is also applied to the phenomena of intelligence. Although the idea was considered as a thing distinct from the intellect, yet, as the intellect is perfected by it, and placed in relation with the thing represented, they said that the intellect was the same as the thing known. We must thus explain passages in St. Thomas and other scholastics, since, although their expressions, if considered in isolation, would be inexact, they are not so, if regard be had to the meaning which they attributed to them, and which clearly follows from their fundamental principles. Thus St. Thomas (Quodlibet. 7 A. 2), to prove that the created intellect cannot know many things at the same time, says:

"Sed quod intellectus simul intelligat plura intelligibilia, primo et principaliter, est impossibile. Cujus ratio est quia *intellectus secundum actum est omnino, id est, perfecte res intellecta*: ut dicitur in 3 de anima. *Quod quidem intelligendum est non quod essentia intellectus fiat res intellecta* vel species ejus; sed quia complete informatur per speciem rei intellectæ, dum eam actu intelligit. Unde intellectum simul plura intelligere primo, idem est ac si res una simul esset plura. In rebus enim materiabilus videmus quod una res numero non potest esse simul plura in actu, sed plura in potentia.

"Unde patet quod sicut una res materialis non potest esse simul plura actu, ita unus intellectus non potest simul plura intelligere primo. Et hoc est quod Alga, dicit, quod sicut unum corpus non potest simul figurari pluribus figuris; ita unus intellectus non potest simul plura intelligere. Nec potest dici quod intellectus informatur perfecte simul pluribus speciebus intelligibilibus, sicut unum corpus simul informatur figura et colore; quia figura et color non sunt formæ unius generis, nec in eodem ordine accipiuntur quia non ordinantur ad perficiendum in esse unius rationis; sed omnes formæ intelligibiles in quantum hujusmodi, sunt unius generis, et in eodem ordine se habent ad intellectum, in quantum perficiunt intellectum in hoc quod est esse intellectum in actu. Unde plures species intelligibiles se habent sicut figuræ plures, vel plures colores, qui simul in actu in eodem esse non possunt secundum idem."

By the first passage, we see that the meaning of identity of the intellect with the thing known, is the same as explained in the beginning of this note; to wit, the intimate union of the idea of intelligible species with the intellect, as the form with its matter,—a form which perfects the intellect, makes it pass from potentiality to actuality, and places it in relation with the thing represented.

ON CHAPTER XII.

(12) The doctrine of immediate intelligibility is susceptible of still further illustration; but as this cannot be clearly done without examining at length the nature of ideas, which does not pertain to our present treatise, we shall reserve it for its proper place.

ON CHAPTER XIII.

(13) Enough, perhaps, was not said in the text to enable all readers to form clear and complete ideas of the representation of causality; but this doctrine, as regards the first intelligence, is closely allied to the questions on the foundation of the possibility even of non-existent things,—questions which we cannot here investigate without reversing the order of subjects.

ON CHAPTER XIV.

(14) The distinction of geometrical and non-geometrical orders of ideas is of the utmost importance in ideology. We have given this distinction in order that the examination of a truth fundamental among purely ideal truths might not remain incomplete. But its explanation and foundation will be given in our treatise on the of space and extension.

ON CHAPTER XV.

(15) The word *instinct*, when applied to the intellect, is clearly taken in a different sense than it is when applied to irrational animals. It has here no ignoble meaning; and this is in accordance with the use made of it when

divine things are spoken of. One meaning given it by the dictionary is, *"impulse, or movement of the Holy Ghost, in speaking of supernatural inspirations."* The Latin, *instinctus*, means *inspiration*. Thus: "Sacro mens *instincta* furore."

ON CHAPTER XVI.

(16) The confusion of ideas upon this point originates in that tendency to unity of which we spoke in our Fourth Chapter. We first suppose there must be one only principle, and we ask what it is; whereas, before inquiring what it is, we should ascertain if there be one only, as is supposed. We have already seen that Fichte's system rested on the same supposition. Thus the cause of innocent disputes in the schools may lead to more transcendental errors.

ON CHAPTER XVII.

(17) We have, we think, faithfully interpreted the thought of Descartes, but lest there should be some doubt as to this, we subjoin a notable passage from his answer to the objections collected by *Père Mersenne* from various philosophers and theologians, against the Second, Third, Fourth, Fifth, and Sixth Meditations.

"When we know that we are something that thinks, this first notion *is taken from no syllogisms*; and when any one says: *I think, therefore I am*, or exist, *he does not infer* his existence from thought, as *by the force of a syllogism*, but as a thing known by itself; *he sees it by a simple inspection of the mind*; for if he deduced it from a syllogism, he would have to know beforehand this major; whatever thinks, is, or exists. On the contrary, this proposition is manifested to him by his own sentiment that he cannot think without existing. It is a property characteristic of our mind to form general propositions from the knowledge of particular propositions." Descartes does not always explain himself with this clearness; the objections of his adversaries made him examine his doctrine more thoroughly, and this contributed to clear up his ideas.

ON CHAPTER XVIII.

(18) To form an accurate estimate of Descartes' views, let us listen to his own explanation of his system.

"As the senses sometimes deceive us, I wished to *suppose* that nothing of what they make us imagine appeared; as there are men who are deceived, and make paralogisms even when reasoning upon the simplest matters of geometry, I judged myself as liable to err as they are, and I rejected as false all those reasons I had before held to be demonstrations; and also considering that even the thoughts which we have while awake may come to us while asleep, although no one of them may be true, I resolved to *feign* that all things which had entered my mind contained no more truth than illusory dreams. But I immediately observed that, while I wished to think that every thing was false, it was necessary for me, who thought this, to be something; and, noting that this truth: I think, therefore I am, was so firm and secure, that the most extravagant suppositions could not shake it, I judged that I might, without scruple, receive it as the first truth of philosophy." —*Discours sur la Méthode. P.* 4ieme.

We said that the doubt of Descartes was a *supposition,* a *fiction,* and these are the very terms he himself uses. In his reply to the objections of *Père Mersenne,* we find the following confirmatory extract: "I have read with great satisfaction your observations upon my treatise on philosophy, for they show your good-will towards me, your piety towards God, and your zeal for the advance of his glory. I cannot but rejoice that you have judged my arguments worthy of your criticism, but also that you say nothing not easily answerable.

"In the first place, you remind me that I have rejected the ideas of phantasms of bodies, *not truly, but only by a mere fiction,* in order to conclude that I am something that thinks, fearing, perhaps, that I should believe it followed from this that I am only something that thinks; but I have already shown, in my Second Meditation, that I agreed with this, and I said: 'But these things, which I *suppose* not to be, because I do not know them, may not really be any thing different from me who know them; of this I can say nothing, I have at present nothing to do with it.'" * * * * * * *

We here see that Descartes did not deny his doubt to be a mere fiction; he even says that he does nothing but apply a method, the necessity of which all philosophers admit.

"I pray you," he continues, "to remember that with respect to matters of the will, I have always made a broad distinction between the contemplation of truth and the uses of life; as regards the latter, I am so far from thinking that we must follow only things very clearly known, that I believe we must not always consider even what is most probable, but that we must, among things wholly unknown or uncertain, sometimes choose one, and hold firmly to it, so long as we see no reason for not doing so, just as if we had chosen it from evident and certain motives, as I have already explained in the *Discours sur la Méthode;* but when we treat only of the contemplation of truth, *who ever doubted that it was necessary to suspend the judgment upon things that are obscure or not distinctly known?"*

In what, then, consists Descartes' merit? In having *applied* a rule known to all, and employed by few, and in so doing at the very time that prejudices in favor of the Aristotelian doctrine were the strongest. Descartes plainly says so; his method of doubting is not new, only the application of it was wanting; for, as regards its fundamental principle, "who ever doubted that it was necessary to suspend the judgment upon things that are obscure or not distinctly known?"

Understanding Descartes' method in this sense, that is, taking the doubt as a supposition, a mere fiction, it is not opposed to sound religious and moral principles. The profound philosopher does not seem to disdain to set his readers at rest upon this point; he ingenuously shows, in commencing his investigations, that his religious belief was safe. "Finally, as before undertaking to rebuild the house wherein one lives, it is not enough to demolish the old one, and provide materials and workmen, or to exercise one's self in architecture, and to carefully trace the design of the new house; but it is also necessary to have another house in which to live, while the new one is building; so that my actions might not be unresolved, like my judgments, and that I might, in the meantime, live as happily as possible, I made a provision for myself; it consists of three or four maxims. The first is, to observe the laws and customs of my country, *and constantly to preserve the religion in which, by the grace of God, I have been instructed from my infancy.* * * * * * * After having assured myself of these maxims, and laid them aside with *the truths of faith which have always been first in my belief,* I judged that I might freely reject the rest of my opinions." —*Discours sur la Méthode*, P. 3ieme.

ON CHAPTER XIX.

(19) With respect to the distinction between the testimony of consciousness and that of evidence, as in the analysis of the proposition: I think, therefore I am; there can be no doubt that Descartes did not express himself with sufficient precision and exactness. See, for example, this extract: "After this, I considered in general what is necessary for a proposition to be true and certain; for, although I had not yet met such a one, I nevertheless thought I ought to know in what this certainty consisted; and observing that in the proposition, I think, therefore I am, there is nothing to assure me of its truth, except the clear perception that in order to think I must be, I judged that I could take it to be a general rule that things clearly and distinctly conceived are all true; only there is some difficulty in ascertaining what things we do distinctly conceive." —*Discours sur la Méthode.* Partie 4me.

ON CHAPTER XX.

(20) The *apodictical* certainty of which Kant speaks in the passage cited, is the result of the intrinsic evidence of ideas, or, in other words, it is what the schoolmen called metaphysical certainty.

ON CHAPTER XXI.

(21) Besides the questions on the principle of contradiction as the only foundation of certainty, there are others as to its scientific utility and importance. We shall, when we come to treat of the idea of *being* in general, examine these points at length; wherefore we will now pass them by.

ON CHAPTER XXII.

(22) We see by a passage from the fourth part of the *Discourse on Method*, by Descartes, cited in note xv., that besides the principle, I think, therefore I am, he admitted the principle of the legitimacy of evidence; for, asking what is necessary in order that a proposition may be true and certain, he says, that having remarked that if he was certain of the truth of this proposition (I think, therefore I am), he was so only because he saw it to be so; he believed that he could take it to be a general rule *that things known clearly and distinctly are all true.* This shows two principles, closely connected, although very unlike, to enter into Descartes' system. The first is the fact of consciousness of thought; the second is the general rule of the legitimacy of the criterion of evidence.

It is also to be remarked that there is here some confusion of ideas, which we have already pointed out. It is not exact to say that the principle, I think, therefore I am, is evident: the evidence relates to the *consequence*; but there is, properly speaking, no evidence of the act of thought, excepting consciousness. Evidence is a criterion, but not the only one.

ON CHAPTER XXIII.

(23) What we have said of the second proposition of this chapter is independent of the mode in which the soul and body exercise their mutual influence. These questions belong elsewhere. This influence is, in every system, a fact attested by experience; and this is all that is needed for what we propose to establish here.

ON CHAPTER XXIV.

(24) For the better understanding of what we have said in this chapter on evidence, it will be well to consider what will be advanced in chapters XXVI. to XXXI., inclusive.

ON CHAPTER XXV.

(25) What has been said in this chapter shows the truth of what we said in the twenty-fourth chapter, upon the connection of the different criteria, and the necessity of not confining one's self to an exclusive philosophy.

Consciousness serves as the basis of the other criteria, as an indispensable fact; but if we deny the others, we also deny consciousness.

ON CHAPTERS XXVI., XXVII., AND XXVIII.

(26) Dugald Stewart in his *Elements of the Philosophy of the Human Mind*, (P. II., C. II., Section 3, §2,) cites a passage from a dissertation printed at Berlin in 1764, which does not appear so unreasonable as he pretends. We subjoin it, because the German philosopher's opinion seems to us the same that we gave in the text.

"Omnes mathematicorum propositiones sunt identicæ et representantur hac formula, A=A. Sunt veritates identicæ, sub varia forma expressæ, imo ipsum quod dicitur contradictionis principium vario modo enuntiatum et involutum; si quidem omnes hujus generis propositiones revera in eo continentur. Secundum nostram autem intelligendi facultatem ea est propositionum differentia, quod quædam longa ratiociniorum serie, alia autem breviore via, ad primum omnium principiorum reducantur, et in illud resolvantur. Sic. v. g. propositio 2 + 2=4 statim huc cedit: 1 + 1 + 1 + 1=1 + 1 + 1 + 1; id est, idem est idem; et, proprie loquendo, hoc modo enuntiari debet,—si contingat adesse vel existere quatuor entia, tum existunt quatuor entia; nam de existentia non agunt geometræ, sed ea hypothetice tantum subintelligitur. Inde summa oritur certitudo ratiocinia perspicienti; observat nempe idearum identitatem; et hæc est evidentia assensum immediate cogens, quam mathematicam aut geometricam vocamus. Mathesi tamen sua natura priva non est et propria; oritur etenim ex identitatis perceptione, quæ locum habere potest, etiamsi ideæ non repræsentent extensum."

ON CHAPTERS XXX AND XXXI.

(27) We have shown that Dugald Stewart had perhaps in view Vico's doctrine; but without wishing to bring against him the charge he brought against his master, Reid, that of resuscitating the doctrines of the Jesuit Buffier, we would, in order that the reader may judge with full knowledge of the cause, subjoin a remarkable extract from the Scotch philosopher, which will show coincidence between some of his doctrines and those of the Neapolitan. Had Stewart read Vico, we are inclined to believe that he would not have complained of the *confusion* with which various ancient and modern authors have explained this doctrine.

"The peculiarity of that species of evidence which is called demonstrative, and which so remarkably distinguishes our mathematical conclusions from those to which we are led in other branches of science, is a fact which must have arrested the attention of every person who possesses the slightest acquaintance with the elements of geometry. And yet, I am doubtful if a satisfactory account has hitherto been given of the circumstance in which it arises. Mr. Locke tells us, that 'what constitutes a demonstration is intuitive evidence of every step;' and I readily grant, that if in a single step such evidence should fail, the other parts of the demonstration would be of no value. It does not, however, seem to me that it is on this consideration that the demonstrative evidence of the conclusion depends, not even when we add to it another which is much insisted on by Dr. Reid,—that 'in demonstrative evidence our first principles must be intuitively certain.' The inaccuracy of this remark I formerly pointed out when treating of the evidence of axioms; on which occasion I also observed, that the first principles of our reasonings in mathematics are not axioms, but definitions. It is in this last circumstance (I mean the peculiarity of reasoning from definitions) that the true theory of mathematical demonstration is to be found; and I shall accordingly endeavor to explain it at considerable length, and to state some of the more important consequences to which it leads.

"That I may not, however, have the appearance of claiming, in behalf of the following discussion, an undue share of originality, it is necessary for me to remark that the leading idea which it contains has been repeatedly started, and even to a certain length prosecuted, by different writers, ancient as well as modern; but that, in all of them, it has been so blended with collateral considerations, although foreign to the point in question, as to divert the attention both of writer and reader, from that single principle on which the solution of the problem hinges. * * * * * * *

"It was already remarked, in the first chapter of this part, that whereas, in all other sciences, the propositions which we attempt to establish, express facts real or supposed,—in mathematics, the propositions which we demonstrate only assert a connection between certain suppositions and certain consequences. Our reasonings, therefore, in mathematics, are directed to an object essentially different from what we have in view, in any other employment of our intellectual faculties;—not to ascertain truths with respect to actual existences, but to trace the logical filiation of consequences which follow from an assumed hypothesis. If, from this hypothesis, we reason with correctness, nothing, it is manifest, can be wanting to complete the evidence of the result; as this result only asserts a necessary connection between the supposition and the conclusion. In the other sciences, admitting that every ambiguity of language were removed, and that every step of our deductions were rigorously accurate, our conclusions would still be attended with more or less of uncertainty, being ultimately founded on principles which may, or may not, correspond exactly with the fact." (*Elements of the Philosophy of the Human Mind*. P. II., C. II., S. 3, § 1.)

This is exactly Vico's doctrine of the cause of the difference in the degrees of evidence and certainty; although he makes a general system, in order to explain the problem of intelligence, what the Scotchman only assigns as a fact to show the reason of mathematical evidence. Père Buffier (Trait. des prem. Vérités, P. I., C. II.) explains the same thing with great clearness.

We have said that, considering the indefatigable laboriousness which distinguishes the Germans, it would not be strange if they had read the scholastics. In confirmation of this, we notice that Leibnitz urgently recommends the reading of them, and the more modern Germans are not likely to forget the advice of so able an author.

Among various passages of Leibnitz, we select the following extract, because it seems to us rather curious: "Truth is more spread than one would believe; but it is often colored, also often covered over, and even weakened, mutilated, and corrupted by additions which spoil it, or render it less useful. By observing the traces of truth in the ancients, or, to speak more generally, in all who have preceded us, we dig gold from dirt, and draw the diamond from its mine, light from darkness, and this would really be *perennis quædam Philosophia*.

"It may even be said that some progress would be observable in knowledge. The Orientals have great and beautiful ideas of the Divinity; the Greeks added reasoning and a form of science; the Fathers of the Church rejected whatever was bad in Greek philosophy; but the scholastics labored to usefully employ whatever was acceptable in Pagan philosophy. I have frequently said: *aurum latere in stercore illo scholastico barbariei*, and I wish we could find some one versed in the Irish and Spanish philosophy, to cull from it what is good; I am sure he would find his labor repaid by many and beautiful truths. There was once a Swiss who *mathematized* scholastically; his works are but little known; although, from what I have seen of them, I should judge them to be profound and worthy of consideration." (Lettre 3ieme à M. Remond de Montmort.)

Thus speaks Leibnitz, one of the most eminent men of modern times, and of whom Fontenelle said: "He led the van in all the sciences." See, then, if he was wrong in recommending the study of those authors to all desirous of acquiring a profound knowledge of philosophy. This study, setting aside its intrinsic utility, is of great advantage in judging, with knowledge of the cause, a school, which, whatever its worth, occupies a page in the history of the human mind.

ON CHAPTER XXXII.

(28)The author to whom I allude (317) is Fenelon, who, under the name of common sense, includes also the criterion of evidence, as may be seen by this extract: "What is common sense? Does it not consist in the first notions which all men have of the same things? This common sense, which always and everywhere is the same, which precedes all examination, and even holds it in ridicule on certain questions, in which one laughs instead of examining; which renders man unable to doubt, no matter how great his efforts may be; this sense which belongs to all men, which only waits to be consulted in order to discover itself and show us the *evidence* or the absurdity of the question, *is not this what I call my ideas?* Here, then, are these general ideas or notions which I cannot contradict or examine, but according to which I examine and judge every thing, so that, instead of replying, I laugh when any thing is proposed clearly in opposition to what these *immutable ideas* represent." — *Existence de Dieu*, P. II., v. 33.

There is no doubt that Fenelon speaks of evidence in this extract, since, besides using this very term, he refers to immutable ideas; by common sense he understands the general ideas by which we judge of all things, or in other words, the ideas from which evidence proceeds.

NOTE TO BOOK SECOND

ON CHAPTER II.

(29) The immateriality of the souls of brutes is not a discovery of modern philosophy, the scholastics maintained it, and carried their ideas on this subject so far as to assert that no vital principle can be a body. In this sense they taught that even the principle of life, or the soul of plants, was something superior to the body. St. Thomas (P. I., Q. LXXV., A. I.) asks, in general, if the soul is a body: "Utrum anima sit corpus," and answers as follows:

"Respondeo dicendum, quod ad inquirendum de natura animæ, oportet præsupponere, *quod anima dicitur esse primum principium vitæ,* in iis quæ apud nos vivunt. Animata enim viventia dicimus, res vero inanimatas vita carentes; vita autem maxime manifestatur duplici opere, scilicet cognitionis, et motus. Horum autem principium antiqui philosophi imaginationem transcendere non valentes, aliquod corpus ponebant, sola corpora res esse dicentes, et quod non est corpus, nihil esse, et secundum hoc, animam aliquod corpus esse dicebant. Hujus autem opinionis falsitas, licet multipliciter ostendi possit, tamen uno utemur, quo etiam communius et certius patet animam corpus non esse. Manifestum est enim, quod non quodcumque vitalis operationis principium est anima; sic enim oculus esset anima, cum sit quoddam principium visionis, et idem esset dicendum de aliis animæ instrumentis: sed primum principium vitæ dicimus esse animam. Quamvis autem aliquod corpus possit esse quoddam principium vitæ, sicut cor est principium vitæ in animali; tamen non potest esse primum principium vitæ aliquod corpus. Manifestum est enim, quod esse principium vitæ, vel vivens, non convenit corpori ex hoc quod est corpus, alioquin omne corpus esset vivens, aut principium vitæ, convenit igitur alicui corpori quod sit vivens, vel etiam principium vitæ, per hoc quod est tale corpus. Quod autem est actu tale, habet hoc ab aliquo principio, quod dicitur actus ejus. *Anima igitur quæ est primum principium vitæ, non est corpus, sed corporis actus,* sicut calor qui est principium calefactionis, non est corpus, sed quidam corporis actus."

Notwithstanding this doctrine, it might still be doubted whether matter does not enter as a component element in the soul, although the soul itself is not corporeal, and, therefore, the holy doctor (Ib., A. 5) asks if the soul is composed of matter and form; and here he is speaking of the soul in general as the principle of life, and not of the intellectual soul alone. He answers in the negative, as follows:

"Respondeo dicendum, quod *anima non habet materiam*, et hoc potest considerari dupliciter. *Primo quidem, ex ratione animæ in communi*, est enim de ratione animæ, quod sit forma alicujus corporis. Aut igitur est forma secundum se totam, aut secundum aliquam partem sui. Si secundum se totam, impossibile est quod pars ejus sit materia, si dicatur materia aliquid ejus in potentia tantum, quia forma, in quantum forma, est actus. Id autem quod est in potentia tantum, non potest esse pars actus, cum potentia repugnet actui, utpote contra actum divisa. Si autem sit forma secundum aliquam partem sui, illam partem dicemus esse animam, et illam materiam cujus primo est actus, dicemus esse primum animatum. Secundo specialiter ex ratione humanæ animæ, in quantum est intellectiva."

Although these passages are clear enough, there is another where it is expressly asserted that the souls of perfect animals are absolutely indivisible, so that division can be predicated of them neither *per se* nor *per accidens*. He asks, (Q. LXXVI., art. 8,) if the soul in general is in any part of the body; and he answers, yes: distinguishing between essential and quantitative totality:

"Sed forma, quæ requirit diversitatem in partibus, sicut est anima, *et præcipue animalium perfectorum*, non equaliter se habet ad totum et ad partes; unde *non dividitur per accidens, scilicet per divisionem quantitatis*. Sic ergo totalitas quantitativa, non potest attribui animæ, nec per se, nec per accidens. Sed totalitas secunda, quæ attenditur secundum rationis et essentiæ perfectionem, proprie et per se, convenit formis."

It seems, however, that this doctrine of St. Thomas met with opposition, from some persons who could not conceive how the soul of brutes could be inextensive, as they regarded this as the exclusive property of the intellectual soul. Cardinal Gaetano, in his comments on St. Thomas, undertakes his defence. He shows that he understood the doctrine of St. Thomas concerning the indivisibility of the souls of brutes, in its strictest sense. He gives the objection in the following words:

"Dubium secundo est circa candem totalitatem quoniam S. Thomas a communi opinione discordare videtur hoc in loco, eo quod ponat *præter animam intellectivam*, aliquam aliam formam in materia *inextensam, scilicet animam sensitivam animalium perfectorum*, cum tamen vix possit sustineri, quod anima intellectiva de foris veniens, informet secundum esse, et sit inextensa."

Instead of more or less plausible interpretations of the text in order to solve the objection, the learned commentator boldly maintains the indivisibility of the souls of brutes, and treats almost with contempt those who think differently:

"Ad secundum dubium dicitur, quod doctrina hic tradita, *est quidem contra modernorum communem phantasiam, sed non contra philosophicas rationes, parum est autem de horum aucthoritate curandum.* Cum autem dicitur, quod sine ratione hoc est dictum, respondetur quod ratio insinuata est a posteriori, quia scilicet diversam totaliter habet habitudinem ad totum et partem ipsa forma ex propria ratione. Si enim habet totaliter diversam habitudinem ad totum et ad partes, *hoc provenit ex indivisibilitate formæ.* Quia si divideretur forma ad divisionem totius, jam pars formæ proportionaretur parti corporis, et cum pars quantitativa formæ sit tota essentia formæ, ergo ipsa forma secundum rationem suæ essentiæ non habet totaliter diversam habitudinem ad totum et ad partes: sed utrumque, scilicet tam totum quam partem respicit, ut proportionatum perfectible. Et confirmari potest ista ratio, quia forma extensa ex vi solius divisionis, non desinit esse secundum illam partem quam habet in parte decisa: imo quæ quodammodo erat per modum potentiæ, perficitur, et fit actu seorsum, ut patet in formis naturalibus, ergo a destructione consequentis, si ex sola divisione pars decisa non potest retinere eandem speciem, *ergo non erat extensa et divisibilis ad divisionem subjecti.* **

* * * * * * * *

Non est ergo sine ratione dictum, quod animæ aliquæ præter intellectivam sunt tantæ perfectionis quod sunt inextensæ, tam per se quam per accidens: quamquam potentiæ omnes earum sint extensæ per accidens: qualitates enim, sunt corporis partibus accommodatæ."

NOTES TO BOOK THIRD

ON CHAPTER X.

(30) Leibnitz and Clarke had a very interesting dispute on space, from which I shall extract a few passages. Leibnitz wrote a letter to the Princess of Wales, in which he repeated the expression of Newton, that space was the organ which God uses in his sensations of things. Leibnitz argued against this opinion, that if God, in order to perceive things, needs any medium, they do not depend entirely on him, and are not produced by him.

Clarke Answered:

"M. le chevalier Newton ne dit pas que l'espace est l'organe dont Dieu se sert pour apercevoir les choses; il ne dit pas non plus que Dieu ait besoin d'aucun moyen pour les apercevoir. Au contraire, il dit que Dieu, étant présent partout, aperçoit les choses par sa présence immédiate, dans tout l'espace où elles sont, sans l'intervention ou le secours d'aucun organe ou d'aucun moyen. Pour rendre cela plus intelligible, il l'éclaircit par une comparaison. Il dit que comme l'âme, étant immédiatement présente aux images qui se forment dans le cerveau par le moyen des organes des sens, voit ces images comme si elles étaient les choses mêmes qu'elles représentent; de même Dieu voit tout par sa présence immédiate, étant actuellement présent aux choses mêmes, à toutes les choses qui sont dans l'univers, comme l'âme est présente à toutes les images qui se forment dans le cerveau. M. Newton considère le cerveau et les organes des sens comme le moyen par lequel ces images sont formées, et non comme le moyen par lequel l'âme voit ou aperçoit ces images lorsqu'elles sont ainsi formées. Et dans l'univers il ne considère pas les choses comme si elles étaient des images formées par un certain moyen ou par des organes, mais comme des choses réelles que Dieu lui-même a formées et qu'il voit dans tous les lieux où elles sont sans l'intervention d'aucun moyen. C'est tout ce que M. Newton a voulu dire par la comparaison dont il s'est servi lorsqu'il suppose que l'espace infini est, pour ainsi dire, le *sensorium* de l'Etre qui est présent partout."

Leibnitz Replied:

"Il se trouve expressément dans l'appendice de l'*Optique* de M. Newton que l'espace est le *sensorium* de Dieu. Or le mot *sensorium* a toujours signifié l'organe de la sensation. Permis à lui et à ses amis de s'expliquer maintenant tout autrement, je ne m'y oppose pas.

"On suppose que la présence de l'âme suffit pour qu'elle s'aperçoive de se qui se passe dans le cerveau; mais c'est justement ce que le P. Malebranche et toute l'école cartésienne nient et ont raison de nier. Il faut toute autre chose que la seule présence pour qu'une chose représente ce qui se passe dans l'autre. Il faut pour cela quelque communication explicable, quelque manière d'influence. L'espace, selon M. Newton, est intimement présent au corps qu'il contient, et qui est commensuré avec lui; s'ensuit-il pour cela que l'espace s'aperçoive de ce qui se passe dans le corps, et qu'il s'en souvienne après que le corps en sera sorti? Outre que l'âme étant indivisible, sa présence immédiate, qu'on pourrait s'imaginer dans le corps, ne serait que dans un point. Comment donc s'apercevrait-elle de ce qui se fait hors de ce point? Je prétends d'être le premier qui ait montré comment l'âme s'aperçoit de ce qui se passe dans le corps.

"La raison pourquoi Dieu s'aperçoit de tout n'est pas sa simple présence, mais encore son opération; c'est parce qu'il conserve les choses par une action qui produit continuellement ce qu'il y a de bonté et de perfection en elles. Mais les âmes n'ayant point d'influence immédiate sur les corps, ni les corps sur les âmes, leur correspondance mutuelle ne saurait être expliquée par la présence."

Clarke Answered:

"Le mot de *sensorium* ne signifie pas proprement l'organe, mais le lieu de la sensation. L'œil, l'oreille, etc., sont des organes, mais ce ne sont pas des *sensoria*. D'ailleurs M. le chevalier Newton ne dit pas que l'espace est un *sensorium*, mais qu'il est (par voie de comparaison) *pour ainsi dire* le *sensorium*, etc.

"On n'a jamais supposé que la présence de l'âme suffit pour la perception; on a dit seulement que cette présence est nécessaire afin que l'âme aperçoive. Si l'âme n'était pas présente aux images des choses qui sont aperçues, elle ne pourrait pas les apercevoir; mais sa présence ne suffit pas, à moins qu'elle ne soit aussi une substance vivante. Les substances inanimées, quoique présentes, n'aperçoivent rien; et une substance vivante n'est capable de perception que dans le lieu où elle est présente; soit aux choses mêmes, comme Dieu est présent à tout l'univers; soit aux images des choses, comme l'âme leur est présente dans son *sensorium*. Il est impossible qu'une chose agisse ou que quelque sujet agisse sur elle dans un lieu où elle n'est pas présente, comme il est impossible qu'elle soit dans un lieu où elle n'est pas. Quoique l'âme soit indivisible, il ne s'ensuit pas qu'elle n'est présente que dans un seul point. L'espace fini ou infini es absolument indivisible, même par la pensée; car on ne peut s'imaginer que ses parties se séparent l'une de l'autre sans s'imaginer qu'elles sortent, pour ainsi dire, hors d'elle-mêmes; et cependant l'espace n'est pas un simple point.

"Dieu n'aperçoit pas les choses par sa simple présence, ni parce qu'il agit sur elles, mais parce qu'il est non-seulement partout, mais encore un être vivant et intelligent. On doit dire la même chose de l'âme, dans sa petite sphère, ce n'est point par sa simple présence, mais parce qu'elle est une substance vivante, qu'elle aperçoit les images auxquelles elle est présente, et qu'elle ne saurait apercevoir sans leur être présente."

Reply of Leibnitz.

"Ces messieurs soutiennent donc que l'*espace* est un *être réel absolu*; mais cela les mène à de grandes difficultés, car il paraît que cet être doit être éternel et infini. C'est pourquoi il y en a qui out cru que c'était Dieu lui-même, ou bien son attribut, son immensité. Mais comme il a des parties, ce n'est pas une chose qui puisse convenir à Dieu.

"Pour moi, j'ai marqué plus d'une fois que je tenais l'espace pour quelque chose de *purement relatif*, comme le temps, pour un *ordre des coexistences*, comme le temps est un *ordre de succession*. Car l'espace marque, en terms de possibilité, un ordre des choses qui existent en même temps, en tant qu'elles existent ensemble, sans entrer dans leurs manières d'exister. Et lorsqu'on voit plusieurs choses ensemble, on s'aperçoit de cet ordre des choses entre elles.

"Pour réfuter l'imagination de ceux qui prennent l'espace pour une substance, ou du moins pour quelque être absolu, j'ai plusieurs démonstrations; mais je ne veux me servir à présent que de celle dont on me fournit ici l'occasion. Je dis donc que si l'espace était un être absolu, il arriverait quelque chose dont il serait impossible qu'il y eût une raison suffisante, ce qui est contre notre axiome. Voici comment je le prouve. L'espace est quelque chose d'uniforme absolument; et sans les choses y placées, un point de l'espace ne diffère absolument en rien d'un autre point de l'espace. Or il suit de cela (supposé que l'espace soit quelque chose en lui-même outre l'ordre des corps entre eux) qu'il est impossible qu'il y ait une raison pourquoi Dieu, gardant les mêmes situations des corps entre eux, ait placé les corps dans l'espace ainsi et non autrement; et pourquoi tout n'a pas été pris à rebours (par exemple), par un échange de l'orient et de l'occident. Mais si l'espace n'est autre chose que cet ordre ou rapport, et n'est rien du tout sans les corps, que la possibilité, d'en mettre, ces deux états, l'un tel qu'il est, l'autre supposé à rebours, ne différeraient point entre eux. Leur différence ne se trouve donc que dans notre supposition chimérique de la réalité de l'espace en lui-même. Mais dans la vérité, l'un serait justement la même chose que l'autre, comme ils sont absolument indiscernables; et par conséquent il n'y a pas lieu de demander la raison de la préférence de l'un à l'autre.

"Il en est de même du temps. Supposé que quelqu'un demande pourquoi Dieu n'a pas tout créé un an plus tôt, et que ce même personnage veuille inférer de là que Dieu a fait quelque chose dont il n'est pas possible qu'il y ait une raison pourquoi il a fait ainsi plutôt qu'autrement: on lui répondrait que son illation serait vraie, si le temps était quelque chose, hors des choses temporelles; car il serait impossible qu'il y eût des raisons pourquoi les choses eussent été appliquées plutôt à de tels instants qu'à d'autres, leur succession demeurant la même. Mais cela même prouve que les instants hors des choses ne sont rien, et qu'ils ne consistent que dans leur ordre successif; lequel demeurant le même, l'un des deux états, comme celui de l'anticipation imaginée, ne différait en rien, et ne saurait être discerné de l'autre qui est maintenant....

"Il sera difficile de nous faire accroire que, dans l'usage ordinaire, *sensorium* ne signifie pas l'organe de la sensation....

"La simple présence d'une substance même animée ne suffit pas pour la perception; un aveugle et même un distrait ne voit point. Il faut expliquer comment l'âme s'aperçoit de ce qui est hors d'elle.

"Dieu n'est pas présent aux choses par situation, mais par essence; sa présence se manifeste par son opération immédiate. La présence de l'âme est toute d'une autre nature. Dire qu'elle est diffuse par le corps, c'est la rendre étendue et divisible; dire qu'elle est tout entière en chaque partie de quelque corps, c'est la rendre divisible d'elle-même. L'attacher à un point, la répandre par plusieurs points, tout cela ne sont qu'expressions abusives, *Idola Tribus.*"

Clarke's Answer:

"Il est indubitable que rien n'existe sans qu'il y ait une *raison suffisante* de son existence, et que rien n'existe d'une certaine manière plutôt que d'une autre, sans qu'il y ait aussi une *raison suffisante* de cette manière d'exister. Mais à l'égard des choses qui sont indifférentes en elles-mêmes, la *simple volonté* est une raison suffisante pour leur donner l'existence, ou pour les faire exister d'une certaine manière; et cette volonté n'a pas besoin d'être déterminée per une cause étrangère....

"L'espace n'est pas une substance, un être éternel et infini, mais une propriété ou une suite de l'existence d'un être infini et éternel. L'espace infini est l'immensité mais l'immensité n'est pas Dieu;[60] donc l'espace infini n'est pas Dieu. Ce que l'on dit ici de l'espace n'est point une difficulté. L'espace infini est absolument et essentiellement indivisible, et c'est une contradiction dans les termes que de supposer qu'il soit divisé; car il faudrait qu'il y eût un espace entre les parties que l'on suppose divisés; ce qui est supposer que l'espace est divisé et non divisé en même temps.[61] ...

"Il ne s'agit pas de savoir ce que Goclenius[62] entend par le mot de *sensorium*, mais en quel sens M. le chevalier Newton s'est servi de ce mot dans son livre. Si *Goclenius* croit que l'œil, l'oreille, ou quelque autre organe des sens est le *sensorium*, il se trompe. Mais quand un auteur emploie un terme d'art et qu'il déclare en quel sens il s'en sert, à quoi bon rechercher de quelle manière d'autres écrivains ont entendu ce même terme? *Scapula* traduit le mot dont il s'agit ici, *domicilium*, c'est-à-dire le lieu ou l'âme réside."

Reply of Leibnitz:

"Si l'espace infini est l'immensité, l'espace fini sera l'opposé de l'immensité, c'est-à-dire la mensurabilité ou l'étendue bornée. Or l'étendue doit être l'affection d'un étendu. Mais si cet espace est vide, il sera un attribut sans sujet, une étendue d'aucun étendu. C'est pourquoi, en faisant de l'espace une propriété, l'on tombe dans mon sentiment, qui le fait un ordre des choses et non pas quelque chose d'absolu.

"Si l'espace est une réalité absolue, bien loin d'être une propriété ou accidentalité opposée à la substance, il sera plus subsistant que les substances. Dieu ne le saurait détruire, ni même changer en rien. Il est non-seulement immense dans le tout, mais encore immuable et éternel en chaque partie. Il y aura une infinité de choses éternelles hors de Dieu.

"Dire que l'espace infini est sans parties, c'est dire que les espaces finis ne le composent point, et que l'espace infini pourrait subsister quand tous les espaces finis seraient réduits à rien. Ce serait comme si l'on disait, dans la supposition cartésienne, d'un univers étendu sans bornes, que cet univers pourrait subsister quand tous les corps qui le composent seraient réduits à rien ...

"Je serais bien aise de voir le passage d'un philosophe qui prenne *sensorium* autrement que *Goclenius*.

"Si *Scapula* dit que *sensorium* est la place où l'entendement réside, il entendra l'organe de la sensation interne; ainsi il ne s'éloignera point de Goclenius.

"*Sensorium* a toujours été l'organe de la sensation. La glande pinéale serait, selon Descartes, le *sensorium* dans le sens qu'on rapporte de *Scapula*.

"Il n'y a guère d'expression moins convenable sur se sujet que celle qui donne à Dieu un *sensorium*: il semble qu'elle le fait l'âme du monde. Et on aurait bien de la peine à donner à l'usage que M. *Newton* fait de ce mot un sens qui le puisse justifier."

Clarke's Answer:

"On revient encore ici à l'usage du mot de *sensorium*, quoique M. Newton se soit servi d'un correctif lorsqu'il a employé ce mot. Il n'est pas nécessaire de rien ajouter à ce que j'ai dit sur cela ...

"L'espace destitué de corps est une propriété d'une substance immatérielle; l'espace n'est pas borné par les corps, mais il existe également dans les corps et hors des corps. L'espace n'est pas renfermé entre les corps; mais les corps étant dans l'espace immense sont eux-mêmes bornés par leurs propres dimensions.

"L'espace vide n'est pas un attribut sans sujet; car par cet espace nous n'entendons pas un espace où il n'y a rien, mais un espace sans corps. Dieu est certainement présent dans tout l'espace vide, et peut-être qu'il y a aussi dans cet espace plusieurs autres substances qui ne sont pas matérielles, et qui par conséquent ne peuvent être tangibles ni aperçues par aucun de nos sens.

"L'espace n'est pas une substance, mais un attribut; et si c'est un attribut d'un être nécessaire, il doit (comme tous les autres attributs d'un être nécessaire) exister plus nécessairement que les substances mêmes, qui ne sont pas nécessaires. L'espace est immense, immuable et éternel; et l'on doit dire la même chose de la durée. Mais il ne s'ensuit pas de là qu'il n'y ait rien d'éternel hors de Dieu, car l'espace et la durée ne sont pas hors de Dieu, ce sont des suites immédiates et nécessaires de son existence, sans lesquelles il ne serait point éternel et présent partout.

"Les infinis ne sont composés de finis que comme les finis sont composés d'infinitésimes; j'ai fait voir ci-dessus en quel sens on peut dire que l'espace a des parties ou qu'il n'en a pas. Les parties dans le sens que l'on donne à ce mot, lorsqu'on l'applique au corps, sont séparables, composées, désunies, indépendantes les unes des autres et capables de mouvement. Mais quoique l'imagination puisse en quelque manière concevoir des parties dans l'espace infini, cependant, comme ces parties, improprement ainsi dites, sont essentiellement immobiles et inséparables les unes des autres, il s'ensuit que cet espace est essentiellement simple et absolument indivisible."[63]

Reply of Leibnitz:

"Comme j'avais objecté que l'espace pris pour quelque chose de réel et d'absolu, sans les corps, serait une chose éternelle, impassible, indépendante de Dieu, on a tâché d'éluder cette difficulté en disant que l'espace est une propriété de Dieu. J'ai opposé à cela, dans mon écrit précédent, que la propriété de Dieu est l'immensité; mais que l'espace, qui est souvent commensuré avec les corps, et l'immensité de Dieu, n'est pas la même chose.

"J'ai encore objecté que, si l'espace est une propriété, et si l'espace infini est l'immensité de Dieu, l'espace fini sera l'étendue ou la mensurabilité de quelque chose finie. Ainsi l'espace occupé par un corps sera l'étendue de ce corps, chose absurde, puisqu'un corps peut changer d'espace, mais qu'il ne peut point quitter son étendue.

"J'ai encore demandé: si l'espace est une propriété, de quelle chose sera donc la propriété, un espace vuide borné, tel qu'on s'imagine dans le récipient épuisé air? Il ne paraît point raisonnable de dire que cet espace vuide, rond ou quarré, soit une propriété de Dieu. Sera-ce donc peut-être la propriété de quelques substances immatérielles, étendues, imaginaires, qu'on se figure (se semble) dans les espaces imaginaires?

"Si l'espace est la propriété ou l'affection de la substance qui est dans l'espace, le même espace sera tantôt l'affection d'un corps, tantôt d'un autre corps, tantôt d'une substance immatérielle, tantôt, peut-être, de Dieu, quand il est vuide de toute autre substance matérielle ou immatérielle. Mais voilà une étrange propriété ou affection, qui passe de sujet en sujet. Les sujets quitteront ainsi leurs accidents comme un habit, afin que d'autres sujets s'en puissent revêtir. Après cela comment distinguera-t-on les accidents et les substances?

"Que si les espaces bornés qui y sont, et si l'espace infini est la propriété de Dieu, il faut (chose étrange) que la propriété de Dieu soit composée des affections des créatures; car tous les espaces finis, pris ensemble, composent l'espace infini.

"Que si l'on nie que l'espace borné soit une affection des choses bornées, il ne sera pas raisonnable non plus que l'espace infini soit l'affection ou la propriété d'une chose infinie. J'avais insinué toutes ces difficultés dans mon écrit précédent, mais il ne paraît point qu'on ait tâché d'y satisfaire.

"J'ai encore d'autres raisons contre l'étrange imagination que l'espace est une propriété de Dieu. Si cela est, l'espace entre dans l'essence de Dieu. Or l'espace a des parties; donc il y aurait des parties dans l'essence de Dieu, *spectatum admissi.*

"De plus des espaces sont tantôt vuides, tantôt remplis; donc il y aura dans l'essence de Dieu des parties tantôt vuides, tantôt remplies, et par conséquent sujettes à un changement perpétuel. Les corps remplissant l'espace rempliraient une partie de l'essence de Dieu, et y seraient commensurés; et, dans la supposition du vuide, une partie de l'essence sera dans le récipient. Ce dieu à parties ressemblera fort au dieu stoïcien, qui était l'univers entier, considéré comme un animal divin.

"Si l'espace infini est l'immensité de Dieu, le temps infini sera l'éternité de Dieu; il faudra donc dire que ce qui est dans l'espace est dans l'immensité de Dieu, et par conséquent dans son essence; et que ce qui est dans le temps est dans l'éternité de Dieu. Phrases étranges, et qui font bien connaître qu'on abuse des termes.

"En voici encore une autre instance. L'immensité de Dieu fait que Dieu est dans tous les espaces. Mais si Dieu est dans l'espace, comment peut-on dire que l'espace est en Dieu, ou qu'il est sa propriété? On a bien ouï dire que la propriété soit dans le sujet; mais on n'a jamais ouï dire que le sujet soit dans la propriété. De même, Dieu existe en chaque temps, comment donc le temps est-il dans Dieu, et comment peut-il être une propriété de Dieu? Ce sont des *alloglossies perpétuelles*....

"Comme j'avais objecté que l'espace a des parties, on cherche un autre échappatoire en s'éloignant du sens reçu des termes, et soutenant que l'espace n'a point de parties; parce que ses parties ne sont point séparables et ne sauraient être éloignées les unes des autres par discerption. Mais il suffit que l'espace ait des parties, soit que ces parties soient séparables ou non; et on les peut assigner dans l'espace, soit par les corps qui y sont, soit par les lignes ou surfaces qu'on peut mener....

"On s'excuse de n'avoir point dit que l'espace est le *sensorium* de Dieu, mais seulement *comme* son *sensorium*. Il semble que l'un est aussi peu convenable et aussi peu intelligible que l'autre....

"Si Dieu sent ce qui ce passe dans le monde, par le moyen d'un *sensorium*, il semble que les choses agissent sur lui, et qu'ainsi il est comme on conçoit l'*âme du monde*. On m'impute de répéter les objections, sans prendre connaissance des réponses; mais je ne vois point qu'on ait satisfait à cette difficulté; on ferait mieux de renoncer tout à fait à ce *sensorium* prétendu."

For the rest of this interesting discussion, I refer the reader to the works of Leibnitz. These extracts may serve to show what importance eminent philosophers attributed to the questions on space.

ON CHAPTER XVII.

(31) In order that the reader may form a perfect conception of Kant's opinion of space, and judge for himself whether there is or not the contradiction which we have intimated, I extract a few passages from his works.

"The transcendental conception of phenomena[64] in space is a critical observation that, in general *nothing* perceived in space *is any thing in itself*; that space is, moreover, a form of things, and would belong to them if considered in themselves; but that objects in themselves are wholly unknown to us, and those things which we call *external objects, are only the pure representations of our sensibility*, whose form is space, and whose true correlative, that is to say, the thing in itself, is for this reason wholly unknown, and will always remain so; for experience can tell us nothing of it.

* * * * * * * *

"It is altogether certain, and not merely possible or probable, that space and time, as the necessary conditions of all experience, both internal and external, are purely subjective conditions of all our intuitions. It is therefore equally certain that *all objects in relation with space and time, are only simple phenomena and not things in themselves,* if considered according to the manner in which they are given us. Much may be said *a prior* of the form of objects, but nothing of the thing in itself, which serves as the ground of these phenomena."—*Transc. Æsth.* I.

This doctrine of Kant's brought upon him the charge of idealism, and drew from the German philosopher explanations which some look upon as a manifest contradiction.

Here is how Kant defends himself from idealism: "When I say that in space and time the intuitions of external objects, and of the mind, represent these two things as they affect our senses, *I do not mean to say that objects are a pure appearance;* for in the phenomenon, the objects, and even the properties which we attribute to them, are always considered as something really given; but that as this quality of being given depends only on the manner of perception of the subject in its relation with the object given, this object as phenomenon, is different from what it is as object in itself. *I do not say that bodies merely seem* to be external, or that my soul *merely seems* to have been given me in consciousness. When I assert that the qualities of space and time (in conformity to which I place the body and the soul as the condition of their existence) exist only in my mode of intuition, and not in the objects themselves, I should do wrong to convert into a mere appearance what I must take for a phenomenon; but this does not occur, if my principle of the ideality of all our sensible intuitions is admitted. On the contrary, if an objective reality is given to all these forms of sensible representations, every thing is inevitably converted into a pure appearance; for, if space and time are considered as qualities which, as to their possibility, must be found in the things themselves, and we reflect on the absurdities which follow, since two infinite things, which can neither be substances, nor any thing inherent in a substance, but which are still something existent, and even the necessary condition of the existence of all things would still subsist, though all the rest were annihilated, we cannot blame Berkeley for reducing bodies to a mere appearance."—*Ibid.* 2d Edition.

In the *Transcendental Logic* there is also a reputation of idealism. There Kant establishes this theorem:

"The mere consciousness of my own existence, empirically determined, proves the existence of objects outside of me in space."

It is not possible for me to give here the doctrines of Kant's *Transcendental Logic*; it is enough to have given his remarks on the reality of objects; others call them retractations or contradictions, and give various causes for them, which, however, do not belong to the field of philosophy.

ON CHAPTER XIX.

(32) The scholastics always carefully separated the sensible order from the intelligible. Kant was not the first to discover the limits which divide the intelligible from the sensible, things in themselves as objects of the understanding, *noumena*, as he calls them, from things as represented in sensible intuition, *phenomena*. The scholastics were so far from regarding sensible representations as sufficient for intelligence, that they denied that they were intelligible. The intellect might know sensible things, but it was necessary for it to abstract them from material conditions. On account of its limitation, it required the intuition of objects in sensible representation, *conversio ad phantasmata*; but these intuitions were not the intellectual act, they were only its necessary conditions. Hence proceeded the theory of the *intellectus agens*, which some have laughed at, because they did not understand it. This hypothesis has strong reasons in its favor, whatever may be its intrinsic value, if, setting aside the form in which it is expressed, we attend only to its ideological profoundness.

In reading some passages in Kant's *Transcendental Logic* on phenomena and noumena, on the necessity of sensible intuition in pure conceptions, and the distinction of the intuition from the conception, and on the sensible and intelligible worlds corresponding to the sensitive and intellective faculties, we might suppose that the German philosopher had read the scholastics. True, he departed from their doctrines, but what of that? The authors from whom we learn the most, are not always those whose opinions we follow.

In the treatise on ideas, I shall have occasion to explain my opinion on this point; for the present I shall only make a few extracts from St. Thomas, the most illustrious representative of the scholastic philosophy. The reader will find that he clearly explains our necessity of sensible representations, (*phantasmata,*) and the line which divides these representations from the purely intellectual order.

"(Pars 1, Q. LXXIX., art. 3.) Sed quia Aristoteles non posuit formas rerum naturalium subsistere sine materia, *formæ autem in materia existentes non sunt intelligibiles actu*; sequebatur, quod naturæ, seu formæ rerum sensibilium, quas intelligimus, non essent intelligibiles actu. Nihil autem reducitur de potentia in actum, nisi per aliquod ens actu: sicut sensus fit in actu per sensibile in actu. Oportet igitur ponere aliquam virtutem ex parte intellectus, quæ faceret intelligibilia in actu per abstractionem specierum a *conditionibus materialibus*. Et hæc est necessitas ponendi intellectum agentem.

"(P. 1, Q. LXXIX., art. 4). Ad cujus evidentiam considerandum est, quod supra animam intellectivam humanam, necesse est ponere aliquem superiorem intellectum, a quo anima virtutem intelligendi obtineat.

* * * * * * * *

"Nihil autem est perfectius in inferioribus rebus anima humana. Unde oportet dicere, quod in ipsa sit aliqua virtus derivata a superiori intellectu, per quam possit *phantasmata illustrare*. Et hoc experimento cognoscimus, dum percipimus *nos abstrahere formas universales a conditionibus particularibus, quod est facere actu intelligibilia.*

"(P. 1. Q., LXXXIV., art. 1.) Hoc autem necessarium non est: quia etiam in ipsis sensibilibus videmus, quod forma alio modo est in uno sensibilium, quam in altero; puta cum in uno est albedo intensior, in alio remissior, ut cum in uno est albedo cum dulcedine, in alio sine dulcedine. Et per hunc etiam modum, forma sensibilis alio modo est in re, quæ est extra animam, et alio modo in sensu, qui suspicit formas sensibilium absque materia, sicut colorem auri sine auro. Et similiter intellectus species corporum, quæ sunt materiales et mobiles, recipit immaterialiter, et immobiliter, secundum modum suum, nam receptum est in recipiente per modum recipientis. Dicendum est ergo, quod anima per intellectum cognoscit corpora, *cognitione immateriali, universali et necessaria.*

"(P. I, Q. LXXXIV., art. 6.) Et ideo ad causandam intellectualem operationem secundum Aristotelem non sufficit sola impressio sensibilium corporum, sed requiritur aliquid nobilius, quia agens est honorabilius patiente, ut ipse dicit. Non autem quod intellectualis operatio causetur ex sola impressione aliquarum rerum superiorum, ut Plato posuit, sed illud superius, et nobiliŭs agens, quod vocat intellectum agentem, de quo jam supra diximus quod *facit phantasmata a sensibus accepta intelligibilia in actu,* per modum abstractionis cuiusdam. Secundum hoc ergo, ex parte phantasmatum intellectualis operatio a sensu causatur. Sed quia phantasmata non sufficiunt immutare intellectum possibilem, sed oportet quod fiant intelligibilia actu per intellectum agentem, non potest dici quod sensibilis cognitio sit totalis, et perfecta causa intellectualis cognitionis, sed magis quodammodo est materia causæ."

FOOTNOTES

[1] Fichte, *Grundlage der gesammten Wissenschaftslehre*. Theil. i., § 1. Ed. Berlin, 1845, p. 92.

[2] *Treatise of Human Nature*, vol. i., p. 467.

[3] *Saggio sull' origine delle idee*, p. 5, c. iv., tr. 11, p. 285, where he cites the theoretico-chemical observations on the cataracts of those born blind, by Luigi de' Gregori, professor of chemistry and opthalmia, published at Rome in 1826.

[4] *Wissenschaftslehre, Th. 1, § 1*

[5] *Ibid.*

[6] P. 1a, Q. 87a, A. 1o

[7] P. 1a, Q. 14a, A. 5o.

[8] Q. 12a, A. 8o

[9] Descartes. *Principes de la Philosophie*, 1ière partie.

[10] Descartes. *Principes de la Philosophie*, 1ière partie, N. 7.

[11] *Les Principes de la Philosophie*. Preface, p. 13.

[12] *Les Principes de la Philosophie*. 1ière. partie, N. 9.

[13] *Essay on the Human Understanding*. Prologue.

[14] *Essay on the Human Understanding*. Book iv., Chap. I., § 1.

[15] *Essai sur l'Origine des Connaissances*. Première partie, C. 1., § 1.

[16] *Transcendental Logic*, B. ii., C. 2, Sect. 1, pp. 140-141. Ed. Leipsic. 1828.

[17] *Critic of Pure Reason*. Introduction, Sect. 4. p. 9.

[18] *Summa Theologica*. P. 1a, Q. 2a, A. 1o, in corp.

[19] 1a 2dae, Q. 94a, A. 2o, in corp.

[20] P. 1a, Q. 25a, A. 3.

[21] *Wissenschaftslehre*. Erster Theil. § 3.

[22] Part II., Chap. II., Sect. 3, § 2, pages 436-7.

[23] *Critik der reinen Vernunft*. Einleitung.

[24] Ibid..

[25] Kant, *ubi supra*, § 5.

[26] *Ancient Wisdom of Italy*, L. 1, C. 1.

[27] Ibidem, § 1.

[28] Ancient Wisdom of Italy, L. 1, C. 1.

[29] Respondeo dicendum, quod in Verbo importatur respectus ad creaturam. Deus enim cognoscendo se, cognoscit omnem creaturam. Verbum igitur in mente conceptum est representativum omnis ejus, quod actu intelligitur. Unde in nobis sunt diversa verba, secundum diversa, quæ intelligimus. Sed quia Deus uno actu et se, et omnia intelligit, unicum verbum ejus est expressivum, non solum Patris sed etiam creaturarum. Et sicut Dei scientia, Dei quidem est cognoscitiva tantum, creaturarum autem cognoscitiva et factiva; ita verbum Dei, ejus quod in Deo Patre est, est expressivum tantum, creaturarum vero est expressivum et operativum, et propter hoc dicitur in Psal. 32; Dixit, et facta sunt, quia importatur in Verbo ratio factiva eorum quæ Deus facit. *Summa Theologiæ*, P. 1a, Qa, 34a, A 3o.

[30] Pater enim intelligendo se, et Filium, et Spiritum Sanctum, et omnia alia quæ ejus scientia continentur, concipit Verbum, ut sic tota Trinitas Verbo dicatur, et etiam omnis creatura. P. 1a, Q. 34a, A. 1o, *ad*. 3un.

[31] Quicunque autem intelligit, ex *hoc ipso quod intelligit,* procedit aliquid intra ipsum, quod est conceptio rei intellectæ ex vi intellectiva proveniens et ex ejus notitia procedens. Quam quidem conceptionem vox significat, et dicitur verbum cordis, significatum verbo vocis. P. 1a, Q. 27a, A. 1o.

[32] *Ibid.*

[33] Lamennais, *Essai sur l'Indifference en Matière de Religion.* T. 2, C. 13.

[34] Ibid.

[35] See Bk. II., Ch. XXIII., § 226.

[36] P. 1. C. xi.

[37] See Book 1, § 56.

[38] Essai sur l'Indifference, Tome II., Part III., Ch. I.

[39] Book II. Ch. ix.

[40] See Ch. I.

[41] Descartes, *Principes de la Philosophie.* P. 2, § 18.

[42] Descartes, Ibid., § II, p. 21.

[43] Leibnitz, *Nouveaux Essais.* L. II., C. XIII., § 17.

[44] Leibnitz, Ibid., § 21.

[45] Fragment of a Letter.—(I do not know what letter the author here refers to, but the same opinion in almost the same words may be found in Clarke's fourth and fifth letters to Leibnitz, *Tr.*)

[46] I take no notice in this place of the different manner in which the idea of being is applicable to God and to creatures.

[47] See Book II., Chap. xv.

[48] Kant, *Transc. Æsth.* I. Absch. § 2, 1.

[49] Bk. II., Chs. VII., VIII., and IX., and Bk. III., Ch. IV.

[50] Bk. II., Ch. VIII., and Bk. III., Ch. VI.

[51] Bk. II. Chap. VIII.

[52] Chap. v.

[53] XII., XIII., XIV., and XV.

[54] *Sum. Theol.* P. I., Q. viii., Art. 1.

[55] *Sum. Theol.* Q. LII., Art. I.

[56] Dialecticians understand by an *equivocal* term one which in different things has an entirely different meaning. They give as an example the term lion which is applied *equivocally* to an animal, or a constellation. Æquivoca sunt quorum nomen commune est, et ratio per nomen significata, simpliciter diversa, is the scholastic definition.

[57] *Sum. Theol.* Q. lxxvi., Art. 8.

[58] B. II., Ch. II.

[59] Ch. II.

[60] In this proposition Clarke is either inexact and obscure, or else he falls into a serious error. The immensity of God is God himself. Every attribute of God is God.

[61] Here Clarke confounds *divisibility* with *separability.* See chapters X. and XI. of this book.

[62] Goclenius is the author of a philosophical dictionary quoted by Leibnitz.

[63] Here Clarke falls again into the confusion we have spoken of, and making *divisibility* the same thing as *separability*, he asserts contradictory propositions.

[64] Kant defines phenomenon, "the indeterminate object of an empirical intuition." He calls empirical intuition, "that which relates to an object by means of sensation." He understands by sensation, "the effect of an object on the representative faculty, in so far as we are affected by it." —*Transcend. Æsthet.* I.